SELECTED SHORT SUBJECTS
From Spanky to the Three Stooges

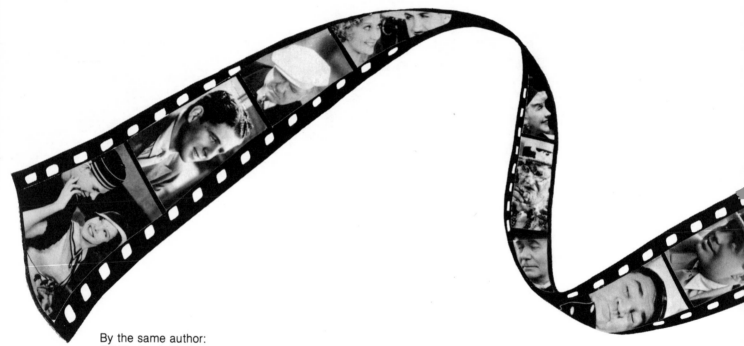

By the same author:
TV Movies (editor)
Movie Comedy Teams
The Art of the Cinematographer (Behind the Camera)
The Disney Films
Our Gang: The Life and Times of the Little Rascals (co-author)
The Great Movie Comedians
Of Mice and Magic: A History of American Animated Cartoons
The Complete Guide to Home Video (co-author)
The Whole Film Sourcebook (editor)
The Real Stars (editor)
The Laurel and Hardy Book (editor)

SELECTED SHORT SUBJECTS
From Spanky to the Three Stooges

by Leonard Maltin

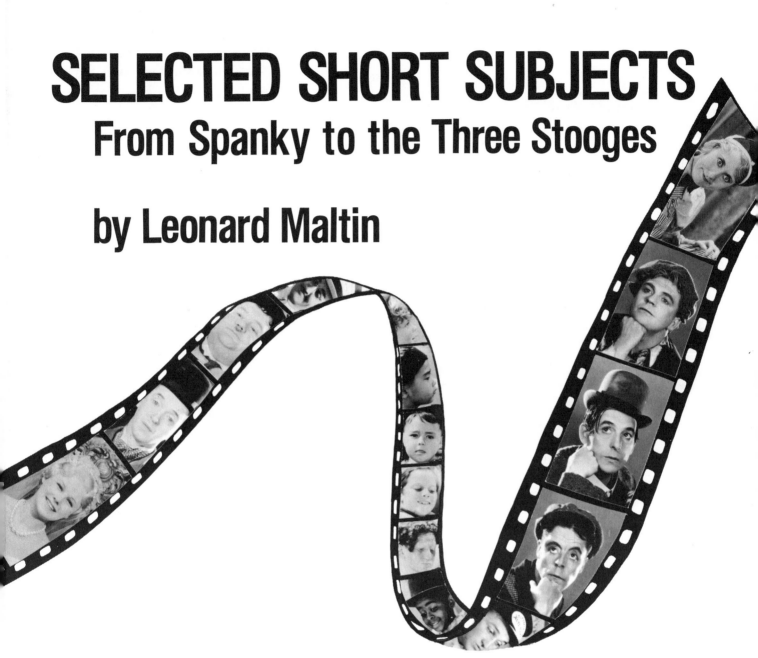

FOREWORD BY PETE SMITH

A DA CAPO PAPERBACK

Dedicated to the gang at Joe's Place,
who like short subjects too.

Library of Congress Cataloging in Publication Data

Maltin, Leonard.
  Selected short subjects.

  (A Da Capo paperback)
  Reprint. Originally published: Great movie shorts. New
York: Bonanza Books, 1972.
  Bibliography: p.
  Includes index.
  1. Comedy films—United States—History and criticism. I.
Title.
PN1995.9.C55M34 1983ı   791.43′09′0917   83-7580
ISBN 0-306-80204-X (pbk.)

This Da Capo Press paperback edition of *Selected Short
Subjects: From Spanky to the Three Stooges* is an un-
abridged republication of the edition published in New York
in 1972, originally entitled *The Great Movie Shorts*. It is re-
printed by arrangement with the author.

Published by Da Capo Press, Inc.
A Subsidiary of Plenum Publishing Corporation
233 Spring Street, New York, N. Y. 10013

Manufactured in the United States of America

Acknowledgments

Photograph credits and acknowledgments: Allied Artists, Columbia Pictures (Gary Shapiro), Hal Roach Studios (Herbert Gelbspan, Richard Feiner), MGM, Paramount Pictures, RKO Radio Pictures, Warner Brothers, United Artists; Richard L. Bare, Dorothy Granger, Lou Gross, Vitaprint, Miles Kreuger, Hal LeRoy, Erik Magnuson, Bernard Maltin, Pete Smith, Lou Valentino, D. Victorek.

Portions of this book have been adapted from articles that appeared in *Film Fan Monthly*.

contents

foreword

At last!

The saga of the movie short subject has been written.

For decades, countless millions of theatre-goers the world over were short-subject fans.

When the main title of a popular minifilm or personality was flashed on a theatre screen the cash customers generally burst into happy applause and, often, screams of delight.

An exhibitor would no more think of omitting one or more shorts and a newsreel from his program than he would have kept his theatre closed on New Year's Eve. Today a short in a theatre is practically as rare as a tick on a rubber duck.

Historians of the cinema have written dozens of tomes about glamorous personalities, the productions and events that blazed across the feature-film firmament over the years. And now comes a young man—a very young man—who has captured for the first time the comprehensive story of the colorful characters, incidents, and data that vitalized the one- and two-reelers.

Leonard Maltin began writing about movies for publication at the ripe old age of thirteen. And in due time various metropolitan publications made the bright young writer in Teaneck, New Jersey, the subject of feature articles. Now in his very early twenties, he is still at it with more enthusiasm than ever. Among other literary endeavors he writes, edits, and publishes his own magazine, *Film Fan Monthly*.

The fact that the author was not yet around when short subjects were at the height of their popularity is significant. Like Leonard, thousands of young film buffs will enjoy delving into this form of earlier screen entertainment. For those older ones who, as kids, howled at shorts and mimicked their favorite performers, this book should provide a nostalgic tug. Then, too, the statistical-minded should rejoice in it as a reference source.

Shorts of former days, of course, were not all pie-in-the-face and pratfalls. Dramatic and romantic stories as well as historic events were told in the short span of a thousand or two (or fewer) feet of film, as were the achievements of noted figures in science, history, music, and government. This involved brevity and to-the-point writing that demanded specialized craftsmanship. And not to be forgotten were the memorable shorts furthering patriotic causes in times of war.

Many celebrated stars, writers, and directors of multi-million-dollar feature productions started and learned their art in the field of short subjects. Other exponents of the "shorties" preferred to be proverbial big frogs in small puddles and gained fame, popularity, and happiness in what they were doing. To some, indeed, shorts were practically a religion.

And so, Leonard Maltin, let's have it.

PETE SMITH*

*Pete Smith, who generously provided the foreword for this book in 1972, died in 1979 at the age of 86. He made an indelible contribution to the field of "selected short subjects," and his kind words about this author were a source of great encouragement.
—LEONARD MALTIN, May 1983

preface

They say this is the age of specialization. Well, my specialty is the short subject. I first learned to love shorts when I grew up with the comedies of Our Gang, Laurel and Hardy, and the Three Stooges on television. I loved these films long before I was old enough to realize that they were "old movies." When I acquired a serious interest in films of the past, I sought out more and more one- and two-reelers from the 1930s and 1940s.

It wasn't easy; time has not been kind to these shorts. They are seldom revived, and are hardly ever shown on television. The movie companies themselves have little or no interest in their accumulated backlogs of shorts.

I found researching the shorts even more difficult. Very little was written about them at the time, and not all *that* has been saved. In the recent flood of film literature, the talkie short has been pretty much ignored. There are virtually no reference sources one can consult to obtain the simplest facts.

Yet it was precisely these factors that made me all the more intrigued with shorts. Seeking them out became a challenge; researching them became a giant jigsaw puzzle. Eventually, most of the pieces fell into place.

Other than the films themselves, one of the best sources of information turned out to be the people who made them. While that might sound like an obvious statement, many actors, directors, and technicians are often forgetful, or have little to say, when one asks about certain films they made. On the other hand, virtually everyone I interviewed opened up when I mentioned short subjects, for most of them had had a ball making them.

Therefore, I am deeply indebted to Goodman Ace, Gertrude Astor, Lucien Ballard, Richard L. Bare, Nathaniel Benchley, George Chandler, Ann Doran, Gordon Douglas, Richard Fleischer, Billy Gilbert, Dorothy Granger, Moe Howard, Patsy Kelly, Hal LeRoy, Gloria Morgan, George Sidney, Don Siegel, Joe Smith, the late Ralph Staub, George Stevens, Grady Sutton, Elwood Ullman, Jules White, Jean Yarbrough, and Robert Youngson for sharing with me their memories of working in this fascinating field. I owe a special debt of thanks to Edward Bernds, who rendered service above and beyond the call of duty in providing material on filming two-reel comedies. I am especially grateful to Pete Smith for his foreword.

For access to the shorts themselves, information about them, and general moral support, I am grateful to Gordon Berkow, Rudi Blesh, John Cocchi, Jon Davison, William K. Everson, Herb Graff, Ron Hall, Alan Hoffman, Joel Jacobson, Al Kilgore, Don Koll, Milton Menell, Don Miller, Charles Pavlicek, Carl Rons, Patrick Sheehan and the staff of the Library of Congress, and the staff of the Theater Collection of the New York Public Library.

Special thanks must go to Dick Bann, who was of great help on the Our Gang chapter, and responsible for its filmography; George Geltzer, who did the basic filmography on Charley Chase for *Film Fan Monthly;* and D. Victorek, whose generous help was largely responsible for the Pete Smith chapter, and who provided the Smith filmography.

Now comes the copout. The familiar phrase has always been "selected short subjects," and in keeping with that motto, I have selected which shorts to include in this volume. There were many thousands of shorts released between 1930 and 1950, the approximate years I have covered; to discuss or list them all would have been impossible. The first to go were cartoons; they too have been neglected, but they deserve a book all their own. And while I have included chapters on musical shorts, newsreels, and documentaries, all three are enormous subjects in themselves, and my summaries are just that —summaries, not in-depth surveys. Another tremendous subject which was impossible to include was World War II shorts.

What is needed is an encyclopedia of short subjects listing not only facts but offering a fresh evaluation of the shorts. This cannot be compiled until the movie companies realize that there is much value in their old shorts and thus make prints available; until the archives learn that shorts are as worthy of preservation as features; and until all the original data kept on short subjects and now buried is made accessible. The crime is that this material—both the films and the data—exists, but no one is interested enough to do anything about it. The Laurel and Hardy and W. C. Fields shorts are widely available because they have always been in demand. If a demand existed for Charley Chase and Joe McDoakes shorts, they too would be in general release.

Finally, compiling an encyclopedia would require someone with infinite patience to screen all the shorts, for it should be made clear right now that not all shorts were great. Many were mediocre, and many others worse than that. In tracking down shorts for this book, I would often sit through four flops, wondering just why I was interested in this field in the first place. Then would come the fifth short, a little unknown gem, and my faith would be restored.

Now you have before you the fruits of my labor of love. I hope you will find it interesting reading, and informative. Most of all, I hope it will make you want to see the shorts yourself; perhaps someday this won't be such a difficult task.

LEONARD MALTIN

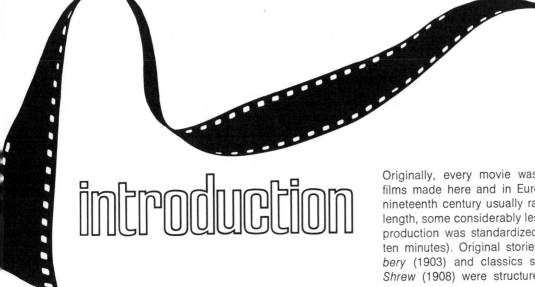

introduction

Originally, every movie was a short subject. The first films made here and in Europe in the latter part of the nineteenth century usually ran no more than a minute in length, some considerably less. Before too long, however, production was standardized at one reel (approximately ten minutes). Original stories like *The Great Train Robbery* (1903) and classics such as *The Taming of the Shrew* (1908) were structured to meet the time restrictions.

D. W. Griffith was a principal figure in expanding the horizons of filmmaking by demanding longer running times on his films. American Biograph, his studio, finally agreed to let him make two-reel films so long as each reel could be released separately. It was a considerable compromise, but a step in the right direction. European filmmakers took the first giant step in producing feature films running as long as an hour. In 1913, Griffith followed suit with his *Judith of Bethulia*. Other feature films followed, but it was not until *Birth of a Nation* that the feature was firmly and irrevocably established as the staple of film production.

Gradually, the short films, which had been the main item on film programs, became merely an extra added attraction on the bill. One notable exception was the short comedy, for the greatest clowns of the era—Chaplin, Lloyd, Keaton, Arbuckle—worked primarily in two-reelers until the early 1920s, and, for many audiences, they were still the drawing card at the local theatre. Any feature accompanying the shorts was incidental.

But by the mid-1920s, even the comedians turned to feature films, and those left in short-subject production faced the facts: they might still be popular, and profitable, but they would never enjoy the prestige of the feature films they supported.

Still, no theatre owner would dream of showing a feature without accompanying shorts, and the standard billing "Also Selected Short Subjects" became a welcome cliché for most American moviegoers.

By the start of the sound era, circa 1929, where our study begins, short subjects were many things to many people in the motion-picture business. To exhibitors, they were a necessity to fill out their programs. To the studios, they were part of the regular production schedule, usually quite profitable and therefore worthy of decent budgets and a fair amount of publicity. But at the same time, shorts were only shorts, and the studio executives let the specialists in charge of their production work as an autonomous unit, without interference. As long as the product came out on time, was fairly well received, and turned a profit, there was no need to get involved as they would in feature-film production. The only direct usefulness the studio found in its short subjects was as a training ground for newcomers, both in front of and behind the camera, and indeed, the number of actors, writers, directors, and technicians who graduated from short-subjects units is most impressive.

For the audience, the short subject was frequently the brightest spot on the program. To be sure, there were more bad shorts than good ones being turned out by a variety of fly-by-night companies as well as established studios, but most intelligent theatre owners came to know which series their patrons preferred, and often would advertise especially popular ones above the feature film on the marquee and in newspaper ads. In the 1930s, a life-size cutout of Laurel and Hardy in front of a theatre would often bring a crowd sooner than most program features (just as Chaplin's cutout had done in the teens and early 1920s), and when Bing Crosby, just making a name for himself on radio and on records, starred in two-reelers for Mack Sennett, fans flocked to see them without caring what feature was being shown.

For the filmmakers, the short-subject unit was perhaps the most creative place to work in Hollywood. Because there were none of the pressures of a major production, there was always time to experiment and try different ideas, to listen to suggestions, and to have fun. Since the same people worked on most of the series, each unit became a family. It was for most of them a happy experience, fondly remembered today. When time and effort and love go into a film, they show on the screen. This is what makes so many of the short subjects of the 1930s and 1940s a delight to watch, and what will keep them fresh for many years to come.

the studios

Each short-subject company had its own individual style during the 1930s and 1940s. This was determined by many factors: the people themselves, the executives, the facilities, the budgets, and certain intangibles that combine to produce a distinct personality.

Hal Roach

The Hal Roach studio was the greatest comedy-production company of the 1930s. Ask anyone who worked there at that time what it was like, and their faces will brighten.

"We were all young and gay," says actress Gertrude Astor. "They had the top floor of the studio, where they would write the films, and we used it for a drinking spot." Asked if there was a stigma in the industry about doing short subjects, she replies, "Oh yes; people would say 'Oh, she's working in the Roach comedies.' They were looked down upon, but were great fun to make."

"I don't remember any schedules," says director Gordon Douglas. "They [the shorts] usually ran a week, eight days. In those days there was no big rush."

"You didn't have to be in makeup at seven for an eight-thirty shooting," actress Dorothy Granger recalls. "You came maybe at ten and they would shoot until three, and then the gag writers would go into conference, and they'd send you home."

Says Patsy Kelly, "Mr. Roach was a wonderful man; kind, considerate. The best boss I've ever had, and I've had quite a few."

In this relaxed, friendly working atmosphere, people got together to do what they did best: create comedy.

Hal Roach was born in 1892 in Elmira, New York. As a teen-ager, he set out on his own and worked up and down the West Coast, holding an incredible variety of jobs, from truck driver to mule-train superintendent. While in Los Angeles, he noticed an advertisement for Western extras on a film being shot the next day; he applied for the job, and that was his introduction to the movie business. An ambitious young man, he worked his way into the production end of movies, and with aggressiveness, and later the help of a small inheritance, he set up his own studio. His first star was a fellow extra named Harold Lloyd.

A portrait of Hal Roach, circa 1929.

quality. Leo McCarey, Fred Guiol, Charley Chase and his brother James Parrott, and George Stevens were among those who helped to develop this style, which reached a peak of perfection in the late 1920s. Roach's own invention, "Our Gang," enjoyed sustained popularity all during this time; Charley Chase made it to the top with his breezy, sophisticated comedies, and the inspired teaming of Laurel and Hardy gave the world one of the great comic duos of all time.

By the time sound came to Hollywood, Roach was ready for any challenge. A strong alliance with MGM (which distributed his shorts) plus some of the top comedy stars of the day, made him a leading producer in Hollywood. His talented staff wrestled with the problems of talking pictures for a short while, and finally adapted their style to the new medium with great success.

There were no rules at the studio; everyone did everything. Stan Laurel, Charley Chase, and Billy Gilbert, who starred in Roach comedies, all worked as gag writers at the same time. Gilbert directed on occasion, Laurel later became his own producer, and Chase directed himself as well as other comics. Gagman Charley Rogers often appeared in the comedies, and frequently tried his hand at directing. Gordon Douglas, who headed the casting department, played in the "Boy Friends" comedies and later became a gagman and director. The extras in various scenes of the films were often the brothers, sisters, wives, and husbands of people on the payroll!

Hal Roach's "All-Star" Trio of the mid-1930s: Don Barclay, Douglas Wakefield, and Billy Nelson.

By the 1920s, Hal Roach was an established producer, and his comedies were reasonably successful. Mack Sennett, the "King of Comedy," acknowledged Roach as "my only rival." By 1930, however, Sennett was facing hard times, while Roach had long surpassed him to become the *new* King of Comedy. Roach developed his own stars and series, fostered bright young talent, and generally stayed out of their way.

One reason for Sennett's decline was his failure to successfully develop his basic style. Audiences of the 1920s, who were treated to Hollywood films that glimmered with polish and filmmaking know-how, no longer cared for the frenetic, roughhouse antics that had put Sennett on the map ten years before. Slapstick, it seemed, was a dirty word.

The people at the Roach studio, however, realized that what was needed was slapstick with finesse—a greater emphasis on characterization, better overall photographic

"We used to charter a bus to go to Tijuana over weekends," Douglas recalls. "There would be third-assistant prop men as well as these big directors. It was a fun group, and nobody wore their medals, if you know what I mean. Everybody was there to make the picture as good and as fast as possible, and as funny. Nobody was there to hurt anybody else. I've never run into as many nice people in one spot as existed at Hal Roach."

Dorothy Granger recalls, "At the time I was at Roach they had a small wardrobe department, mostly duplicate costumes for the girls and their doubles to wear. At that time only stunt *men* were used to double the women. And even if you didn't need a double or stunt man you would usually need a dress—two or sometimes three of the same thing, when you had to get a pie in the face, or be doused with water, or whatever. And sometimes it was just a scene that was so hectic you ruined the dress you had on. It was at this point that Mrs. Hal Roach took over as head of the wardrobe department. She would take us out to the department stores and pick out the clothes for us."

Several years later, when Thelma Todd and ZaSu Pitts were making their two-reelers, Thelma recommended her friend, costume designer Edward Stevenson, for a position at the studio. Stevenson later explained, "I told Thelma, 'Roach won't pay for a dress designer,' but Thelma said, 'I can sell him on the idea; they've been buying my dresses at the May Company, and it would be much funnier for me to fall in a mud puddle wearing a beautiful gown that fits than in an ordinary dress.'" Stevenson was hired.

Roach remained something of an enigma. Charley Rogers told John McCabe in his book *Mr. Laurel and Mr. Hardy,* "Roach had a terrific ability to spot talent. He knew what a good gag was but he usually let someone else work it out. He'd get an idea, talk it over with us, and then when it came to actually putting the gag on film, he'd say, 'That's the idea, boys. Work it out. Know what I mean?' Then he'd walk away and too many times we didn't know what he'd meant—not that that ever stopped us."

Roach's hot-and-cold attitude toward directing films himself was responsible for most of his staff's graduation to the director's post. Often Roach would start a film in the morning and be bored by noon, or simply have other things to attend to. In such a case, whoever was handy would be called upon to complete the film; men like George Stevens and Gordon Douglas got their first chances in this manner.

With several established series running on their own steam, Roach tried to inaugurate new stars and series

Billy Gilbert as Mr. Schmaltz, the famous director, with Charlie Hall and James C. Morton in *Movie Daze.*

during the 1930s, with varying degrees of success. Among the more interesting groups of films, the "All-Star Comedies" and "Hal Roach Musicals" gave some of the supporting comics on the lot a chance to star in their own films and experiment with some offbeat ideas.

By 1935, Roach sensed that short subjects were on the way out. The double feature was increasingly popular, cutting down the market for quality two-reel shorts. He tested his stars in feature films; those who succeeded, like Laurel and Hardy, stayed with him. Those who did not, like Charley Chase, were eased out. In 1938 he sold "Our Gang" to MGM and set up a new distribution system for feature films with United Artists. His features were successful until the early 1940s, when his idea for "Streamliner" films, a compromise between shorts and features, petered out at the box office.

After World War II, Roach was never able to regain his footing in the industry. He had some success with television, ironically enough doing what were essentially two-reelers padded out to a half hour. But even here, financial problems overcame the producer and his partner-son, and by the early 1960s the Roach studio was demolished. With it went a storehouse of memories of a corps of workers whose dedication to comedy had made the Hal Roach studio great.

Columbia Pictures

Columbia Pictures started out on Poverty Row, and it took many years to erase the B-picture stigma from its name. But by the mid-1930s, with the help of such pictures as *One Night of Love* and *It Happened One Night,* Columbia was able to expand, both physically and artistically. One major step was the formation of a short-subject unit. To head it, Columbia's chieftain Harry Cohn hired Jules White.

White grew up in California around the same time that the motion picture industry was taking root there. When he was eight he worked for D. W. Griffith, and he subsequently appeared in many silent films, including the original version of *The Spoilers* (1914) with William Farnum and Tom Santschi. Jules's older brother Jack (born in 1899) got the movie bug at an early age, directed his first film at the age of seventeen, and two years later was in charge of his own comedy unit, working with Educational Pictures. In the 1920s, Jack White became one of the biggest names in comedy production, producing the "Mermaid" series and Lloyd Hamilton comedies for Educational. He gave his brother Jules his first directing job in 1922. Another brother, Sam White, became a comedy director at RKO some years later.

By 1934, Jules White was a veteran in the comedy field, but like so many of his contemporaries, he had a difficult time finding work. Educational Pictures was no longer the prosperous studio it had been in the 1920s, although it still produced a lot of two-reelers. White's golden opportunity came when Harry Cohn hired him to head the short-subject department at Columbia.

White's first step was to hire experts to work for him. One of his first directors was James Horne, a veteran of Hal Roach and Universal comedies; his brother Jack came to work for him, using the pseudonym "Preston Black." Among his first stars were Andy Clyde and Leon Errol. While directing at MGM in the early 1930s, White had worked with Ted Healy and his Stooges. He decided to star the Three Stooges in their own short subjects, and thus began one of the longest-running comedy series of all time. He starred the fading Harry Langdon in a new series of shorts as well. And when he found one of Mack Sennett's greatest directors selling used cars, he hired him immediately. The man was Del Lord, who was responsible for a large majority of the great comedies that Columbia made for the next fifteen years.

Says actress Ann Doran about Del Lord, "Without a doubt, he was the most even-tempered man I have ever known. He never tired, he was inventive. His sense of humor and timing was infallible. Charley [Chase] and

Roscoe Karns in one of his two Columbia shorts, *Half Shot at Sunrise,* with Bobby Larson and Ann Doran.

Del knew what they were doing every minute; they proved ways to open a door, to sit, to put on a hat, to drink a glass of water, to answer a phone. The tiniest thing can make a scene funny. A shrug or a lifted eyebrow at the precise moment can make a scene hilarious. Charley and Dell had the same marvelous feeling for timing that Jack Benny has. It is an inborn sense."

Before long, Columbia became the mecca for experienced comedy creators who needed work. Clyde Bruckman, one of the all-time great comedy writers, who had been responsible for many of Buster Keaton and Harold Lloyd's greatest hits, and later worked with W. C. Fields and Laurel and Hardy as a director, joined Columbia in the mid-1930s. When Hal Roach fired Charley Chase, Bruckman came to Columbia and functioned as a comic, writer, director, and associate producer. Buster Keaton spent several years at Columbia with his own starring series, happily reunited with Clyde Bruckman. Veteran Sennett director Harry Edwards joined Columbia, and worked with Harry Langdon, whom he had directed when Langdon first came to Hollywood in the 1920s. Veterans Polly Moran, Charlie Murray and George Sidney, Smith and Dale, Tom Kennedy, and Monty Collins all made comedy shorts for Columbia in the 1930s.

The shorts were also a proving ground for untried talent. Lucille Ball, Walter Brennan, Bruce Bennett, Lloyd Bridges, Linda Winters (later Dorothy Comingore), and many others got their start in Columbia shorts. Cameraman Lucien Ballard found it invaluable experience photographing the two-reelers. There was also the fine stock company of supporting players, headed by Bud Jamison and Vernon Dent, who added so much to the comedies.

The comedy unit hit its stride in the late 1930s and early 1940s. There was abundant use of location shooting at this time; the gags were ingenious, the performers fresh, and the pace unexcelled. Del Lord harked back to his freewheeling Sennett days in a short called *Free Rent* (1936) with Tom Kennedy and Monty Collins doing elaborate sight gags with a runaway trailer, without the aid of miniatures or process photography. When Lord teamed with writer Clyde Bruckman and star Buster Keaton on *The Pest from the West* (1939), the results were glorious.

Says Ann Doran, "We had no regularly scheduled number of days, though most of the shorts were filmed in three to five days. The hours were backbreaking—twelve to sixteen hours a day. The important day came when we took the picture for preview. We usually went to Ingle-

Cohn. The two men operated separate units throughout the 1940s. This left White more time to direct films himself, and McCollum followed suit in the late 1940s. But unfortunately, as the decade wore on, economic factors began to erode the quality of the Columbia shorts. Less time was available for each short's production, and the former leisurely pace was tightened so each short would be completed in three to four days' time. This left less time for experimentation and forced the comedies to become a bit more studied and less improvisational. Spontaneity was at a minimum in these shorts, and many of the gags have a cut-and-dried, mechanical look to them.

One of Columbia's rare dramatic series was *Fools Who Made History*. This 1939 episode starred young Robert Sterling (*right*) as Charles Goodyear, with Robert Fiske.

Even Billie Burke did two-reelers for Columbia; this 1949 short is *Billie Gets Her Man*, with Dick Wessel, Emil Sitka, and Patsy Moran.

wood, Glendale, or Santa Monica. They had rigged a recording machine that ran at the same speed as the film. It was placed in the audience and recorded the laughs of the people viewing the film. The next day we ran the film and the recording in the studio. If the laugh didn't come where we thought it would, or if one laugh overrode another, the picture was recut. On rare occasions we reshot a scene to retime it. We wanted perfection."

Jules White split his producing chores in the late 1930s with Hugh McCollum, a former secretary to Harry

There was more and more borrowing from the past; Shemp Howard remade most of Charley Chase's shorts in the mid-1940s, for example.

Comedy writer Elwood Ullman explains, "You could do much more with two-reelers of the late 1930s than you could later on, when costs began to soar. You could, for instance, go out and shoot stuff around a railroad locomotive and a train of cars, or get into a wild chase with automobiles, go out on the Columbia ranch and shoot night stuff."

There was also a heavy reliance on stock footage, but one can only marvel at the ingenious way it was used. In *In the Sweet Pie and Pie* (1941), the Three Stooges are ex-convicts married to society debutantes. At one point they are told to go for their dance lesson. The picture fades and we see Geneva Mitchell giving them their instructions—from a 1935 film, *Hoi Polloi.* Only the most careful examination (or knowledge of the earlier film) reveals the deception.

Such chicanery became more intricate as years went by. For a 1952 Andy Clyde comedy, *A Blissful Blunder,*

Director Edward Bernds (*center*) discusses a script on the set with Shemp Howard and Tom Kennedy at Columbia.

Columbia reconstructed a set and rehired actor Fred Kelsey so they could match up scenes for Clyde's 1940 endeavor *A Bundle of Bliss* without anyone noticing. By 1958 Jules White was able to film *one day's* worth of new footage and create a new two-reeler, using older stock shots.

The 1940s also saw new faces in Columbia comedies. Hugh Herbert and El Brendel both had long-running series; each had been top-name supporting actors in the 1930s. Radio stars Vera Vague and Harry Von Zell starred in two-reelers, and many actors came to the department for brief stays between more prestigious assignments: Roscoe Karns, Alan Mowbray, Una Merkel, Sterling Holloway, Billie Burke, etcetera. Many of their comedies were simply remakes of earlier shorts which had starred other Columbia contractees.

Jules White did the largest number of comedies at this time; Del Lord curtailed his activities as the decade progressed. White says of his style, "I had a theory: make 'em move so fast, if they're not funny, no one will have time to realize it or get bored." In general, this theory worked, but, unfortunately, White's tendency to have a loose shooting script and make up ideas on the spot, under pressure, made for a lot of protracted and unfunny sequences, often excessively violent in nature.

White was quite a character to work for, as well. Says Dorothy Granger, "He would think up some of the darndest things for you to do, and you would have to scream your head off before he would get a double for you. He always said, 'I never ask an actor to do anything I wouldn't do.' And then he would proceed to go on the set and do the stunt. I remember one I did with him; I believe it was called *Pardon My Lamb Chop,* with Gus Schilling and Dick Lane. During the course of the action my fanny catches on fire and I jump, or one of them dumps me, into a sink full of water. I didn't want to do it, but Jules went through the whole thing with flames and all. They had me padded with asbestos all up and down my back, but one thing none of us realized was that he had short hair and mine was in a long bob at the time. So as we are shooting the scene the flames are running up my back and then I start smelling hair burning! Well, I really did some screaming and dashed for the water. But he got his scene—and I got a hair singeing job!" Another colleague says succinctly, "You could write a whole book about Jules White—but no one would believe it."

It was a shame that Hugh McCollum didn't direct more films, for his style was distinctly different from White's—gentler, and more tasteful. His Three Stooges comedy *Hula La La* (1951) bears his own distinctive mark.

Unfortunately, many of the comedy veterans who were at Columbia at this time had seen better days; drinking problems and sloppy filming techniques were among the hazards the comedy unit faced for employing some of these former greats. Clyde Bruckman's penchant for "borrowing" from his earlier work was hardly unique, but when, for one short, he took the magician's coat sequence from Harold Lloyd's *Movie Crazy* out of the original script, word for word, Columbia faced a lawsuit from Lloyd.

One of the few newcomers to attain success within the unit was Edward Bernds, who had been Columbia's chief

One of the studio's last attempts at a series was in the 1950s with Max Baer and Maxie Rosenbloom.

sound technician since 1929. Speaking of his work in preparing each short, he says today,

Since I wrote, co-wrote, or re-wrote almost all of the two-reelers I directed, I was preparing as I wrote. For instance, I frequently checked the feasibility of a gag with the special effects men before I wrote it. Thus alerted, *they* were able to prepare, too. I had a good relationship with these people, and they would give me the best possible break on cost, frequently shifting costs to the million-dollar epics that Columbia made, which, they reasoned, were much better able to absorb their charges. In the rare instances where I got a script without prior writing work on it, I suppose I prepared for ten days to two weeks—if that much time was available. That included conferences about sets, casting, wardrobe, and, most important in two-reelers, with prop men, stunt men, and special-effects men.

As for improvisation, I tried to be as well prepared as possible, and that meant having the script as complete and as good as I could make it, and having all the mechanical gags thoroughly prepared and ready to go when needed. So I guess you would say that I was much less inclined to improvise than many of the old-timers. I was certainly willing to improvise, and I did; but I like to think that I did it from a solid foundation of script preparation. If you can't think of a good gag when you're writing a script, why should you be able to do it on the set, with the pressures of a tight schedule working against you? We worked on a four-day shooting schedule during my time on two-reelers, which was ample if you didn't waste time, but since so many of our gags required mechanical preparation—breakaway walls, breakaway props, wirebelt rigging and the like—it was disastrous not to figure them out and prepare for them in advance.

By the 1950s, most other studios had dropped their comedy short subjects, but Columbia's continued. One reason was Jules White's relationship with his boss. "I

am one man who *liked* Harry Cohn," he says. "We got along fine because I was not afraid of him, didn't try to fool him, and always made money for Columbia. He was a character, but knew his business. I learned much from him. He never interfered with me or the shorts department. I did exactly as I chose from the day I started to the day I quit. When he died I was so wrought up I didn't want to stay at Columbia. In fact, I just wanted to quit the business. Why wait to drop dead in your harness? For years I had begged *him* to quit."

White and coproducer McCollum had frequent clashes throughout the 1940s, but by the early 1950s they became so violent that a showdown was inevitable. When it occurred, McCollum was fired and White continued as sole head of the short-subject unit. At that point, he made the operation a family affair. His brother Jack wrote many scripts, Jules produced and directed virtually every one (the number was cut from twenty-five a year to fifteen), and his son Harold White edited them. In 1959 he left Columbia, where he had spent the last 25 years, and the short-subjects department closed. White could have gone with Columbia's television department, Screen Gems, and worked on new series ideas, but after one brush with TV (a series with the Wiere Brothers called "Oh, Those Bells") he retired, saying, "Who needs such a rat race?"

Working at Columbia was difficult and, for some, grueling. But in its heyday it offered many people the satisfaction of working with their peers toward a common goal, that of good comedy. Elwood Ullman recalls Del Lord explaining, "You don't have to be nuts to work here, but it helps."

RKO

In the early days of sound, several companies—FBO, Pathé, and Radio Pictures—were gradually merged together. At first, RKO, Pathé, and Radio Pictures tried to maintain separate entities, but finally they came together as RKO Radio Pictures. In the merger stages, a permanent short-subject department was formed under the direction of Harry Sweet, a writer-director-comic. Gloria Morgan, a script supervisor on the shorts, remembers him as "a very gentle, funny man with a delicious sense of humor."

Sweet initiated several series, most notably Edgar Kennedy's "Mr. Average Man" comedies, and directed many himself. He also starred in a number of shorts and supervised other comedies being made at the time with Clark and McCullough, the Masquers Club, etcetera.

When he died in a plane crash, producer Lou Brock took over the short-subject program and stayed on for many years.

Among the directors working on RKO shorts at this time was Mark Sandrich, a bright, inventive director with a keen mind for gimmickry. His imaginative handling of a short called *So This Is Harris,* starring Phil Harris, won the three-reeler an Academy Award as Best Short Subject of the Year in 1933 (the first year that award was given). It also was his stepping-stone to feature films, and after a delightful "B" with Harris called *Melody Cruise,* he went on to direct some of the best musical comedies of the decade, including most of the Fred Astaire and Ginger Rogers vehicles.

After leaving Hal Roach, George Stevens went first to Universal and then to RKO, where he directed six two-reelers and got *his* break at doing a feature film. The influence of his training at Roach was evident in a new series he started at RKO, "The Blondes and the Red-heads."

One thing that set RKO shorts apart from those of rival companies was pictorial quality. RKO was always known as Hollywood's chic studio, and the shorts people had access to the elegant sets and backgrounds that graced the studio's feature films. In addition, the cameramen on these comedies included Ted McCord and Nicholas Musuraca, both of whom went on to great acclaim as cinematographers on some of the top feature films of the 1940s, '50s, and '60s. The lighting, editing, and overall look of the RKO comedies was very polished, something that could never be said of many other two-reelers being made at this time.

This also fit in with the general feel of the comedies, which, especially after Sandrich and Sweet left the department, veered away from slapstick and were more firmly rooted in situation comedy. To be sure, slapstick remained an ingredient, but it was hardly as dominant as it was at Columbia, or even Hal Roach.

Practically every comedy director in Hollywood worked for RKO at one time or another. George Marshall had a brief stay after serving time with both Sennett and Roach, and before making a success in feature films. Jean Yarbrough, who had also worked for Roach and Sennett, acted as writer and director on many RKO comedies in the mid- and late 1930s. "It was quite difficult at times, due to the physical things we did," he recalls, "but with comics like [Edgar] Kennedy and Leon [Errol], we usually came up with a funny show." Yarbrough went on to become one of the most prolific directors of B pictures, and later turned his energies to television, where he is still active.

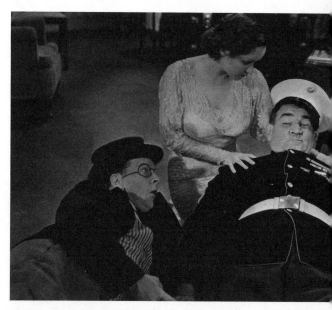

Bobby Clark and Dorothy Granger with another RKO comedy star, Tom Kennedy, in *In the Devil's Doghouse.*

Leigh Jason, a would-be songwriter who had done some of Hal Roach's musical comedies, brought his own touch to RKO and did some musically oriented comedies there. His brother Will, who later did many of the "Pete Smith Specialties" at MGM, also directed for RKO. When Chic Sale was making two-reelers for RKO, his vaudeville straight man, Ben Holmes, worked behind the scenes and became a very competent comedy director. Lloyd French, Alf Goulding, comedy writer Al Boasberg, scenarists Leslie Goodwins and Charles E. Roberts, and assistant director Clem Beauchamp, all took their turns directing the RKO comedy product.

In the 1930s, RKO did a wide variety of miscellaneous shorts called "Headliners," starring Ruth Etting, Tom Kennedy, Chick Chandler, Betty Grable, Tony Martin, Louis Prima, Gene Austin, and Billy Gilbert, among others. Quality varied sharply, from abysmal (*A Quiet Fourth,* starring young Grable) to delightful (*Swing Fever,* with Gilbert and Jack Norton). In 1937 the studio inaugurated a series starring Ray Whitley and his Six Bar Cowboys, a country-western musical group; the films were successful enough to last as a series for six years. They were, by this time, nearly unique items in a field that had gone from the widest range of subjects in the early 1930s to a set of standard types by the early 1940s.

In the 1940s, the RKO comedy output boiled down to two series: Leon Errol and Edgar Kennedy. After 1945, these were made almost entirely by one writer-director, Hal Yates. In the meantime, various producers and directors were doing shorts series for RKO-Pathé, a subsidiary of the studio, such series as "Information Please," based on the popular radio show, "Picture People," RKO's contribution to the Hollywood-behind-the-scenes genre, and "Flicker Flashbacks," a long-running series that showed early silent film clips with hokey narration and gag titles. The originator of this series, and its producer-director, was Richard Fleischer, the son of cartoon-producer Max Fleischer (Popeye, Betty Boop) and later the director of such films as *Fantastic Voyage, The Boston Strangler,* and *Tora! Tora! Tora!*

"Pathé didn't own anything," Fleischer explains about the films he used in "Flicker Flashbacks." "I had to dig it all up myself, from various sources all over the country and, in fact, all over the world. I made a trip to Buenos Aires to pick up a few reels. When I read the Library of Congress had found these old films that were printed

An on-the-set shot while filming *Baby Makes Two,* **with Carol Hughes, Gil Lamb, Frank Nelson, and Claire Carleton.**

Jed Prouty in one of his RKO two-reelers, *Coat Tales.*

on paper, I went down there and made a deal with them. I got some through private sources. I went everywhere to get the films. While I was working on these short subjects, Ike Kleinerman was my assistant, and he is now one of the biggest producers in television; he did 'The 21st Century.' Also when I worked out here on the films, Carl Hunt was cutting them, and he is now the president of DeLuxe Labs."

Fleischer also wrote and directed many entries in the "This Is America" series, a two-reel documentary series inspired by "The March of Time." Produced by Frederic Ullman, Jr., the films recorded various aspects of American life, some serious and some lighthearted. They were generally quite good, and one of the two-reelers got Fleischer his chance to direct feature films for RKO.

As the 1940s drew to a close, and most studios were curtailing or discontinuing short-subject production, RKO moved ahead. No less than three new series were initiated, and new musical shorts were added to the schedule. None of them were exceptionally good, although Gil Lamb's comedies were up to RKO's usual standard. When Leon Errol and Edgar Kennedy died, the studio put many of their older shorts into reissue to meet the apparent demand, and continued to do so until the studio folded in the mid-1950s. To the very end, the RKO shorts had a professional sheen that belied their low budgets and shooting schedules. They always had a look of quality.

Educational Pictures

Hollywood has never been a particularly logical place, so it seemed perfectly natural to most people that one

Left: **Earle W. Hammons, founder and president of Educational Pictures.**

Right: **Broadway star Joe Cook, who made some of Educational's best shorts.**

of the leading producers of comedy shorts was named Educational Pictures. Actually, when Earle W. Hammons established the company in 1919, it was with the idea of making films for schools. This enterprise soon fizzled out, and Hammons turned instead to comedies.

In the 1920s, Educational grew to become a leading contender in the comedy field, with chief producer Jack White, and such stars as Lloyd Hamilton and Lupino Lane, both of whom were very popular. But by the 1930s, Educational's position in the industry had changed somewhat, and it became one of the most curious studios of the era.

If one searched for a key word to describe the Educational comedies of the 1930s, the best one might be "cheap." Educational films almost always looked cheap, even though they were made in most cases by seasoned veterans. One problem was the claustrophobia of shooting at the company's eastern studio in Astoria, Long Island. In addition, one suspects that the largest chunk of the small budgets went to pay the stars' salaries, leaving very little for sets, costumes, and technical frills. Nevertheless, the comedies (which were distributed by 20th Century Fox) always made money, despite the fact that the quality of the material was often downright poor.

The studio's ad copy boasted "the best of the old comedy favorites, the brightest of the new stars . . ."

and that was its claim to fame. Throughout the 1930s, people on the way up and people on the way down always found work at Educational. Among the former group were Edward Everett Horton, Charlotte Greenwood, Bert Lahr, Milton Berle, the Ritz Brothers, Imogene Coca, Danny Kaye, June Allyson, and Barry Sullivan; among the latter were Harry Langdon, Buster Keaton, and (behind the scenes) Mack Sennett. There were also vaudevillians and stage comedians like Ernest Truex, Tom Howard and George Shelton, Buster West and Tom Patricola, Tim and Irene Ryan, and Joe Cook, who were not down on their luck, but whose stage success meant little in the movie world.

Worst of all were Educational's own stars—unknowns and young hopefuls who were starred and featured in an endless procession of unfunny comedies and excruciating musicals. Even people like Billy Gilbert got involved in some of the studio's endeavors, including a heavy-handed musical satire of Communism called *Hail, Brother* (1935). With newcomers as well as old-timers, the material was often below par, and little could be done with it. It took the hilarious dialect comedy of young Danny Kaye, in films like *Getting an Eyeful,* the contagious good-naturedness of Joe Cook, or the sheer professionalism of Charlotte Greenwood to overcome bad scripts.

Bert Lahr's two-reelers were made for Educational at a time when he was enjoying great success on Broadway. When they were good (as with *Off the Horses*) they were very good, but when they were bad (as with *No More West*) the most generous helping of Lahr's mannerisms and mugging was useless.

Grinding out some sixty shorts a year, the Educational team was bound to do something right once in a while, but more often than not the Educational shorts were tired slapdash affairs, and the studio died a quiet death in the late 1930s.

MGM

MGM was the Tiffany of motion picture studios, and never more so than in the 1930s and 1940s. To maintain the MGM image, it was important that every film that opened with the famous Metro lion carry with it the integrity and overall "class" that characterized the studio. This included short subjects as well as feature films, and during those two decades, no short subjects were as meticulously made as MGM's. Certainly none looked so good.

In the early 1930s, short-subject production at the studio was rather limited, since MGM distributed Hal

Delightful long-legged Charlotte Greenwood, in the Educational comedy *Girls Will Be Boys*.

Roach's product and advertised it with its own product. Thus, the only shorts that the studio itself made were the occasional "MGM Oddities" and offbeat one-shots.

One special short, released for Christmas of 1932, was called "Jackie Cooper's Christmas." It ran nine minutes and had little Jackie wanting to give a Christmas party for his football team, but being unable to manage such an ambitious enterprise. He brings his problem to Norma Shearer, who arranges with Louis B. Mayer for the use of an empty sound stage. There, hundreds of youngsters are treated to a tremendous party, with such stars as Marion Davies, Lionel Barrymore, Clark Gable, Leila Hyams, Wallace Beery, Polly Moran, and Marie Dressler serving food and acting as chaperones. The one-reeler was distinctively MGM's.

The studio also released a series of musicals, comedies, and travelogues in Technicolor throughout the 1930s; they were another example of traditional Metro opulence. One of the first homegrown series at MGM was the invention of comedy directors Zion Myers (the brother of silent-screen star Carmel Myers) and Jules White. Called the "Dogville" comedies, they featured trained canines acting out spoofs of current movies. One of the earliest entries was *The Dogway Melody,* which actually used the "Singin' in the Rain" soundtrack from *Broadway Melody,* with Cliff Edwards and the Brox Sisters. Another entry that year was *All Quiet on the Canine Front.* These shorts, like the later "Speaking of Animals" comedies, were strictly one-joke items however, and after the initial novelty wore off, there was little to shout about.

Another man who was to figure prominently in the development of MGM shorts was Pete Smith, who in the early 1930s headed the studio's advertising department. When someone was needed to put together the studio's then-current series of sports films, Smith was given the assignment. He added his own sense of humor to the otherwise standard footage of football, fishing, diving, golfing, etcetera. As his shorts became more popular, the subject matter became more freewheeling, and by 1935 they were known as the "Pete Smith Specialties." The series, under that name, continued for the next twenty years.

A man named Jack Chertok, who had started as script clerk at the studio, was made head of short-subject production in the mid-1930s. It was at this time that four other successful series were initiated at the studio: "Crime Does Not Pay," "John Nesbitt's Passing Parade," "Carey Wilson Miniatures," and the Robert Benchley

MGM starlet Irene Hervey is pressed into service for a 1934 Pete Smith short, *Taking Care of Baby.*

shorts. With these series the MGM shorts department flourished and developed a great deal of formidable talent.

George Sidney, who was in charge of shooting the studio's screen tests, was a teen-ager when he got his first directorial assignment from Pete Smith. He says of his work in the shorts department,

Writing, preparation, budgeting, shooting, and editing were done with the same thoroughness as a feature. From the idea to the answer print would be several months. We had access to most facilities so long as we did not get in the way.

Mr. Mayer was too busy to be active [in the department]. He built and ran the most successful film factory the world has ever, or will, know. He allowed and guided more talents to be developed in every phase than any single person in the history of motion pictures. A few of the graduates of the shorts department were Fred Zinnemann, Buddy Adler, Jack Chertok, David Miller, Jerry Bresler, John Farrow, Joseph Losey, Jules Dassin, Robert Taylor, Roy Rowland, etc. The shorts department was a great training arena for so very many, and a stimulating way of life.

Fred Zinnemann has said that the shorts were prepared meticulously in order to compensate for small budgets, and that the young directors considered it a challenge to make up for the minimal budgets by using their imaginations.

In this, Zinnemann and his many colleagues succeeded. The shorts that were made at MGM in the 1930s and 1940s showed genuinely creative minds at work, covering a wide range of subject matter in ingenious ways, with the best cinematography, art direction, sets, music, and casts that Hollywood had to offer. There was often more "production" in a ten-minute MGM short than in an eighty-minute Monogram feature.

Shorts were also a proving ground for actors on the studio lot. Notable examples include Robert Taylor's appearance in *Buried Loot,* the first "Crime Does Not Pay"; James Stewart in a Chic Sale short, *Important News;* and Judy Garland costarring with Deanna Durbin in a musical short, *Every Sunday.*

Most of the directors in the department graduated to feature films; as they did, new recruits like Jacques Tourneur, Cyril Endfield, and Walter Hart were brought in to take their place. The quality of the MGM shorts remained consistently good through the late 1940s; by the 1950s, only Pete Smith was carrying on a regular production schedule.

The only sour apple in this otherwise untarnished group

A small sample of MGM opulence, from a "Crime Does Not Pay" short, *Pound Foolish;* Roy Gordon is toasting Neil Hamilton.

was "Our Gang," which MGM bought from Hal Roach in 1938. For six years the studio produced these one-reel comedies, proving once again that, for all its gloss and expertise, MGM was amazingly bereft of comedy know-how. In 1944 the series was discontinued, much to the relief of those who had come to love the shorts as they once were.

Over the years, MGM shorts proved to be unfailingly popular with audiences; they won countless awards; and they produced a great deal of talent—outstanding achievements for any films, and a particular credit to the studio's fine short subjects.

Paramount

One of two studios with a major production facility in the east (the other was Warner Brothers), Paramount made use of this site to lure as many Broadway and vaudeville names as possible to appear in their films. Many of the performers went into feature films and, if suc-

cessful, moved to Hollywood and greater success. An equal number appeared in Paramount shorts, which had the biggest lineup of top names of any studio during the early 1930s. When the studio abandoned its Astoria sound stages and made its shorts in Hollywood, the focus shifted from stars to big bands.

Some of the early Astoria-made shorts show no imagination at all. *Radio Rhythm* (1929), directed by Joseph Santley, has two cameras filming Rudy Vallee and his Connecticut Yankees on a small platform. One gets a head-on shot of the entire group, and the other, angled off to the side, shows a closer view of Vallee himself. The shots are intermingled throughout the reel, and once when the camera cuts to close-up, Vallee is off-center and the camera jerkily moves over to regain composition.

Any shorts calling for exterior shots were also in trouble. An Ethel Merman one-reeler from 1931, *Roaming,*

MGM adds glamour to a traditional Pete Smith pool short with Willie Mosconi and Jimmy Caras; the girls are Corinne Calvet and Joi Lansing, and the film is *Super Cue Men*.

casts her as the daughter of a medicine-show man who always is on the road. Since it was absolutely necessary to have a great deal of outdoor footage, this was filmed silent, badly overdubbed later, and then intercut with interior mock-ups showing the same scenes in a tighter shot. The result is quite haphazard, and the reel itself is rather silly. But as with the Vallee short, what counts in the long run is the value of having Ethel Merman on film; one tends to forgive the cinematic shortcomings in consideration of the entertainment value.

Occasionally, entire vaudeville sketches, combining a story or comedy with music, would be filmed. An example is Eddie Cantor's *Insurance* (1930), an entertaining reel in which Eddie goes to a doctor for a physical examination and gives him a hard time. Eddie tells him he can't sleep. "Oh, insomnia," the doctor replies. "No," says Eddie, "I can't sleep." "Why can't you sleep?" the doctor persists. "I can't find a place!" Later in the discussion Cantor is distracted by the nurse's pretty legs and tells her that she's out of style. He sings a song, "Now That the Girls Are Wearing Long Dresses (Men Can Keep Their Minds on Their Work)." The short is probably a faithful recreation of one of Cantor's vaudeville routines and, as such, is a valuable record of what it must have been like to see a headliner at the Palace.

Jack Benny, Burns and Allen, Lillian Roth, Irene Bordoni, Charlie Ruggles, Harry Richman, Ruth Etting, Smith and Dale, Helen Kane, Jack Haley, George Jessel, Victor Moore, and other top stars all appeared in one- and two-reel shorts for Paramount filmed at the Astoria studio. The money was good, the work was easy, and the schedule didn't interfere with most nighttime performances, so most players were more than happy to be approached by the studio.

When Paramount moved all its operations to the West Coast, the nature of their short subjects changed drastically. Fewer vaudeville headliners appeared, and the studio began relying more and more on big bands: Louis Armstrong, Ben Bernie, Cab Calloway, Duke Ellington, and most of the other name bands of the day.

The studio also had a great affection for songwriters, and made innumerable subjects with them. As early as 1929, Rodgers and Hart starred in a two-reeler called *Makers of Melody,* in which they were called upon to act out preposterous skits showing how they got the inspiration for such tunes as "Manhattan" and "Blue Room." The studio's resident songsmiths, Mack Gordon and Harry Revel, appeared in a number of shorts during the 1930s, as well as the 1936 feature *Collegiate*. Gordon, an ingratiating ham, loved to sing his own tunes while Revel accompanied him on the piano. Paramount worked up a one-reeler in 1934 called Hollywood Rhythm, supposedly showing them hard at work creating songs for Lyda Roberti and Jack Oakie to sing in the feature *College Rhythm*. Engaging in its silliness, the film helped to maintain the public image of the happy-go-lucky, hardworking Hollywood songwriters.

There were endless other shorts, mostly in the "Paramount Pictorial" series, with Hoagy Carmichael, Ralph Rainger and Leo Robin, Harold Arlen, Con Conrad, and other top tunesmiths. Several shorts featured Sigmund Spaeth, the "tune detective," demonstrating his encyclopedic knowledge of songs and their origins.

The studio also favored a large number of miscellany shorts. "Paramount Pictorial" was a screen magazine covering such diverse topics as "Artistry in Glass Making" and "Ann Leaf at the Organ." These shorts frequently included short sequences of entertainers, either snatched from other Paramount products or filmed especially for the series. "Screen Souvenirs" was one of the first series to make use of early silent footage, both factual and fictional; and unlike some other series of this kind, it avoided mocking the silent footage, presenting it instead as it was originally meant to be seen. Occasional compilations, such as *Fashions in Love,* showing lovemaking on the screen from the Edison film *The Kiss* through the

early 1930s, and "Movie Milestones," which collected great scenes from Paramount silent features, were of special interest.

After leaving Pathé, Grantland Rice brought his "Sportlights" series to Paramount, amassing 206 reels during his stay there. "Unusual Occupations" was a forerunner of several TV panel shows depicting ordinary Americans whose jobs ranged from making artificial eyes to constructing furniture from cactus plants. In the 1940s, this series had the added interest of being shot in color.

Paramount made several stabs at entering the behind-the-scenes rally, first with "Broadway Highlights," narrated by Ted Husing, then with the sucessful "Hollywood on Parade," in the early 1930s, and finally with the short-lived "Hedda Hopper's Hollywood," in the early 1940s. But the studio seemed to fare best with its always intriguing one-shot items, such as *Rube Goldberg's Travelgab,* a Goldberg's-eye view of New York City; *Find What's Wrong,* a collection of movie mistakes revealed to the audience; *Lucky Stars,* showing a variety of Paramount screen tests; and the unforgettable *Hollywood Extra Girl,* a promotional short for *The Crusades* showing Cecil B. De Mille as a wise, benevolent director who gives a break to an extra-girl. The short is gloriously phony—as when De Mille, on an interior set, addresses

Burns and Allen in one of their starring shorts, *Babbling Book*.

a crowd of extras who are shown in a reaction shot to be on an exterior location!

In 1930, Paramount entered another unusual field within the realm of short subjects: the commercial short. Commercials in movie theatres were nothing new at this time; many filmmakers, including Walt Disney, had broken into the motion-picture business by making such films for local theatres around the country. But studios had not gotten involved in the field to any great extent until Paramount took the plunge. One short for a well-known toothpaste, for example, was made at a cost of $7,500. Paramount charged the client $15,000 to show the film in one hundred Paramount theatres (that's $150 a theatre), to an estimated three to four million people. Many of Paramount's commercial shorts, such as *A Jolt for General Germ,* an eight-minute animated commercial for Lysol produced in 1930, were made by their resident cartoon producer, Max Fleischer.

By the end of the year, Paramount was doing quite a number of these films, and Warner Brothers was getting in on the act with a Liggett and Myers tie-in. The Warners shorts were more subtle, however, giving the viewer a full reel of entertainment (one short starred Clark and McCullough) and only showing the sponsor's name at the beginning and end.

In 1931, at least one theatre began announcing in its newspaper ads that patrons would see no advertising except coming attractions on its screen. *Variety* and some other trade papers spoke harshly of the blatantly commercial films that the studios were forcing on exhibitors, and in so doing alienating their customers. The studios took the hint and production dropped sharply, but the practice did not die out entirely. As late as 1941, Paramount made a two-reel short called *There's Nothing to It,* starring Charles Butterworth, promoting Westinghouse washing machines.

The 1940s brought new series to Paramount, including the Robert Benchley comedies; a group of Technicolor two-reel musicals starring unknowns, new contractees, and a generous helping of character actors; "Speaking of Animals," Jerry Fairbanks's clever but tiresome series showing animals wisecracking (just their mouths were animated): and a short-lived series of "Pacemakers" starring Tom Ewell, Patsy Kelly, and Red Barber, among others, in lightly amusing human-interest films.

What Paramount had, more than most studios producing short subjects, was genuine variety, and it was this that maintained interest in their shorts over the years.

Mack Sennett

Mack Sennett pioneered screen humor, and by the second decade of this century had more than earned the title "King of Comedy." One need hardly recount the fact that Sennett learned the filmmaking craft under the tutelage of D. W. Griffith, and that when he formed his own studio he discovered and fostered such talents as Mabel Normand, Charlie Chaplin, Ford Sterling, Chester Conklin, Hank Mann, "Fatty" Arbuckle, Ben Turpin, Edgar Kennedy, Charley Chase, Al St. John, Slim Summerville, Charlie Murray, Gloria Swanson, Wallace Beery, Louise Fazenda, Polly Moran, Billy Bevan, Andy Clyde, Harry Langdon, and Carole Lombard, to name a few. The Sennett studio was the birthplace of the greatest screen comedy of its day, and the springboard for most of the great comic talents who flowered during the 1920s.

Nobody could top Sennett at his own game: fast-moving, belly-laugh comedies with nonstop action, slapstick, and sight gags. Unfortunately, Sennett didn't realize that audience tastes were beginning to change in the 1920s and that screen comedy was coming to depend more and more on characterization and deliberate pacing rather than on breakneck speed. What is more, Sennett had an uncanny knack of losing his biggest properties

The King of Comedy, Mack Sennett.

as soon as they became stars. So, while his films of the mid- and late 1920s were filled with talented people, they seldom had star attractions to draw box-office crowds.

By the time sound came to the movie industry, Mack Sennett's name no longer carried the weight it once had. He moved from Pathé distribution to Educational, a significant change, for, while his films still appeared in many theatres, the stigma of being associated with Educational was a sure sign that Sennett was no longer the king who reigned over screen comedy.

Sound opened some new vistas for Sennett, however. The tie-in with Educational relieved him of many administrative duties, and he was able to return to directing, his first love. He tried to avoid the "old-fashioned" tag by doing more modern comedies, with youth-oriented plots and new faces, but he inevitably returned to the type of humor that had made him famous. And, surprisingly enough, he added a few more names to the roster of his notable discoveries.

One new experiment for Sennett was the use of color. He called his particular process "natural color" and used it on several two-reelers, including a "special" in 1931 called *Movie Town,* in which Sennett appeared as himself, along with contractees Marjorie Beebe, Frank Eastman, Virginia Whiting, and Marion Sayers.

Another was the use of music. Sennett tried to interpolate songs into a number of his shorts, and hired George Olsen's popular band on at least one occasion to perform in a two-reeler. He also starred Irish tenor Donald Novis in a short-lived series of musical comedies. But Sennett's biggest success in this department, and his biggest success of the sound era, was a series of two-reelers starring Bing Crosby.

Crosby was trying to launch a solo career, after achieving success as part of Paul Whiteman's Rhythm Boys. He was singing at the Coconut Grove in Los Angeles and making quite a splash with his unique singing style and listenable songs like "I Surrender, Dear" and "Wrap Your Troubles in Dreams," written for him by his ex-partner Harry Barris. With no particular offers coming his way, he decided to accept an offer made by Mack Sennett to star in some two-reelers. In his autobiography, *Call Me Lucky,* Bing recalled,

The way we made those Sennett shorts reads like a quaint piece of Americana. For two days we'd have a story conference. I was in on it. In fact, everybody was in on it—actors, cameramen, gagmen, and Sennett. . . . For our title we used the name of the basic song in the picture, like "I Surrender, Dear," "At Your Command," or "Just One More Chance." . . . [Sennett] put nothing down on paper. His story was really a series of gags. We always would end up with somebody falling in a fish pond or some other device with "punch" possibilities. . . . The songs we used were usually shot against a nightclub background or in a radio station or at a microphone. We weren't clever or adroit about working the songs subtly into the action. Sennett just said, "Now we'll have a song," and we had one.

This carefree formula was perfect for showcasing Crosby's easygoing style and natural charm, and the fact that he sang many hit songs of the day made them doubly popular. *Blue of the Night,* the fifth of his six Sennett shorts, made in 1933, was probably the best, featuring the title tune (which became Bing's theme), "Auf Wiedersehn," and a frothy plot involving sprightly Marjorie "Babe" Kane and Franklin Pangborn. The Crosby shorts remained in perpetual re-release through the 1940s, under their original titles as well as many new monickers. They were spliced together by Astor Pictures into a "feature" called *The Road to Hollywood.*

Sennett's other major "discovery" of the sound era was W. C. Fields. Fields had been in movies sporadically since 1915, never with any outstanding success. His four shorts for Sennett were not generally appreciated at the time of their release, but they have survived over the years as some of the Great Man's funniest films.

Bing Crosby and players in one of his starring two-reelers.

The Sennett staff at this time included such first-rate writers and directors as Del Lord, William Beaudine, Lewis R. Foster, George Marshall, Clyde Bruckman, Felix Adler, and Eddie Cline. But since they had to turn out as many as thirty-five two-reelers a year, the quality of the product varied sharply from film to film. Oddly enough, Sennett tried to veer away from slapstick so sharply that when he returned to it in a big way, as in Andy Clyde's *Don't Bite Your Dentist* (1930) or the classic *Great Pie Mystery* (1931), the films were received as nostalgic reminders of comedy's golden age.

One suspects that Sennett never really wanted to drop slapstick, and probably, if he had stayed with it, he could have survived through the 1930s. But his semisituation comedy shorts and romantic two-reelers were incredibly unfunny, despite the presence of cast members such as Walter Catlett, Franklin Pangborn, Joyce Compton, Dorothy Granger, Marjorie Beebe, Harry Gribbon, and Grady Sutton. In trying to be more "modern," Sennett was not being himself, and that is where his films failed.

Even when others handled the direction, however, Sennett was personally involved. " 'The Old Man,' as he was called behind his back, was always around and knew every minute what was going on," Dorothy Granger recalls. "He used to leave occasionally and take his boat and go fishing. But he always had a few spies on the set to keep him posted. He directed a few of the comedies. I was petrified when I learned he was going to direct me for the first time. I had heard from others that he was a real s.o.b. to actors when he directed them. But he was as nice as pie (custard, that is) to me."

George Chandler, who acted in several Sennett shorts, including *The Fatal Glass of Beer,* says succinctly, "He *knew* comedy."

In mid-1932 Sennett and Educational parted company, and Paramount began distributing the comedies. This association lasted only one year, however, at which time Sennett shut down his studio. He was generally inactive, although a familiar figure on the Hollywood scene, until 1935, when he took a brief flier at directing again, for Educational Pictures. Here, for the only time, he worked with Buster Keaton, on a two-reeler called *The Timid Young Man.*

His last film, a short called *Way up Thar,* introduced Joan Davis to the screen in a delightful hillbilly musical comedy which also gave wonderful opportunities to Myra and Louise Keaton, Buster's mother and sister, and to a group called "The Sons of the Pioneers" (including a young man later to be called Roy Rogers).

Precisely why Sennett left Educational is not clear; it *is* clear that there was nowhere to go once he had left that studio. Jules White claims that he once bought a script for a Columbia short from Sennett, using a *nom de plume.* And Sennett continued to be a part of Hollywood social life, even appearing as himself in a number of films over the years (*Hollywood Cavalcade, Down Memory Lane, Abbott and Costello Meet the Keystone Kops, etcetera*). But it seems sad that one of cinema's giants should have been put out to pasture so early in life. He lived to be eighty and died in Hollywood in 1960.

Like D. W. Griffith and other film pioneers, Sennett was responsible for establishing a good part of the foundation of American filmmaking, but once having laid that foundation, he found himself gradually being bypassed by younger entrepreneurs who were able to take what he had invented and develop it more fully. His contribution to American film cannot be underestimated, but, unfortunately, by the sound era, Mack Sennett was no longer the King of Comedy.

Two of Sennett's talking stars of the early 1930s: Lloyd Hamilton and Marjorie Beebe.

The Sennett style hadn't changed that much by the 1930s. Franklin Pangborn eyes a messy Walter Catlett.

Warner Brothers

When Warner Brothers secured the rights to the Vita-phone sound-on-disc process for talking pictures, they prepared a gala program to launch this movie milestone. On the evening of August 7, 1926, moviegoers at New York's Piccadilly Theater were treated to an evening of Vitaphone products, beginning with introductory remarks spoken from the screen by Will Hays, the president of the Motion Picture Producers and Distributors of America, and proceeding with musical pieces performed by the New York Philharmonic Orchestra, Metropolitan Opera singer Marion Talley, entertainer Roy Smeck, Anna Case, Mischa Elman and, for a finale, Giovanni Martinelli sing-ing "Vesti la Giubba" from *I Pagliacci.* This program of shorts was a prelude to *Don Juan,* a silent film with syn-chronized sound effects and a musical score.

Thus, while *Don Juan* had a sound track, the first all-talking films made with the new process were short sub-jects. The Vitaphone Corporation (70 percent owned by Warner Brothers), which had its name on these films, was involved with all Warners' initial talking pictures, but after a studio was set up on Avenue M in Brooklyn, the sub-sidiary devoted itself to short subjects exclusively for the rest of its existence.

In 1928, the head of Vitaphone production in New York set about to film a series of "Vitaphone Acts." By the end of the following year, the company had churned out hundreds of short films featuring famous and unknown vaudeville performers doing songs, dances, novelty acts, dramatic sketches, etcetera. By 1930, it was obvious that a little more finesse would be helpful in producing the shorts, and quantity was allowed to diminish as quality was augmented.

When Sam Sax took over as production manager of the eastern studio in 1931, he continued to recruit as many New York headliners as possible, but tried to make the shorts better than the rather nondescript "Vitaphone Varieties." The performers were happy to work for Vita-phone; it was easy work and good money.

Vitaphone's forte was musicals. With musical director David Mendoza, young songwriters Sammy Cahn and Saul Chaplin, ex-hoofer-turned-director Roy Mack, and a host of top Broadway and vaudeville performers, the Vitaphone musical product was generally quite good.

One of the studio's top musical stars was the delightful dancer Hal LeRoy, who made his first Vitaphone short with his partner, Mitzi Mayfair after starring in the 1931 *Ziegfeld Follies;* he continued to star in two-reelers for the studio throughout the decade.

"We did the shorts in three days," he recalls. "Two and a half days shooting, a half day scoring. The first half day you'd score all the musical numbers, which were written especially for the shorts. Some of the great choreographers were out there in those days. Harlan Dixon was considered one of the great eccentric dancers of all time, and he was a choreographer out there. As far as my dancing was concerned, I was an ad-lib dancer, so it was very hard for me to set a routine and match it. So all they did was score the music, and when I shot the dance, they put mikes on the side and recorded the taps during the playback."

Ziegfeld Follies stars Hal LeRoy and Mitzi Mayfair in a Vita-phone short, *Use Your Imagination.*

The scripts were fairly complete, enabling the produc-tion crew to arrange an orderly shooting schedule. "We'd start on a Monday and by Wednesday night at 5:00 we were through," LeRoy explains. "If you were in a show, and you were going to run overtime, they'd shoot around you, get you out of the way, so you could leave the studio around 5."

He admits that the scripts were pretty silly—"just there to utilize the talents." But every once in a while something fresh and original would emerge. "They had me one time as a bellhop, and I had these shoes to shine that be-longed to Pat Rooney. I had a row of shoes lined up, and as I was shining shoes with the rhythm of the cloth, the other shoes started to tap, and I did a dance with all the shoes dancing around me—which was a cute idea. They did it with wires. Roy Mack got that idea."

Another highlight was an entertaining short called *The Prisoner of Swing,* an elaborate spoof of *The Prisoner of Zenda,* with LeRoy in the dual role. One young man who played extra roles in some of these musicals was Phil Silvers. LeRoy's leading ladies included Toby Wing, June Allyson, Dorothy Lee, and Betty Hutton. All were at the outset of their careers; June Allyson was one of Sam Sax's brightest discoveries. She worked in many Vitaphone shorts while establishing a name for herself on Broadway.

For LeRoy, as for many others, the shorts were also a career springboard. He was already well known on Broadway, but one day Doris Warner was visiting the eastern studios and, after watching LeRoy film one of his shorts, recommended him for the title role in the studio's impending remake of *Harold Teen.* A screen test was made in New York and sent to the Coast, where LeRoy was accepted, and where he filmed the feature later that year.

Of Sam Sax, LeRoy recalls, "You'd have an 8:00 call in make-up, and who would come along with a container of coffee in his hand but Sam Sax. You'd go on the set 8:45, 9:00, and Sam would be there all day long."

Sax was largely responsible for the high quality of the Vitaphone product. In addition to seeking out new talent for the films, he always had his eye open for intriguing ideas. When he realized that Warners, having filmed *Fifty Million Frenchmen* in 1931 minus the Cole Porter score, owned all the show's tunes, he commissioned a two-reel condensation of the show to include as many of the show's songs as possible. The result, *Paree, Paree* (1934), starred Bob Hope and Dorothy Stone, included the hit "You Do Something to Me," and looked like a *Reader's Digest* version of the original play. Similarly, the studio did two-reel versions of previously filmed musicals such as *Spring Is Here,* calling it *Yours Sincerely,* featuring Lanny Ross, *The Flame Song* (from *Song of the Flame*), and *The Red Shadow* (from *The Desert Song*) with Alexander Gray and Bernice Claire, among others.

When Mack Sennett had great success starring Bing Crosby in two-reelers, Sam Sax hired Crosby's "rival," Russ Columbo, for an entertaining short called *That Goes Double,* featuring the singer's biggest hits, "Prisoner of Love," and "You Call It Madness."

Ruth Etting, who had a prolific career in short subjects, made a large number for Vitaphone, along with Donald Novis, Phil Harris, Morton Downey, Eddie Foy, Jr., Bill "Bojangles" Robinson, Jane Froman, Grace and Peter Lind Hayes, Lillian Roth, the infant Sammy Davis, Jr.,

Hal LeRoy and a very young June Allyson in *The Prisoner of Swing,* an elaborate spoof of *The Prisoner of Zenda.*

Dorothy Lamour, Frances Langford, Nick Lucas, The Frazee Sisters, June and Cherry Preisser, Fifi D'Orsay, Bernice Claire, Irene Bordoni, Gertrude Niesen, Molly Picon, Wini Shaw, The Yacht Club Boys and Harriet Hilliard, to name just a few.

In the field of drama, Vitaphone petered out after the initial "Vitaphone Acts," which had featured performers as diverse as Helen Broderick (with Lester Crawford) and Dame Judith Anderson. A notable exception was the studio's S. S. Van Dine mystery series in 1931 and 1932, featuring Donald Meek and John Hamilton, a so-so series of whodunits which at least had novelty value, if not the quality of the Philo Vance features which were being made at the same time. Drama pretty much left the picture until the Hollywood studio took over short-subject production in 1940. Of that, more later.

As far as comedy was concerned, Vitaphone was prolific but not especially adept. Joe Penner, Ken Murray, Jack Haley, Joe Frisco, Ben Blue, Shemp Howard, Benny Rubin, William Demarest, Henry Armetta, and supporting players Johnny Berkes, Lionel Stander, and Charles Judels all starred in Vitaphone comedies that were more often bad than good. Alf Goulding and Lloyd French were the principal directors.

One of the feathers in Sam Sax's hat, however, was the rediscovery of Roscoe "Fatty" Arbuckle. The collapse of Arbuckle's screen career following a notorious scandal in 1922, even though he was completely exonerated, is one of the blackest pages in Hollywood history, a shameful disgrace. Contrary to popular opinion, Arbuckle did

work quite a bit after the scandal, primarily as a comedy director at Educational studios during the early 1930s, in addition to accepting odd jobs like the direction of Marion Davies's *The Red Mill*. This was all under the name of William Goodrich (his friend Buster Keaton had suggested the original pseudonym Will B. Good, but it was thought a bit too obvious), and the public never suspected the director's true identity.

On October 11, 1932, *Film Daily* reported, "And mebbe you think Sam Sax, manager of the Warner Vitaphone stude, isn't feeling chipper these days after the showing that the first Roscoe 'Fatty' Arbuckle film scored when they ran it cold in two theaters in New Jersey the other nite, the Fabian in Hoboken and the Ritz in Jersey City. Fatty had the customers fairly rolling in their seats, so it looks as if the rotund comic has scored his comeback decisively. In back of it all is a story of a careful and well-planned build-up for months on the part of Arbuckle's managers, Leo Morrison and Joe Rivkin, who spotted him in on key spots for stage appearances. Then, Sam Sax went to work over at Vitaphone on the first of

Young Bob Hope and Johnny Berkes in *Calling All Tars*.

the shorts series. Now the rest is history. Mr. A. is definitely back."

Arbuckle made only six shorts for Vitaphone, but they were generally quite good, fondly reminiscent of the silent comedies, and showing Arbuckle to good advantage. The best of the group was the last, *Buzzin' Around,* directed by Alf Goulding and costarring Arbuckle's longtime crony, Al St. John. Involving Fatty's formula that makes fragile china unbreakable, the short, filmed mostly outside the Brooklyn Warner studio, moves at a brisk pace and is filled with inventive sight gags. Arbuckle's death shortly after completing this two-reeler put an end to hopes that his career would flower once again.

Another of Sax's discoveries was Bob Hope, who had scored a hit on Broadway in *Roberta* and had appeared in a few odd shorts for Educational and Universal. Hope was still several years away from achieving nationwide fame on radio and in films when he made his string of two-reelers for Vitaphone. They show a brash young comic (usually teamed with fall guy Johnny Berkes) who has a good sense of delivery, but no material to deliver.

In his recent autobiography, George Murphy recalled working wtih Hope in *Roberta* and wrote, "Doc Shurr got Bob a contract to make several movie shorts out on Long Island [it was actually Brooklyn]. Hope asked me if I'd like to appear in one of them. My instincts told me to thank the gentleman and decline. The shorts turned out to be pretty dreadful." Hope didn't like his films either, and, after seeing one, told Walter Winchell, "When they catch John Dillinger, they're going to make him sit through it twice."

One of the brighter spots in the Vitaphone comedy field was the Edgar Bergen–Charlie McCarthy series. When Bergen first began filming the shorts in 1930 he was virtually unknown, and the quality was variable. But as his fame grew and his material improved, the shorts got better and better. In the mid- and late 1930s, Bergen-McCarthy shorts, such as *Double Talk,* were a delight.

Worthy of mention for historical purposes only is a short-lived "Joe Palooka" series that Vitaphone attempted in the mid-1930s. Starring Robert Norton as brawny but pea-brained fighter Joe Palooka, Shemp Howard as his manager Knobby Walsh, Johnny Berkes as his second, and Beverly Phalon as his girl friend, nine two-reelers were made before Vitaphone threw in the towel. Viewers must have given up long before that, after watching these clumsy attempts to turn the well-known comic strip into a series of infantile comedies.

Around 1935, Warners started to revitalize short-subject production in its Hollywood studio; the two major directors involved were Crane Wilbur and Ralph Staub. Staub, the entrepreneur of "Screen Snapshots," had worked with Sennett during the 1920s and was a good comedy director; his two-reelers, such as *Lonesome Trailer,* with El Brendel, easily outshone most of the New York comedy product. In 1935, he directed a film that was to become a movie milestone, *Keystone Hotel.* As he recalled, shortly before his death several years ago,

The picture, including all the chases, was made in seven days. I personally knew Ford Sterling, Ben Turpin, Chester Conklin, and others appearing in the film. I sold them on starting a new slapstick series. Jack Warner would only permit me to contract with the players for *one* picture. After the preview at Warner's Hollywood theater, Warner said "sign them for a series," but this was not possible. Their agents were there at the preview and when I approached them, they wanted *triple* the salary they received in *Keystone Hotel.* Jack Warner would not go for the hike in salary (I couldn't blame him).

The short was a brilliant revival of the Keystone slapstick formula, featuring Sterling, Turpin, Conklin, Hank Mann, Marie Prevost, Jack Duffy, Vivien Oakland, Dewey Robinson, and the Keystone Kops. It has some wonderful chase footage and concludes with perhaps the greatest pie-throwing melee ever filmed. It is so good, in fact, that ever since 1935, whenever anyone has used supposed-Mack-Sennett footage for a documentary, it has usually been from *Keystone Hotel,* minus the sound track!

Crane Wilbur had been the leading man in the legendary "Perils of Pauline" series in 1914, but writing and directing always interested him more than acting. He began to do shorts for Warners that combined comedy, drama, and human-interest material, often shooting them in Technicolor. Color must have been the only interest factor in many of them, which today are cloying and difficult to sit through, particularly those starring a precocious British youngster named Sybil Jason. *A Day at Santa Anita* has minimal value beyond its hackneyed story line, with quick shots of various Warner Brothers stars (Edward G. Robinson, Bette Davis, Olivia de Havilland, etcetera) supposedly watching the race—and shot in Technicolor.

In 1940, the Brooklyn Vitaphone studio was closed; Sam Sax joined the sales department of Warner Brothers, and short-subject production, although not as vigorous, was continued on the West Coast. In the last days of the New York operation, Vitaphone had started filming some of the best big-band musical reels of the day, with Artie Shaw, Eddy Duchin, Woody Herman, Freddy Martin, Clyde McCoy, Glen Gray, Hal Kemp, Isham Jones, Vincent Lopez, etcetera. One of the studio's last "discoveries" in the field of comedy was Red Skelton, shown at his very best in a fine two-reeler called *Seein' Red* (1939).

The Hollywood production team, topped by producer Gordon Hollingshead, issued a very different kind of product—mostly miniature dramas, Westerns, and musicals, all with impressive production value and frequently filmed in Technicolor. The most successful shorts of this kind were the Warners historical two-reelers, led by *Sons of Liberty* (1939), a "special" starring Claude Rains and Gale Sondergaard, directed by Michael Curtiz, filmed in color, and the winner of an Academy Award.

Warners continued to turn out these patriotic shorts, which usually favored fiction over fact, covering the Bill of Rights, the Declaration of Independence, the Monroe Doctrine, and the stories of Clara Barton, Patrick Henry, Andrew Jackson, Buffalo Bill Cody, and Francis Scott Key. Directed mostly by Crane Wilbur (who also wrote the scripts), these films were audience-minded hokum at its best, full of cute coincidences (At the end of *Old*

Hickory, the Andrew Jackson story, two observers cheer Jackson on, and one tells the other that he too will lead his people some day—cutting to a shot of the young Abraham Lincoln).

Not accidentally, one of the best in this series was *not* done by Wilbur, but instead by B. Reeves "Breezy" Eason, the legendary second-unit director. *Wild West Days,* filmed in color, was a highly fictionalized account of the pony express and one of its riders, Bill Cody (George Reeves). It makes no more sense than any of the Warners historical shorts, but it moves like lightning and packs more into two reels than many feature films do in an hour and a half.

The original musicals made at this time must be seen to be believed. They are ridiculous, in an amusing sort of way, and most contain songs written by Jack Scholl and M. K. Jerome, two songsmiths who were under studio contract (they wrote "Knock on Wood" for Dooley Wilson to sing in *Casablanca*). *Royal Rodeo,* filmed in color, stars John Payne, Scotty Beckett, and Cliff Edwards, with little Scotty as the ruler of a mythical kingdom and the others, stars of a Wild West show, helping him avert sabotage in his country. *The Singing Dude* stars Dennis Morgan and Fuzzy Knight in an amiable Western tale. *Swingtime in the Movies* has Fritz Feld as a nutty director whose perfectionism drives everyone crazy.

And apparently those three films, augmented by a few others, were responsible for all the Warners musical shorts that followed during the 1940s. If Columbia was masterful at using old comedy footage in its shorts, Warners was unrivaled in mixing and matching old and new footage to create musical two-reelers. After *Swingtime in the Movies,* Fritz Feld repeated his role—with some of the same footage—in another short called *Quiet Please.* For this one he used an extended sequence showing a typical day in the life of a young actress, pegged to the song "So You Want to Be in Movies," and followed by a terrible production number, "Springtime in Vienna." Five years later, James Kern shot new color footage of two tour guides giving a musical tour of a movie studio (the male guide was none other than Mel Tormé) for *Movieland Magic,* which used the entire "So You Want to Be in Movies" and "Springtime in Vienna" numbers, as well as sequences from *The Singing Dude, Royal Rodeo,* and a Jane Wyman musical Western called *The Sunday Round-Up.* The following year, Jack Scholl reassembled all this material, and still more footage, framed by the two tour guides, for another short called *Hollywood Wonderland.* And so it went.

Some of the Warners dramatic shorts were interesting and featured new talent (Dane Clark, Nina Foch, Dorothy Malone, Andrea King, Janis Paige, etcetera) and such

A poster for one of Warners historical dramas, *Sons of Liberty,* with Gale Sondergaard and Claude Rains; this one won an Oscar.

directors as Jean Negulesco and Don Siegel. Siegel, who had headed Warners' montage department, had not worked in about a year due to a feud with Jack Warner. When Warner suggested that they forget their differences, and Siegel begin anew by directing short subjects, Siegel decided to propose two ideas that he was sure Warner would turn down: one, a modern parable on the life of Christ, *Star in the Night;* the other, a propagandistic short called *Hitler Lives.* To his amazement, Warner gave the go-ahead for both, Siegel made them, and both won Academy Awards!

Warners easily took preeminence in the short-subject field during the 1950s with its exceptional travelogues (especially those made in CinemaScope by Owen Crump), the "Joe McDoakes" comedies (one of the last original comedy series), and Robert Youngson's multiple-award-winning documentaries on America's past. Much of the WB short subject quality was due to the integrity of the shorts' sales manager, Norman Moray, who earned the respect of everyone who worked for him.

Warners continued to produce first-rate short subjects well into the 1950s, until it became economically unfeasible for both the studio and the filmmakers to continue, especially with Warners becoming involved in television production. But the studio proved that there was always a demand for quality short subjects, and met that demand longer than anyone else in Hollywood.

Other Studios

The companies detailed above were responsible for the bulk of the short subjects on the market during the 1930s, '40s, and '50s. But every studio had *some* short-subject product, no matter how limited.

Universal Pictures never distinguished itself in the short-subject field, although it always had something cooking. In the early talkie days, it had a popular comedy series starring Slim Summerville. In 1932 and 1933, it hired Warren Doane, who had left Hal Roach, to supervise a series of two-reelers. Doane, in turn, hired two other ex-Roach employees, directors George Stevens and James Horne, to pilot the comedies; to star in them he got most of the major comedy names in Hollywood: Louise Fazenda, James Gleason, Billy Gilbert, Henry Armetta, James Finlayson, Vince Barnett, Walter Catlett, Frank Albertson, Marie Prevost, Grady Sutton, Max Davidson, and Sterling Holloway, as well as a flock of short-subject stalwarts (Vivien Oakland, Fred Kelsey, Tiny Sandford, Eddie Dunn, Anita Garvin, Mickey Daniels, Johnny Arthur, etcetera). What a shame that these shorts are not made available today; they certainly *sound* fascinating.

Universal also released the Thalians comedies, sponsored by the Hollywood-based acting club. In addition to such regulars as Arthur and Florence Lake, Monty Collins, and Vernon Dent, they featured such guests as Buddy Rogers, John Wayne, Noah Beery, Johnny Mack Brown, Betty Compson, and Franklin Pangborn. One of the studio's most durable series was John Hix's "Strange As It Seems," a parallel to the Robert Ripley "Believe It Or Not" subjects in showing oddities from around the world.

Where the studio did take a leading position was in its big-band series of the late 1940s. Although filmed without much imagination, they were glossy productions and featured such bands as those of Stan Kenton, Desi Arnaz, Woody Herman, Jimmy Dorsey, Buddy Rich, Duke Ellington, Gene Krupa, Les Brown, and even Lawrence Welk.

20th Century Fox was content to release the product of Educational Pictures, and later "The March of Time," for the bulk of its shorts. Movietone, its newsreel division, did supply some good live-action material over the years, but one of the spin-offs from the newsreel, Lew Lehr's "Dribble Puss Parade," was about as dull a series as ever conceived, filmed very cheaply and off the cuff.

Most of the B-picture factories had little regard for short subjects, although judging from the speed with which they made feature films, they probably could have turned out a two-reeler in an hour. Republic did have the short-lived "Meet the Stars" series in the early 1940s, but aside from this and occasional one-shots, Republic, Monogram, and their peers steered clear of short subjects.

There were also several enterprising independent producers who made short-subject series and often sold them to the major studios. One of the most prominent was Ben K. Blake. His shorts ranged from musical sing-alongs to dramatic series like the "Voice of Experience," a Mr. Anthony kind of sob-story series. Most of these shorts were economically filmed in New York and contained little of merit.

Just as audiences today feel cheated when a theatre runs a sponsored short, so audiences at better theatres of the 1930s and 1940s felt shortchanged when one of these cheapies would appear. Most smart exhibitors (aside from those chain-theatre managers who were forced to take certain shorts along with a feature block) learned to book from the major-studio product when it came to shorts—and moviegoers were seldom disappointed.

the series

"Our Gang"

For fifteen years, children of the television age have been enjoying the antics of "The Little Rascals." Run over and over again, the comedies never grow tiresome, and the youthful audience for the films is perhaps bigger today than it has ever been. At no time does anyone feel impelled to explain that the films are thirty to forty years old; for they are timeless, as timeless as childhood itself.

Hal Roach has said that he always had the idea of making "kid comedies." He experimented with the idea several times in the early stages of his producing career. Then, in the early 1920s, he happened upon an extremely talented Negro child, Ernie Morrison, who was nicknamed "Sunshine Sammy." He worked in several Roach comedies and received a tremendous response. The producer and one of his younger directors, Robert McGowan, scouted around for other talented kids. They wanted natural children, however, not professionals. Mary Kornman was the daughter of Harold Lloyd's still photographer, and Jackie Davis was the younger brother of Mildred Davis, Lloyd's wife and leading lady; they both had infectious personalities, and were signed to appear in the new kiddie series. Freckle-faced Mickey Daniels, Jackie Condon, chubby Joe Cobb, and Allen Clayton Hoskins (known as Farina) were other early members of the troupe.

Robert McGowan was given charge of the series. He played with the kids, became an unofficial "uncle," and learned how to get the best reactions from them. In 1922, "Our Gang" was born. McGowan and Anthony Mack directed the series through the 1920s, as the Gang grew in popularity to become one of the top comedy attractions in films. The kiddie personnel stayed essentially the same through the late 1920s, with occasional newcomers broken in.

We join the story of "Our Gang" in 1929, at the turning point of the sound era. Heads were rolling in Hollywood as the inevitable talkie revolution ended many careers and wreaked havoc at every studio in town. Any apprehensions people may have had about the Gang adjusting to sound were unwarranted, however. First, McGowan was still directing (occasionally acting as "supervising director" when someone else would pilot one short), and by now he had an infallible knack of working with the kids. Second, in 1929 there was a changeover in cast, easing out most of the familiar kids and building up a new troupe. These newcomers would have an even easier time starting out in talkies, not having to unlearn any silent film techniques.

Among the new kids were Jackie Cooper, Bobby "Wheezer" Hutchins, and Mary Ann Jackson (the latter two had appeared in some late silents), Norman "Chubby" Chaney (who won a nationwide contest to replace Joe Cobb as the "fat kid" in the series), Dorothy De Borba, and Matthew "Stymie" Beard. They took to film like fish to water, whereas Hal Roach's staff had to adapt themselves to the talkie medium, and here the road was rough. The first sound films were released as both silents and talkies; the latter versions were hampered by their silent footage, however, producing a most curious effect. In *Boxing Gloves* (1929), for instance, everything is silent unless a character is talking; in the key boxing sequence we see the juvenile audience cheering, but the sound track is silent. As clumsy as these techniques seem today, they were accepted in 1929 by audiences who were so excited about any sound at all that most considerations of quality were laid aside.

After the technical bugs were straightened out, and continuous sound recording was used, another problem came up: timing. The blame here must go to the editor, more than anyone else, for the early "Our Gang" talkies are plagued by arid stretches between jokes and lines of dialogue. Almost every shot is held too long, with many superfluous reaction shots. The situation was not helped by including vaudevillelike dialogue in most of the films, which slowed the pace even further. Director George Stevens, then working for Roach, has said, "We were *inept* with dialogue," explaining that scripts at this time were conceived in visual terms and then were passed on to H. M. Walker, who would sandwich funny dialogue between the sight gags.

As late as 1931, all semblance of action stops dead in its tracks in *Shiver My Timbers* to allow a long exchange of gag dialogue between Stymie and sea captain Billy Gilbert. Stymie asks if he can have a cutlass when he signs on board Gilbert's ship. "What kind of a cutlass?" the captain asks. "I want a veal cutlass," Stymie says, smiling.

However, the men behind the scenes knew that it would be foolish to sacrifice all visual humor for dialogue in the Gang comedies. One of the first all-talkies, *Shivering Shakespeare,* is highlighted by a pie-throwing melee. Other entries from 1930 rely heavily on Edgar Kennedy in the key role of Kennedy the cop. *When the Wind Blows* is really a vehicle for the comic, who steadfastly repeats his slogan, "Kennedy always gets his man!" even though he bungles the job all through a long night.

One of the best early talkies is *Pups Is Pups* (1930). It makes excellent use of audio and visual techniques, and is one of the most charming of all "Our Gang" films. The main plot has the Gang sprucing up their pets (everything from a parrot to a pig) to enter them in the city pet show, where Farina is working as a page. The show is a high-society affair, however, and the Gang's unruly animals make a shambles of the event. Worst of all are the white mice, which cause one matron to fall into a fountain, and send most of the ladies scurrying. For his efforts in helping the Gang, Farina is fired. Several subplots are working at the same time. One involves little Wheezer, who adores his affectionate puppies, and has found that he attracts their attention every time he rings a bell. When he loses the bell, the dogs start to run after any similar noise they hear; a train whistle sends them in one direction, a Good Humor man the other way, etcetera. All the while, Wheezer is desperately trying to find a bell himself; every time he does (there's one on a nearby bicycle) it's counteracted by a bell from the opposite direction. Finally, he rings a giant church bell, which apparently doesn't work. He sits distraught on the church steps, as the dogs, who *did* hear it, scamper up to him for a happy reunion. The final subplot involves Jackie Cooper's bratty kid sister, who can't stay out of a large mud puddle. Jack fears he'll be blamed every time she messes up her clothes, but he can't do anything about it. In the final scene of the film, Little Sister, in a new dress, hops into the puddle. Her mother thinks Farina has pushed her in, and stalks over to scold him; as she does, she trips and falls into the puddle herself.

Here, in one film, are most of the essential ingredients that made "Our Gang" popular. First, the kids are poor, but unfailingly happy. What they lack in material things is more than compensated for in ingenuity. Second, they are never fooled by pomp or pretentiousness, and have a knack for puncturing dignity. Thus, all the elegant people at the Pet Show are no match for this little group of kids, who manage to wreck the exhibition without even trying. Finally, the Gang always seems to have the last laugh on unpleasant adults, like Jackie's mother, and these characters invariably get their just deserts in the end.

The "Our Gang" kids are reflections of what we'd all like to be as children. In all probability, most of us never had as many adventures in five years as the Gang does in every comedy. There is a beguiling fantasy world for us on the screen as we watch these kids, without money or help from adults, build their own fire engine, run a clubhouse, organize a band, or do any of the thousand-and-one things we wish we could have done ourselves. The puncturing of dignity is a timeless yearning in all audiences, and here again we experience the vicarious pleasure of seeing the Gang emerge victoriously after doing battle with snooty matrons, cruel guardians, and the like. Nor is this limited to the adult world. Throughout the "Our Gang" films, there is an active dislike for rich kids, and even more so for consciously cute kids—something the remarkable youngsters in these comedies never became.

Unfortunately, director-mentor Robert McGowan had some unusual thoughts about the Gang films at this time. He started relying more and more on sentiment, and too often went with something cute instead of something funny. To his credit, it must be said that most of the sentiment was honest, and not cheap-jack tearjerker material. Nevertheless, films like *Big Ears* (1931), in which Wheezer's parents are in the midst of an angry divorce, were hardly as appealing as films that concentrated on the kids and *their* problems. Curiously enough, even when McGowan was sentimental, the kids remained "themselves." In *Birthday Blues* (1932), Dickie Moore is upset because his mean, inconsiderate father refuses to buy his wife a present on her birthday. Dickie and younger brother Spanky go to the store to buy something themselves; while window-shopping, Spanky is only interested in cowboy gear, and suggests that they could buy their mother a swell gun.

"What would she do with a gun?" groans Dickie. "Shoot papa," says Spanky.

One of the best turnabouts on a sentimental theme occurs in *Dogs Is Dogs* (1931), in which Wheezer and Dorothy live with a cruel stepmother who abuses and mistreats them. At the end of the film, their loving aunt arrives to take them away. She dresses them in handsome new clothes, buys the dog Pete a jeweled collar, and for good measure gives the stepmother a swift kick in the derrière as she departs. As their chauffeured car is about to pull away, Wheezer sighs and says, "Gee, I hate to leave my old pal Stymie; I wish he was going along with us." And as the car drives off, there is Stymie, smiling gaily, perched inside the spare tire on the back.

One of the best ideas introduced at this time was the character of Miss Crabtree, the Gang's schoolteacher, portrayed by June Marlowe, an attractive, demure young blonde with limited thespian abilities. She first appeared in *Teacher's Pet* (1930), whose story line had the Gang envisioning a hawkish old woman as their new teacher— after all, how could anyone with a name like Crabtree be anything but? In addition, they all have fond memories of their last teacher, Miss McGillicutty. They decide in advance to give her a hard time on the first day, planning all sorts of practical jokes. On the way to school, Jackie is given a lift by a pretty young woman, to whom he relates the whole story of Miss Crabtree—never dreaming that she and the woman seated next to him are one and

Jackie Cooper and "Miss Crabtree" (June Marlowe) in *Teacher's Pet*.

the same. When the new teacher introduces herself later that morning, Jackie does a whopping double take and tries to shrink out of sight as his numerous practical jokes are carried out. He's even arranged to be dismissed early that day—and therefore misses out on a surprise ice-cream party Miss Crabtree holds for the class. Ashamed, he sits next to a tree in the yard and starts to cry, but after a few minues Miss Crabtree comes out to bring him his ice cream and let him apologize. He looks up and sobs, "Gee, you're pretty, Miss Crabtree. You're prettier 'an Miss McGillicutty."

Jackie's crush on Miss Crabtree continues through several shorts, concluding wtih *Love Business,* in which the teacher rents a room from Jackie's mother. Jack is plagued by mixed emotions; on the one hand, he'll be with Miss Crabtree all the time from now on, but on the other hand, he'll have to wash his ears every day, and undergo even more unpleasant tortures. The situation gets worse when Chubby, who is also stuck on Miss Crabtree, comes to call on her one evening to ask her to marry him. Jackie is furious and does this best to disrupt their intimate conversation, succeeding to a large degree, until his mother stops him. Then his mother senses that Chubby's dialogue is somehow familiar; it turns out that Wheezer, Jackie's younger brother, sold Chubby his mother's old love letters, and Chubby has memorized them all for this occasion!

An amusing sidelight to this sequence is that the letters, shown in close-up, are addressed to a "Miss May Wallace." Indeed, the name of the actress playing Jackie's and Wheezer's mother was May Wallace. One

Chubby makes love to a cut-out of Greta Garbo as Dorothy and Pete stand by in *Love Business.* Note the romantic couple in the photo at left: Thelma Todd and Charley Chase!

finds this use of real names, often with amusing twists, throughout Hal Roach comedies.

The juvenile cast of "Our Gang" was constantly changing during the early 1930s. In 1931 Jackie Cooper left the Gang to achieve stardom on his own with such pictures as *The Champ* and *Skippy.* For a while, Wheezer was made the center of attention in the shorts, and then a new "star" was brought in, Dickie Moore, one of the top child actors of the 1930s who, like Cooper, enjoyed considerable success after leaving the Gang.

Probably Moore's best short in the series was *Free Wheeling* (1932) in which he plays the son of wealthy parents, all of whose money can't seem to do anything about Dickie's stiff neck; it holds rigid in one position, and he cannot move it around. One doctor has the courage to tell the overprotective mother that she's spoiling him, and that if she let the youngster go out and play, get some exercise, the neck would probably heal itself. The indignant mother refuses to listen to such talk. But

that afternoon, Dickie sneaks away for a ride in Stymie's makeshift taxi. Just then, Stymie's mule, which propels the car, runs away. Dickie can't see it, however. "Where?" he asks excitedly. "Down there!" says Stymie, grabbing Dickie's head and twisting it in the right direction—thereby curing Dickie's stiff neck! For a free tow, the kids proceed to tie their taxi to a truck parked in front of it. As the truck climbs over the crest of a steep hill, however, the taxi starts rolling downhill on its own, and the rope breaks. Stymie's efforts to steer and brake the car are futile; when Dickie asks where they're headed, Stymie replies, "I don't know, brother, but we're on our way!" The car finally comes to a stop after it goes off the road at the bottom of the hill and crashes into a bale of hay.

That same year, 1932, another member, who became one of the most durable members of the series, was added to the cast: Spanky McFarland. Actress Dorothy Granger recalls working on the Roach lot when director James Horne came in one day and corralled everyone in sight to see a test he had filmed with a new kid, saying, "You've *got* to see this." Horne had discovered Spanky, and trained his camera on him for the length of one reel. He asked him a few questions, and then had Spanky recite a fairy tale. Everyone in the screening room was captivated with this three-year-old, and Spanky was signed immediately for the "Our Gang" series.

He was outfitted with miniature golfing togs, including a beret, and was made the perennial kid brother in his first "Our Gang" endeavors. The Roach staff knew they had a good thing, and featured him in a two-reeler named *Spanky.* He was an instant hit and blended in with the other kids perfectly; here was a youngster who was irresistibly cute, yet never coy or phony. In addition, he was young enough that his screen character could be altered as he grew up in the films, with plenty of time ahead before worrying about his being too old for the series.

Another discovery at this time was Scotty Beckett. If the words "natural," "cute," and "charming" seem to be popping up with great frequency in this discussion, let the reader be advised that these words are being used sparingly, and with accuracy. The kids who populated "Our Gang" were outstanding little performers.

Proof that children as good as they were difficult to come by can be obtained by viewing almost any subsequent film with juveniles in its cast. Television commercials constitute conclusive proof.

Like Spanky and Dickie Moore, Scotty Beckett was a "natural." Someone had the inspired idea of teaming him and Spanky, since they both were slightly younger than the rest of the Gang members. The results, in a string of shorts over the next two years, were most rewarding. Another strong asset of the series at this time was a new director, Gus Meins. Meins was one of the top directors on the Hal Roach lot; he piloted some of the best comedies of Laurel and Hardy, Thelma Todd and Patsy Kelly, and Charley Chase. In addition, his "Our Gang" two-reelers from the mid-1930s are probably the best in the series' history. Meins never was as fond of pathos or cuteness as his predecessor, Robert McGowan; he had a keen mind for gags but, more importantly, an innate sense of comedy construction. His two-reelers are the most rounded of the Hal Roach output; they move smoothly, with a logical beginning, middle, and end.

His first-rate comedies include *The First Round-Up* (1934), in which the Gang goes on a week's camping trip, leaving Spanky and Scotty behind because they're too young. When they arrive at the campsite, the older kids find everything going wrong, while the two younger boys, who have made it to camp under their own steam, are prepared for everything. In *Hi, Neighbor* (1934), Wally Albright loses his girl friend to a rich kid who moves onto the block with a shiny red toy fire engine. Not to be outdone, the Gang decides to build its own fire engine—an incredible contraption made up of wheels from perambulators, a ladder taken from under the feet of a painter, and sundry ornaments "borrowed" from the neighborhood. *Honky Donkey* (1934) centers around a stubborn mule named Algebra, who causes trouble when wealthy Wally Albright brings it, and the Gang, to his family's mansion, particularly ruffling the dignity of chauffeur Don Barclay.

Mike Fright (1934) is a delightful short with the Gang forming the International Silver String Submarine Band in the hope of getting on a radio amateur show. They are invited down to the station by a program director who has no idea what's in store for him. The Gang arrives and makes a shambles of the broadcast, as well as the studio, before finally going on the air and becoming the hit of the show when they perform "The Man on the Flying Trapeze." One sequence is absolutely priceless: The Gang, scheduled to go on last, has to sit through an interminable series of polished and professionally cute kiddie acts. During each one, the camera cuts to reaction shots of Scotty, Spanky, and the other kids, registering disdain for these affected youngsters. These shots tell the whole story, as far as "Our Gang" is concerned.

Another amateur show, this one on a theatre stage, was the theme of *Beginner's Luck* (1935), with approximately the same results. In this one, Spanky's mom is an insufferable stage mother determined to push her son into the limelight even if it kills him. Arguing with Grandma (May Wallace) about her ambitious plans, Mother asks, "Why, what has Clark Gable or Barrymore got that Spanky hasn't got?" "A moustache!" answered Spanky defiantly.

Like all Hal Roach comedies, "Our Gang" benefited greatly from performances by adult supporting players. We have already mentioned the work of Edgar Kennedy and June Marlowe in the early talkies. Billy Gilbert contributed some memorable moments as a jewel thief in *Free Eats,* a salty sea captain in *Shiver My Timbers,* and a villainous neighbor in *Dogs Is Dogs.* Franklin Pangborn proved a hilarious foil for Spanky as a portrait photographer in *Wild Poses,* as did James Finlayson in *Mush and Milk. Wild Poses* also featured an unusual unbilled guest appearance by Laurel and Hardy, dressed in baby clothes. Johnny Arthur, a very amusing character comedian, excelled as Spanky's father in *Anniversary Trouble* and later as Darla Hood's father in *Feed 'Em and Weep,* and Gay Seabrook, a sort of poor man's Gracie Allen, had some good moments as Spanky's scatterbrained mother in *Wild Poses* and *Bedtime Worries,* with Emerson Treacy as her harried husband. Clarence Wilson, the archetypical mean old man in countless films, was perfect as the nasty orphanage head in *Shrimps for a Day,* and later played an evil school superintendent in *Come Back, Miss Phipps.* Comedy veteran Dell Henderson was left at the mercy of the Gang in *Choo Choo,* and Roach regular James C. Morton suffered a similar fate as theatre pianist in *Beginner's Luck.*

Specific scenes stand out as one surveys the vast "Our Gang" output from the 1930s: Chubby making love to a giant Greta Garbo cutout in *Love Business,* as Dorothy parodies everything he says; little Spanky enjoying the courtesy of the house at a sidewalk diner taken over by a monkey named Cotton in *A Lad an' a Lamp;* Tommy Bond, before he grew up to play Butch, singing a hilariously determined rendition of "Friends, Lovers No More" in *Mush and Milk;* Chubby's mother (Lyle Tayo) coaching him from the audience during the performance in *Shivering Shakespeare,* and eventually receiving a pie in the face; Spanky trying to distract Robert McKenzie long enough to snatch a plate of food in front of him in *Teacher's Beau;* two supposedly truant children turning out to be midget entertainers (George and Olive Brasno) in *Arbor Day;* former members of "Our Gang" raising a glass to toast their successors in the opening scene of *Reunion in Rhythm.*

Wheezer and Dorothy are about to be given what-for by Blanche Payson in *Dogs Is Dogs.*

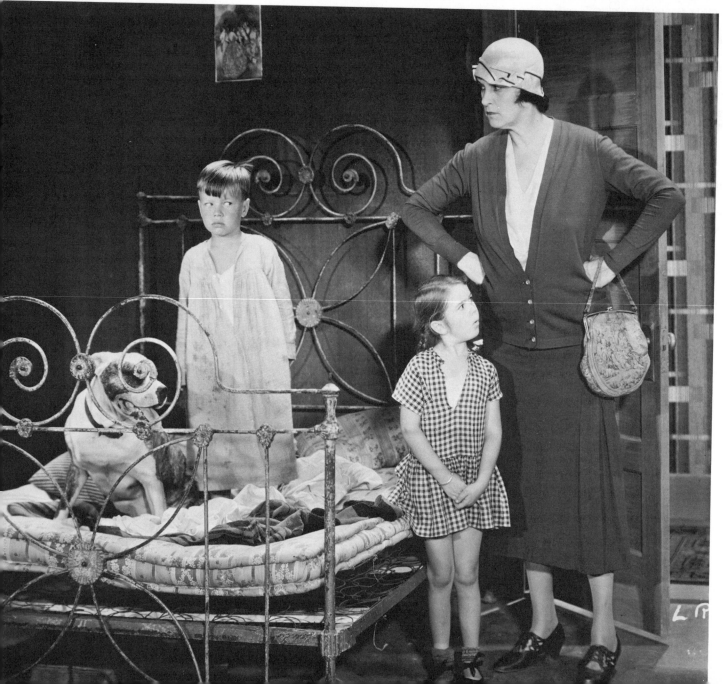

One of the most unusual shorts of the series was *Mama's Little Pirates,* directed by Gus Meins in 1935. It is a fantasy, sparked by the Gang reading a newspaper story about buried treasure at a nearby cave. They decide to investigate, and Spanky goes along even though his mother has locked him in his room for disobeying her. (He is talked into going by his devilish alter ego, who stands next to him and asks, "Well, what are we? Mice or men?") The cave turns out to be a nightmarish place, inhabited by a surly giant who jealously guards his roomful of gold and jewels and prepares to punish the young intruders, when Spanky wakes up to find it all a dream. For a finale, he knocks his alter ego down to show him who's boss. The beauty of *Mama's Little Pirates* is that the cave sequences are truly suspenseful, with all the fantasy elements vividly realized (the kids literally swimming in gold coins, the overpowering giant, etcetera).

In 1935 the Gang started working with a musical format, which was reused a number of times during the next few years. It usually involved the Gang putting on a show for the neighborhood kids, with the core of the film devoted to the performance itself. *Our Gang Follies of 1936* (1935) is refreshing because it never gets too slick, a fault of several subsequent endeavors of this kind. In this one, the Gang stages a show, the highlight of which is to be a number by the Florydory Girls. When the girls don't show up, Spanky, Scotty, and the other kids have to take their place. Spanky tells the others to follow his every move, unaware that a pet monkey holding a large pin has just slipped into the bustle of his costume. As the animal starts to fidget around, Spanky goes into wild gyrations, and the others follow suit for an unexpected finale to the Gang's production.

Pay As You Exit (1936) is another amusing outing with Alfalfa spoiling his "Romeo and Juliet" performance with Darla by insisting on eating onions before the show. Buckwheat, of all people, takes Darla's place, making a shambles of the show but pleasing the audience nevertheless. *Reunion in Rhythm* (1937) has the Gang staging a show for a class reunion (including former cast members such as Mickey Daniels and Joe Cobb). The production is a bit too polished, however, the numbers carefully and elaborately staged; the danger here is that the Gang comes close to being the kind of professional entertainers they used to heartily dislike in films like *Mike Fright.*

By far the best of these miniature musicals is the last one made for Roach, *Our Gang Follies of 1938* (1937), an incredibly lavish and delightfully conceived two-reeler directed by Gordon Douglas. The film opens naturally enough, with the Gang producing a show; Spanky is in charge, Buckwheat is leading the band, and Darla is the

Spanky warns Buckwheat to stick to the script in *Reunion in Rhythm.*

featured female vocalist. But the star of the show, heralded on a poster outside the "theatre," is Alfalfa, the King of the Crooners. When he makes his entrance, instead of going into a song, he proceeds to sing, "I'm the Barber of Seville," bringing a chorus of boos and catcalls from the youthful audience. Spanky rings down the curtain and demands to know what's going on. Alfalfa explains that a voice such as his is a gift, and he isn't going to waste it any more on anything but opera. He signs a contract with operatic impresario, Henry Brandon, despite the warnings of Spanky that before long he'll be singing in the street for pennies. Alfalfa takes a nap, and dreams that his name is in lights on Broadway, announcing his debut in *The Barber of Seville.* Comes opening night, he makes his entrance and sings the first aria, only to be greeted by a hostile audience that razzes him and throws vegetables at the stage. The curtain falls, and Alfalfa decides to get out while he can. But the evil entrepreneur reminds him of his ironclad contract and tells him he will have to sing opera in the street from now on. Alfalfa trudges outside, where it has begun to snow, and holds out a tin cup as he sings over and over again, "I'm the Barber of Seville." Then, who should drive up in a chauffeured limousine but Spanky, dressed in top hat, white tie, and tails, about to enter the prominent Club Spanky.

He takes Alfalfa inside, where the plush cabaret is filled with customers, and "Cab" Buckwheat is leading the swing band. The star of the floor show, needless to say, is Darla, who heads a large-scale production number based on the song "The Love Bug Will Get You If You

Don't Watch Out.'' Darla and Spanky prevail upon Alfalfa to toss his pride away and croon for the customers; but before he can begin, in steps the leering impresario, who drags Alfalfa back into the streets, laughing wickedly. At this point Alfalfa wakes up, realizes it's all been a dream, and goes on stage for the finale of Spanky's show, singing the Bing Crosby number, ''Learn to Croon.''

Our Gang Follies of 1938 is a delightful departure from the norm for the series, a very clever spoof of 1930s musicals, with the kids playing the roles usually played by adult stars in completely serious films. The comedy is doubly good because it stands out in a period when the quality of the series was slipping considerably.

One reason for this was the cast. In the past, few Gang members had stayed with the series long enough to lose the basic spontaneity of their performances. Having a large number of kids also enabled the series to focus on different ones in different comedies, a decided advantage. By 1936, both ideas were abandoned in favor of sticking with the five basic characters who had fared the best over the past few seasons: Spanky, Alfalfa, Buckwheat, Porky, and Darla. Carl ''Alfalfa'' Switzer joined the series in 1935, at the age of eight, as part of an amateur hillbilly singing act with his brother Harold. They appeared together in *Teacher's Beau, Beginner's Luck,* and *The Lucky Corner,* after which it was decided to explore Alfalfa's possibilities as a leading player in the shorts. Darla Hood joined the series in 1935 at the age of four and became the ''leading lady,'' the apple of Alfalfa's eye, and, like him, a singer.

Billy ''Buckwheat'' Thomas was the latest in the series of black youngsters who had been a fixture in the Gang since its inception. He was usually teamed with Eugene ''Porky'' Lee, who joined the series around the same time. The two remained inseparable pals through the next few years in most of the ''Our Gang'' shorts.

One cannot overlook the importance of a black child in the makeup of ''Our Gang.'' In an age before even tokenism was heard of, Hal Roach chose to show black and white children playing together, without prejudice, and without calling attention to it. Like everything else in ''Our Gang,'' the subject was treated *naturally,* and if there were occasional lapses into stereotype, one must remember the positive aspects of an integrated group of kids—especially at a time when few films depicting adults would ever dare show friendship between black and white men.

Gordon Douglas, who headed the casting department at the Roach studio before becoming a director there, recalls, ''A lot of those kids came in through the casting office. We used to have interviews every Saturday morning

for kids, because in the Gang when they were ten years old we had to move them on. That's where Buckwheat came from, Porky, Alfalfa, Scotty Beckett, Darla Hood. Spanky was the only set member.'' Douglas maintains that even the kids who stayed with the films for several years remained fresh. ''They were all great kids. We tried to keep them away from the greasepaint; we worked it so they weren't acting, trying to make it real. We tried to make the kids just kids—we didn't use make-up. The only one who was made up was the dog, with that ring around his eye.''

Nevertheless, in 1936 several changes came about in ''Our Gang.'' For one, many of the shorts were cut from two reels (approximately twenty minutes) to one (approximately ten) in length; this left less time for mood and characterization, putting greater emphasis on the story line. Second, as noted above, the cast became standardized. And finally, the shorts became surprisingly slick. In many cases, this may have been a direct result of the one-reel format, which made it necessary to eliminate the ''rough edges'' that in large part gave ''Our Gang'' its charm.

Oddly enough, the very first one-reel ''Our Gang'' short won the series its only Academy Award. *Bored of Education* was named the Best Short Subject of 1936. It was also the first short in the series directed by Gordon Douglas, who comments today, ''I figured if at 22 I could get an Oscar, I had this town made.'' He alternated responsibility for the shorts with a comedy veteran, Fred Newmeyer, for the next two years.

Bored of Education was a fairly good little comedy, probably one of the best of the later group, but hardly as good as the shorts from the early 1930s. Nevertheless, it had a charm of its own, and proved that the one-reel format was a feasibility for ''Our Gang.''

Some of the shorts that followed maintained that quality: *Spooky Hooky* (1936) has the four boys writing a phony absence note for school so they can go to the circus the next day. When they discover that the teacher is planning to take the class anyway, they must return to the schoolhouse that night and retrieve the note; the results are disastrous. *Pigskin Palooka* (1937) is an excellent comedy, in which Alfalfa writes home from military school that he's a gridiron hero and then has his tall tales backfire when he returns home and is pressed into service on the Gang's football team. *Hide and Shriek* (1938), the last Hal Roach ''Our Gang,'' is also one of the best, with Alfalfa heading a detective agency which accepts the case of Darla's box of candy being stolen. Alfalfa, with his assistants Porky and Buckwheat, inadvertently ends up in an amusement park house of horrors, where the three are subjected to all sorts of "tortures" before escaping and fleeing back to headquarters, where Alfalfa decides to abandon the detective business for good.

There were also some below-par comedies in this late group, several of which, like *The Awful Tooth,* betrayed the whole essence of "Our Gang" by introducing adult characters who would get the last laugh on the kids—something that would never have been tolerated in the early 1930s comedies. What prompted the scriptwriters to make this unfortunate move is not clear.

It is clear, however, that by the late 1930s the Gang's days were numbered. What is surprising is that they lasted as long as they did on the Hal Roach lot. The producer started easing short subjects off his production schedule as early as 1935, making a clean sweep by the end of the following year, with the "Gang" a notable exception. Roach saw the market for high-quality shorts declining and decided his future was in feature films. One by one, he tested out his short-subject stars in features to see if they would pass muster. Laurel and Hardy had proven themselves much earlier and had no worries at this time. Patsy Kelly's teammate Thelma Todd had died, but on her own, and with Lyda Roberti, Patsy Kelly managed to headline several Roach feature films. Unfortunately, Charley Chase could not sustain an hour-long film, and was fired.

In 1936, Roach put "Our Gang" into a feature called *General Spanky.* It was not a success. Its codirector, Gordon Douglas, explains, "In those days, you didn't have to have too much story in a two-reeler, but you had to have a lot of story in a feature. Now today, a lot of features don't have too much story—they're just set up with people. But Hal Roach features in the early days suffered from too little story, for that time; the audiences then wanted a beginning, a middle, and an end." *General Spanky* could have meant the end of "Our Gang" altogether, but apparently the series was too profitable to write off so quickly. It stayed in production through 1938 at Roach studios, at which point the producer sold the property lock, stock, and barrel to MGM, which had been distributing the shorts for the past eleven years. Included in the sale was the right to the name "Our Gang," which is why the original Roach comedies are called "The Little Rascals" on television.

Initially, the main stars of the series, the director (Douglas), and two writers (Robert McGowan and Harold Law) went to MGM to continue the shorts. Douglas bailed out early in the game. "The big difference there was that at Roach we made the stories about a kid's problem; for instance, a kid getting an ice-cream cone could be

the story. When they went to Metro, I felt they involved the kids with adult problems, and I think it was a mistake. I only stayed there for about two pictures. Later on, when I left Metro and went back to Roach, they became even more involved with adult stories; they were going back to the mortgage-on-the-farm plots. And we never made fun in Roach days of any physical deformities, anything about what a kid was born with, and Metro did, in a few pictures I remember. Laughs were based on cross-eyed kids, and other things."

The first shorts, directed by Douglas, such as *Aladdin's Lantern* (1938), are virtually indistinguishable from the Roach product. But most later ones are in a class by themselves. If Robert McGowan tended to be sentimental when he was directing the series, his scripts became

Darla sings her heart out in a number from *Our Gang Follies of 1938.*

downright mawkish at MGM. Some were absolutely unbearable, made more so by the addition of a new child actor, Mickey Gubitosi, who delivered every line with a whine in his voice. A good example of the deterioration of the series is a 1940 gem called *All About Hash,* in which Mickey joins the kids on the verge of tears. He explains that every Monday night his mother serves Sunday's leftovers in the form of hash, which invariably precipitates an argument between her and his father. He can't take it any more. So the Gang, ever ready to do the right thing, goes on the radio and stages an unsubtle skit dramatizing the silliness of getting into bitter arguments about such petty things as serving hash on Mondays. Everything ends happily—except for Mickey, who even manages to sound whiny when he's pleased. [Gubitosi soon changed his name to Bobby Blake, and became a familiar face in 1940s movies before disappearing from the scene, only to return some years later as Robert Blake, the star of *In Cold Blood, Tell Them Willie Boy Is Here,* etcetera.]

The MGM crew eventually turned the "Our Gang" comedies into ten-minute morality plays, stressing mother love, patriotism, pedestrian safety, and other American virtues in such a maudlin way that the studio's Andy Hardy films seem anarchistic by comparison.

Only on rare occasions did the MGM unit come up with a winner. One such short was *Goin' Fishin'* (1940), in which the Gang decides that the only way to get to the river early enough to get in on the good fishing is to camp out by the bus stop overnight. After encountering various problems in carrying out this plan, they board the bus the next morning and match wits with an irate conductor (Paul Hurst) and passenger (Arthur Hoyt). Another unusual endeavor was *Cousin Wilbur* (1939), in which Scotty Beckett returned to the series as Alfalfa's cousin. He is outwardly a sissy, but when threatened by Butch (Tommy Bond), he proves himself a worthy member of the Gang by licking him handily.

Inevitably, the original "Our Gang" kids had to be replaced. MGM took its time about it, with Spanky and Alfalfa literally growing out of their clothes in some of the later comedies; but eventually everyone was eased out. The new principals included Mickey Gubitosi, Janet Burston, and "Froggy" Laughlin, whose distinctive voice was his major asset.

True to form, the MGM shorts were done without the benefit of the easygoing atmosphere that made the Hal Roach studio such a pleasant place to work. There was no improvisation. One of the series' directors during the 1940s was George Sidney, who says today, "The 'Our Gang' scripts were completely planned to the most minute detail, and it is very possible that doing that series conditioned me to hate all kids. At the time I was only seven years older than the oldest kid. They didn't know . . . neither did I."

One suspects that the unbearably wholesome nature of the MGM "Our Gangs" was due to the influence of studio boss Louis B. Mayer, but Sidney says, "Mr. Mayer was not involved in the making of the 'Our Gangs,' although he viewed them all, as well as all shorts, as he was always searching for any new talent . . . directors, actors, writers, etc. New talent in any area he referred to as 'The New Breed.' He watched us progress and develop or fail."

By 1944, MGM had produced fifty-two "Our Gang" comedies, and, at that point, decided to let the series expire. The reasons for this are not apparent, since the series continued to appear in the *Motion Picture Herald's* annual poll of top moneymaking shorts. But for the sake of the viewer, it was probably just as well that the series stopped when it did, instead of continuing to turn out products at the level it had reached.

In 1950, Monogram Pictures reissued twenty-six Hal Roach two-reelers to theaters under the title "The Little Rascals"; they were very successful, and in 1958 Allied Artists (Monogram's new name) edited several shorts into a makeshift feature called *Little Rascals Varieties,* which received limited theatrical play at the time. In 1955, Roach sold ninety-odd shorts, including several late silents with musical tracks, to Interstate Television for a sum total of $27,000. Stations in forty-six cities around the country immediately bought the series, and the films have been telecast ever since, continuing to play for years when many new kiddie series barely last a few months.

During its heyday, "Our Gang" was imitated by numerous fast-buck producers; the most successful was Larry Darmour, with his "Mickey McGuire" comedies, which starred a young Mickey Rooney. Others enjoyed varied degrees of success, including one series called "The McDougall Alley Kids" which patterned itself so closely after "Our Gang" that the black youngster was named Oatmeal!

Similarly, there have been many attempts to revive "Our Gang" in recent years, mostly by Hal Roach himself. One proposed "Little Rascals" TV series went so far as to make a merchandising splash, with comic books, records, and toys, using freshly drawn caricatures of the original kids, but no program ever materialized. Nor is it likely that a new "Our Gang" will ever appear on the horizon; the series belongs to an age of innocence that is long behind us. One would have to search far and wide to find children to match the wonderful kids who populated the series during its peak years.

Fortunately, the original "Our Gang" comedies are still with us, just as marvelous as ever, appealing to the child in each of us as few other films have ever been able to do.

The "Our Gang" Talkie Shorts

Following is a complete listing of the talking shorts made in the "Our Gang" series, including the early 1929 releases which were also distributed as silents. All the films are two reels in length unless otherwise noted (the series switched to one-reelers in the late 1930s). For purposes of expediency, when a child in the series was

A flashy production number from one of the later shorts, *Ye Olde Minstrels.* Spanky at front row center, with Darla and Buckwheat above him; Mickey Gubitosi barely visible at extreme left, Froggy at extreme right.

known primarily by nickname, his full name is given the first time it appears, and subsequently he is referred to only by the nickname (i.e., George "Spanky" McFarland will be called "Spanky" in the cast listings of all but the first of his films in this index). Director's name follows release date. In the cast listings, the child actors are separated from the adult supporting cast by a semicolon.

1. *Small Talk.* Roach-MGM (4/18/29), Robert McGowan. Bobby "Wheezer" Hutchins, Joe Cobb, Allan Clayton "Farina" Hoskins, Mary Ann Jackson, Jean Darling, Harry Spear; Lyle Tayo, Helen Jerome Eddy, Pat Harmon. Wheezer and the rest of the Gang are taken from their orphanage and adopted by high society matrons.

2. *Railroadin'.* Roach-MGM (6/15/29), Robert McGowan. Wheezer, Joe Cobb, Farina, Mary Ann Jackson, Harry Spear, Norman "Chubby" Chaney, Jean Darling; Helen Jerome Eddy. The Gang's adventures at the railroad yard.

3. *Lazy Days.* Roach-MGM (8/15/29), Robert McGowan. Farina, Joe Cobb, Harry Spear, Wheezer, Jannie Hoskins, Chubby, Jean Darling, Mary Ann Jackson, Bobbie Burns. Farina and the Gang enter their brothers and sisters in a baby contest.

4. *Boxing Gloves.* Roach-MGM (9/9/29), Anthony Mack, supervised by Robert McGowan. Joe Cobb, Chubby, Farina, Mary Ann Jackson, Harry Spear, Jackie Cooper, Jean Darling, Wheezer, Bobby Mallon, Donnie, Billy Schuler, Johnny Aber, Charlie Hall. Harry and Farina promote a boxing match between Joe and Chubby.

5. *Bouncing Babies.* Roach-MGM (10/12/29), Robert McGowan. Wheezer, Mary Ann Jackson, Jackie Cooper, Farina, Jean Darling, Chubby, Harry Spear, Bobby Mallon; Eddie Dunn, Lyle Tayo. With Wheezer's new baby brother receiving all his parents' attention, he tries to send the baby back to heaven.

6. *Moan and Groan, Inc.* Roach-MGM (12/7/29), Robert McGowan. Farina, Jackie Cooper, Mary Ann Jackson, Chubby, Wheezer, Jay R. Smith, Bobby Mallon; Edgar Kennedy, Max Davidson. The Gang ignores the warnings of Kennedy the Cop and go to a local haunted house.

7. *Shivering Shakespeare.* Roach-MGM (1/25/30), Anthony Mack, supervised by Robert McGowan. Chubby, Farina, Jackie Cooper, Mary Ann Jackson, Wheezer, Donald Haines, Edith Fellows, Gordon Thorpe, Jack McHugh, Douglas Greer, Georgie Billings, Johnny Aber; Gertrude Sutton, Edgar Kennedy, Carlton Griffin, Mickey Daniels (latter two in costume as animals), Lyle Tayo, Charles McAvoy. A school play, *The Gladiator's Dilemma,* turns into a pie-throwing melee.

8. *The First Seven Years*. Roach-MGM (3/1/30), Robert Mc-Gowan. Jackie Cooper, Wheezer, Mary Ann Jackson, Donald "Speck" Haines, Farina, Chubby, Jannie Hoskins; Edgar Kennedy, Otto Fries, Joy Winthrop. Jackie engages in a duel for the affections of Mary Ann. One of several "Our Gang" shorts made in Spanish-language versions.

9. *When the Wind Blows*. Roach-MGM (4/5/30), James Horne. Jackie Cooper, Farina, Wheezer, Mary Ann Jackson, Chubby; Edgar Kennedy, Charles McAvoy, Mary Gordon. Jackie foils a nocturnal burglary, despite the bumbling of Kennedy the Cop. Filmed in Spanish.

10. *Bear Shooters*. Roach-MGM (5/17/30), Robert Mc-Gowan. Leon Janney, Wheezer, Farina, Jackie Cooper, Mary Ann Jackson, Chubby; Bob Kortman, Charlie Hall, Fay Holderness. During a camping trip, the Gang encounters a couple of poachers.

11. *A Tough Winter*. Roach-MGM (6/21/30), Robert Mc-Gowan. Farina, Mary Ann Jackson, Wheezer, Jackie Cooper, Chubby; Stepin Fetchit. Stepin tries to help the Gang clean up a mess after a taffy pull.

12. *Pups Is Pups*. Roach-MGM (8/30/30), Robert McGowan. Wheezer, Farina, Jackie Cooper, Chubby, Dorothy De Bora, Mary Ann Jackson, Buddy MacDonald, The Hill Twins; Charlie Hall, William Gillespie, Lyle Tayo, Charles McAvoy. The Gang decides to enter their animals in a local pet show.

13. *Teacher's Pet*. Roach-MGM (10/11/30), Robert Mc-Gowan. Jackie Cooper, Farina, Chubby, Wheezer, Matthew "Hercules" Beard (later known as Stymie), Dorothy De Bora, Buddy MacDonald, Mary Ann Jackson, Donald Haines, Artye Folz, Bobby Mallon; June Marlowe, Baldwin Cooke. Jackie prepares an elaborate series of practical jokes for his new teacher, Miss Crabtree.

14. *School's Out*. Roach-MGM (11/22/30), Robert Mc-Gowan. Jackie Cooper, Farina, Chubby, Mary Ann Jackson, Donald Haines, Douglas Greer, Buddy MacDonald, Bobby "Bonedust" Young, Wheezer, Stymie, Dorothy De Borba, Bobby Mallon; June Marlowe, Creighton Hale. The kids mistake Miss Crabtree's brother for a suitor, and try to discourage him.

15. *Helping Grandma*. Roach-MGM (1/3/31), Robert Mc-Gowan. Wheezer, Stymie, Farina, Mary Ann Jackson, Chubby, Jackie Cooper, Shirley Jean Rickert, Bonedust, Dorothy De Borba, Donald Haines; Oscar Apfel, Margaret Mann, Dell Henderson, William Gillespie. The Gang's adopted grandma can't decide to whom to sell her store.

16. *Love Business*. Roach-MGM (2/14/31), Robert Mc-Gowan. Jackie Cooper, Chubby, Wheezer, Mary Ann Jackson, Farina, Stymie, Dorothy De Borba, Donald Haines, Bonedust, Shirley Jean Rickert; June Marlowe, May Wallace. Miss Crabtree becomes a boarder at Jackie's house, causing complications—he's got a terrible crush on her.

17. *Little Daddy*. Roach-MGM (3/28/31), Robert McGowan. Farina, Stymie, Jackie Cooper, Chubby, Wheezer, Bonedust, Mary Ann Jackson, Dorothy De Borba, Shirley Jean Rickert, Donald Haines, Douglas Greer; George Reed, Otto Fries, June

Marlowe. Officials try to take Stymie away from his only guardian, Farina.

18. *Bargain Days*. Roach-MGM (5/2/31), Robert McGowan. Stymie, Wheezer, Shirley Jean Rickert, Farina, Jackie Cooper, Chubby, Mary Ann Jackson, Dorothy De Borba, Douglas Greer, Donald Haines; Tiny Sandford, Harry Bernard, Baldwin Cooke, Otto Fries. Wheezer and Stymie, door-to-door salesmen, meet a lonely little rich girl.

19. *Fly My Kite*. Roach-MGM (5/30/31), Robert McGowan. Farina, Wheezer, Mary Ann Jackson, Stymie, Dorothy De Borba, Georgie Ernest, Shirley Jean Rickert, Chubby; Margaret Mann, James Mason, Mae Busch, Broderick O'Farrell. A despicable man tries to put his mother-in-law in an old folks' home until he discovers she has a fortune in stock.

20. *Big Ears*. Roach-MGM (8/29/31), Robert McGowan. Wheezer, Stymie, Dorothy De Borba, Donald Haines, Sherwood Bailey; Ann Christy, Creighton Hale, Wilfred Lucas, Gordon Douglas. Wheezer feigns illness in order to bring his quarreling parents together again.

21. *Shiver My Timbers*. Roach-MGM (10/10/31), Robert McGowan. Stymie, Wheezer, Dorothy De Borba, Sherwood Bailey, Jerry Tucker, Georgie Ernest, Carolina Beard; Billy Gilbert, June Marlowe, Harry Bernard, Dick Gilbert, Cy Slocum. The Gang has been playing hooky to listen to a friendly sea captain's tall tales.

22. *Dogs Is Dogs*. Roach-MGM (11/21/31), Robert Mc-Gowan. Wheezer, Stymie, Sherwood "Spud" Bailey, Dorothy De Borba; Billy Gilbert, Blanche Payson, Lyle Tayo, Harry Bernard. Wheezer and Dorothy are forced to live with an evil stepmother and her spoiled-brat son.

23. *Readin' and Writin'*. Roach-MGM (2/2/32), Robert Mc-Gowan. Kendall "Breezy Brisbane" McComas, Wheezer, Stymie, Dorothy De Borba, Spud, Donald Haines, Carolina "Marmalade" Beard; June Marlowe, May Wallace, Lyle Tayo, Harry Bernard, Otto Fries. Tired of school, Breezy concocts a scheme to get himself expelled.

24. *Free Eats*. Roach-MGM (2/13/32), Raymond McCarey. Stymie, Wheezer, Breezy, George "Spanky" McFarland, Donald Haines, Dorothy De Borba, Spud; Billy Gilbert, Paul Fix, May Wallace, Belle Hare, Lilyan Irene, Lillian Elliott, Otto Fries, Harry Bernard, Eddie Baker. The Gang attends a lawn party and helps to capture a family of thieves.

25. *Spanky*. Roach-MGM (3/26/32), Robert McGowan. Spanky, Breezy, Stymie, Dorothy De Borba, Wheezer, Spud, Speck, Bobby Mallon; Billy Gilbert. While staging a play, Spanky finds his father's hiding place for the family "fortune."

26. *Choo Choo*. Roach-MGM (5/7/32), Robert McGowan. Spanky, Stymie, Breezy, Donald Haines, Wheezer, Dorothy De Borba, Spud, Georgie Billings, Wally Albright, Harold "Bouncy" Wertz; Dell Henderson, Harry Bernard, Belle Hare, Lyle Tayo, Otto Fries, Baldwin Cooke, Eddie Baker. The Gang changes places with a group of orphans about to take a train ride.

27. *Pooch*. Roach-MGM (6/14/32), Robert McGowan. Stymie, Spanky, Dorothy De Borba, Wheezer, Breezy, Spud, Artye Folz, Bouncy; May Wallace, Belle Hare, Harry Bernard, Dick Gilbert, Baldwin Cooke. The Gang tries to save Pete the Pup from a mean dogcatcher.

28. *Hook and Ladder*. Roach-MGM (8/27/32), Robert McGowan. Dickie Moore, Stymie, Spanky, Breezy, Dorothy De Borba, Spud, Bouncy, Speck. The Gang plays firemen and actually succeed in putting out a fire.

29. *Free Wheeling*. Roach-MGM (10/1/32), Robert McGowan. Dickie Moore, Stymie, Spanky Dorothy De Borba, Breezy, Jackie Lynn, Douglas Greer; Creighton Hale, Belle Hare, Lillian Rich, Wilfred Lucas. Stymie takes Dickie for a ride in his runaway auto and cures his stiff neck.

30. *Birthday Blues*. Roach-MGM (11/12/32), Robert McGowan. Dickie Moore, Stymie, Spanky, Dorothy De Borba, Breezy, Bobbie "Cotton" Beard, Jackie Lynn, Donald Haines, Edith Fellows, Georgie Billings, Carolina Beard, Douglas Greer, Bobby Mallon. Dickie throws a party to raise enough money to buy his mother a birthday present.

31. *A Lad an' a Lamp*. Roach-MGM (12/17/32), Robert McGowan. Dickie Moore, Stymie, Spanky, Wheezer, Dorothy De Borba, Donald "Toughie" Haines, Georgie Billings, Cotton; James C. Morton, Harry Bernard, Lillian Rich, Dick Gilbert. The Gang thinks they've found a magic lamp, and among other things, Spanky turns Cotton into a monkey.

32. *Fish Hooky*. Roach-MGM (1/28/33), Robert McGowan. Stymie, Dickie Moore, Spanky, Wheezer, Dorothy De Borba, Cotton, Farina, Joe Cobb, Donald Haines, Georgie Billings, Mildred Kornman; Mary Kornman, Mickey Daniels, Baldwin Cooke. The Gang tries to evade a truant officer in an amusement park.

33. *Forgotten Babies*. Roach-MGM (3/11/33), Robert McGowan, Spanky, Dickie Moore, Stymie, Wheezer, Dorothy De Borba, Tommy Bond, Cotton; Harry Bernard, Dick Gilbert, Belle Hare, Ruth Hiatt. Spanky plays baby-sitter while the Gang goes fishing.

34. *Kid from Borneo*. Roach-MGM (4/15/33), Robert McGowan. Spanky, Stymie, Dickie Moore, Dorothy De Borba, Tommy Bond, Wheezer; May Wallace, Otto Fries, Harry Bernard, Dick Gilbert. The Gang goes to the sideshow to visit their uncle, but mistake him for a wildman.

35. *Mush and Milk*. Roach-MGM (5/27/33), Robert McGowan. Stymie, Dickie Moore, Spanky, Tommy Bond, Dorothy De Borba, Edith Fellows, Wheezer; Gus Leonard, James Finlayson, Rolfe Sedan. When Cap's back pension finally comes in, he treats the kids of Bleak Hill Boarding School to a day at an amusement park.

36. *Bedtime Worries*. Roach-MGM (9/9/33), Robert McGowan. Spanky, Stymie, Tommy Bond, Jerry Tucker, Georgie Billings; Emerson Treacy, Gay Seabrook, Harry Bernard, Lee Phelps. The first night Spanky sleeps alone in a bedroom, he encounters a burglar.

Dickie Moore and Stymie prepare a very unusual birthday cake in *Birthday Blues*.

37. *Wild Poses*. Roach-MGM (10/28/33), Robert McGowan. Spanky, Stymie, Tommy Bond, Jerry Tucker, Georgie "Darby" Billings; Franklin Pangborn, Emerson Treacy, Gay Seabrook, Stan Laurel, Oliver Hardy. Spanky balks at having his picture taken by a studio photographer; Laurel and Hardy make a gag appearance as babies.

38. *Mike Fright*. Roach-MGM (2/25/34), Gus Meins. Spanky, Scotty Beckett, Stymie, Tommy Bond, Leonard Kibrick, Alvin Buckelew, Billy Lee, the Five Meglin Kiddies; James C. Morton, Charlie Hall, William Irving, Marvin Hatley, Frank H. LaRue. The Gang goes to a radio station amateur show.

39. *Hi Neighbor*. Roach-MGM (3/3/34), Gus Meins. Wally Albright, Spanky, Stymie, Scotty Beckett, Tommy Bond, Jackie "Jane" Taylor, Jerry Tucker, Marvin "Bubbles" Trin, Donald Proffitt, Tommy Bupp, Cotton; Tiny Sandford, Jack "Tiny" Ward, Charlie Hall, Harry Bernard, Ernie Alexander. When a rich kid with a shiny new fire engine steals Wally's girl friend, the Gang decides to build its own fire engine.

40. *For Pete's Sake*. Roach-MGM (4/14/34), Gus Meins. Spanky, Scotty Beckett, Wally Albright, Stymie, Marianne Edwards, Tommy Bond, Jackie Taylor, Leonard Kibrick, Bubbles, Carolina "Buckwheat" Beard, Billie Thomas, Philbrook Lyons; William Wagner, Fred Holmes, Lyle Tayo. The Gang tries to raise enough money to buy a doll for Marianne.

41. *First Round-Up*. Roach-MGM (5/5/34), Gus Meins. Spanky, Scotty Beckett, Wally Albright, Stymie, Tommy Bond, Willie Mae "Buckwheat" Taylor, Philbrook Lyons, Cullen Johnson, Bubbles, Billie Thomas, Jackie Taylor; Billy Bletcher, Zoila Conan. The Gang goes on a camping trip but doesn't want the company of the two little kids, Spanky and Scotty.

42. *Honkey Donkey*. Roach-MGM (6/2/34), Gus Meins. Wally Albright, Stymie, Spanky, Scotty Beckett, Tommy Bond, Willie Mae "Buckwheat" Taylor, Philbrook Lyons; Don Barclay,

William Wagner, Bess Flowers, Natalie Moorhead, Charles Mc-Avoy. Rich-kid Wally brings the Gang, and their pet mule, back home with him.

43. *Washee Ironee.* Roach-MGM (9/29/34), James Parrott. Spanky, Wally "Waldo" Albright, Scotty Beckett, Stymie, Jackie Taylor, Tommy Bond, Leonard Kibrick, Billie Thomas, Willie Mae "Buckwheat" Taylor, Jerry Tucker, Jackie White, Alvin Buckelew, Yen Wong, Tony Kales, Tommy McFarland; Sam Adams, Ellinor Vanderveer, Tiny Sandford, James C. Morton, William Irving, Natalie Moorhead, Gertrude Astor, Symona Boniface, Sam Baker, Ernie Alexander, Lester Dorr. Waldo gets his clothes dirty playing football with the Gang—just before he is to be introduced at his mother's society party.

44. *Mama's Little Pirates.* Roach-MGM (11/3/34), Gus Meins. Spanky, Scotty Beckett, Stymie, Jerry Tucker, Billie "Buckwheat" Thomas (the first time he essayed this role, which remained his thereafter), Mary Ann Breckell; Claudia Dell. The Gang goes after treasure hidden in a cave.

45. *Shrimps for a Day.* Roach-MGM (12/8/34), Gus Meins. Spanky, Stymie, Scotty Beckett, Buckwheat, Jackie Taylor, Marialise Gumm, Barbara Goodrich, Marianne Edwards, Jackie White, Harry Harvey, Jr., Leonard Kibrick, Jerry Tucker, Alvin Buckelew, Tommy McFarland, Donald Proffitt; Clarence Wilson, Rosa Gore, George and Olive Brasno, Wilfred Lucas, Joseph Young, Doris McMahan, Ray Turner. A magic lamp lets a married couple become kids again and expose a nasty old man who runs his orphanage like a prison.

46. *Anniversary Trouble.* Roach-MGM (1/1/35), Gus Meins. Spanky, Scotty Beckett, Buckwheat, Leonard Kibrick, Jerry Tucker, Cecelia Murray, Donald Proffitt, Sidney Kibrick, Alvin Buckelew; Johnny Arthur, Claudia Dell, Hattie McDaniel. The Gang's treasury, entrusted to Spanky, is confused with some money of his father's.

47. *Beginner's Luck.* Roach-MGM (2/23/35), Gus Meins. Spanky, Scott Beckett, Buckwheat, Stymie, Jerry Tucker, Carl Switzer, Harold Switzer, Alvin Buckelew, Marianne Edwards, Donald Proffitt, Sidney Kibrick, Leonard Kibrick, Jackie White, Cecelia Murray, The Five Cabin Kids, The Five Meglin Kiddies; James C. Morton, May Wallace, Robert McKenzie, Fred Holmes, Ernie Alexander, Jack "Tiny" Lipson, Tom Herbert, Kitty Kelly, Bess Flowers, Charlie Hall, Ruth Hiatt. Spanky's mother goads him into taking part in a local theatre's amateur night.

48. *Teacher's Beau.* Roach-MGM (4/27/35), Gus Meins. Spanky, Scotty Beckett, Carl "Alfalfa" Switzer, Buckwheat, Stymie, Jerry Tucker, Alvin Buckelew, Donald Proffitt, Rex Downing, Harold Switzer, Marianne Edwards, Dorian Johnston, Jackie White, The Five Cabin Kids; Arletta Duncan, Edward Norris, Robert McKenzie, Billy Bletcher, Gus Leonard, Charlie Hall, Robert "Bobby" Burns, Fred Holmes, Ernie Alexander, Lon Poff. The Gang tries to discourage their teacher from marrying.

49. *Sprucin' Up.* Roach-MGM (6/1/35), Gus Meins. Spanky, Alfalfa, Scotty Beckett, Buckwheat, Marianne Edwards, Jerry "Percy" Tucker, Alvin Buckelew, Dorian Johnston, Donald Proffitt, Harold Switzer; Dick Elliott, James Burtis, Lillian Rich,

Gertrude Sutton, Leota Lorraine, Harry Bernard, Bess Flowers. When the truant officer moves into the neighborhood, everyone tries to get friendly with his daughter.

50. *Little Papa.* Roach-MGM (9/21/35), Gus Meins. Spanky, Alfalfa, Scotty Beckett, Buckwheat, Donald Proffitt, Alvin Buckelew, Sidney Kibrick, Dickie De Nuet, Patsy Dittemore, Eva Lee Kuney; Ruth Hiatt. Before the Gang can play football, Spanky has to put his baby sister to sleep.

51. *Little Sinner.* Roach-MGM (10/26/35), Gus Meins. Spanky, Buckwheat, Eugene "Porky" Lee, Alfalfa, Sidney Kibrick, Jerry Tucker, Donald Proffitt, Rex Downing; Clarence Wilson. Rather than go to church, Spanky goes fishing, which turns out to be a spooky experience.

52. *Our Gang Follies of 1936.* Roach-MGM (11/30/35), Gus Meins. Spanky, Alfalfa, Scotty Beckett, Philip Hurlic, Rex Downing, Darla "Cookie" Hood, Buckwheat, Porky, Jackie White, Donald Proffitt, Harold Switzer, Sidney Kibrick, Jerry Tucker, Dickie De Nuet, Marvin Trin, Janet Comerford, Dickie Jones, Leonard Kibrick. The Gang stages a revue.

53. *Pinch Singer.* Roach-MGM (1/4/36), Fred Newmeyer. Spanky, Alfalfa, Darla Hood, Buckwheat, Porky, Dickie De Nuet, Billy Winderlout, Jerry Tucker, Marianne Edwards, Sidney Kibrick, Harold Switzer, Dorian Johnston, Dickie Jones, Rex Downing, Delmar Watson; Blair Davis, Eddie Craven, Charlie Hall, Gail Goodson, David Sharpe, Bill Madsen, Lester Dorr, Marvin Hatley. Darla is supposed to represent the Gang on a radio talent contest, but Alfalfa is forced to substitute.

54. *Divot Diggers.* Roach-MGM (2/8/36), Robert McGowan. Spanky, Alfalfa, Buckwheat, Darla Hood, Porky, Harold Switzer, Baby Patsy May; Billy Bletcher, Tom Dugan, Thomas Pogue, David Thursby, Leonard Kibrick, Matty Roubert, Jack Hatfield, Hubert Diltz. The Gang volunteers to work as caddies for a golfing foursome.

55. *The Lucky Corner.* Roach-MGM 3/14/36), Gus Meins. Spanky, Scotty Beckett, Buckwheat, Alfalfa, Marianne Edwards, Leonard Kibrick, Harold Switzer, Alvin Buckelew, Donald Proffitt, Tommy McFarland, Gloria Mann; Gus Leonard, William Wagner, James C. Morton, Fred Holmes, Sam Lufkin, Jack "Tiny" Lipson, Lester Dorr, Joe Bordeaux, Bobby Dunn, Ernie Alexander. The Gang helps Gus when he's forced to move his lemonade stand to a remote part of town.

56. *Second Childhood.* Roach-MGM (4/11/36), Gus Meins. Spanky, Alfalfa, Darla Hood, Buckwheat, Porky, Dickie De Nuet; Zeffie Tilbury, Sidney Bracey, Greta Gould. The Gang encounters a crochety old woman and gradually make her thaw into a fun-loving, zesty lady.

57. *Arbor Day.* Roach-MGM (5/2/36), Fred Newmeyer. Alfalfa, Spanky, Buckwheat, Darla Hood, Harold Switzer; George Guhl, Rosina Lawrence, May Wallace, George and Olive Brasno, Maurice Cass, Hattie McDaniel, Bobby Dunn, Rolfe Sedan, Kathryn Sheldon. The truant officer mistakes two midgets for delinquent schoolchildren.

58. *Bored of Education.* Roach-MGM (8/29/36), Gordon

Douglas. Spanky, Alfalfa, Buckwheat, Porky, Darla Hood, Sidney Kibrick, Harold Switzer, Donald Proffitt, Dickie De Nuet, Dorian Johnston; Rosina Lawrence, Jack Egan. Spanky and Alfalfa contrive to get out of school via a toothache, only to find that the teacher has planned an ice-cream party. Academy Award winner.

59. *Two Too Young*. Roach-MGM (9/26/36), Gordon Douglas. Spanky, Alfalfa, Porky, Buckwheat, Donald Proffitt, Jerry Tucker, Dickie De Nuet, Sidney Kibrick, Harold Switzer, Rex Downing; Rosina Lawrence. Spanky and Alfalfa try to talk Porky and Buckwheat out of their firecrackers.

60. *Pay As You Exit*. Roach-MGM (10/24/36), Gordon Douglas. Spanky, Alfalfa, Porky, Buckwheat, Darla Hood, Joe Cobb, Sidney Kibrick, Rex Downing, Harold Switzer, Bobs Watson, Robert Winkler, Marvin Trin. The Gang stages a production of *Romeo and Juliet*.

61. *Spooky Hooky*. Roach-MGM (12/5/36), Gordon Douglas. Spanky, Alfalfa, Porky, Buckwheat; Rosina Lawrence, Sam Mc-Daniels. The Gang plants a phony absence note on the teacher's desk for the next day, then has to retrieve it when they hear the class is going to the circus.

Spanky calls attention to a major operation in *Washee Ironee*. Behind him, Tommy Bond, Jerry Tucker, Leonard Kibrick, and Matthew "Stymie" Beard.

62. *Reunion in Rhythm*. Roach-MGM (1/9/37), Gordon Douglas. Spanky, Alfalfa, Porky, Darla Hood, Buckwheat, Sidney Kibrick, Harold Switzer, Georgia Jean LaRue; Rosina Lawrence, Mickey Daniels, Mary Kornman, Joe Cobb, Matthew "Stymie" Beard, Ernie Alexander. The Gang stages a musical show at a reunion for some of the former Gang kids.

63. *Glove Taps*. Roach-MGM (2/20/37), Gordon Douglas. Alfalfa, Tommy "Butch" Bond, Spanky, Porky, Buckwheat, Sidney "Woim" Kibrick, Jerry Tucker, Harold Switzer, Darwood Kaye, Rex Downing, Larry Harris, Hugh Chapman, Donald Proffitt, Robert Winkler. Butch challenges Alfalfa to a fight.

64. *Three Smart Boys*. Roach-MGM (3/13/37), Gordon Douglas. Spanky, Alfalfa, Buckwheat, Porky, Darwood "Waldo" Kaye, Darla Hood, Shirley Coates; Sidney Bracey, Rosina Lawrence, Jack Egan, Nora Cecil. The Gang decides to stage a phony epidemic to close down the school.

65. *Hearts Are Trumps*. Roach-MGM (4/3/37), Gordon

Douglas. Alfalfa, Spanky, Darla Hood, Buckwheat, Sidney Kibrick, Waldo, Porky, Beverly Lorraine Smith, Shirley "Henrietta" Coates, Robert Winkler; Rosina Lawrence. The Gang vows to keep away from girls on Valentine's Day—but Alfalfa can't resist Darla's affections.

66. *Rushin' Ballet*. Roach-MGM (4/24/37), Gordon Douglas. Spanky, Alfalfa, Butch, Buckwheat, Porky, Woim, Waldo, Harold Switzer, Maria Ayres; Kathryn Sheldon, Fred Holmes. While tracking down Butch and Woim, Spanky and Alfalfa get tangled up in a dance recital.

67. *Roamin' Holiday*. Roach-MGM (6/12/37), Gordon Douglas. Spanky, Alfalfa, Buckwheat, Porky, Darla Hood; May Wallace, Fred Holmes. The Gang runs away from home, but learns their lesson from two kindly old people.

68. *Night 'n' Gales*. Roach-MGM (7/24/37), Gordon Douglas. Spanky, Alfalfa, Buckwheat, Porky, Darla Hood, Gary "Junior" Jasgar; Johnny Arthur. Due to a storm, the Gang spends the night at Darla's and wrecks her father's nerves.

69. *Fishy Tales*. Roach-MGM (8/28/37), Gordon Douglas. Alfalfa, Spanky, Butch, Porky, Buckwheat, Waldo, Darla Hood, Junior, Woim, Dickie De Nuet, Dorian Johnston. Alfalfa tries to back out of a fight with Butch by pretending to be incapacitated.

70. *Framing Youth*. Roach-MGM (9/11/37), Gordon Douglas. Spanky, Alfalfa, Buckwheat, Porky, Darla Hood, Butch, Junior; Jack Mulhall, Ernie Alexander. Butch fixes it so he'll win over Alfalfa in a radio amateur contest.

71. *Pigskin Palooka*. Roach-MGM (10/23/37), Gordon Douglas. Alfalfa, Spanky, Darla Hood, Porky, Buckwheat, Freddie Walburn, Sidney Kibrick, Dickie Jones, Harold Switzer, Alvin Buckelew, Delmar Watson, Waldo, Junior, Larry Harris, Rex Downing, Donald Proffitt, Marvin Trin. Alfalfa's been away at military school, pretending in his letters to be a football star; returning home, he has to prove it.

72. *Mail and Female*. Roach-MGM (11/13/37), Fred Newmeyer. Spanky, Alfalfa, Buckwheat, Porky, Darla Hood, Alvin "Spike" Buckelew, Harold Switzer, Waldo, Freddie Walburn, Hugh Chapman, Robert Winkler, Joe "Corky" Geil. When Alfalfa is made president of the He-Man Woman Haters' Club, he rushes to Darla to retrieve a love note he's sent her.

73. *Our Gang Follies of 1938*. Roach-MGM (12/18/37), Gordon Douglas. Alfalfa, Spanky, Darla Hood, Buckwheat, Porky, Dickie Jones, Alvin Buckelew, Harold Switzer, Darwood Kaye, Kenneth Wilson, Philip Mac Mahon, Josephine Roberts, Tommy McFarland, Georgie Jean La Rue, Patsy Currier, Robert Winkler, Bobs Watson, Corky, Annabella Logan; Henry Brandon, Gino Corrado, Wilma Cox, Doodles Weaver. Alfalfa spoils the Gang's revue when he tells Spanky he'd rather sing opera than croon.

74. *Canned Fishing*. Roach-MGM (2/12/38), Gordon Douglas. Spanky, Alfalfa, Buckwheat, Porky, Junior; Wilma Cox. Spanky and Alfalfa's plans to play hooky are foiled when they have to baby-sit with Junior.

75. *Bear Facts*. Roach-MGM (3/5/38), Gordon Douglas. Spanky, Alfalfa, Darla Hood, Buckwheat, Porky. Alfalfa seeks a job taming wild animals in a circus, but changes his mind when he encounters a live bear.

76. *Three Men in a Tub*. Roach-MGM (3/26/38), Nate Watt. Alfalfa, Spanky, Darla Hood, Waldo, Buckwheat, Porky, Junior, Jerry Tucker, Sheila Brown, Tommy McFarland. A boat race between Alfalfa and Waldo becomes a contest for Darla's affections.

77. *Came the Brawn*. Roach-MGM (4/16/38), Gordon Douglas. Alfalfa, Spanky, Porky, Buckwheat, Darla Hood, Waldo, Butch, Woim, Alvin Buckelew, Patsy Currier, Raymond Rayhill Powell, Billy Mindy, Betsy Gay, Corky. Alfalfa's fight with the Masked Marvel is rigged—or so he thinks.

78. *Feed 'em and Weep*. Roach-MGM (5/27/38), Gordon Douglas. Alfalfa, Porky, Darla Hood, Philip Hurlic, Junior, Percy; Wilma Cox, Johnny Arthur. Darla's father's birthday dinner is ruined by a visit from the Gang.

79. *The Awful Tooth*. Roach-MGM (5/28/38), Nate Watt. Alfalfa, Buckwheat, Porky, Spike; Jack Norton. The Gang believes that if they have all their teeth pulled, the Tooth Fairy will leave them a fortune.

80. *Hide and Shriek*. Roach-MGM (6/18/38), Gordon Douglas. Alfalfa, Buckwheat, Porky, Darla Hood, Junior, Percy; Fred Holmes. The Gang plays detective, and ends up in a spooky amusement-park fun house.

81. *The Little Ranger*. MGM (8/6/38), Gordon Douglas. Alfalfa, Butch, Shirley "Mugsy" Coates, Darla Hood, Porky, Buckwheat, Waldo, Woim, Alvin Buckelew, Harold Switzer. Alfalfa goes to a Western movie and dreams that he is the hero.

82. *Party Fever*. MGM (8/27/38), George Sidney. Alfalfa, Butch, Waldo, Darla Hood, Porky, Buckwheat, Woim, Harold Switzer; Frank Jaquet. Alfalfa and Butch run for office in a local boys' government project, to win Darla's affections.

83. *Aladdin's Lantern*. MGM (9/17/38), Gordon Douglas. Spanky, Alfalfa, Buckwheat, Darla Hood, Waldo, Porky, Gary Jasgar, Corky, Alvin Buckelew. Porky and Buckwheat continually interrupt the Gang's play.

84. *Men in Fright*. MGM (10/15/38), George Sidney. Spanky, Alfalfa, Darla Hood, Buckwheat, Porky, Gary Jasgar, Sonny Bupp; Barbara Bedford, Bess Flowers, Jack Rice, Margaret Bert. The Gang visits Darla in the hospital, bringing her food they know she can't eat—so *they* do.

85. *Football Romeo*. MGM (11/12/38), George Sidney. Alfalfa, Spanky, Darla Hood, Butch, Buckwheat, Porky, Gary Jasgar, Woim; Barbara Bedford. Alfalfa is downhearted, thinking that he hasn't a chance with Darla, but she and Alfalfa's mother concoct a scheme to dissuade him.

86. *Practical Jokers*. MGM (12/17/38), George Sidney. Spanky, Alfalfa, Darla Hood, Porky, Buckwheat, Butch. Butch has perpetrated a series of practical jokes on the Gang, but then the tables are turned.

87. *Alfalfa's Aunt*. MGM (1/7/39), George Sidney. Alfalfa,

Spanky, Porky, Buckwheat, Gary Jasgar; Marie Blake, William Newell, Barbara Bedford. Alfalfa reads one of his aunt's mystery stories and thinks she wants to murder him.

88. *Tiny Troubles.* MGM (2/18/39), George Sidney. Alfalfa, Spanky, Darla Hood, Buckwheat, Porky; Fred Kelsey, Emory Parnell, Jerry Marenghi, Barbara Bedford, Sue Moore, Edward and Jimmy Marazone. Alfalfa "trades" his whiny baby brother for another child—a midget criminal.

89. *Duel Personalities.* MGM (3/11/39), George Sidney. Alfalfa, Spanky, Butch, Darla Hood, Porky, Buckwheat, Mugsy,

Woim, Butch, Alfalfa, Darla, Spanky, Porky, and Buckwheat in a confrontation from *Dog Daze.*

Woim, Waldo; John Davidson, Doodles Weaver, Lester Dorr. While under a hynotic spell, Alfalfa thinks he's D'Artagnan and challenges Butch to a duel.

90. *Clown Princes.* MGM (4/15/39), George Sidney. Spanky, Alfalfa, Darla Hood, Porky, Buckwheat, Mugsy, Gary Jasgar, Harold Switzer; Clarence Wilson. The Gang stages a circus to raise rent money for Porky.

91. *Cousin Wilbur.* MGM (4/29/39), George Sidney. Alfalfa,

Scotty Beckett, Spanky, Butch, Darla Hood, Buckwheat, Porky, Woim, Philip Hurlic, Harold Switzer, Waldo, Freddie Chapman, Gary Jasgar. Cousin Wilbur organizes a protection agency; Butch thinks he can take over, since Wilbur is a sissy—but he's proven wrong.

92. *Joy Scouts.* MGM (6/24/39), Edward Cahn. Alfalfa, Spanky, Porky, Buckwheat, Mickey Gubitosi; Forbes Murray. Too young to join the Boy Scouts, the Gang decides to camp out on their own.

93. *Dog Daze.* MGM (7/1/39), George Sidney. Alfalfa, Spanky, Scotty Beckett, Porky, Buckwheat, Darla Hood, Butch, Woim; Wade Boteler, John Power. Having received a reward for caring for a lost dog, the Gang tries to raise more money by rounding up all the stray dogs they can.

94. *Auto Antics.* MGM (7/22/39), Edward Cahn. Alfalfa, Spanky, Darla Hood, Buckwheat, Porky, Butch, Woim, Mickey Gubitosi; Baldwin Cooke, Major James H. McNamara, Joe Whitehead. Butch sabotages the Gang's car just before a kiddie-car race.

95. *Captain Spanky's Show Boat.* MGM (9/9/39), Edward Cahn. Spanky, Alfalfa, Darla Hood, Butch, Buckwheat, Woim, Mugsy, Mickey Gubitosi, Waldo, Clyde Wilson. When Butch is turned down to apear in Spanky's show, he seeks revenge.

96. *Dad for a Day.* MGM (10/21/39), Edward Cahn. Mickey Gubitosi, Spanky, Alfalfa, Buckwheat, Waldo; Louis Jean Heydt, Milton Parsons, Mary Treen, Hugh Herbert, Peggy Shannon, Walter Sande. Orphaned Mickey feels left out when the Gang arranges a Father-Son picnic.

97. *Time Out for Lessons.* MGM (12/2/39), Edward Cahn. Alfalfa, Spanky, Darla Hood, Mickey Gubitosi, Buckwheat, Mugsy, Sidney Kibrick, Waldo, Hugh Chapman, Valerie Lee, Harold Switzer; Si Wills. Alfalfa's father tells him what life will be like if he continues to neglect his school work in favor of football.

98. *Alfalfa's Double.* MGM (1/20/40), Edward Cahn. Alfalfa, Darla Hood, Spanky, Buckwheat, Mickey Gubitosi; Hank Mann, Barbara Bedford, Anne O'Neal, Milton Parsons. Alfalfa meets a wealthy lookalike named Cornelius and changes places with him.

99. *The Big Premiere.* MGM (3/9/40), Edward Cahn. Spanky, Alfalfa, Darla Hood, Buckwheat, Mickey Gubitosi, Waldo, Mugsy, Harold Switzer; Charles Evans. After being kicked out of a local premiere, the Gang decides to film their own movie and stage a gala event.

100. *All About Hash.* MGM (3/30/40), Edward Cahn. Mickey Gubitosi, Spanky, Alfalfa, Darla Hood, Buckwheat, Janet Burston; Louis Jean Heydt, Barbara Bedford, William Newell, Ferris Taylor, Peggy Shannon. The Gang stages a radio skit to stop Mickey's parents from continually quarreling because she serves hash every Monday night.

101. *The New Pupil.* MGM (4/27/40), Edward Cahn. Spanky, Alfalfa, Juanita "Sally" Quigley, Darla Hood, Mickey Gubitosi, Billy "Froggy" Laughlin, Buckwheat, Waldo, Patsy Currier; Anne

O'Neal, May McAvoy. Spanky and Alfalfa vie for the attentions of a pretty new girl in school— who doesn't like boys.

102. *Bubbling Trouble.* MGM (5/25/40), Edward Cahn. Alfalfa, Darla Hood, Spanky, Butch, Buckwheat, Mickey Gubitosi; William Newell, Barbara Bedford, Hank Mann. To impress Darla, Alfalfa drinks Butch's homemade "dynamite" brew.

103. *Good Bad Guys.* MGM (9/7/40), Edward Cahn. Spanky, Alfalfa, Buckwheat, Mickey Gubitosi, Freddie Walburn; George Lessey, Al Hill, Byron Foulger, Emmett Vogan, Hugh Beaumont, William Newell, Barbara Bedford, Margaret Bert. Deciding to become criminals, the Gang inadvertently gets mixed up with a real burglar.

104. *Waldo's Last Stand.* MGM (10/5/40), Edward Cahn. Spanky, Froggy, Alfalfa, Waldo, Darla Hood, Mickey Gubitosi, Buckwheat, Janet Burston. The Gang puts on a show to attract customers to Waldo's lemonade stand. A reworking of *The Lucky Corner*.

105. *Goin' Fishin'.* MGM (10/26/40), Edward Cahn. Alfalfa, Spanky, Buckwheat, Mickey Gubitosi; Paul Hurst, Robert Homans, Anne O'Neal, Arthur Hoyt. The Gang sleeps on the sidewalk overnight in order to catch an early-morning bus and go fishing.

106. *Kiddie Cure.* MGM (11/23/40), Edward Cahn. Spanky, Alfalfa, Darla Hood, Buckwheat, Mickey Gubitosi, Froggy; Thurston Hall, Josephine Whittell, Gerald Oliver Smith. The Gang retrieves a baseball that went through a window, and they meet a strange hypochondriac.

107. *Fightin' Fools.* MGM (1/25/41), Edward Cahn. Spanky, Froggy, Mickey Gubitosi, Buckwheat, Ray "Boxcar" Smith, Freddie "Slicker" Walburn, Joe "Tubby" Strauch, Jr. The Gang challenges Slicker's bunch of rowdies to a fight to settle their disputes.

108. *Baby Blues.* MGM (2/15/41), Edward Cahn. Mickey Gubitosi, Spanky, Froggy, Buckwheat, Janet Burston, Betty Scott, Freddie "Bully" Chapman, Billy Ray Smith; Hank Mann, Margaret Bert, William Edmunds. Mickey's mother is pregnant, and Mickey is worried, having read that every fourth child born in the world is Chinese.

109. *Ye Olde Minstrels.* MGM (3/18/41), Edward Cahn. Spanky, Darla Hood, Froggy, Mickey Gubitosi, Buckwheat, Joline Karol, Jackie Salling, David Polonsky, Valerie Lee, Marlene Mains; Walter Wills. The Gang stages a show (with Froggy's Uncle Walter) to raise money for the Red Cross.

110. *1-2-3 Go!* MGM (4/26/41), Edward Cahn. Spanky, Froggy, Mickey Gubitosi, Buckwheat, Freddie Walburn; Barbara Bedford, Margaret Bert, Arthur Hoyt, Anne O'Neal, Charles Evans, William Tannen. After Mickey is hit by a car, the Gang decides to form a safety society.

111. *Robot Wrecks.* MGM (7/12/41), Edward Cahn. Spanky, Froggy, Darla Hood, Buckwheat, Mickey Gubitosi, Slicker, Boxcar; Emmett Vogan, Billy Bletcher, Margaret Bert. The Gang decides to build a robot.

112. *Helping Hands.* MGM (9/27/41), Edward Cahn. Spanky,

Three would-be mechanics in *Auto Antics*.

Darla Hood, Froggy, Mickey Gubitosi, Buckwheat, Leon Tyler, Freddie Chapman, Billy Ray Smith, Mickey Laughlin; Sam Flint, Byron Foulger, Margaret Bert. The Gang does their bit at home by organizing a scrap drive.

113. *Come Back, Miss Pipps.* MGM (10/25/41), Edward Cahn. Spanky, Mickey Gubitosi, Froggy, Buckwheat, Darla Hood, Leon Tyler, Teresa Mae Glass; Sara Haden, Christian Rub, Byron Foulger, Billy Bletcher, Barbara Bedford. The Gang springs into action to save their teacher from losing her job after she has been fired by a mean school superintendent.

114. *Wedding Worries.* MGM (12/13/41), Edward Cahn. Spanky, Froggy, Darla Hood, Mickey Gubitosi, Buckwheat; Byron Shores, Barbara Bedford, Chester Clute, William Irving, Jack "Tiny" Lipson, Margaret Bert, Stanley Logan. The Gang tries to sabotage Darla's father's marriage when they hear terrible things about stepmothers in general.

115. *Melodies Old and New.* MGM (1/24/42), Edward Cahn. Spanky, Froggy, Mickey Gubitosi, Buckwheat, Janet Burston; Walter Wills. The Gang stages a show to raise money for football uniforms.

116. *Going to Press.* MGM (3/7/42), Edward Cahn. Darryl Hickman, Spanky, Froggy, Sally, Mickey Gubitosi, Buckwheat, Freddie Chapman, Boxcar. The Gang, running a crusading newspaper, tries to pin the identity of a mysterious "boss" running a tough gang.

117. *Don't Lie.* MGM (4/4/42), Edward Cahn. Buckwheat, Spanky, Froggy, Mickey Gubitosi; Emmett Vogan. The Gang tries to cure Buckwheat of fibbing—not knowing he wasn't kidding when he said he saw a monkey.

118. *Surprised Parties.* MGM (5/30/42), Edward Cahn. Froggy, Spanky, Janet Burston, Buckwheat, Mickey Gubitosi, Leon Tyler, Robert Ferrero; Margaret Bert. In order to prepare a surprise party for him, the Gang is forced to kick Froggy out of their club, temporarily.

119. *Doin' Their Bit.* MGM (7/18/42), Herbert Glazer. Spanky, Froggy, Janet Burston, Buckwheat, Mickey Gubitosi, Billy Finnegan, Freddie Chapman, Jackie Salling, Billy Ray Smith; Walter Wills. The Gang stages a show for all local servicemen.

120. *Rover's Big Chance.* MGM (8/22/42), Herbert Glazer. Spanky, Froggy, Janet Burston, Buckwheat, Mickey Gubitosi, Freddie Chapman, Bobby Anderson; Byron Shores, Horace McNally, Barbara Bedford. A casting director decides to put the Gang's dog in movies.

121. *Mighty Lak a Goat.* MGM (10/10/42), Herbert Glazer. Spanky, Mickey Gubitosi, Froggy, Buckwheat; Anne O'Neal, Charles Evans, William Tannen. After being splashed by mud, the Gang uses a strong-smelling cleaner that makes them unwelcome throughout town.

122. *Unexpected Riches.* MGM (11/28/42), Herbert Glazer. Spanky, Buckwheat, Mickey Gubitosi, Froggy, Barry "Ken" Downing; Emmett Vogan, Willa Pearl Curtis, Margaret Bert, Ernie Alexander, Symona Boniface, Ernestine Wade, Stanley Logan. A rich kid tricks the Gang into doing his work for him.

123. *Benjamin Franklin, Jr.* MGM (2/30/43), Herbert Glazer. Mickey Gubitosi (hereafter known as Bobby Blake), Froggy, Janet Burston, Buckwheat, Mickey "Happy" Laughlin, Barry Downing, Dickie Hall, Billy Ray Smith, Valerie Lee; Barbara Bedford, Margaret Bert, Ernie Alexander. The Gang puts on a skit from Ben Franklin's *Poor Richard's Almanac* that makes the kids understand the importance of the war.

124. *Family Troubles.* MGM (4/3/43), Herbert Glazer. Janet Burston, Froggy, Bobby "Mickey" Blake, Buckwheat, Beverly "Aurelia" Hudson, Dickie Hall, Happy; Barbara Bedford, Byron Shores, Sara Padden, Elspeth Dudgeon. Janet thinks her parents are ignoring her, and leaves home.

125. *Calling All Kids.* MGM (4/24/43), Sam Baerwitz. Froggy, Mickey, Buckwheat, Janet Burston; Mark Daniels. The Gang goes on radio to salute the armed forces.

126. *Farm Hands.* MGM (6/19/43), Herbert Glazer. Froggy, Mickey, Buckwheat, Happy; Murray Alper. The Gang, city slickers all, visit Mickey's uncle's farm.

127. *Election Daze.* MGM (7/31/43), Herbert Glazer. Mickey, Froggy, Buckwheat, Janet Burston, Freddie Chapman, Dickie Hall, Robert Ferrero, Billy Ray Smith, Valerie Lee. Mickey and Froggy continually split the vote in their club elections.

128. *Little Miss Pinkerton.* MGM (9/18/43), Herbert Glazer. Froggy, Mickey, Janet Burston, Buckwheat; Dick Rich, Norman Willis. The Gang helps solve a murder in a local department store.

129. *Three Smart Guys.* MGM (10/23/43), Edward Cahn. Froggy, Mickey, Buckwheat, Janet Burston; Edward Fielding. The boys go fishing instead of to school, but an old-timer convinces them they're wrong.

130. *Radio Bugs.* MGM (4/1/44), Cyril Endfield. Froggy, Mickey, Buckwheat, Janet Burston; Chester Clute, Marie Blake, Jack "Tiny" Lipson, Tiny Hanlon, Morris Ankrum, Red Skelton heard on the radio. The Gang wants to go on the radio, and auditions for potential sponsors.

131. *Tale of a Dog.* MGM (4/15/44), Cyril Endfield. Buckwheat, Cordell Hickman, Mickey, Janet Burston, Froggy, Dickie Hall; Emmett Vogan, Willa Pearl Curtis, Margaret Bert, Dorothy Neumann, Anita Bolster. Trouble begins when the Gang names their dog Smallpox.

132. *Dancing Romeo.* MGM (4/29/44), Cyril Endfield. Froggy, Mickey, Buckwheat, Janet Burston, Valerie "Marilyn" Lee, Billy Ray Smith, Dickie Hall, Bobby "Gerald" Browning. Froggy has to learn to dance in order to win Marilyn's affections.

Laurel and Hardy

It has been said that Laurel and Hardy didn't appeal to anybody but the public. The assertion is true, for in their prime, Laurel and Hardy were ignored by critics. But at the same time, millions of people all over the world were flocking to see their pictures. When a Laurel and Hardy short played a theatre, it was frequently advertised as the main attraction, with the feature film as an incidental bonus. What is more, the Laurel and Hardy shorts have withstood the test of time. They are *still* great.

Why were the Laurel and Hardy two-reelers so superior to most of the contemporary comedy product? Why have their films endured so long? How is it that such popular stars did the bulk of their work in two-reelers instead of feature films? To those unfamiliar with the team, these questions come to mind. To anyone who has watched even a small sampling of their work, the answers are obvious.

The Laurel and Hardy shorts stood out among the many comedy featurettes of the day because they were made with special care. As I mentioned earlier, the Hal Roach studio was an unusual place, unexcelled in providing an outlet for comic talent. There was never any rush, and the films were made by a team of people who cared most of all about good comedy.

The films have endured because Stan Laurel and Oliver Hardy went beyond the superficiality of most screen comedy. They were not content to appear in films and participate in a series of funny gags. They created characters (Stan and Ollie) who were real people, characters the audience came to know and love. Laurel and Hardy's enduring popularity is a tribute to the warmth of their characterizations, which have stayed in people's hearts over the years and enabled new generations to appreciate them all over again.

As to the question of short subjects versus feature films, the simple fact is that Laurel and Hardy did their best work in shorts. The compact nature of the two-reeler enabled them to hit the bull's-eye more often than not with a minimum of wasted time and no superfluous material. When the team went into feature films, they suffered from the necessity to fill seventy minutes with nothing but comedy—in most cases, a burden which was relieved by unwelcome romantic subplots or musical numbers. The two-reeler presented Laurel and Hardy in their purest form, the way most of us would like to remember them.

Stan Laurel was born Arthur Stanley Jefferson in Ulverston, Lancashire, England, in 1890, the son of a famous theatrical producer. He caught stage fever during his youth, and made his debut at the age of sixteen. He set out to join the world of the British music hall, where he received his comic training, most notably in the Fred Karno troupe, which spawned another famous comedian —Charlie Chaplin. When the Karno company toured America, Stan decided to stay. After a career of ups and downs in vaudeville, he settled in California and tried his luck at the movies. Here, too, his career was erratic, although many of his earliest silent comedies still exist and show Stan to be a talented comic from the start. He had some success in the 1920s with a series of popular movie burlesques such as *Dr. Pyckle and Mr. Pryde, Mud and Sand,* and *The Soilers,* but when the opportunity came to work behind the scenes as a gag writer and sometime director for Hal Roach, Stan jumped at the chance. Necessity forced him back in front of the cameras, and fate brought him together with Oliver Hardy.

Oliver Norvell Hardy (he often used his full name when, in character as Ollie, he would try to impress someone) was born in 1892 in Harlem, Georgia. Although his family had no show-business links, young Oliver had a beautiful soprano voice and acquired a local reputation as an outstanding singer. He ran away from home to join a minstrel show at the age of eight, but he was home before long, and after military school he studied law at the University of Georgia. He still was not happy, and in 1910 he decided to open a movie theatre, one of the first in his vicinity. The movies he showed piqued his interest, and he ventured down to Jacksonville, Florida, where the Lubin film company was making short comedies. Once

he made his film debut, he decided the movies were the life for him. Hardy became a familiar screen "heavy" over the next decade, and played opposite Billy West (the famous Charlie Chaplin imitator), Larry Semon, and others.

When both Laurel and Hardy were working for Hal Roach in the late 1920s, Roach had few stars under contract and was producing what were euphemistically tagged "All-Star Comedies." These silent two-reelers featured (besides Laurel and Hardy) such stalwarts as Anita Garvin, James Finlayson, and Noah Young. But before long, it became evident that Laurel and Hardy worked well together, and more and more the All-Star films centered around them. When they were given a chance to star on their own, they proved more than worthy of the honor, and the world's greatest comedy team was born.

By the time sound arrived on the scene, Laurel and Hardy were firmly established, and their characters had come full flower. Probably no one realized at the time how much sound would mean to them. Many have marveled at how *right* their voices were for their characters. But in addition to being appropriate, the voices added a whole new dimension to their personalities. It is one thing to see doorman Ollie bashfully ask to escort Jean Harlow through a hotel lobby in the silent *Double Whoopie,* but it's quite another thing to *hear* his courtly manners when he and Stan approach two young lovelies in *Men o' War.* Watching Stan's amazing look of total nothingness is wonderful, but hearing him rattle off an idea and then be unable to repeat it coherently, as in *Towed in a Hole,* is priceless.

Sound made Laurel and Hardy greater than ever, and unlike some other comics, they refused to let the talkies dictate new methods for creating their comedies. They improvised as much as ever.

"The boys could have done twenty-eight minutes on one scene," says Dorothy Granger, who worked with them several times, "because the director would just turn on the camera, and they would keep it up and keep it up. The only way he'd say 'cut' was if the whole crew would get hysterical and they'd have to cut because of the sound."

Which is not to say that the director was unimportant to the Laurel and Hardy comedies. "They had great support from a couple of people," George Stevens says. "Freddie Guiol was a big help. . . . I think more than anyone else Leo McCarey designed it, because they had been doing entirely different kinds of things. Stan was doing an entirely different kind of character, and it hadn't been working for him. And right from the start, it worked

The boys struggle with a canoe in *Men o' War*; James Finlayson looks on from the dock.

for *them,* right from the very first picture." But he adds, "Stan was the genius on the Laurel and Hardy detail."

Director Gordon Douglas adds, "Stan was the greatest gagman I've ever known—he could think of unbelievably funny business. Stan kind of ran the ship for him and Babe . . . he was there every day, as the guiding hand. Babe (as Hardy was known off screen) would like to play golf, go to the race track; Babe enjoyed life that way, but Stan enjoyed working on scripts."

But if Stan was the pilot behind the scenes, he shared equally on screen with Hardy. It is rare that two performers work together as beautifully as did Laurel and Hardy. "There was no rivalry between them," says Billy Gilbert, who worked closely with the boys, and indeed, neither one dominated on the screen. They were two as one.

There was probably no greater audience for Laurel and Hardy than Stan himself. Another member of the Hal Roach team, Patsy Kelly, recalls, "We used to have to go see our rushes, and I can't stand myself on the screen; my voice makes me climb a wall. But I used to love to go and watch him look at his rushes, because he'd get hysterical at himself; you see, it wasn't him on the screen at all. He used to call him, like Chaplin, the Little Fellow. He'd watch it and he'd say, 'No, the little fellow'—even though it was funny—'wouldn't do that.' Because there was a great deal of pathos, and sweetness, so he wouldn't let him do anything a little risqué or too cruel."

George Stevens adds, "I walked into the projection room once, when a film was being run for one man, and there's a fellow sitting on the edge of his seat, holding onto it to keep from falling down, and it was Stan Laurel watching Babe Hardy on the screen."

Laurel and Hardy also had great support from the marvelous acting troupe at Roach. Casting James Finlayson as their perpetual foil was nothing short of inspired, and such other players as Charlie Hall, Mae Busch, Tiny Sandford, Harry Bernard, Billy Gilbert, Edgar Kennedy, and Thelma Todd, to name a few, worked as a team with Stan and Ollie to make magical things happen on screen.

Only with this kind of relaxed, noncompetitive atmosphere could improvisation really work. "They could get strong on a physical piece of business," Gordon Douglas explains, "and things would happen. In rehearsal you kind of generalize, but if a glass fell over, let's say, both of these men were so much at ease that they would make something of the glass falling over that didn't happen in rehearsal. Sometimes the funniest stuff would come out of things like that that weren't rehearsed, sometimes weren't even discussed."

Out of such spontaneous business came shorts like *A Perfect Day* (1929), one of the team's all-time funniest endeavors. In it, the family sets out for a Sunday picnic and spends all their time dealing with a stubborn car and overly friendly neighbors. In this kind of short, a picnic plot was thought of in advance, but once everyone saw the possibilities of just getting started, the focus of the short was altered.

And while visual comedy remained the principal ingredient in the Laurel and Hardy comedies, there was frequently great dialogue as well. One of their earliest talkies, *Men o' War* (1929), has a hilarious exchange between sailor Ollie and a pair of cute young girls. Ollie has found a pair of women's panties on the ground (lost from a laundry basket), and thinks they belong to one of the girls. Meanwhile, the girl has lost her gloves, and thinks that Ollie is referring to them in his conversation.

"Can you describe them?" he asks sheepishly. "Well, they button on the side," she answers. Ollie takes out a moment to study the garment again, then he persists, "I'll bet you miss them." "Well, you can just *imagine*," replies the girl. "Good thing we're having warm weather!" Ollie laughs, as the misunderstanding continues until a policeman finds the gloves and returns them to the lady.

Slapstick was a dirty word in the 1930s, considered passé by most people in the movie industry, but Laurel and Hardy kept it alive and brought to the genre their own special refinements. In *Helpmates* (1931), slapstick is used as a device for showing mounting frustration. The premise of the short is that everything goes wrong for Ollie the day his wife is due home from a trip, so instead of one slapstick sequence, there are many—each one building in laughs from the one preceding it. Seltzer bottles, explosions, dishwater, chinaware, flour, bureau drawers, and soot all gang up on Ollie just in his hour of need, and the results are side-splitting.

Another unique occurrence took place in the early days of sound. Laurel and Hardy, along with many other Hollywood stars, made as many as four different foreign-language versions of their films for showing overseas; their dialogue would be written out in phonetic French, German, Spanish, or whatever language, on a blackboard next to the camera. *Variety* summed up the result in a review of *Glueckliche Kindheit,* the German version of *Brats:* "Away from the U.S., in foreign countries, Laurel and Hardy appear to be the ace film attraction. Though in shorts, they are heavily billed, with the foreign theatre where one of their shorts is playing seemingly certain of a profitable period. In Spanish territories Laurel and Hardy are a panic the minute they commence to speak. This is regardless of any action. They speak with a comical accent to the natives; their Spanish must sound like Milt Gross does to Americans. . . . This is *The Brats* in its original English version so far as action is concerned. Comedy team speaks German. L&H's German occasionally possesses a decided American twang."

Even when Hal Roach decided to experiment with a three-reel format, Laurel and Hardy came out on top. There was talk in the film business of making the short subject a more prominent part of the movie program, and to that end several producers tried out featurettes running up to forty-five minutes instead of the usual twenty. Roach hopped on the bandwagon and featured most of his stars in thirty-minute comedies, but the results, for the most part, were disappointing. The Roach staff obviously had been steeped in the two-reel tradition so long that the extra length acted as a hindrance instead of a help.

One notable exception was the Laurel and Hardy short *The Music Box* (1932), which not only remains one of the funniest three reels ever filmed, but won an Academy Award as best short subject of the year. *The Music Box* is a marvel of pacing; it shows how Laurel and Hardy built a gag to a veritable crescendo of laughter through artful repetition and an unhurried tempo that for all its steadiness was *never* slow.

Alas, just as Laurel and Hardy hit their stride in talkies, Hal Roach decided to move them into feature films. It was a gradual progression, with the team doing about one feature a year until 1935, filling out the rest of each year with short subjects. The features are not bad, by any means, and some of them are wonderful, but the two-reelers were so satisfying to everyone concerned that it seems a shame they had to be abandoned.

The very last short the team made, *Thicker Than Water* (1935), shows the kind of inventiveness that still existed in the making of their little comedies and how this creativity could have been used indefinitely instead of being

Professor Billy Gilbert demands the right of way in *The Music Box*.

diluted in the tougher task of expanding the Laurel and Hardy format for features. In *Thicker,* every time the setting changes and the boys walk out of a room, Stan "pulls" the new scene across the movie screen in a very clever optical effect. At one point, he loses his grip and the new scene falls back like a vertical window shade. Stan has to go back and get hold of it again.

But at least for Roach, it didn't pay to make "quality" short subjects any longer, and it was economically foolish to have his top attraction appearing in anything other than feature-length films. Thus ended one of the greatest chapters in the history of short subjects; seldom, if ever, would there be a series of shorts made with such love and care, with two such funny men to make them glow as the little gems they were.

The Laurel and Hardy Talkie Shorts

This list comprises all the starring talkie short subjects Laurel and Hardy made for Hal Roach that were released by MGM. The status of Laurel and Hardy's 1929 releases has confused many people. During the first half of the year, their films were conceived and designed as silents; some of these films were "gimmicked up" so that they could be released as part-talkies. They remained, in essence, silent films. During the latter half of the year, the shorts were planned and executed as talkies, and then reedited and titled for simultaneous release as silent films, to accommodate theatres not equipped for sound. These films, for all intents and purposes, were talkies. Further confusion arises because the films were not released in the order in which they were made; the silent *Angora Love* was issued in December, for instance. This index includes Laurel and Hardy's *talkie* shorts only, beginning with their first all-sound endeavor, *Unaccustomed As We Are.*

This index does not include Laurel and Hardy's guest appearances in such shorts as *Stolen Jools* (*The Slippery Pearls*), an all-star fund-raising short; *Wild Poses,* an "Our Gang" comedy in which they appeared as babies; *On the Loose,* a Thelma Todd–ZaSu Pitts comedy; and *On the Wrong Trek,* a Charley Chase short in which they made a gag appearance as hitchhikers.

1. *Unaccustomed As We Are* (5/4/29), Lewis Foster. Mae Busch, Thelma Todd, Edgar Kennedy. The boys have an innocent encounter with the wife of a jealous neighbor. Reused virtually intact in their feature film *Block Heads.*

2. *Berth Marks* (6/1/29), Lewis Foster. Charlie Hall, Harry Bernard, Baldwin Cooke, Pat Harmon. Reportedly, Paulette Goddard appears as an extra. A train ride becomes a major calamity for traveling musicians Stan and Ollie.

3. *Men o' War* (6/29/29), Lewis Foster. James Finlayson, Charlie Hall, Harry Bernard, Baldwin Cooke. Sailors on leave, the boys join two young cuties for a day's amusement.

4. *Perfect Day* (8/10/29), James Parrott. Edgar Kennedy, Kay Deslys, Isabelle Keith, Harry Bernard, Lyle Tayo, Baldwin Cooke, Charley Rogers. The family sets out for a picnic that never comes off.

Now they've done it! A leaky radiator and the boys to blame, in *The Hoose Gow.*

5. *They Go Boom* (9/21/29), James Parrott. Charlie Hall. Stan plays nursemaid when Ollie catches a cold.

6. *The Hoose Gow* (11/16/29), James Parrott. James Finlayson, Tiny Sandford, Leo Willis, Dick Sutherland, Blackie Whiteford, Elinor Vandivere, Sam Lufkin, Baldwin Cooke, Eddie Dunn, Charlie Hall. The boys' adventures in a prison camp.

7. *Night Owls* (1/4/30), James Parrott. Edgar Kennedy, James Finlayson, Anders Randolph, Harry Bernard, Charles McAvoy. Kennedy the Cop induces the boys to perform a bogus robbery.

8. *Blotto* (2/8/30), James Parrott. Anita Garvin, Tiny Sandford, Charlie Hall, Frank Holliday, Baldwin Cooke. The boys sneak away from their wives to go to a nightclub. This, along with other shorts of this period, was filmed in more than one language for foreign distribution, with the boys doing their dialogue phonetically. The Spanish version of *Blotto* costarred Linda Loredo; the French version, Georgette Rhodes.

9. *Brats* (3/22/30), James Parrott. Laurel and Hardy play their own children.

10. *Below Zero* (4/26/30), James Parrott. Charlie Hall, Frank Holliday, Leo Willis, Tiny Sandford, Bob O'Conor, Kay Deslys, Vivien Oakland, Blanche Payson, Lyle Tayo, Baldwin Cooke,

Edgar Kennedy talks the boys into a little scheme in *Night Owls*.

Robert "Bobby" Burns. Sidewalk musicians Stan and Ollie find a walletful of money.

11. *Hog Wild* (5/31/30), James Parrott. Fay Holderness, Dorothy Granger. Ollie tries to install a radio aerial with Stan's help. Originally titled *Hay Wire*.

12. *The Laurel-Hardy Murder Case* (9/6/30), James Parrott. Fred Kelsey, Tiny Sandford, Stanley Blystone, Dell Henderson, Robert "Bobby" Burns, Dorothy Granger, Frank Austin, Lon Poff. The boys go to an eerie mansion to claim an inheritance. Three reels.

13. *Another Fine Mess* (11/29/30), James Parrott. Thelma Todd, James Finlayson, Harry Bernard, Eddie Dunn, Charles Gerrard, Gertrude Sutton, Bill Knight, Bob Mimford. To escape the police, the boys duck into a mansion and then pose as its owners. Three reels.

14. *Be Big* (2/7/31), James Parrott. Anita Garvin, Charle Hall, Isabelle Keith, Baldwin Cooke. The boys want to go to a lodge meeting, but can't get into their special outfits.

15. *Chickens Come Home* (2/21/31), James Horne. Mae Busch, James Finlayson, Thelma Todd, Charles French, Frank Holliday, Baldwin Cooke, Gertrude Pedlar, Elizabeth Forrester. Ollie, running for mayor, is blackmailed by an old flame. A remake of the boys' silent *Love 'em and Weep*. Three reels.

16. *Laughing Gravy* (4/4/31), James Horne. Charlie Hall, Harry Bernard. The boys try to keep a dog in their apartment, over the protests of their landlord. A remake of their silent *Angora Love*.

17. *Our Wife* (5/16/31), James Horne. Babe London, James Finlayson, Ben Turpin, Charley Rogers, Blanche Payson. Ollie tries to elope.

18. *Come Clean* (5/19/31), James Horne. Mae Busch, Charlie Hall, Gertrude Astor, Linda Loredo, Eddie Baker, Tiny Sandford. The boys save a woman from drowning and then can't get rid of her.

19. *One Good Turn* (10/31/31), James Horne. Mary Carr, James Finlayson, Billy Gilbert, Dorothy Granger, Lyle Tayo, Snub Pollard. The boys try to save a sweet old lady from eviction.

20. *Beau Hunks* (12/12/31), James Horne. Charles Middleton, Leo Willis, Broderick O'Farrell, Harry Schultz, Charlie Hall, Robert Kortman, Tiny Sandford, Baldwin Cooke, Dick Gilbert, Abdul Kasim Khorne (James Horne), 3,987 Arabs, 1,944 Riffians, four native swede gilders [*sic*]. The boys join the Foreign Legion. Four reels.

21. *Helpmates* (1/23/32), James Parrott. Blanche Payson, Robert "Bobby" Burns. Ollie asks Stan's help in straightening up the house after a wild party.

22. *Any Old Port* (3/5/32), James Horne. Jacqueline Wells (Julie Bishop), Walter Long, Harry Bernard, Arthur Housman, Charlie Hall, Robert "Bobby" Burns, Sam Lufkin, Dick Gilbert. Ollie volunteers Stan's services to a boxing promoter.

23. *The Music Box* (4/16/32), James Parrott. Billy Gilbert,

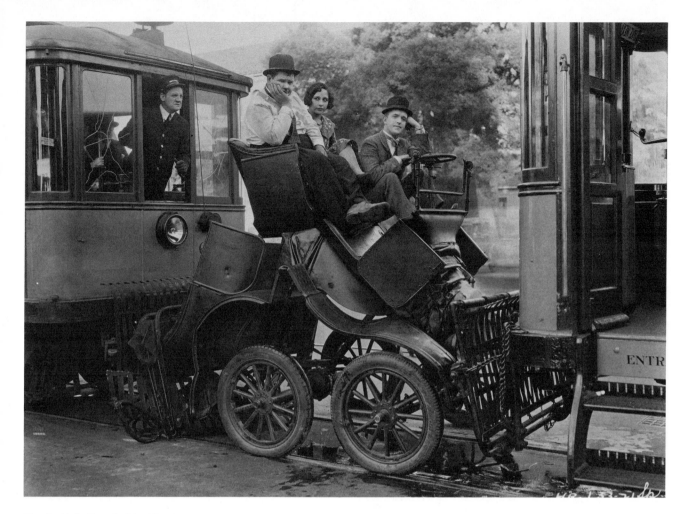

Charlie Hall, Sam Lufkin. The boys try to deliver a piano to a hilltop home. An Academy Award winner. Three reels.

24. *The Chimp* (5/21/32), James Parrott. Billy Gilbert, James Finlayson, Tiny Sandford, Charles Gamora (in the title role), Martha Sleeper, Robert "Bobby" Burns. A circus folds, and Laurel and Hardy's severance pay is a chimp.

25. *County Hospital* (6/25/32), James Parrott. Billy Gilbert, Sam Lufkin, Baldwin Cooke, May Wallace, Frank Holliday. Stan visits Ollie in the hospital.

26. *Scram* (9/10/32), Raymond McCarey. Arthur Housman, Richard Cramer, Vivien Oakland, Sam Lufkin, Baldwin Cooke. The boys are invited home by a drunk, who takes them to the wrong house.

27. *Their First Mistake* (11/5/32), George Marshall. Mae Busch, Billy Gilbert, George Marshall. To smooth over marital discord, Ollie adopts a baby.

28. *Towed in a Hole* (12/31/32), George Marshall. Billy Gilbert. The boys try to renovate an old fishing boat.

29. *Twice Two* (2/25/33), James Parrott. Charlie Hall, Baldwin Cooke. The boys play each other's wives; May Wallace is the voice of Mrs. Laurel.

30. *Me and My Pal* (4/22/33), Charles Rogers and Lloyd French. Marion Bardell, James Finlayson, James C. Morton, Eddie Dunn, Charlie Hall, Bobby Dunn. Ollie gets so involved in a jigsaw puzzle that he forgets about his own marriage.

31. *The Midnight Patrol* (8/3/33), Lloyd French. Bob Kortman, Charlie Hall, Harry Bernard, Tiny Sandford, Frank Brownlee, James C. Morton, Eddie Dunn. Stan and Ollie, new to the force, arrest their own police chief.

32. *Busy Bodies* (10/7/33), Lloyd French. Tiny Sandford, Charlie Hall, Dick Gilbert. A string of gags at a lumber company.

33. *Dirty Work* (11/25/33), Lloyd French. Lucien Littlefield, Sam Adams. The boys work as chimney sweeps for a mad scientist.

34. *Oliver the Eighth* (1/13/34), Lloyd French. Mae Busch, Jack Barty. Ollie marries a wealthy widow with diabolical plans. Charlie Hall's role as a laundryman was cut from the final release print.

35. *Going Bye Bye* (6/23/34), Charles Rogers. Walter Long, Mae Busch, Elinor Vandivere, Baldwin Cooke, Sam Lufkin, Fred Holmes, Harry Dunkinson. Having testified against a killer, the boys decide to leave town.

36. *Them Thar Hills* (7/21/34), Charles Rogers. Billy Gilbert, Charlie Hall, Mae Busch, Bobby Dunn, Eddie Baker. The boys go to the mountains for Ollie's health.

The boys get drunk with Mae Busch in _Them Thar Hills_.

37. _The Live Ghost_ (12/8/34), Charles Rogers. Walter Long, Mae Busch, Charlie Hall, Arthur Housman, Leo Willis, Harry Bernard, Charlie Sullivan, Jack ''Tiny'' Lipson, Sam Lufkin, Pete Gordon, Dick Gilbert, Baldwin Cooke, Arthur Rowlands, Hubert Diltz, John Power. The boys get involved with a rough-and-tumble sea captain.

38. _Tit for Tat_ (1/5/35), Charles Rogers. Mae Busch, Charlie Hall, James C. Morton, Bobby Dunn, Pete Gordon, Elsie Mac-Kaye. A sequel to _Them Thar Hills_ with Charlie Hall and the boys as neighboring storekeepers. Nominated for an Academy Award.

39. _The Fixer-Uppers_ (2/9/35), Charles Rogers. Mae Busch, Charles Middleton, Arthur Housman, James C. Morton, Bobby Dunn, Noah Young, Dick Gilbert. Stan and Ollie are greeting-card salesmen who help a customer make her husband jealous.

40. _Thicker Than Water_ (3/16/35), James Horne. Daphne Pollard, James Finlayson, Harry Bowen, Charlie Hall, Grace Goodall, Bess Flowers, Lester Dorr, Gladys Gale, Allen Caven. The boys squander their household money at an auction.

Perpetual drunk Arthur Housman is _The Live Ghost;_ with him are Walter Long, Mae Busch, and our heroes.

Charley Chase

It seems criminal that a man who starred in nearly two hundred shorts and devoted his life to comedy, both as an actor and a writer-director, should be nearly forgotten today. Yet that would be the sad fate of Charley Chase had not a handful of enthusiasts worked during the past few years to bring his name back into the spotlight. Most prominently, Robert Youngson has included the cream of the Chase footage from the silent era in virtually all his feature-length compilations (*When Comedy Was King, Laurel and Hardy's Laughing 20s,* etcetera), and he gave Chase equal billing with Stan Laurel, Oliver Hardy, and Buster Keaton in his latest film, *Four Clowns.*

While Chase never quite ranked alongside Keaton in the 1920s, he was not very far behind, for his bright, breezy little comedies were extremely popular from their inception, in 1924, until Chase's death in 1940. And the more one sees of Chase's own films, as well as those he directed with other stars, the more one realizes the extent of his comic mind. There are films, and individual sequences, that rate alongside the best work Keaton or Chaplin ever did.

By the time Chase embarked upon his own starring series in 1924, he was well steeped in the comedy tradition. Born in Baltimore, Maryland, in 1893, he took to the vaudeville circuits as a young man where, according to Sam Gill, he "gave an Irish monologue, sang, danced, and played several instruments." In other words, like so many others who received their training in vaudeville, he became a compleat entertainer, able to tackle with élan any kind of performing task. He appeared in at least one Broadway show in 1912 before venturing to the West Coast and breaking into the movies.

Reportedly, his first job was for Al Christie. But if so, his stay there was short, for by mid-1914 he was working for Mack Sennett. Always willing to give a potential comic a try, Sennett hired the young, handsome Charles Chase, who decided to use Charley Chase as a screen name. During his first year at the studio, he appeared in the cast of a handful of films starring Charlie Chaplin, although his contribution to these films was negligible. He also appeared with such other Sennett comics as Fatty Arbuckle, Fritz Schade, and Mae Busch. But at this point he was just one more supporting comic who had no real personality of his own.

The most important aspect of his career with Sennett was that he was given a chance to direct. Using the name Charles Parrott, he codirected several comedies with Fatty Arbuckle and Ford Sterling, and by 1916 he was working on his own. After reaching this milestone in his career, he left Sennett for a writer-director berth at Fox Pictures' comedy unit. Over the next few years, he abandoned acting entirely in favor of behind-the-scenes work at several studios, with actors like Hank Mann, Billy West, Mr. and Mrs. Carter DeHaven, and Lloyd Hamilton.

In early 1921, Charley had his first contact with Hal Roach when the producer hired him to direct the Snub Pollard comedies. The series of films that resulted are among the funniest two-reelers made during the 1920s, full of wild, ingenious gags that stand as a testament to Chase's rare ability as a comedy director. In *Sold at Auction* (1923), for instance, a character punches Snub in the jaw and knocks him out cold. He gets a dazed look in his eyes, and suddenly the screen picture "melts" into blankness. Moments later, when Snub recovers, the picture reassembles and the action resumes!

(Another comic on the Roach lot around this time was named Paul Parrott. There has been much confusion about the link between him and Chase. Paul Parrott was actually Chase's brother, who, as James Parrott, became one of Roach's top directors, and who, to make matters more confusing, also appeared for a while as Jimmie Parrott. The fact that Chase also used the last name of Parrott when he directed would seem to indicate that it was the real family name, but surprisingly enough, Chase was actual, and Parrott, assumed.)

In 1924, for reasons unknown, Chase was lured in front of the cameras again, to star in his own one-reel comedies. These were erratic little comedies, with occasional flashes of brilliance. Two things, however, changed the course of Chase's career: one was his association with a young director named Leo McCarey; the other was a move into two-reel comedies. McCarey and Chase worked together on each comedy in a relaxed and friendly atmosphere and produced some of the best silent comedies ever made—films like *Bad Boy, His Wooden Wedding, Dog Shy, Mighty Like a Moose,* etcetera.

They established the Chase character: a dapper, basically intelligent but incredibly naïve young man who inevitably found himself in some outlandish circumstances through no fault of his own. They alternated between comedies that presented him as a single man-about-town with an eye for the girls, and a married man under the thumb of his wife. In both silent and sound films, the first formula came off better, because so many other comics were using the marriage idea in their comedies. Nevertheless, Chase always made the most of the genre.

The Chase comedies got better and better as the 1920s drew to a close. McCarey was elevated to a supervisory position, and directors Fred Guiol and James Parrott continued the Chase winning streak. When sound came in there were some awkward moments as the production people at Roach tried to get their bearings, but Chase's voice was fine, and was immediately acceptable along with his already-established screen character. Nevertheless, Billy Gilbert has said that Charley "felt uncomfortable in talking pictures; his great forte was pantomime and a funny way of handling his body. He liked to work with me as I was a 'talking' actor and he could lean on me."

Sound, however, provided one new horizon for Chase—he was able to sing in his films. Music was always his first love, and, needless to say, he jumped at the chance of vocalizing on film. Thus, many of his comedies were spiced by diverting little tunes such as "Smile When the Raindrops Fall," a catchy song used in *Whispering Whoopee* and *What a Bozo,* and subsequently a standard used as background music in many Roach comedies; "You've Got to Give Credit to Love," sung with Betty Mack in *The Chases of Pimple Street;* "Let's Make It a Big Day," sung with Rosina Lawrence in *On the Wrong Trek;* "I'm in a Doghouse," from *Poker at Eight;* and "The Sun-Sun-Sunny South," from *Southern Exposure.*

These songs, plus the infectious background music played for all the Roach talkies by "The Hal Roach Happy-go-Lucky Trio" and composed by Marvin Hatley, helped to give the talkies a charm all their own. Another aid was the wonderful Roach stock company: Billy Gilbert, James Finlayson, Edgar Kennedy, Charlie Hall, Harry Bowen, James C. Morton, Harry Bernard, Rolfe Sedan, Tiny Sandford, Leo Willis, and Fred Kelsey, among others. Although they were seldom billed, at least one, and usually more, of these actors appeared in every Hal Roach film, and, in the spirit of a true repertory company, every once in a while each player would get a role that would allow him to shine, if just for a few minutes.

Chase also had an impressive array of leading ladies during the 1930s at Roach. One of his first, and his best, was Thelma Todd, whose beauty and vivacity were exceptional and whose rapport with Chase made their co-starring films a special treat. Dorothy Granger, who made a career out of comedy, was still a novice when she worked with Chase, and wasn't given much to do. Blander yet was Jacqueline Wells, who changed her name to Julie Bishop and achieved moderate success in feature films. Joyce Compton, who became one of movies' most delightful dumb blondes, was ironically little more than an attractive "straight man" for Chase in her films with him. Constance Bergen was moonlighting

from B Westerns when she made her Chase comedies. Dorothy Appleby was pert and quite winning, but she remained in B pictures until 1940, when she became Columbia's all-purpose comedy heroine. June Marlowe, best known as Miss Crabtree in the "Our Gang" shorts, was a surprisingly lifeless heroine for Charley in *Fast Work.* Rosina Lawrence was being groomed for bigger things when she appeared opposite Charley in 1936. Another leading lady known as Antoinette Lees, *did* graduate to big things when she left Roach and changed her name to Andrea Leeds. While her work opposite Charley Chase doesn't rate alongside her stunning portrayal in *Stage Door,* she was an extremely attractive heroine in his comedy shorts.

Charley's two favorite leading ladies, judging from the number of films they made with him, were Betty Mack and Muriel Evans. Both came out of Westerns, where Miss Evans was leading lady to Buck Jones, John Wayne, and other cowboy stars, and Miss Mack played opposite Tom Tyler and Harry Carey. It is safe to say that neither lady would be remembered today by any but the staunchest Western buffs if not for their fine, and prolific, work with Charley Chase. Miss Evans started with Chase in 1932; her beauty, poise, and wry sense of humor wear extremely well, and one wonders why she left the series at all. One possibility is that she did not sing, which Betty Mack did. An attractive, but not beautiful, woman, Betty had a pleasant singing voice and a subdued personality which becomes increasingly appealing as one sees more and more of her work.

Thus, Charley had a lot of support in making his two-reelers for Hal Roach during the 1930s. Even so, his first talkie efforts were largely disappointing. The addition of sound seemed to throw off the timing of many Roach comedies, with ample evidence in Charley's *The Real McCoy,* a hillbilly comedy with a barren sound track (the background music was to come later) and practically no laughs. An early sound effort that came off much better was *Whispering Whoopee,* which is played for farce as Charley hires three good-time girls (Thelma Todd, Anita Garvin, Dolores Brinkman) to help him close a big business deal with three executives. The execs turn out to be stuffy, sober types, but the girls gradually win them over, with the help of some drinks, and before long they are all playing post office. Feeling lightheaded, one of the businessmen turns to Charley and asks, "Have you ever seen Niagara Falls?" Charley says no, and the questioner douses him with seltzer. This turns into a free-for-all, with even the girls getting doused. Charley's landlord comes up to complain, and he is royally splattered. Finally, as the landlord kicks them all out, Charley gets

Charley is trying to sneak his fiancée (Thelma Todd) past his c.o. (Carlton Griffin) in *Rough Seas*—but it doesn't look as if it's going to work.

with a newly captured prisoner of war. In *Rough Seas* the war is over, and Charley tries to smuggle a French coquette (Thelma Todd) onto his homebound boat. He puts her into his duffel bag and carries her over his shoulder. After passing the C.O. at the gangplank, however, Thelma's leg breaks through the bag, making a most unusual sight for the soldiers on deck.

In 1931, Charley really hit his stride with a film called *The Pip from Pittsburgh.* Costarred with Thelma Todd, Carlton Griffin, and Dorothy Granger, Chase combined a clever story idea with basic slapstick and sight-gag elements in perfect harmony. The *Motion Picture Herald* wrote, "This is perhaps the funniest comedy Charley Chase has ever made. It starts in with real laughs, they are there all the way and in at the finish. James Parrott gets the credit for directing a corking good comedy."

Charley Chase and Thelma Todd in *The Pip from Pittsburgh.*

the three men to sign his contract, but a moment later, as the picture fades, the document is covered with seltzer.

This was the formula that the Roach people were seeking to find—a happy medium between the sight gag and the newly added soundtrack. After some false starts, the better directors (like James Horne, who did *Whoopee*) got the feel of it, and were able to maintain some continuity from picture to picture. It took others longer to catch on to the new talkie formula, and so Chase's 1930 comedies varied sharply in quality.

That same year saw an experiment that turned out to be a flop. Hal Roach, along with other short-subject producers, decided to try out a three- and four-reel short format, making the films more like featurettes, which would warrant greater attention from theatres around the country. Unfortunately, most of the three-reel Roach films that ensued showed a marked use of padding to make up for lack of material to carry the extra length.

One interesting duo, however, was provided by Charley Chase. *High C's,* a 1930 three-reeler, and *Rough Seas,* a 1931 three-reeler, were designed as companion pieces, the latter picking up where the former left off, and using the identical cast and setting. In a World War One background, Charley and his musical group, The Ranch Boys, go to war, but find it much more fun to sing than to fight—thus, the film is full of barbershop-type songs, including some German tunes that are performed

The story has Griffin fixing up the reluctant Chase with a blind date for a dance; having been stung once (with plump Kay Deslys), Charley decides to make himself as distasteful as possible by wearing Griffin's old suit, not shaving, and munching on garlic all afternoon. Griffin, in turn, borrows Charley's new suit to make a good impression on his girl, Dorothy. When Charley sees that his blind date is Thelma Todd, he does his best to undo everything, getting "mouthwash" from a perfume dispenser, shaving by using a man's shiny jacket for his mirror, and finally snatching his suit, piece by piece, from Griffin. All ends happily in this delightful little film.

1931 also brought one of Chase's strangest shorts, *The Panic Is On,* a spoof of the Depression. The highlight comes when Leo Willis holds up Charley in a deserted alley, saying, "Your money or your life." "Sorry pal," Charley apologizes, "but I'm hit by the Depression. I've got no money." "You think *you've* got it bad," replies Willis, opening his gun. "Look at this—no bullets!" Audiences at the time were not amused.

By 1932, the Charley Chase comedies started to be more consistent, with good products outweighing the bad. *The Tabasco Kid* has Charley in a dual role as a ranch hand and a notorious Mexican bandit. *In Walked Charley* is notable mainly for Dell Henderson's portrayal of a father who pretends to be insane in order to keep his family from going away on vacation. *Young Ironsides* was the best film of that year, with Charley hired to stop Muriel Evans from entering a beauty contest and disgracing her society family. It's a brisk, clever comedy with a hilarious cameo by Billy Gilbert as a pansy, and young, blonde Paulette Goddard as "Miss Hollywood." *Now We'll Tell One* features a new scientific discovery: a belt that can transmit the personality of the wearer to anyone wearing a copy of the same belt. Charley unwittingly wears the fixture and alternately becomes a motorcycle trick rider, a sheik, a drunk, a classical dancer, and a prizefighter, all in time to get him in and out of trouble with his girl (Muriel Evans) and her family.

1933's first release, *Fallen Arches,* ranks as one of Chase's all-time bests. In it, Charley, a clerk in Billy Gilbert's office, takes everything he is told literally. After several silly examples, Gilbert sends him out West with the parting remark, "Remember—get a good grip on yourself, keep a stiff upper lip, and never let your right hand know what your left hand is doing!" Charley proceeds to grab his jacket, tighten his upper lip, and keep one hand inside his jacket as the other opens the door. Told to "hike" out to the West Coast office, he does it, in the company of several dozen other hitchhikers. When he hits upon a scheme to limp as he hikes down the road, a crutch is thrown to him from a passing car. The

last half of the film reworks one of Chase's best silent gags, from *All Wet:* the car stuck in a water-filled ditch. It was even worth one more exposure, several years later, in his Columbia comedy *The Awful Goof.*

The good shorts continued, one after another: *Nature in the Wrong,* a Tarzan takeoff; *His Silent Racket,* with a classic scene of bankrupt James Finlayson persuading Charley to buy into his cleaning business by putting on a charade of a typical busy morning; *Midsummer Mush,* which casts Charley as a boy-scout leader; and *Luncheon at Twelve,* pure slapstick with Charley hired by Billy Gilbert as a house painter. (The material here was so good that Chase reused it for the Three Stooges several years later, in *Tassels in the Air.*)

1934's best entry was *The Chases of Pimple Street,* also one of his best films. In it Charley fights a never-ending battle with his obnoxious sister-in-law, and, in a fit of anger at her pampered dog, grabs it off screen and bites it. "Now *that's* news," he tells her. Another 1934 gem, *Four Parts,* has Charley playing four identical brothers, each of whom runs into Betty Mack at different times during the day, sending her into a state of utter confusion.

The best Chase films of 1935 were his last two releases, *Manhattan Monkey Business* and *Public Ghost No. 1,* both with Joyce Compton as leading lady. In the former, Charley dines at a swanky restaurant and finds he has accidentally tipped a doorman with his only twenty-dollar bill. (When he goes to retrieve it he is told that the doorman has left his job—"He said something about going to Europe.") Forced to work as a waiter in the French restaurant to pay his bill, he makes a mess of a Welsh rarebit and, with his hand full of the sticky goo, manages to lift off James Finlayson's toupee and accidentally tear off Joyce's dress. *Public Ghost No. 1* features Edwin Maxwell as an escaped lunatic with a host of strange inventions. He demonstrates to Charley his fly exterminator, a complicated device wherein the fly, after going through an incredible series of tortures, ends up on a soft pillow and "crawls away to die of embarrassment." The climax takes place in a mansion owned by Joyce and her father (Clarence Wilson) and which Charley has been hired to "haunt."

While these shorts certainly stand out as first-rate comedies, it is important to note that by this time, Charley's personality, and the expertise of the Roach gagmen, directors, and repertory company, made even the minor endeavors a pleasure to watch. Chase's personality could carry weak material and make it look good, and when compared to some of the most ambitious efforts of other comedy studios, diverting shorts like Chase's *You Said a Hatful* and *Nurse to You* are practically masterpieces.

All he did was give the car a push; now Muriel Evans and James C. Morton are sinking fast in *Fallen Arches*. Note the use of the same setting from Laurel and Hardy's *The Hoose Gow*.

Charley's last year at Hal Roach was highlighted by a scene in *On the Wrong Trek*. With his wife and mother-in-law, he is traveling cross-country by auto. Mother suggests that they pick up some of the hitchhikers along the way; Charley refuses, saying he doesn't want that type of person in his car. "Oh, Charley," she answers, "there are two men over there who don't look so bad." And there, hitchhiking in opposite directions on the side of the road, are Stan Laurel and Oliver Hardy. Charley is more adamant than ever, muttering, "They look like a couple of horse thieves to me!"

The Charley Chase comedies were always well re-ceived by the press and public, and though, as Stan Laurel once pointed out, Chase never aimed for higher things, he was a king of his domain—the two-reel comedy. The problem was that Hal Roach *was* setting his sights higher, hoping to ease out of short-subject production and concentrate on feature films. So Roach put Chase, along with his other stars, into a feature comedy to see what the results would be. The fifty-five-minute film, *Neighborhood House,* was shown to the trade press, but was apparently so weak that Roach decided to withdraw it, edit it down, and release it as a standard two-reel comedy. The result was a fair, if somewhat abrupt, spoof of moviegoing in the 1930s. It spelled the end of Chase's association with Hal Roach.

Why Roach was unable to find a berth for Charley Chase in his plans for the future is something of a puzzlement, considering Chase's acknowledged popularity and the fact that he had contributed noteworthy supporting performances in Laurel and Hardy's feature *Sons of the Desert* (1933) and in *Kelly the Second* (1936), Roach's feature-film test for Patsy Kelly. For whatever reasons, Chase was dropped from the Roach roster after fifteen years, and he sought refuge, as did so many others, at Columbia.

Chase joined Columbia as writer, producer, director, and comedian. He was able to work on his own films as well as on those starring Andy Clyde, the Three Stooges, and other comics; he was working with people like himself, who knew nothing but comedy, and he was able to borrow freely from his own sizable backlog of experience.

The Columbia Chase comedies are generally good, but they lack the distinctive charm of the Hal Roach series. The supporting players are sorely missed, as are the background music and Charley's own inevitable songs. The Columbias rely more on action and slapstick, with varying degrees of success. Some are quite good by any standards. In *Calling All Doctors,* Charley is an incurable hypochondriac who is taught a lesson by his wife, his doctor, and his best pal, who pretend that he has just a few hours to live. *The Big Squirt* is also a lot of fun. Charley plays a soda jerk with a passion for detective magazines. One memorable sequence has him fixing an ice-cream soda without once watching what he's doing. He cavalierly throws scoops of ice cream into the air, tosses cherries on top of the soda, and ruins his perfect record by sliding it down the counter onto a pretty customer's lap.

Chase was drinking quite heavily at this time, and age was beginning to take its toll. He began to dye his hair for every screen appearance. Even so, he remained a perfectionist, and producer Jules White recalls him as being a one-take actor. Moe Howard, of the Three Stooges, says, "Charley Chase was not only one of the best actors in the field of household or family comedies but was even a more competent director—soft-spoken, gracious, and very knowledgeable. His own statement to me personally was that he had never worked with comedians who were so cooperative and with such wonderful timing. He played a guitar and sang very well, and we would all harmonize together real barbershop harmony, with Vernon Dent, who sang a beautiful tenor, and sometimes with Buddy Jamison, both of whom worked with Chaplin. They are all gone; what a sextet they must be having somewhere on high!"

Chase also directed Smith and Dale in two shorts. Joe Smith recently recalled, "We were out on location, and I remember having a box lunch with him. He told me that the week before he had been shooting a film down at a department store, and they had hired a lot of extras

Charley and friend (as the usual caption goes) in *Nature in the Wrong.*

to be in a scene looking in the window. This one guy kept bothering him, asking him what he should be saying . . . he couldn't just be looking in the window, he wanted something to say. So, to get him out of his hair, Chase gave him something to say. Then, the next day, when it came time to pay the extras, instead of getting $8 a day, this guy had to get $22 because he had said a line in the film! Well, in this short [*A Nag in the Bag*], Charlie [Dale] and I are playing owners of a drive-in restaurant, and there's a guy who plays the chef—you know, in a cubbyhole where we would tell him the order. And he says to me, 'Wouldn't it be cute if when you yelled in the order I answered "Coming right up"?' I said yes, it would be cute. Of course, you'd never work for Charley Chase again . . .''

Chase took some of his old comedies and revamped them for himself, and others, at Columbia. *His Wooden*

Wedding, one of his best silents, was reworked for Andy Clyde as *Ankles Away,* but somehow what was charming and funny in the original was tasteless and most unfunny in this remake. On the other hand, the 1930 *Fast Work* was redone, starring Charley himself, as *Many Sappy Returns,* and the remake actually improved on the original, with John T. Murray as an escaped lunatic whom Charley believes to be the father of his girl friend (Ann Doran). One scene in which Charley and Murray discuss gourmet food while stuffing their mouths full of crackers is quite funny.

At Columbia, Charley was working most often with Del Lord, one of the all-time great comedy directors. Together, near the end of Chase's stay at Columbia, they made two classic comedies. The first, in 1939, was *Rattling Romeo.* No talkie Chase comedy, either at Roach or at Columbia, ever came closer to the feel and atmosphere of silent comedy than did this. The plot has Charley winning a contest prize of $250 and fulfilling his girl friend's (Ann Doran) wish that he buy a car. Meanwhile, at the used-car lot, the dealer has just repainted a junk heap he bought for $10, and plans to sell it for $150. He decides to change it to $250 (painting the price on the windshield), and is about to alter the two into a four when Charley comes by and purchases the auto with his $250 prize money. The next morning, he drives his girl friend to work and, as he does, the car starts to fall apart, piece by piece, until there is practically nothing left. He ends up back on the streetcar, with a bundle of accessories on his back, breaking windows and poking people right and left until a lucky move knocks out a criminal on the lam and all is forgotten. This simplified synopsis cannot capture the film's charm, but *Rattling Romeo* is a light, wholly entertaining little gem.

The other film that hit the bull's-eye was *The Heckler,* one of Charley's all-time funniest, and a complete departure from the normal Chase formula. Charley plays an obnoxious loudmouth who attends all the baseball games and throws the local team off balance with his constant heckling. Two con men spot him and try to use him to guarantee some bets, with disastrous results. Several scenes in the bleachers are incredibly funny, with Charley managing to pester everyone within a three-row radius of his seat. At one point he yells for a hot dog, has everyone in the row pass it down, and then pass it back for mustard. "Not too much," he instructs, adding, "of course, not too little either . . . you know, just right . . ." Then, grabbing the hot dog on its way down the row he spills some of the mustard on a woman's dress. "That's all right," he explains amiably. "There was too much on it anyway."

Charley's leading lady at Columbia, Ann Doran, says of him, "I have a special place in my heart for Charley Chase. He was a warm, helpful, easygoing, intense, gifted man who approached his job with a rare dedication." She recalls shooting the next-to-last film Chase ever made, *South of the Boudoir:*

The weather was miserable, and we couldn't do any outside filming, so it was decided we would find situations around an ordinary house to construct a picture. Part of the action was in the kitchen. Charley had ground his tie along with the meat in a hand-turned grinder. We had bickered a bit. We had a stack of breakaway plates left over from a previous picture. They were being used as dressing in the cupboards. In frustration, because none of us could think of a funny situation, Charley threw down one of the dishes. That was it! We bickered over the amount of dishes he used in preparing anything, which I claimed I always had to wash. To punctuate a point, we started throwing dishes to the floor. Del just let the camera run while Charley and I argued. When the camera ran out of film, we had made a shambles of the kitchen, every dish was broken, everything was stripped from the shelves, and we were glaring at each other in utter frustration. It was one of the funniest sequences we ever shot.

Unfortunately, it was also one of the last films Charley ever made. Billy Gilbert, perhaps his closest friend, has explained, "Charley was a loner. He was polite and kind

With girl friend Ann Doran in his newly acquired car, Charley is a *Rattling Romeo.*

Charley in one of his funniest roles, *The Heckler,* with Monty Collins and Vernon Dent on either side of him, Richard Fiske over Dent's left shoulder.

to people but he let very few of them get close to him. I was one of the few. We both belonged to a club called The Masquers. It was for men alone. I was a bachelor and it was my hangout; it was his too but he was no bachelor. He had been married for years. He and his wife had some understanding—he was too much of a gentleman to discuss it but there was something wrong there. Toward the end of his life his doctor told him he had to stop drinking or he would die. He stopped for a few months, then started drinking harder than ever. He told me that if he couldn't drink he didn't want to live.''

On June 20, 1940, he suffered a heart attack and died in Hollywood.

''He was a sweet, sad man who felt among other things that his talent was not fully appreciated. He wasn't bitter about it, he just wondered why people didn't rank him with Laurel and Hardy, Keaton, Chaplin, and Lloyd. He knew his style of comedy was more sophisticated than theirs, but he felt that there was an audience for him, too. I think he was ahead of his time . . .'' concludes Billy Gilbert.

Time has proven that Charley Chase *does* rank alongside the great men of screen comedy. His comedies, some over forty years old, are fresh, funny, and wondrously inventive today. It is a pity that more people didn't realize it when he was still alive.

Charley Chase's Talkie Shorts

This list includes all Chase's starring short subjects from the sound era; it does not include his other appearances, in feature films and such shorts as MGM's *Hollywood Party,* nor does it include the short subjects he wrote, produced, and directed, both at Roach and Columbia studios. All films are two reels in length unless otherwise noted.

1. *The Big Squawk.* Roach-MGM (5/25/29), Warren Doane. Nena Quartaro, Gale Henry. Bashful Charley tries to win his girl.

2. *Leaping Love.* Roach-MGM (6/22/29), Warren Doane. Isabelle Keith, Dixie Gay, Barbara Leonard, Maurice Black. Charley falls in love with both mother and daughter.

3. *Snappy Sneezer.* Roach-MGM (7/29/29), Warren Doane. Thelma Todd, Anders Randolf. Charley's hay fever makes him a public nuisance. Originally titled *Hay Fever.*

4. *Crazy Feet.* Roach-MGM (9/7/29), Warren Doane. Thelma Todd, Anita Garvin. Charley plays a dancer.

5. *Stepping Out.* Roach-MGM (11/2/29), Warren Doane. Thelma Todd, Anita Garvin. Charlie goes out for an evening without the wife.

6. *Great Gobs.* Roach-MGM (12/28/29), Warren Doane. Edgar Kennedy, Linda Loredo, Mildred Costello, William Guiler. Songs: ''La Borrachita,'' ''In a Little Spanish Town,'' ''Home Sweet Home,'' ''La Violetera.''

Ann Doran and Charley improvise a scene in *South of the Boudoir.*

7. *The Real McCoy*. MGM-Roach (2/1/30), Warren Doane. Thelma Todd, Edgar Kennedy, Charlie Hall, Nelson McDowell. Charley poses as a hillbilly, to woo country-girl Thelma. He sings a hillbilly song about a girl who drowns.

8. *Whispering Whoopee*. MGM-Roach (3/8/30), James W. Horne. Thelma Todd, Anita Garvin, Dolores Brinkman, Kay Deslys, Eddie Dunn, Dell Henderson, Carl Stockdale, Tenen Holtz, Eddie Dillon. Charley hires three good-time girls to help him put over a business deal. Songs: "Smile When the Raindrops Fall," "The Rockaway Booster Song."

9. *All Teed Up*. MGM-Roach (4/19/30), Edgar Kennedy. Thelma Todd, Tenen Holtz, Dell Henderson, Carl Stockdale, Nelson McDowell, Edgar Kennedy, Harry Bowen. Thelma invites Charley to play golf at her father's country club. Song: "Golfer's Blues."

10. *Fifty Million Husbands*. MGM-Roach (5/24/30), Edgar Kennedy and James W. Horne. Ruth Hiatt, Christine Maple, Tiny Sandford, Edgar Kennedy, Charlie Hall, Eddie Dillon. An estranged couple comes to see their old apartment, now Charley's, and the wife misunderstands.

11. *Fast Work*. MGM-Roach (6/28/30), James W. Horne. June Marlowe, Dell Henderson, Charles K. French, Broderick O'Farrell, Pat Harmon, Gus Kerner, William Gillespie, Bill Elliott (dance extra). Charley mistakes an escaped lunatic for the father of a girl he's interested in. Originally titled *The Fast Worker*. Remade as *Many Sappy Returns*.

12. *Girl Shock*. MGM-Roach (8/23/30), James W. Horne. Carmen Guerrero, Edgar Kennedy, Jerry Mandy, Elinor Vandivere, Caesar Varoni, Catherine Courtney. Charley is terribly bashful with girls, and goes into hysterics if he is touched by one—including his fiancée.

13. *Dollar Dizzy*. MGM-Roach (10/4/30), James W. Horne. Thelma Todd, Edgar Kennedy, James Finlayson, Dorothy Granger, Charlie Hall, Dick Granger, Ted Strobach, Dorothy Dix, Ida Schumacher, Ann Lewis, Lorema Carr. Thelma and Charley are millionaires, each trying to elude possible fortune hunters. Three reels.

14. *Looser Than Loose*. MGM-Roach (11/15/30), James W. Horne. Thelma Todd, Dorothy Granger, Dell Henderson, Wilfred Lucas, Edgar Kennedy, Eddie Dunn, Wilfred Lucas, Gordon Douglas (extra). Charley's boss orders him to entertain an out-of-town client on the eve of Charley's engagement to Thelma.

15. *High C's*. MGM-Roach (12/27/30), James W. Horne. Thelma Todd, Carlton Griffin, Oscar Smith, Harry Schultz, Lucien Prival, The Ranch Boys including Jimmy Adams. World War One is fine with Charley as long as he can sing barbershop ballads with his pals. Songs: "My Pretty Quadroon," "Down by the Old Mill Stream," "Where, Oh, Where Has My Little Dog Gone?" (in German), "Du, Du, Liegst Mir im Herzen," "Eleven More Months and Ten More Days." Three reels.

16. *Thundering Tenors*. MGM-Roach (2/7/31), James W. Horne. Lillian Elliott, Elizabeth Forrester, Dorothy Granger, Lena Malena, Eddie Dillon, Dell Henderson, Sidney Bracy. Radio singer Charley, "America's Boyfriend," makes a mess out of a fancy dinner party.

17. *The Pip from Pittsburgh*. MGM-Roach (3/21/31), James Parrott. Thelma Todd, Dorothy Granger, Kay Deslys, Carlton Griffin, Charlie Hall, Harry Bernard, Baldwin Cooke, Frank Holliday. Charley, forced to go on a blind date, makes himself as disagreeable as possible. A Spanish-language version of this film, called *La Senorita De Chicago*, featured Manuel Granado (Paul Ellis), Linda Loredo, Mona Rico, Charles Dorety, and Carmen (Carmita) Tarrazo.

18. *Rough Seas*. MGM-Roach (4/25/31), James Parrott. Thelma Todd, Carlton Griffin, Frank Brownlee, Harry Bernard, Charlie Hall, Jerry Mandy, The Ranch Boys including Jimmy Adams. A sequel to *High C's;* with the war in France over, Charley wants to take his French girl friend home with him. Songs: "When Johnny Comes Marching Home," "You're My Love Unspoken," "Asleep in the Deep," "You're My Ideal." Three reels. A Spanish-language version of this film, called *Monerias,* featured Angelica Benitez, Enrique Acosta, and Manuel Granado (Paul Ellis).

19. *One of the Smiths*. Roach-MGM (5/23/31), James Parrott. James Finlayson, Louise Carver, Leo Willis, Harry Bowen, Eddie Baker, Harry Bernard. Charley is sent out to hillbilly country to investigate why the people there keep ordering musical instruments through the mail and never pay for them. Three reels. Song: "Handsome Jim."

20. *The Panic Is On*. MGM-Roach (8/15/31), James Parrott. Virginia Whiting, Billy Gilbert, Margaret Mann, Charlie Hall, Leo Willis, Harry Bernard. Charley, hit by the depression, accepts a job offer, not knowing he's involved with a blackmail ring.

21. *Skip the Maloo!* MGM-Roach (9/26/31), James Parrott. Jacqueline Wells (Julie Bishop), Gale Henry, Dell Henderson, Eddie Dunn, Leo Willis, Fern Emmett, Harry Bernard, Jerry Mandy. Charley is a duke who is hired by the unsuspecting father of his fiancée to impersonate himself. A remake of the 1927 Chase comedy *One-Mama Man*.

22. *What a Bozo!* MGM-Roach (11/7/31), James Parrott. Gay Seabrook, Elizabeth Forrester, Charlie Hall, Harry Bowen, Bill Elliott, Sidney Bracy. Bandleader Charley has been neglecting his girl friend for the aristocratic Mrs. Van Forrester. Song: "Smile When the Raindrops Fall."

23. *The Hasty Marriage*. MGM-Roach (12/19/31), Gil Pratt. Lillian Elliott, James Finlayson, Gay Seabrook, Eddie Dunn, Lyle Tayo, Harry Bernard, Harry Bowen, Georgie Billing, Billy Gilbert. Charley can't work for the trolley company unless he's married.

24. *The Tabasco Kid*. MGM-Roach (1/30/32), James W. Horne. Frances Lee, Billy Gilbert, Wilfred Lucas, Julian Rivero, Leo Willis, Marvin Hatley, Frank Gage, The Ranch Boys featuring Jimmy Adams. Charley is a dead ringer for a notorious Mexican bandit. Songs: "In the Good Old Summertime," "Welcome, Mary Jones," "Marquita."

25. *The Nickel Nurser*. MGM-Roach (3/12/32), Warren

Doane. Thelma Todd, Billy Gilbert, Harry Bowen, Belle Hare, Eddie Dillon. Efficiency expert Charley is called in to teach a millionaire's daughters the value of money.

26. *In Walked Charley.* MGM-Roach (4/23/32), Warren Doane. Jacqueline Wells, Gertrude Astor, Dell Henderson, Billy Gilbert, Eddie Dunn, Harry Bernard. Charley, a travel agent, is unwittingly pulled into a situation where he has to humor an apparent lunatic. Song: "Aren't You the Girl I Met the Other Night?"

27. *First in War.* MGM-Roach (5/28/32), Warren Doane. Luis Alberni, Carlton Griffin, Nancy Torres, Billy Gilbert, Eddie Parker. Charley writes a national anthem for the country of

Charley draws disapproving looks from James Finlayson and Eddie Dunn when he tries to get a ride the hard way in *The Hasty Marriage.*

Nicarania and accidentally gets involved with a revolution there. Songs: "Fight On, Pennsylvania," "Fight On, Nicarania."

28. *Young Ironsides.* MGM-Roach (9/3/32), James Parrott. Muriel Evans, Clarence H. Wilson, Heinie Conklin, Billy Gilbert, Charlie Hall, Harry Bernard, Eddie Dillon, Paulette Goddard, Baldwin Cooke, May Wallace. Charley is hired to stop Muriel from entering a beauty contest and thereby disgracing her aristocratic family.

29. *Girl Grief.* MGM-Roach (10/8/32), James Parrott. Muriel Evans, Nora Cecil, Fanny Cossar, Ida Schumacher. Although afraid of girls, Charley is forced to take a job teaching in a girls' school. Song: "I Was Seeing Nellie Home."

30. *Now We'll Tell One.* MGM-Roach (11/19/32), James Parrott. Muriel Evans, Lillian Elliott, Frank Darien, Gale Henry, Eddie Baker, Major Sam Harris. Charley unwittingly wears a belt that has the power to change his personality. Gale Henry sings "I Loved You As I Never Loved Before."

31. *Mr. Bride.* MGM-Roach (12/24/32), James Parrott. Muriel Evans, Dell Henderson, Charlie Hall, Gale Henry, Harry Bernard. Charley's boss stages a "rehearsal honeymoon," with Charley as guinea pig.

32. *Fallen Arches.* MGM-Roach (2/4/33), Gus Meins. Muriel Evans, Billy Gilbert, Eddie Dunn, Charlie Hall, James C. Morton, Harry Bernard, Pat Harmon. Told to "hike" out to his firm's West Coast office, Charley does so—literally.

Charley and Joyce Compton are sidewalk acquaintances in *Public Ghost No. 1.*

33. *Nature in the Wrong.* MGM-Roach (3/18/33), no director credited. Muriel Evans, Carlton Griffin, Nora Cecil, Mary Gordon. Charley discovers he is a direct descendant of Tarzan of the Apes. Original title: *Tarzan in the Wrong.*

34. *His Silent Racket.* MGM-Roach (4/29/33), no director credited. Muriel Evans, James Finlayson, Anita Garvin, Harry Bernard, Leo Willis, Charlie Hall, James C. Morton, Harry Schultz, Jack Raymond, Eddie Baker. Charley buys what he thinks is a thriving cleaning business.

35. *Arabian Tights.* MGM-Roach (6/3/33), no director credited. Muriel Evans, Carlton Griffin, Rolfe Sedan, Eddie Baker, Harry Schultz, Jerry Bergen, Russ Powell, The Ranch

Boys with Jimmy Adams. A sultan holds Charley and his pals prisoners in the desert. Songs: "Mademoiselle from Armentieres," "I'll Forget You."

36. *Sherman Said It.* MGM-Roach (9/2/33), Charles Parrott. Nita Pike, Luis Alberni, The Ranch Boys (Jimmy Adams, Marvin Hatley, Frank Gage), Harry Bernard, Eddie Dunn. World War One is over, but Charley can't seem to get out of France. Songs: "Sidewalk Sam, the Sweeping Man," "Mine, All Mine."

37. *Midsummer Mush.* MGM-Roach (10/21/33), Charles Parrott. Betty Mack, The Ranch Boys (Jimmy Adams, Marvin Hatley, Frank Gage), Eddie Baker. Boy Scout leader Charley falls in love with Betty on a camping trip. Song: "I'm Sorry."

38. *Luncheon at Twelve.* MGM-Roach (12/9/33), Charles Parrott. Betty Mack, Gale Henry, Billy Gilbert, James Barty, Rolfe Sedan, Harry Bernard, Major Sam Harris, Charlie Hall, Billy Franey. Charley unwittingly becomes a house painter. Song: "Oh, Desdemona."

39. *The Cracked Iceman.* MGM-Roach (1/27/34), Charles Parrott and Eddie Dunn. Betty Mack, Billy Gilbert, Harry Bowen, Florence Roberts, Harry Bernard, Spanky McFarland, Tommy Bond, Stymie Beard. Charley faces sundry problems on his first day of work as a kindergarten teacher. Song: "One Times One Is Only One but One and One Are Two."

40. *Four Parts.* MGM-Roach (3/17/34), Charles Parrott and Eddie Dunn. Betty Mack, Florence Roberts, Stymie Beard. Charley is one of four identical brothers—which drives Betty crazy. Songs: "Auntie's Got Ants in Her Pantry," "When the Band Around My Hat Plays Home Sweet Home." Charley plays nine parts in all in this film.

41. *I'll Take Vanilla.* MGM-Roach (5/5/34), Charles Parrott and Eddie Dunn. Betty Mack, Tommy Bond, Harry Bowen, Gertrude Astor, James C. Morton, Tiny Sandford, Charlie Hall. Ice-cream man Charley gets involved with customer Betty and her bratty nephew. Song: "The Ice-Cream Song."

42. *Another Wild Idea.* MGM-Roach (6/16/34), Charles Parrott and Eddie Dunn. Betty Mack, Frank Austin, Tiny Sandford, Harry Bowen, Harry Bernard, Carlton Griffin, Charlie Lloyd, Harry Dunkinson, James C. Morton, Kay McCoy, George Nardelli, Baldy Cooke, Pat Harmond, Arthur King Singers; Billy Gilbert's voice is heard on a radio broadcast. Betty's father uses Charley to test out a new ray-gun which releases its subjects inhibitions. Songs: "Henry, the King," "I Love You."

43. *It Happened One Day.* MGM-Roach (7/7/34), Charles Parrott and Eddie Dunn. Betty Mack, Oscar Apfel, Charlie Hall, James C. Morton, Harry Bowen, Eddie Baker, Stanley Price. Charley keeps annoying a man on his way to work—only to discover that the man is his new boss. Song: "This Salesman So Gay."

44. *Something Simple.* MGM-Roach (9/8/34), Charles Parrott and Walter Weems. Betty Mack, Dell Henderson, Arthur Housman, Lew Kelly, Harry Bowen, James C. Morton, Charlie Hall, Harry Bernard, Snowflake, Charles Sullivan, Jack Cheatham, Eddie Baker. Charley is mistaken for an escaped lunatic.

45. *You Said a Hateful!* MGM-Roach (10/13/34), Charles Parrott. Dorothy Appleby, Oscar Apfel, Clarence H. Wilson, Harry Bowen, Harry Bernard, Tiny Sandford, Benny Baker, Tommy Bond, James C. Morton, Lester Dorr, Bobby Burns. For business reasons, Charley and his boss exchange identities during a trip out of town.

46. *Fate's Fathead.* MGM-Roach (11/17/34), Charles Parrott. Dorothy Appleby, Dorothy Granger, Dick Alexander, Margaret Nearing, Baby Tonia Brady, Hattie McDaniel. An old friend of Charley's wife accuses Charley of having flirted with her in the park. Song: "How About Another Cup of Coffee?"

47. *The Chases of Pimple Street.* MGM-Roach (12/22/34), Charles Parrott. Betty Mack, Ruthelma Stevens, Gertrude Astor, Wilfred Lucas, Arthur Housman, Hattie McDaniel, Harry Bernard, May Wallace, Eddie Baker, Kay Hughes, Margaret Nearing, Harry Bowen, James C. Morton, Eddie Borden, Jack Hill (Charley's double), Charlie Hall, John Binns. (Stanley Blystone and Bess Flowers were cut from the final print of this film.) Charley is fed up with his good-for-nothing sister-in-law. Song: "You've Got to Give Credit to Love."

48. *Okay Toots!* MGM-Roach (2/2/35), Charles Parrott and William Terhune. Jeanie Roberts, Constance Bergen, Ferdinand Munier, Harry Bernard, Polly Chase, Hattie McDaniel, Elinor Vandivere, Stanley Price, Harry Bernard, Gertrude Astor, Charlie Hall, Grace Goodall, Emma Tansey, Ben Taggart, Allan Cavan, Scott Mattraw, May Wallace. Charley and his wife mysteriously exchange personalities—her voice and mind in his body, and vice versa. Song: "I've Found My Place in the Sun."

49. *Poker at Eight.* MGM-Roach (3/9/35), Charles Parrott. Constance Bergen, Bernardene Hayes, Tom Dugan, Ben Taggart, Harry Bowen, Harry Bernard, Jack Raymond, Lester Dorr, James C. Morton, Charlie Hall. Charley thinks he has hypnotic powers. Song: "I'm in the Doghouse."

50. *Southern Exposure.* MGM-Roach (4/6/35), Charles Parrott. Constance Bergen, Bob Burns, Louise Carver, Fern Emmett, Ben Taggart, Noah Young, Jessie Arnold, Max Davidson, Carl (Alfalfa) Switzer, Jay Eaton, Louis Natheaux, Carlton Griffin, Leo Willis, Lee Phelps, Lester Dorr, Charlie Hall, Harry Bernard. Charley discovers he's an official Kentucky colonel, and goes home to visit. Charley plays himself and "Pappy." Song: "The Sun-Sun-Sunny South."

51. *The Four-Star Boarder.* MGM-Roach (4/27/35), Charles Parrott. Constance Bergen, T. Roy Barnes, Grace Goodall, Charles Lloyd, Jessie Arnold, Louis Natheaux (voice only), Wesley Girard, Hattie McDaniel, Matty Roubert, Polly Chase, Jay Belasco, Colin Kenny, Harry Wilde, Lester Dorr (Harry Bowen was cut from the final print). Connie's aunt wants to give her niece half of her fortune—but she thinks Connie married her old boyfriend.

52. *Nurse to You.* MGM-Roach (10/5/35), Charles Parrott and Jefferson Moffitt. Muriel Evans, Clarence H. Wilson, Frank Darien, Billy Gilbert, Fred Kelsey, Harry Bowen, Carlton Griffin. Charley thinks he has six months to live.

Charley is flustered by the attentions of Anita Garvin in *His Silent Racket.*

53. *Manhattan Monkey Business.* MGM-Roach (11/9/35), Charles Parrott and Harold Law. Joyce Compton, James Finlayson, Milton Owen, Gertrude Astor, Ben Taggart, Harry Bernard, Ivan Linow, Elinor Vandivere. Charley becomes a French waiter when he is unable to pay his bill at a restaurant. Song: "When I Grow Too Old to Dream."

54. *Public Ghost No. 1.* MGM-Roach (12/14/35), Charles Parrott and Harold Law. Joyce Compton, Edwin Maxwell, Clarence H. Wilson, Ray Turner, Ben Taggart, Harry Bowen. Charley is hired to haunt a house.

55. *Life Hesitates at 40.* MGM-Roach (1/18/36), Charles Parrott and Harold Law. Joyce Compton, James Finlayson, Brooks Benedict, Antoinette Lees (Andrea Leeds), Edward Earle, Lee Phelps, Harry Bowen, Carl "Alfalfa" Switzer, Harry Bernard, Gus Leonard, Sam Lufkin. Charley has strange spells during which everything around him seems to stop.

56. *The Count Takes the Count.* MGM-Roach (2/22/36), Charles Parrott and Harold Law. Antoinette Lees, Kewpie Morgan, Harry Bowen, Ben Taggart, Dorothy Granger, Harry Hol-

man, Edgar Dearing, Alan Bride. Charley, an insurance salesman, has to make sure that a young heiress goes through with her marriage to a count.

57. *Vamp till Ready.* MGM-Roach (3/28/36), Charles Parrott and Harold Law. Wilma Cox, Zeffie Tilbury, Brooks Benedict, Mary McLaren, Harry Bowen, Vesey O'Davoren. Charley's straight-laced wife pretends to be a good-time girl. Remade by Leon Errol as *Let's Go Stepping.*

58. *On the Wrong Trek.* MGM-Roach (4/18/36), Charles Parrott and Harold Law. Rosina Lawrence, Bonita Weber, Clarence H. Wilson, Bud Jamison, Leo Willis, Bob Kortman, Harry Wilson, Harry Bernard, Frances Morris, Pat West, Charlie Sullivan, Lester Dorr, Harry Bowen, Eddie Parker, Charles McAvoy. Special guest appearance by Laurel and Hardy. Charley's auto-trip vacation is just one mishap after another. Song: "Let's Make It a Big Day."

59. *Neighborhood House.* MGM-Roach (5/9/36), Charles Parrott and Harold Law. Rosina Lawrence, Darla Hood, George Meeker, Ben Taggart, Dick Elliott, Harry Bowen, Bill Madsen, Charlie Hall, Barney Carr, Frances Morris, Harry Bernard, Lester Dorr, Bobby Dunn, David Sharpe. The audience suspects something fishy when Charley wins at "bank night" at the local movie house. Originally a fifty-eight-minute feature, edited down to standard two-reeler for release.

60. *The Grand Hooter.* Columbia (5/7/37), Del Lord. Peggy Stratford, Nena Quartaro, Harry Semels, Bud Jamison. Charley's wife thinks he's more devoted to the Lodge of Hoot Owls than he is to her. Song: "Cielito Lindo." Remade with Shemp Howard as *Open Season for Saps.*

Florence Roberts consoles Charley as his brothers look on in *Four Parts.*

61. *From Bad to Worse*. Columbia (6/4/37), Del Lord. Peggy Stratford. Charley's honeymoon, on a train, is complicated by another woman and her jealous husband.

62. *The Wrong Miss Wright*. Columbia (6/18/37), Charles Lamont. Peggy Stratford, John T. Murray, Bud Jamison, Robert, Eva, and Ella McKenzie. Charley tries to break off an arranged marriage so he can wed another girl, not knowing they are one and the same. A remake of the Chase silent, *Crazy Like a Fox*, remade with Vera Vague as *You Dear Boy*.

63. *Calling All Doctors*. Columbia (7/22/37), Charles Lamont. Lucille Lund, John T. Murray, Bobby Watson, Fern Emmett, James C. Morton, Vernon Dent, Lon Poff, William Irving, Lynton Brent. Charley is a hopeless hypochondriac. Remade with Vera Vague as *Doctor, Feel My Pulse*.

64. *The Big Squirt*. Columbia (9/17/37), Del Lord. Lucille Lund, Leora Thatcher, Eddie Fetherstone, Bud Jamison, Theodore Lorch, Carol Tevis. Soda-jerk Charley is a mystery buff who gets entangled in a real-life manhunt. Song: "I'm a Daring Drugstore Desperado." Remade with Bert Wheeler as *The Awful Sleuth*.

65. *Man Bites Lovebug*. Columbia (12/24/37), Del Lord. Mary Russell, John T. Murray, Frank Lackteen, Etta McDaniel, Bud Jamison. Marriage expert Charley is asked to fix up a friend's marriage by letting him pretend to be jealous. Remade with Billy Gilbert as *Wedded Bliss*.

66. *Time Out for Trouble*. Columbia (3/18/38), Del Lord. Louise Stanley, Ann Doran, Dick Curtis, Bess Flowers, Eddie Fetherstone, Vernon Dent, Bud Jamison. When his girl friend jilts him, Charley tries to have himself killed.

67. *The Mind Needer*. Columbia (4/29/38), Del Lord. Ann Doran, Bess Flowers, Vernon Dent, John T. Murray. Charley, hopelessly absentminded, tries to remember his wedding anniversary.

68. *Many Sappy Returns*. Columbia (8/19/38), Del Lord. Ann Doran, John T. Murray, Fred Kelsey, John Sheehan, Vernon Dent, Lane Chandler, Kernan Cripps. Charley mistakes a lunatic for the father of a girl he's interested in. Screenplay by Chase, a remake of *Fast Work*.

69. *The Nightshirt Bandit*. Columbia (10/28/38), Jules White. Phyllis Barry, Eva McKenzie, James C. Morton, Snowflake. Professor Chase goes snooping for a notorious nightshirt bandit on the college campus. Remade by Andy Clyde as *Go Chase Yourself*.

70. *Pie a la Maid*. Columbia (12/25/38), Del Lord. Ann Doran, John Tyrrell, Lionel Belmore, Gaylord Pendleton. A waitress mistakes Charley for a fresh underworld character. Screenplay by Chase.

71. *The Sap Takes a Wrap*. Columbia (3/10/39), Del Lord. Gloria Blondell, Ethel Clayton, The Astor Trio, George Cleveland, Gene Morgan, Harry Wilson, Bud Jamison, James Millican, John T. Murray. Charley is forced to give his girl friend a mink coat which he is supposedly protecting. Screenplay by Chase.

72. *The Chump Takes a Bump*. Columbia (5/5/39), Del Lord.

Bess Flowers, Hollywood's number-one "dress extra," got her best roles in short subjects. Here she is with Charley in *Time Out for Trouble*.

Charley and his boss go to a nightclub where Charley meets his newly blonde wife and doesn't recognize her. Remade with Hugh Herbert as *Who's Hugh?*

73. *Rattling Romeo*. Columbia (7/14/39), Del Lord. Ann Doran, John Tyrrell, Harry Bernard, Bud Jamison, Ben Taggart, Richard Fiske, Stanley Brown, Cy Schindell. Charley buys a car that proceeds to fall apart, piece by piece.

74. *Skinny the Moocher*. Columbia (9/8/39), Del Lord. Ann Doran, John T. Murray, Richard Fiske, Ben Taggart, Stanley Brown, John Tyrrell, James Craig, Cy Schindell. Charley's valet is determined to thwart his boss's romantic endeavors.

75. *Teacher's Pest*. Columbia (11/3/39), Del Lord. Richard Fiske, Ruth Skinner, Chester Conklin, Bud Jamison, Hank Bell, Bill Wolfe, Vernon Dent. Charley takes a job as schoolteacher in a rowdy western town.

76. *The Awful Goof*. Columbia (12/22/39), Del Lord. Linda Winters, Lucille Lund, Dick Curtis, Bud Jamison. Charley can't seem to help running into the wife of a brawny wrestler.

77. *The Heckler*. Columbia (2/16/40), Del Lord. Bruce Bennett, Richard Fiske, Stanley Brown, Don Beddoe, Robert Sterling, Bud Jamison, Beatrice Blinn, Linda Winters, Vernon Dent, Monty Collins, Bess Flowers, Heinie Conklin, John Ince, voice of Jack Mulhall. Charley is an avid sports fan and an unbearable loudmouth. Remade with Shemp Howard as *Mr. Noisy*.

78. *South of the Boudoir*. Columbia (5/17/40), Del Lord. Helen Lynd, Ann Doran, Arthur Q. Bryan. Charley hires a waitress to pose as his wife when he brings his boss home for dinner.

79. *His Bridal Fright.* Columbia (7/12/40), Del Lord. Iris Meredith, Bruce Bennett, Richard Fiske, Stanley Brown, Vernon Dent, Bud Jamison. Charley writes to girls around the world for postage stamps—but gets a carload of fiancées instead.

Harry Langdon

The story of Harry Langdon's movie career is the story of a talent that needed guidance; often it wasn't there, and many times when it was, the stubborn Langdon refused to take it.

When Langdon, a seasoned vaudevillian, came to Mack Sennett in 1923, Sennett immediately realized that he had something special. Sennett later wrote, "It was difficult for us at first to know how to use Langdon, accustomed as we were to firing the gags and the falls at the audience as fast as possible." But, he concluded, "As with Charlie Chaplin, you had to let him take his time and go through his motions."

Sennett's gagmen and directors, notably Frank Capra, Harry Edwards, and Arthur Ripley, worked closely with Langdon and fashioned two dozen two-reelers over the next few years that experimented with Langdon's characterization of the innocent babe in the wods. The comedies were tremendously successful, with such great shorts as *The Luck of the Foolish, All Night Long,* and *Saturday Afternoon* demonstrating beyond a doubt, Langdon's rare abilities as a pantomimist.

Like nearly everyone else who worked for Sennett, Langdon was soon offered more money elsewhere, and he jumped at a lucrative First National Pictures contract that gave him control over his own feature-length comedies. He took Harry Edwards, Arthur Ripley, and Frank Capra with him, and together they came up with the films that show Langdon at the height of his powers: *Tramp Tramp Tramp, The Strong Man,* and *Long Pants.*

But Langdon brought about his own downfall. Flushed with success, he decided to direct himself. He became increasingly uncooperative with his colleagues. His first solo effort, *Three's a Crowd* (1927), perfectly illustrated just how much he needed good direction. He let every comic scene go on interminably, and in trying to build up pathos, only succeeded in becoming boring. Furthermore, he apparently had no firm grasp of the rudiments of film direction—his features were burdened with endless reaction shots and matching shots that do not match.

The film was a disaster, and Langdon's subsequent attempts to duplicate the success of his initial features were doomed to failure. Within a year, he had sabotaged his own career, and between overspending on his budg-

ets and contending with alimony payments, his financial condition was none too secure either.

So it was that with the coming of sound, Langdon was no longer a hot item in Hollywood. Hope for a new start came when Hal Roach offered him the chance to star in a series of talkie two-reelers. William K. Everson has written that Roach directed some of these shorts himself (without taking screen credit) "only because Langdon was impossible for other directors to handle, and Roach assumed that his own friendship with, and understanding of, Langdon might make for an easier rapport. It didn't."

The eight two-reelers that resulted are bad beyond belief. Suspicion, in later years, that the films flopped because Langdon could not adjust to sound would seem to be unjustified. His voice is well suited to his characterization, and indeed, some of the Langdon talkies move quite smoothly, compared to other Roach products being turned out at the same time.

Admittedly, the material in the shorts is not the greatest, but in the long run the blame for these horrible films must rest with Langdon himself. He is incredibly bad. Gone is the innocence he projected so effortlessly in his earlier films; instead, we see a babbling idiot who, instead of creating sympathy, draws impatience and dislike from the viewer. Even the presence of vivacious Thelma Todd in such shorts as *The King* and *The Fighting Parson* does little to liven up the films.

The combination of Langdon's unmanageability and the dismal failure of the shorts made his series one of the shortest in the history of Hal Roach Studios. After one year, Langdon was fired.

The rest of Langdon's career in two-reelers became a challenge, to project once again the babylike innocence that was the hallmark of his initial success. It worked about half of the time. In 1932, a "comeback" was announced as producer-director Arvid E. Gillstrom inaugurated a Langdon series at Educational Pictures, costarring (and cobilling) Harry with his longtime screen cohort Vernon Dent. Of his first short, *The Big Flash, Film Daily* wrote, "Plenty of gags and nice comedy work on the part of Langdon make this look like a strong laugh number."

The Educational comedies made during the next year are not bad at all. They have much of the improvisational, freewheeling quality of the Sennett silent shorts, moving from one gag sequence to another with little rhyme or reason, stopping rather arbitrarily after the allotted two reels. At the end of 1933, Gillstrom let Langdon have his head, to write one two-reeler on his own, *The Stage Hand.* For another year, Langdon and Gillstrom moved to Paramount, where they made five two-reelers.

Throughout his career in talkie two-reelers, Langdon

Harry Langdon is *The King*; Dorothy Granger (in her first short subject) has been dropped for the moment.

was surrounded by former associates—Vernon Dent, Harry Edwards, Arthur Ripley, and so forth. Apparently it was felt, from past experience, that Langdon would work best with old friends and colleagues. There appears to have been little difficulty with the comic during this time.

One would think that working with the men who had created Langdon's screen image would have meant consistently good films, films that maintained the original Langdon character. But Frank Capra has revealed that, as vital as director Edwards and writer Ripley were to the original comedies, neither fully grasped the importance of gearing every gag to Langdon's portrayal. If something was funny, they wanted to use it, even if it meant betraying Harry's innocence. So, not surprisingly, some of Langdon's best talkies were made *not* by Ripley or Edwards, but by other comedy directors.

In 1935 Langdon signed with Columbia, where he starred in two-reelers, on and off, for the next ten years. "On and off" also describes the quality of the shorts, which range from delightful to abysmal. As in Langdon's

earlier work, they often show flashes of inspiration that have gone wrong somewhere along the way. A typical oversight was allowing Harry to grow a moustache; presumably the idea grew out of the fact that he was getting older (one must recall that he was in his fifties at this time) and, without the extreme clown-white facial makeup, it might look more natural for him to sport a moustache. It only made it harder to accept Langdon's childlike characterization.

Counsel on de Fence (1934) is an example of a comedy with good ideas and weak execution. A spoof of the then-popular courtroom melodramas, the film concludes with a takeoff on the famous scene in *The Mouthpiece* in which Warren William, as famed lawyer William Fallon, swallows a vial of acid to prove a point, using a stomach pump afterward to remove the fluid from his system. In *Counsel on de Fence,* Harry tells his assistant to substitute tea for the poison, but unwittingly drinks the real item in court. He wins his case, and only afterward does he realize what has happened. Four different people, worried about his health, insist on treating him with stomach pumps, and after the fourth such exercise, Harry falls out cold.

I Don't Remember (1935) is one of Langdon's most

curious comedies. Written and directed by Preston Black (the pseudonym used by Jack White), it combines some brilliant gags with hopelessly slipshod material. What is more, many of the best gags fail to provoke laughter—because they are more ingenious than funny.

The film opens as Harry's wife (Geneva Mitchell) calls his mother (Mary Carr) to come over and help her out. It seems that Harry's absentmindedness has reached a new peak, and it's driving Geneva crazy. "Why, one night he put his umbrella to bed, and stood in the kitchen all night to let the water run off!" she exclaims. That afternoon, they send Harry down to the furniture company to pay the final installment due on their furniture. On the way, Harry bumps into an old friend (Vernon Dent) who convinces him to split the cost of an Irish Sweepstakes ticket. When Harry returns home, his wife is out, but his mother scolds him for squandering their money, because of which all the furniture has been repossessed. Harry, a would-be artist, gets a brainstorm. He paints furniture on all the walls! Geneva returns home, puts the groceries on the living room "table"—and they slide to the floor. Then she tries to sit down, with similar results. She's so furious she walks out on him, and Harry, despondent, is going to commit suicide. Then, when Vernon calls on him, he decides to commit murder instead!

All of which changes when Vernon tells him that they've won the Sweepstakes. They go to the office to collect their money, but when Harry produces his half of the ticket, it blows out the window. Harry and Vernon chase after it, the wind blows it up, and they run upstairs and try to grab it from the window. It blows down again, and down they go after it. Outside, they scour the streets until Harry discovers the ticket on the ground next to him. As he calls triumphantly to Vernon, a garbage truck passes, sending thousands of pieces of paper all over the street. Then, to make matters worse, a sanitation truck goes by and waters down the whole mess. Harry thinks he's got his eye on the ticket, however, and, when a pile of papers floats down the street and into a sewer, he dives down after it. The picture fades to a view looking out at the ocean, and there in the distance is a head bobbing above the surface. It's Harry, who is yelling from afar, "I've found it!"

I have gone into detail in describing the film to point out an apparent paradox. It sounds funny, and indeed it *is* funny, but it doesn't play funny. The painted-furniture gag is inspired, yet it doesn't provoke laughter. Other good sequences are hurt by the inclusion of gratuitous slapstick—Harry accidentally squirting himself from a paint tube, falling into a bathtub, etcetera. The film shows how the ingredients for a good comedy can be present, but, if not treated carefully, can fall flat.

Langdon's next two-reeler for Columbia was made two years later, and it stands out as his best. For, in *A Dog-gone Mixup,* as in few other shorts, he was given the opportunity to play the Innocent once more, with good gags, and with snappy direction by Charles Lamont. In the film Harry is a compulsive bargain-buyer, and when he gets a good deal on a doghouse and dog collar, he can't resist buying a dog. Unfortunately, the canine, a huge St. Bernard, makes a shambles of his home, nearly destroys his marriage (to Ann Doran), and forces him to move. He buys a trailer (another bargain), and all seems peaceful again, until the dog accidentally causes the trailer to dangle over a cliff. The resulting sight gags are first-rate all the way, and throughout the film, although Harry is a constant bumbler, audience sympathy is with him, who seems so sincere and likeable that one is ready to forgive his ignorance.

Another Columbia short, *Sue My Lawyer* (1938) is also quite good, if not as expert in delineating Harry's characterization. It does repeat a key gag from *The Strong Man,* however, with Harry having to carry an unconscious Ann Doran up a flight of stairs.

Langdon's 1940s comedies for Columbia are not of this caliber. In several, Columbia was apparently using his name to help build up others under contract. He is given star billing in *What Makes Lizzy Dizzy?* (1942), but the film is a showcase for acrobatic comedienne Elsie Ames, with Langdon getting a minimal slice of the footage.

Monty Collins, Bud Jamison, Ann Doran, and Harry in *Sue My Lawyer.*

Harry tried painting furniture on the wall to fool his wife, Geneva Mitchell. It didn't work. Mary Carr looks on, in *I Don't Remember*.

Several years later, he was teamed with El Brendel in a handful of two-reelers in which he sadly received billing among the supporting cast, with Brendel's name going over the title. It was quite a comedown for a man who, twenty years earlier, was being hailed as the new Chaplin.

Langdon's best short from this era was a pleasant little comedy called *To Heir Is Human* (1944), costarring Una Merkel, who seemed to take to slapstick with ease. Although looking old, Harry carried off his footage quite nicely. Unfortunately, the film fell into the trap of relying too heavily on tasteless sight gags that required stunt men or dummies.

After making another El Brendel short, Langdon went to work on *Swingin' on a Rainbow,* a Republic musical starring Jane Frazee. During the shooting he suffered a cerebral hemorrhage, fell into a coma, and died. He was sixty years old.

Truly gifted people come along so rarely that it hurts to see one's potential laid waste. Harry Langdon *had* a great comic gift, but it had to be nurtured and trained. When it was, he was capable of producing comedy that ranked alongside the best in the field. But Langdon's failing was that he couldn't understand that he was not the best judge of his own talent.

Harry Langdon's Talkie Shorts

Following are all Langdon's talkie two-reelers. They do not include guest apearances in such shorts as *Hollywood on Parade*. Three Educational talkies, *Leave It to Dad, Pop's Pal,* and *No Sleep on the Deep,* have been credited to Langdon, but he does not appear in any of them, although they were made by the Mermaid unit which produced his films.

1. *Hotter Than Hot.* Hal Roach-MGM (8/17/29), Lewis R. Foster. Edgar Kennedy, Thelma Todd, Frank Austin, Edith Kramer. Harry is trapped with a blonde in a burning building.

2. *Sky Boy.* Hal Roach-MGM (10/5/29), Charles Rogers. Thelma Todd, Eddie Dunn. Harry lands on an iceberg with his rival.

3. *Skirt Shy.* Hal Roach-MGM (11/30/29), Charles Rogers. May Wallace, Tom Ricketts, Nancy Dover, Charlie Hall. Harry has to pose as a woman to help the woman he works for get a marriage proposal.

4. *The Head Guy.* Hal Roach-MGM (1/11/30), Fred Guiol. Thelma Todd, Nancy Dover, Eddie Dunn, Edgar Kennedy. Harry is recruited as temporary stationmaster in a small town.

5. *The Fighting Parson.* Hal Roach-MGM (2/22/30), Charles Rogers, Fred Guiol. Thelma Todd, Nancy Dover, Eddie Dunn, Leo Willis, Charlie Hall. Harry is mistaken for the famous "fighting parson" in a rough-and-tough western town.

6. *The Big Kick.* Hal Roach-MGM (3/29/30), Warren Doane. Nancy Dover, Edgar Kennedy, Bob Kortman, Sam Lufkin, Baldwin Cooke, Charles McAvoy, Eddie Baker. Gas-station attendant Harry gets mixed up with a gang of runaway bootleggers.

7. *The Shrimp.* Hal Roach-MGM (5/3/30), Charles Rogers. Thelma Todd, Nancy Drexel, James Mason, Max Davidson. Harry is a weakling until a scientist injects a serum into him.

8. *The King.* Hal Roach-MGM (6/14/30), James W. Horne. Thelma Todd, Dorothy Granger. Harry plays a henpecked king with a roving eye.

9. *The Big Flash.* Educational (11/6/32), Arvid E. Gillstrom. Vernon Dent, Lita Chevret, Ruth Hiatt, Matthew Betz, King Baggot, Jack Grey, Bobby Dunn. Harry and Vernon are rival reporters eager to please Ruth, the newspaper's information-desk receptionist.

10. *Tired Feet.* Educational (1/1/33), Arvid E. Gillstrom. Vernon Dent, Shirley Blake, Maidena Armstrong, Eddie Baker, William Irving, Les Goodwin. Mailman Harry goes on vacation with his girl friend and a rival. He proves his devotion when hoboes invade their campsite.

11. *The Hitch Hiker.* Educational (2/12/33), Arvid E. Gillstrom. Vernon Dent, Ruth Clifford, William Irving, Chris Marie Meeker. Harry takes to the air to escape angry director Von Burst after ruining a scene in his new movie, being shot on location.

12. *Knight Duty.* Educational (5/7/33), Arvid E. Gillstrom. Vernon Dent, Matthew Betz, Lita Chevret, Nell O'Day, Eddie Baker, Billy Engle. Harry gets involved in a police chase pursuing jewel thieves. The chase takes them all to a wax museum.

13. *Tied for Life.* Educational (7/2/33), Arvid E. Gillstrom. Vernon Dent, Nell O'Day, Mabel Forrest, Elaine Whipple, Eddie Baker. Harry's rival does everything possible to spoil Harry's marriage and honeymoon.

14. *Marriage Humor.* Paramount (8/18/33), Harry Edwards. Vernon Dent, Nancy Dover, Ethel Sykes, Eddie Schubert. Harry and Vernon get what-for from their wives after a night on the town.

15. *Hooks and Jabs.* Educational (8/25/33), Arvid E. Gillstrom. Nell O'Day, William Irving, Frank Moran, Vernon Dent. Harry is thought to be an ace prizefighter in Dent's saloon.

16. *The Stage Hand.* Educational (9/8/33), Harry Edwards. Marel Foster, Ira Hayward, Eddie Schubert. Stagehand Harry accidentally sets the theatre on fire. Screenplay by Langdon.

17. *On Ice.* Paramount (10/6/33), Arvid E. Gillstrom. Vernon Dent, Eleanor Hunt, Ethel Sykes, Kewpie Morgan, Ruth Clifford,

Instead of ointment, Harry is accidentally applying limburger cheese in *The Hitchhiker;* his fellow passengers don't seem too happy about it. Vernon Dent at right.

Diana Seaby, William Irving. Iceman Harry and a friend "step out" with two girls, but get caught by their wives.

18. *Roaming Romeo.* Paramount (12/29/33), Arvid E. Gillstrom. Vernon Dent, Nell O'Day, Jack Henderson, Les Goodwin. Harry and his girl encounter a so-called model house.

19. *Trimmed in Furs.* Educational (1/5/34), Charles Lamont. John Sheehan, Eleanor Hunt, Dorothy Dix, Louise Keaton, Tom Francis, Harold Berquist, Neal Pratt, Faye Pierre. While trying to find a fur coat for his wife, Harry meets a flamboyant movie star.

20. *Circus Hoodoo.* Paramount (2/16/34), Arvid E. Gillstrom. Vernon Dent, Eleanor Hunt, Matthew Betz, Diana Seaby, James Morton, Tom Kennedy. On the lam from a gang of hoods, Harry and Vernon hide out in a circus.

21. *Petting Preferred.* Paramount (4/27/34), Arvid E. Gillstrom. Vernon Dent, Dorothy Granger, Eddie Baker, Alice Ardell.

Pet-shop owner Harry gets sandwiched between a wife who loves her pet dog and a husband who wants to get rid of it.

22. *Counsel on de Fence.* Columbia (10/25/34), Arthur Ripley. Renée Whitney, Earle Foxe, Jack Norton, Babe Kane. Lawyer Harry represents a woman accused of poisoning her husband.

23. *Shivers.* Columbia (12/24/34), Arthur Ripley. Florence Lake, Dick Elliott. Harry, as mystery writer Ichabod Somerset Crop, moves into a haunted house that provides him with plenty of material.

24. *His Bridal Sweet.* Columbia (3/15/35), Alf Goulding. Billy Gilbert, Geneva Mitchell. Harry and his wife move into a gimmick-laden model house.

25. *The Leather Necker.* Columbia (5/9/35), Arthur Ripley. Wade Boteler. Harry's ex-Marine sergeant runs into him and reminds him of their rivalry over a girl in South America. A remake of Langdon's silent *All Night Long.*

26. *His Marriage Mixup.* Columbia (10/31/35), Preston Black. Dorothy Granger. Bridegroom Harry gets involved with an axe murderess.

27. *I Don't Remember.* Columbia (12/26/35) Preston Black. Geneva Mitchell, Mary Carr, Vernon Dent, Robert "Bobby" Burns. Absentminded Harry drives his wife crazy with his forgetfulness. Remade with Sterling Holloway as *Moron Than Off.*

28. *A Doggone Mixup.* Columbia (2/4/38), Charles Lamont. Ann Doran, Vernon Dent, Bud Jamison, Eddie Fetherstone, Bess Flowers, Sarah Edwards, James C. Morton. Harry buys a huge dog that all but wrecks his marriage.

29. *Sue My Lawyer.* Columbia (9/16/38), Jules White. Ann

Dorothy Granger is an ax murderess; Harry gets involved with her in *His Marriage Mixup.*

Doran, Monty Collins, Bud Jamison, Vernon Dent, Cy Schindell, Don Brodie, Jack "Tiny" Lipson, Robert "Bobby" Burns. Lawyer Harry defends a killer to make a reputation for himself. Story by Harry Langdon.

30. *Goodness, a Ghost.* RKO (3/8/40), Harry D'Arcy. Jack Rice, Tiny Sandford, Kirby Grant. Harry's grandfather's spirit inhabits his old policeman's uniform which is being used in an amateur play. Screenplay by Harry Langdon.

31. *Cold Turkey.* Columbia (10/18/40), Del Lord. Ann Doran, Monty Collins, Vernon Dent, Bud Jamison, Eddie Laughton. Trouble begins when Harry wins a live turkey.

32. *What Makes Lizzy Dizzy?* Columbia (3/26/42), Jules

Una Merkel, working for a missing persons bureau, seems to have found her man, in *To Heir Is Human.*

White. Elsie Ames, Dorothy Appleby, Monty Collins, Bud Jamison, Lorin Raker, Kathryn Sabichi, Kay Vallon. Harry and Monty join their laundress girl friends at a bowling tournament.

33. *Tireman, Spare My Tires.* Columbia (6/4/42), Jules White. Louise Currie, Emmett Lynn, Vernon Dent, Bud Jamison. Traveling salesman Harry meets a runaway heiress.

34. *Carry Harry.* Columbia (9/3/42), Harry Edwards. Elsie Ames, Barbara Pepper, Marjorie Deanne, Dave O'Brien, Stanley Blystone. Harry's fiancée finds him in an apartment with two strange girls.

35. *Piano Mooner.* Columbia (12/11/42), Harry Edwards. Fifi D'Orsay, Gwen Kenyon, Betty Blythe, Stanley Blystone, Chester Conklin. In need of money, Harry becomes a piano tuner.

36. *Blitz on the Fritz.* Columbia (1/22/43), Jules White. Louise Currie, Douglas Leavitt, Vernon Dent, Beatrice Blinn, Jack

Harry, Fifi D'Orsay, and Chester Conklin are living it up in *Piano Mooner*.

El Brendel and Harry are *Defective Detectives;* Vernon Dent is their boss.

"Tiny" Lipson, Charles Berry, Al Hill, Kit Guard, Bud Fine. Harry, classified 4-PDQ by the army, wants to serve his country, and does, when he exposes a ring of saboteurs.

37. *Blonde and Groom.* Columbia (4/16/43), Harry Edwards. Harry's pal comes over with his fiancée; Harry's wife calls on the phone, hears a woman's voice, and misunderstands.

38. *Here Comes Mr. Zerk.* Columbia (7/23/43), Jules White. Harry, a famed scientist, is confused with an escaped lunatic.

39. *To Heir Is Human.* Columbia (1/14/44), Harold Godsoe. Una Merkel, Christine McIntyre, Eddie Gribbon, Lew Kelly, Vernon Dent, John Tyrrell. Would-be detective Una accompanies Harry to an eerie mansion where he's supposed to claim an inheritance.

40. *Defective Detectives.* Columbia (4/3/44), Harry Edwards. El Brendel, Christine McIntyre, Vernon Dent, Eddie Laughton, John Tyrrell, Snub Pollard, Dick Botiller. Private eyes Harry and El get tangled up with the police.

41. *Mopey Dope.* Columbia (6/16/44), Del Lord. El Brendel, Christine McIntyre, Arthur Q. Bryan. Absentminded Harry goes home to the wrong house, incurring the wrath of his neighbor, a jealous husband. Remake of Charley Chase's *The Mind Needer.*

42. *Snooper Service.* Columbia (2/2/45), Harry Edwards. El Brendel, Vernon Dent, Rebel Randall, Dick Curtis, Fred Kelsey, Buddy Yarus. Private eyes Harry and El are assigned to follow a showgirl.

43. *Pistol Packin' Nitwits.* Columbia (4/4/45), Harry Edwards. El Brendel, Christine McIntyre, Dick Curtis, Tex Cooper, Brad King, Victor Cox, Heinie Conklin, Vernon Dent. El and Harry decide to help the lovely owner of a saloon save it from a mortgage foreclosure.

"The Boy Friends"

George Stevens is best known today as the director of such film classics as *Gunga Din, The More the Merrier, A Place in the Sun,* and *Shane.* But in the late 1920s and early 1930s, he was a cameraman at the Hal Roach studio, working with Laurel and Hardy and Charley Chase.

Of Roach, Stevens says today, "He would make one picture a year, or something, and he would always get the wrong story and get into trouble with it. He was directing this one, and about noon he said, 'You direct it.' I said, 'Not for me.' I wouldn't do it, I wouldn't know what the hell to do with it. I thought what he was doing was silly enough, without me trying it. He insisted, and I said 'No, I can't do it, Hal.' So he said, 'Well, what do you want to do?' I said, 'If you want me to direct a picture, let me get my own story, so I'll know what I'm doing.'" The result was a delightful series called "The Boy Friends."

One might best describe The Boy Friends as Our Gang grown up, and the resemblance is more than passing. Two of the mainstays of the series' cast were Mickey Daniels and Mary Kornman, members of the original silent-film Our Gang. Others included David Sharpe, soon to become one of the movies' all-time great stunt men, and who, as nominal leading man of the series, always found an excuse to engage in some eye-popping acrobatics. Grady Sutton, as Alabam, was a special favorite of director Stevens and often provided the best laughs in the films as the slow-witted, naïve southerner. Gertie Messinger, David Rollins, Betty Bolen, Gordon Douglas, Dorothy Granger, and Jacqueline Wells (later known as Julie Bishop) alternated as other members of the group.

Stevens teamed with a former child actor named Warren Burke to prepare a script for the first film in the series, *Doctor's Orders.* It was directed by Arch Heath. "We didn't know too much about it," he says, but concedes it was "all right." The plot had Grady Sutton in love with a girl (Mary Kornman) who did not return his affections. Grady's pal Dave comes up with an idea: Stage a phony auto accident in front of her home, and she'll be forced to take him in and nurse him. Amazingly enough, it works. Seeing his success, Mickey follows suit, with the same results. The only hitch is that Mary's uncle (Edgar Kennedy) is a bit sharper than the girls, and senses something fishy. When Dave shows up as "Dr. Sharpe," to give the patients some phony cures, Edgar tries to catch him off guard. This leads to the film's most prolonged comedy sequence, as Dave somehow masquerades as a nurse to get into the home under another pretext. With the nurse supposedly on one floor and the doctor on another, Edgar keeps going up and down stairs, forcing Dave to leap out the bedroom window and clamber down the side of the house, changing clothes along the way, and vice versa, to maintain both identities.

Doctor's Orders was an auspicious start for the series, but the second film, *Ladies Last,* came as something of a letdown. Although it had its moments, it was burdened with too much talk and too little action. Stevens photographed the first two shorts in the series, and only with the third was he given an opportunity to direct.

"The next one," says Stevens of his series, "was terrible. We tried the wrong kind of story, one where these people were supposed to be comedians rather than people. It was really bad." The film, *Ladies Last*—in which the girls use their wiles to counteract a boycott by their beaus brought about by the girls' insistence that they wear formal dress to their big dance—was probably one of the weakest in the series. But even here, there are some individual gags that are first-rate, and even more importantly, some camera setups that set the film apart from anything else being done at the Roach studio in 1930.

An establishing shot on the beach is taken from overhead, showing Dave Sharpe and Dorothy Granger lying in opposite directions, their heads pressed together, with the ocean washing up against them.

"I guess those shots would look elementary now," Stevens says, "because we've all seen them, but they hadn't then." Other Roach directors were skilled in comedy filming, but the setup of shots was always functional, as it should be in good comedy. Stevens was probably among the first directors at the studio to try something offbeat in shooting his two-reelers.

In 1931, the series hit its stride. The pacing became tighter (even when the films extended into three reels), the gags faster and more elaborate, the cast more assured. In addition, the situation comedy format of the initial shorts was abandoned in favor of a more slapstick and sight-gag-oriented comedy—with delightful results. In fact, the shorts are incredibly close to the "feel" of silent comedies, much closer than many other shorts that strove for that effect.

The shorts' director explains, "The script was really written without any regard for dialogue. The situations were described, with maybe an occasional line. In the silent pictures, they'd do the picture and then the titles would be written. Hiram Walker was the title man; he was very funny. So when the dialogue pictures started, the script was written, then it went to Walker, and he'd do the dialogue. So the three or four pages of script were here, and eight or ten pages of dialogue were here; it was sort of non sequitur. The dialogue was usually very awkward in the Hal Roach pictures, including the Laurel and Hardy pictures. In the Boy Friends pictures, all of a sudden somebody would stop and say something. Because they were not homogeneous, they were two different things, and we depended on situations and sight gags . . . we were inept with dialogue."

Thus, with firmer footing, the production team proceeded to make a succession of truly funny little films. *High Gear* has the gang out for a day's pleasure with Mickey's father's car. Pop (Harry Bernard) has warned Mickey that should there be a scratch on the auto when he returns, he'll be in plenty of hot water. Problems begin when there is an accident with another car, augmented by a run-in with a local traffic cop (played, inevitably, by Edgar Kennedy). As the cop is writing out a ticket for Mickey, the girls (Mary and Gertie) try to talk him out of it—Gertie flatters him by saying, "Why, you're the perfect image of Wallace Beery!" Later, they get caught in a sudden downpour that washes off the car's new paint job and blows away the convertible roof. The gang seeks shelter in a nearby house, which is being used as a gangster's hideout. There follows a wild chase, in and out of doors, up and down stairs, with mistaken identities and Dave Sharpe's acrobatics keeping the sequence moving at a lightning pace. Through it all, poor Alabam repeatedly gets pushed through the same window into a mud puddle outside.

Air Tight is perhaps the best short in the series. The gang has formed a glider club, with enthusiastic response from everyone but Alabam, who's scared to death of heights (or, as one of the kids puts it, "Why, the highest off the ground you've ever been is upstairs."). However he persuades Mary to take his photo sitting in one of the gliders on the field, while Dave goes up for an inaugural flight in the gang's aircraft. Mickey, who's towing the plane with his car, hooks up the wrong one, and, before long, the unsuspecting Alabam is up in the air, screaming for dear life.

In the action that follows, no gag is used twice, and endless variations and complications are brought in to make up a powerhouse comedy. A great asset, as always, is the wonderful Hal Roach music score (by Marvin Hatley); another is the supporting performance of Charlie Hall, as a fellow glider enthusiast whose plane takes

Kennedy the Cop writes out a ticket for the gang: Gertie Messinger, Grady Sutton, Betty Bolen, Mickey Daniels, Mary Kornman, and David Sharpe, in *High Gear*.

Mickey has just been "christened" with a bottle of champagne—it was meant for the plane. Gertie, Grady, and Mary apologize, in *Air Tight.*

Alabam into the blue. (Trying to pacify him, Mary says, "Oh, I'm sorry, Mr. Lind— Oh, I was going to call you Lindbergh. But you *do* look like him.") And while there are some obvious miniature inserts, most of the film's success is due to the incredible reality of the action—not to mention those unique Stevens camera shots, notably one taken from Alabam's point of view, looking down along the rope line to the car towing the glider on the ground.

The short's director and star have vivid memories of the comedy. "You know, we had no process shots," Stevens explains, "so how do you pretend that this glider is up in the air? How do you get it up there in the first place? Do you know those shots that were from some height? There was a cliff, where Loyola, the top of the marina, is now, that had an edge to it, that we could move along. We got one of these big sticks which they use to hoist girders; it's on a caterpillar tractor. We got two of them, and I hooked the glider on a hundred-foot one, and then I took an 80-foot one and put a camera on it; it was just alongside it, and we ran it along the edge of the cliff. We were out over the cliff! It was absolutely terrifying, because when it would start to roll, and you had the camera boom, it was something. The camera platform was really uneasy."

Grady Sutton, who, as Alabam, had to stay in the glider during all that filming, says, "I was in the air, all right. I didn't have any more sense in those days. The little thing was light, and I was in there, going crazy. I wouldn't do it today, but I trusted everybody in those days."

The Kickoff is not a hilarious short, but it is an extremely well-made one. A gang of thugs kidnap the football team's coach (Harry Bernard) and keep the star

player (David Rollins) out of the game. This forces the team to send Mickey and Alabam onto the field, a certain disaster. But by sheer pluck, and happy consequences, they manage to win the game and tackle the two hoodlums on the sidelines to boot. The scenes with Bernard in the gangster's hideout are done seriously, to good effect, and the Stevens touch asserts itself in shots from the middle of the huddle looking up.

In *The Knockout,* Mickey and Mary are having an ice-cream soda when a local hotshot boxer forces his attentions on Mary. She tells Mickey to sock him, but he replies that there are two things he's never done: he's never been kissed by a girl, and he's never punched a boy. She kisses him, and he immediately knocks the intruder out cold. Mickey is then forced to take the pugilist's place in the ring. Unfortunately, the boxing scenes are protracted, and not very funny after a while—not to mention the distracting process screen that serves as an audience behind the ring.

Director Gordon Douglas played Mickey's adversary in *The Knockout,* and recalls ruefully, "I was supposed to win the first round, and he was supposed to win the second, but evidently the director told Mickey something else, because he beat me in the first *and* the second. I used to do a little boxing at prep school, but I never took a beating like this. Mickey Daniels had the great habit of not being able to pull a punch. I came home that night and I had bells ringing for the next three days."

Call a Cop was back in the groove, with the boys annoying Mickey's police-chief father (Harry Bernard) by trying to act heroic instead of calling a cop at the first sign of trouble. Trouble begins anew that night when the girls who live next door think they hear a burglar downstairs. They call across the yard to the boys for help, and also call the police on the phone. The result is a mad chase through darkened rooms and hallways, with the entire gang, and an increasing number of cops every minute, prowling around looking for a nonexistent burglar! The climax was borrowed from the earlier *High Gear,* and in turn, director Stevens took the entire sequence and used it as the conclusion of his Wheeler and Woolsey comedy feature *The Nitwits* four years later.

By this time, "The Boy Friends" was set as a series and sold to exhibitors on the campaign of "youthful frolics." And while the entries in the series varied somewhat in quality from one to the next, the well-established characters carried such charm with them that weak material didn't seem quite so bad. George Stevens has described the cast as "a pretty good bunch of kids," and that they were. Mickey Daniels, with his hyena-laugh trademark, Grady Sutton, whose "reactive sense" (Stevens's de-

78

Thelma Todd and Edgar Kennedy in a "Boy Friends" comedy of errors, *Love Fever*.

scription) was unsurpassed, irresistibly cute Mary Korn-man, and buoyantly athletic Dave Sharpe, along with the Roach stock company (Edgar Kennedy, Harry Bernard, Charlie Hall, Tiny Sandford, etcetera) made the series a lot of fun. So when George Stevens left Roach at the end of 1931 after a dispute over a new project, the immediate impact was not felt. But you could always tell a Stevens short from those made by his colleagues—they weren't always better, although they maintained a very high standard, but they were always distinctive.

In fact, as early as 1930, some of the episodes of the series had been directed by other men, including "Our Gang's" director Robert McGowan. One short was a de-lightfully offbeat item called *Love Fever,* and it bore the marks of McGowan as surely as the others bore those of Stevens. Thelma Todd plays an actress who, seeking solitude to rehearse a new play, moves into the apart-ment house where the gang lives. The boy friends have just been jilted by their girls and, one by one, are swept up by the beauty and charm of Miss Todd. They don't realize at first that she is rehearsing a play. When she learns that they've been jilted, she makes overtures to them and then frightens the daylights out of them, send-ing them packing back to their girls. At the same time, after the girls see their boyfriends playing up to Thelma, they change their minds and are glad to welcome them back.

There are virtually no sight gags in this comedy. It

depends entirely on the verve of the players, led by the always delightful Thelma Todd. And true to McGowan's form, most of the key scenes are played with tight close-ups, something Stevens never favored. *Love Fever* is unique among the "Boy Friends" shorts, and it is great fun.

After Stevens left, some good shorts continued to emerge. *You're Telling Me* is a hilarious film, largely dependent on comic Billy Gilbert for its big belly laughs. The boys graduate from college, and Gordon Douglas (replacing Dave Sharpe as the hero of the series) tells Mickey and Alabam to stop in at his home anytime they wish. They take up his offer immediately, and immediately win over his parents (Gilbert is the father) by inventing some hilarious flattery about Eddie's mother "reminding me of my own mother, standing in the doorway of the old plantation." The boys make themselves at home, proceed to wreck everything in sight (including Gilbert's dress suit, at a party where a gooey cake gets thrown about). By the end of several weeks, Gilbert comes into the kitchen for breakfast a totally shattered man. He tries to hold a cup steady to pour his coffee, but it's impossible—and the scene is impossibly funny.

Too Many Women, one of the last shorts in the series, explores one possibility that should have occurred to

Mary Kornman shows Mickey Daniels her scrapbook, with pictures of them as kids, from "Our Gang," in *Too Many Women*.

someone much sooner. Mary is in love with Mickey, who ignores her because he's got a crush on Sadie, a local lunch-counter waitress. When Sadie gets married, Mickey is broken-hearted; Mary consoles him by taking out a scrapbook and showing him pictures of them as kids, reminding him how they were always sweethearts. The scrapbook's photos, of course, are from ''Our Gang,'' and each photo ''comes to life'' as clips are shown from the early silent comedies that featured Mickey and Mary. It's a charming sequence, and a theme that could have been amplified.

But after one more film, ''The Boy Friends'' series expired. Apparently the series was not a smashing financial success, although it seems likely that Stevens's departure may have had something to do with the demise of the shorts. Without a strong hand to give the films shape, the best directors (James Horne, Lloyd French, etcetera) could not save the series from inconsistency in style and quality. In mid-1932, production stopped on the series.

What is sad is that so few people remember ''The Boy Friends'' shorts. One obvious reason is that they have been out of circulation for such a long time, even though prints do exist. For the sake of comedy, ''The Boy Friends'' should be taken out of mothballs—all the talent that went into them produced a lively and generally delightful group of films that retain their charm today, as part of the innocent, freewheeling comedy world of the 1930s.

''The Boy Friends'' Shorts

Following are all ''The Boy Friends'' comedies, produced by Hal Roach and released by MGM. All are two reels in length unless otherwise noted. The shorts are listed in the order of release, although these dates are often at variance with the time the films were made. One ZaSu Pitts–Thelma Todd short, *Let's Do Things,* is often erroneously credited as a ''Boy Friends'' comedy.

1. *Doctor's Orders* (9/13/30), Arch Heath. Mickey Daniels, Grady Sutton, David Sharpe, Mary Kornman, Dorothy Granger, Gertie Messinger, Edgar Kennedy, Tiny Sandford. The boys stage phony accidents so the girls will have to nurse them back to health.

2. *Bigger and Better* (10/25/30), Edgar Kennedy. Mickey Daniels, Grady Sutton, David Sharpe, Mary Kornman, Dorothy Granger, Gertie Messinger, Edgar Kennedy, Dell Henderson, Dick Granger, Jim Granger. The boys go to work in a department store so they'll be near the girls during summer vacation.

3. *Ladies Last* (12/6/30), George Stevens. Mickey Daniels, Grady Sutton, David Sharpe, Mary Kornman, Dorothy Granger, Gertie Messinger, Edgar Kennedy, Leo Willis, Dick Granger, Blaine Comer. The boys declare a boycott of the girls when they insist that the boys wear tuxedos to their big dance.

4. *Blood and Thunder* (1/17/31), George Stevens. Mickey Daniels, Grady Sutton, David Sharpe, Mary Kornman, Gertie Messinger, Dorothy De Borba, Spec O'Donnell. Mickey overhears the gang rehearsing a play and thinks it's for real.

A mighty melodrama is enacted by the gang in *Blood and Thunder.*

5. *High Gear* (2/28/31), George Stevens. Mickey Daniels, Grady Sutton, David Sharpe, Mary Kornman, Gertie Messinger, Betty Bolen, Edgar Kennedy, Harry Bernard, Tiny Sandford. Out for a Sunday joy ride, the gang unknowingly takes refuge in a gangster's hideout when it rains. Three reels.

6. *Love Fever* (4/11/31), Robert McGowan. Thelma Todd, Mickey Daniels, Grady Sutton, David Sharpe, Mary Kornman, Gertie Messinger, Dorothy Granger, Eddie Dunn, Edgar Kennedy. Actress Thelma is rehearsing a death scene in her apartment; one by one, the boys rush in to save her, and flip for her.

7. *Air Tight* (5/9/31), George Stevens. Mickey Daniels, Grady Sutton, David Sharpe, Mary Kornman, Gertie Messinger, Betty Bolen, Charlie Hall. At the inaugural flight of the gang's glider club, Grady is accidentally up in the air instead of Dave.

8. *Call a Cop* (9/12/31), George Stevens. Mickey Daniels, Grady Sutton, David Sharpe, Mary Kornman, Gertie Messinger,

Mickey and Grady seem to be the main course in *Wild Babies*.

Harry Bernard, Eddie Baker, Baldwin Cooke, Sam Lufkin. The boys rush into action when the girls think there's a burglar in their house.

9. *Mama Loves Papa* (10/24/31), George Stevens. Mickey Daniels, Grady Sutton, David Rollins, Mary Kornman, Gertie Messinger, May Wallace, Harry Bernard, Charlie Hall. May and Harry, both widowed, want to get married, but the kids do their best to stop them.

10. *The Kickoff* (12/5/31), George Stevens. Mickey Daniels, Grady Sutton, David Rollins, Mary Kornman, Betty Bolen, Harry Bernard, Charlie Hall, Leo Willis. Gangsters kidnap the team's football coach and try to throw the game; Mickey and Grady unexpectedly turn out to be heroes by winning.

11. *Love Pains* (2/13/32), James Horne. Mickey Daniels, Grady Sutton, David Rollins, Mary Kornman, Betty Bolen, Harry Bernard, Blanche Payson, Gordon Douglas, Marvin Hatley. Mickey and Grady are left at the starting gate when hotshot Rollins comes to town and wins every girl in sight.

12. *The Knockout* (3/5/32), Anthony Mack. Mickey Daniels, Grady Sutton, Eddie Morgan, Gordon Douglas, Mary Kornman, Jacqueline Wells (Julie Bishop), Harry Bernard, Spec O'Donnell. When Mickey accidentally knocks out a local boxing champ, he's forced to take the fighter's place in a bout.

13. *You're Telling Me* (4/16/32), Anthony Mack and Lloyd French. Mickey Daniels, Grady Sutton, Gordon Douglas, Jacqueline Wells, Betty Bolen, Billy Gilbert, Louise Beavers, May Wallace, Lyle Tayo. Mickey and Grady move in on a friend for a night, and stay several months.

Gordon Douglas, Mickey, and Grady after a melee in *You're Telling Me;* worst of all, the suits they're wearing were borrowed.

14. *Too Many Women* (5/14/32), Anthony Mack and Lloyd French. Mickey Daniels, Grady Sutton, Gordon Douglas, Mary Kornman, Harry Bernard, Tiny Sandford, Charlie Hall, Eddie Baker. Mickey, the baseball team's star pitcher, goes into a slump when a waitress he's in love with gets married. Includes several sequences from silent "Our Gang" comedies with Mickey and Mary.

15. *Wild Babies* (6/18/32), Anthony Mack and Lloyd French. Mickey Daniels, Grady Sutton, Mary Kornman, Charles Rogers, Charlie Hall. Would-be songwriters Mickey and Grady have a nightmare about stealing a song and being captured by jungle natives.

W. C. Fields

In the 1920s and 1930s, one of the most interesting parts of several motion-picture trade magazines was a department in which small-town theatre owners across the country sent in brief comments on the films they had played; this was done for short subjects as well as feature films. Today, these comments are invaluable as a barometer of what the mass movie audience really thought of the films that were being made—unaffected by critical reactions, and uncolored by modern reassessments.

Concerning the W. C. Fields comedies, most exhibitors were unanimous. They stank. Of *The Fatal Glass of Beer,* a Michigan theatre owner wrote, "Two reels of film and 20 minutes wasted," and a North Carolina manager added, "This is the worst comedy we have played from any company this season. No story, no acting, and as a whole has nothing."

Moviegoers today are just as unanimous in their opinions of the shorts: they are among the funniest films ever made.

The reasons for this discrepancy are not difficult to discern. Fields went against the grain of what was then popular humor; in an age when audience sympathy was always with the Little Fellow, when love and justice always triumphed, when anti-heroes were unheard of, Fields dared to be different.

He extolled the joys of drinking; he was mean, selfish, and dishonest. He rebelled against many of the silly conventions Americans held near and dear. And, for the most part, Americans were not ready to accept what he did as humorous. Today, some forty years later, the pendulum has swung the other way, and many people share Fields's views. He has become a popular hero.

But Fields had his problems in Hollywood during the 1920s and 1930s. Few people were willing to let him have his head to do the kind of comedy he wanted to do. Far too often, he was made to contend with Hollywoodized story lines and young-lover subplots. Fortunately, he found his niche often enough to create some pure comic masterpieces such as *It's a Gift* and *The Bank Dick,* that show him at his best, unhampered by studio interference.

One of Fields's greatest opportunities came when he went to work for Mack Sennett. Legend has it that Fields signed on with Sennett at a nominal fee to work as a comedy writer, and starred in his own films only as an afterthought. Whatever the background, it is clear that Sennett let Fields do as he pleased; he took screenplay credit for all four shorts and easily dominated the productions. It is probable that he had a hand in casting the films, choosing some excellent players (Elise Cavanna, Grady Sutton, etcetera) who he knew would be good foils.

The first short, *The Dentist,* consists of three major sequences. The first has Fields doing battle with his daughter (Babe Kane) over breakfast when she announces that she's in love with the iceman. The second has him going out for an early round of golf with a perplexed friend (Bud Jamison) who has to put up with Fields's idiosyncrasies. And the third takes place in the dentist's office, where Fields contends with a motley assortment of patients.

On the golf course, it is clear that Fields plays by his own set of rules. Anxious to tee off, he shouts "Fore!" and proceeds to set up his shot before another foursome has left the green. He makes his shot, and we cut to the green, where one gentleman proclaims, "This game is certainly wonderful for your health!" At which point the golf ball knocks him on the head and lays him out flat. After wrestling with the rule book, losing a ball, arguing with his caddy, and being defeated by a water trap, Fields gives up and goes back to his office.

If there is one word to describe the dentist's office sequence, it is "outrageous." So much so, in fact, that it was heavily edited when the film was shown after 1933, when the Production Code took effect. Original uncut prints today bring gasps along with laughter from modern audiences who can't get over what they're seeing. As Fields is talking to a pal in his office, a female patient (Dorothy Granger) is moaning outside. The nurse looks worried, but Fields continues to chat, unconcerned by the squeals from outside. When his nurse tries to call his attention to it, he mutters, "Ah, the hell with her!"

Fields really works hard at pulling Elise Cavanna's tooth, as nurse Zedna Farley looks on, in *The Dentist.*

Later, while trying to extract a tooth from the mouth of another woman (Elise Cavanna), he pulls her completely out of the chair, her legs straddling him and resting in his pockets! When he drills her tooth (the machine makes a loud buzz-saw sound), her entire body gyrates with what is apparently excruciating pain. Afterward he asks amiably, "Now that didn't hurt, did it?"

The Fields character in *The Dentist* is completely without redeeming qualities, and it is the shock of realizing this as much as anything else that makes the short unusually funny.

The next Fields short, *The Fatal Glass of Beer,* is undoubtedly the wildest, and at the same time the subtlest, of his four for Sennett. Its humor still eludes some people today, who cannot catch the satire and merely find the action dull. As a spoof of the old-fashioned Yukon melodramas, and the "Dangerous Dan McGrew" type of tales, it is without equal. It was directed by comedy veteran Clyde Bruckman.

The film begins as Fields "sings" to sentimental Mountie Richard Cramer a ballad he has written about his son Chester, who went to the Big City, took the Fatal Glass of Beer, was accused of stealing some bonds, and landed in prison. The song is completely formless and without rhyme, not helped by Fields's off-pitch singing.

W. C. shows typical fatherly love for George Chandler in *The Fatal Glass of Beer.*

Barber Cornelius O'Hare uses the latest scientific method to sharpen his razor, in *The Barber Shop.*

A bit later, who should show up at the wintry cabin but Chester (George Chandler), released from prison and come home to make amends with his parents. There are warm greetings all around, and the inane small talk reaches the height of absurdity when Chester, bawling, says, between sniffles, "It's so good to see you both again, and I'm so glad to be back home with you and ma, that I can't talk. I'd like to go to my little bedroom, lay on the bed, and cry like I was a baby again."

"There, there," sobs his mother, "go to your room and have a good cry, dear. I know how you feel."

"I feel so tired," Chester adds pointlessly, "I think I'll go to bed."

"Why don't you lie down and take a little rest first, Chester?" advises Fields.

"Well, good night, pa," says Chester.

"Good night, Chester," he replies.

"Good night, ma," says Chester.

"Good night, Chester," ma answers.

"Sleep well, Chester," says pa.

"Thank you, pa, and you, too," says Chester.

"Thank you, Chester," pa replies.

"Sleep well, Chester," adds ma.

"Thank you, ma, and you sleep well."

"Don't forget to open your window a bit, Chester," says pa.

"Don't forget to open yours a bit, pa."

"I won't, Chester," says pa, as ma adds, "Yes, don't forget to open your window a bit, Chester."

"Open yours a bit, too, ma."

"Good night, Chester," bid both his parents.

"Good night, pa, good night, ma."

"Good night."

"Good night."

"GOOD NIGHT . . . Chester," says pa with finality.

The short is punctuated with Fields's most famous running gag. Whether going in or out of the cabin, or just passing by, he stands at the doorway and says theatrically, "And it ain't a fit night out for man or beast!" as an unseen hand throws a fistful of artificial snow in his face. The gag gets funnier each time he does it, as the pointlessness of it all becomes more and more apparent. At the fade-out, Fields intones the phrase once more, recoiling just slightly as he waits for the snow that does not come.

The Fatal Glass of Beer is filled with a hundred little touches that allow the viewer to enjoy the film more each time he sees it, spotting some comic bit that had escaped notice the last time.

Fields's next short, *The Pharmacist,* was really a blueprint for his classic feature *It's a Gift.* In this short Fields has a dual personality; at home with his family, he is his usual nasty self (daughter Babe Kane complains that he doesn't love her. "Of course I love you," he says harshly as he threatens to slap her), but when he goes downstairs and assumes his role a proprietor of a small-town pharmacy, he not only becomes polite and agreeable, but does so to a preposterous extreme. He takes a telephone order for a box of cough drops and obligingly agrees to deliver it, as the customer gives him directions to travel the highway eighteen miles, make a left, etcetera. His biggest business, it seems, is in selling postage stamps at three cents apiece; but even here, success eludes him. A grumpy customer reluctantly agrees to buy one stamp and then insists that Fields give him one from the middle of the sheet. Anxious to please, the proprietor uses a pair of scissors to cut around the middle of the sheet and ruin a dozen others to supply the man with his one stamp, after which the fellow snaps, "Have you got change for a hundred dollar bill?" When Fields tells him no, the customer says he'll pay up the next time he drops in.

And so it goes during a typical day, as Fields nets a total of three cents for his day's work, and manages to give away three gigantic vases as "souvenirs" to each customer—two of whom have dropped in just to use the ladies' room.

Just as *The Dentist* typifies one side of the Fields screen character, the totally unpleasant man, *The Pharmacist* pinpoints the other, the victim, whom Fields was to portray in many of his later feature films—a man who has everything bad happen to him, but who manages to maintain a cheerful visage, even though the audience *knows* exactly what he is thinking and saying under his breath.

The final Fields-Sennett short, *The Barber Shop,* is the weakest, because it is the most conventional of the batch. Its gags for the most part could be carried out by any number of comics, and don't have as strong a tie to the Fields personality as those in the other two-reelers. There are distinctly Fieldsian gags, and a liberal dose of black humor (a dog sits patiently next to the barber chair ever since Fields cut a customer's ear off and the dog got it), but the comedy is decidedly tame when compared to the previous three endeavors.

Nevertheless, these four two-reel shorts present W. C. Fields in his purest form, creating *his* kind of humor, not someone else's filtered through a script. The attention to detail in *The Fatal Glass of Beer,* the variety of gags in *The Pharmacist,* the combination of verbal and visual humor in *The Dentist,* show what care and skill went into their production.

Fields had made shorts before, among them a notable 1930 two-reeler for RKO called *The Golf Specialist,* which stagily reprised his classic golfing routine; but these four Sennett shorts showed him at the height of his

Fields has a do-it-yourself generator in *The Barber Shop.*

powers. They continue to be shown today, and they remain, as ever, a group of true comedy gems.

W. C. Fields's Talkie Shorts

W. C. Fields made only five starring two-reel shorts in the sound era; they are indexed below. He appeared in one of Bobby Jones's golf shorts, *Hip Action,* two entries of Paramount's "Hollywood on Parade" series, and one episode of RKO's "Picture People," among other guest appearances. Fields also took screenplay credit for Sennett's 1933 short *The Singing Boxer,* with Donald Novis.

1. *The Golf Specialist.* RKO (8/22/30), Monte Brice. A recreation of Fields's classic vaudeville act in which his attempts to play golf are foiled by a series of minor calamities.

Ex-juggler Fields shows Bobby Jones that he hasn't lost his touch in one of Jones's golfing shorts, *Hip Action.*

2. *The Dentist.* Paramount-Sennett (12/9/32), Leslie Pearce. Babe Kane, Elise Cavanna, Zedna Farley, Bud Jamison, Dorothy Granger, Billy Bletcher, Bobby Dunn. Dentist Fields goes golfing in the morning, then returns to his office where he contends with an odd group of patients.

3. *The Fatal Glass of Beer.* Paramount-Sennett (3/3/33), Clyde Bruckman. Rosemary Theby, George Chandler, Richard Cramer. Fields's son returns to his home in the North Woods after serving a jail term.

4. *The Pharmacist.* Paramount-Sennett (4/21/33), Arthur Ripley. Babe Kane, Elise Cavanna, Grady Sutton, Lorema Carr. A typical day in Fields's drugstore. Original title: *The Druggist.*

5. *The Barber Shop.* Paramount-Sennett (7/28/33), Arthur Ripley. Elise Cavanna, Harry Watson, Dagmar Oakland, Frank Yaconelli. There is little peace during an afternoon at Cornelius O'Hare's barber shop.

Thelma Todd–ZaSu Pitts

Thelma Todd–Patsy Kelly

Scholars have been debating for years about what makes something funny. We will not presume to undertake such a discussion here, but there is one point to be made. Comediennes cannot use the same material as comedians and get the same results. Nowhere is this clearer than in the series of shorts produced by Hal Roach during the 1930s in whch he tried to create a "female Laurel and Hardy." Any success the shorts enjoy is due almost entirely to the incomparable personalities of their stars: Thelma Todd, ZaSu Pitts, and Patsy Kelly.

To an extent, the Hal Roach staff knew they were facing certain problems, and tried to create situations that were more suited to women than to men, but far too often they miscalculated. And when they had the girls engage in straight knockabout comedy, the results were often embarrassing.

What the shorts had more than anything else was charm. Thelma Todd, one of the all-time great beauties, also had a rare sense of humor; she was willing to do anything for a laugh, yet at all times she remained completely feminine. ZaSu Pitts was already a screen veteran at the time of these two-reelers, which built up the characterization of a slightly bewildered, not-too-bright young lady implied by the actress's famous fluttery trademarks. They provided the right contrast for a good comedy team, with wise girl Thelma generally having to get the two out of a situation caused by ZaSu's innocent ignorance.

Catch as Catch Can (1931), the duo's second short, is a perfect example of a winning comedy that succeeds without the kind of belly laughs one usually associates with two-reelers. ZaSu is disillusioned with city life until she meets prizefighter Guinn "Big Boy" Williams, who is from her home town of Joplin, Missouri. Meanwhile, Thelma falls in love with Williams's manager, Reed Howe. Guinn is getting homesick and has decided not to fight any more, but vows to do his best at the bout that night if he sees ZaSu in the audience, wearing her new hat. That evening, chaos erupts as ZaSu's hat gets knocked about and thrown from one corner of the arena to another.

The humor here is very mild, but enjoyable just the same, with the spotlight on ZaSu and "Big Boy" Williams. Unfortunately, the Roach people couldn't quite hit the same winning combination again, for none of the other shorts (even the successful ones) ever came close to this one for pure, wistful charm.

The Pajama Party, another early effort, showed that the girls could handle slapstick comedy very well. Staying at a swanky mansion, they are assigned French maids, and Thelma tries to rise to the occasion by acting as chic as possible. The effect is spoiled when she sashays into the bathroom and trips into a sunken bathtub full of water. Momentarily jarred, she looks up, laughs, and says coyly, "Imagine my embarrassment!"

On the Loose also included some funny slapstick material, but is more remarkable for a surprise gag at the end of the film. The only place the girls' boyfriends ever take them is Coney Island, and they are sick and tired of it. Their doorbell rings, and they answer it only to find two new suitors—Stan Laurel and Oliver Hardy! The boys ask the girls out for a date, and suggest that they might go to Coney Island, which results in a violent response from Thelma and ZaSu.

Various directors tried their hands at the comedies. One of the worst, oddly enough, was George Marshall. An extremely talented director with a broad comedy background, he should have known better than to put the girls into roughhouse, physical-comedy situations. Watching ZaSu get tangled up in a hospital cart along with Thelma, a cop, and two male orderlies simply isn't funny—and such protracted scenes abounded in Marshall's shorts with the team.

The best thing that happened to them was Gus Meins. Meins, a man with taste as well as skill was undoubtedly one of Hal Roach's best comedy directors, and he had a good sense of plot as well as of gags. His second short with Todd and Pitts, *Asleep in the Feet,* is one of their most delightful endeavors. To earn some money to help a neighbor who is about to be evicted, the girls take up Anita Garvin on her invitation to work at Billy Gilbert's dime-a-dance emporium. The evening is one long series of mishaps, climaxing when Anita decides to "doll up" ZaSu so she'll be more appealing to the clientele.

The best short the girls made, however, was directed by Charley Chase. *The Bargain of the Century* (1933) also features Billy Gilbert in a hilarious supporting role as a man the girls mistake for a police captain; in reality he's the notorious Schmaltz the Smuggler. The girls have caused policeman James Burtis to lose his job, and he's moved in with them. They think that by flattering "Captain" Gilbert they can reinstate Burtis and get rid of him for good. To amuse the captain, Burtis tries doing a magic trick with Gilbert's pocket watch. ZaSu is supposed to help him switch a fake one for the real item, and in doing so, inadvertently drops the genuine watch into her ice-cream batter. The mistake isn't discovered until later, when dessert is served and Thelma and Burtis

86

discover springs and other machinery as they eat the confection. Gilbert hasn't noticed anything yet, but as he scoops up a spoonful of ice cream, the watch case is revealed. Thelma and Burtis continue to plop more ice cream into his dish so he won't see it, and every time, Gilbert says politely (in his hilarious German dialect), "Zank you, but I don't vant any more ice cream." They persist, and he gets angrier. A major skirmish ensues, with Gilbert finally pleading, "With tears in my ears, I beg you . . . no more ice cream!" When the jig is up, he goes berserk, and the noise that results brings the police, and the realization that they've been treating a bogus captain all along.

Bargain of the Century is a perfect blend of slapstick, sight gag, and situation comedy, with the girls at their best and their supporting cast in top form. After one more two-reeler, however, ZaSu Pitts left the Roach studio, and Hal Roach sought a replacement. While in New York, he saw a hit Broadway musical called *Flying Colors* and invited one of its stars, Patsy Kelly, to come to Hollywood to costar with Thelma Todd.

The Kelly-Todd team was a joy to watch, with cultured, refined Thelma a perfect foil for headstrong, wisecracking Patsy. On the whole, their shorts had more snap than the Todd-Pitts comedies, although they missed the target quite often as well.

The first short in the new series was *Beauty and the Bus,* and Patsy Kelly recalls the hectic experience of shooting her first film. "They took me in a big limousine down to a theatre. And they gave me a little piece of paper, like a note. This was the script. I was supposed to come in the door, drop the ticket, hit my head on the seat, and then I win the raffle, whatever is going on on stage. This is the director saying, 'Now, Patsy, you hit your head, then you go up stage, grab this ticket, and you fall into the drum in the pit.' I said, 'I think you've got me mixed up wth Toto the Clown. . . . I have never fallen in my life.' So anyway, being a little nervous, and looking around, thinking, 'This is a crazy place,' I did it. Thelma was laughing, and she came over and said, 'You know, we have doubles.' I said, 'Now you tell me!' "

That was Patsy's initiation into two-reel comedies, but pretty soon she began to love working at the Roach studio. The enthusiasm comes across in the comedies. Their early films (not, coincidentally, directed by Gus Meins) are among their best: *Backs to Nature* has the girls going on a trouble-prone camping trip; in *Air Fright* they are stewardesses at odds with nutty inventor Don Barclay, who's devised a special ejector seat; and *Babes in the Goods* casts them as salesgirls in a department store who get locked in a display window overnight, much

The girls have an unexpected visitor when they go *Back to Nature*.

to the delight of perpetual-drunk Arthur Housman, who keeps a vigil on a fire hydrant all night so he can enjoy the show.

Later shorts run hot and cold, with some, like *The Misses Stooge* (where the girls are hired as assistants to magician Herman Bing), promising more than they deliver, and others, like *Slightly Static,* providing some unexpected surprises—here, some choice moments of Patsy tap-dancing. In *One Horse Farmers* Patsy falls for a salesman who convinces the girls that they should leave the city and move out to the country—"Heaven on earth," he proclaims. When they arrive at their new home, they find it to be the world's largest sand trap.

There was great harmony on the set of the two-reelers, and Patsy recalls that Stan Laurel "would come in and watch us shoot, and just quickly drop a suggestion that, of course, made the whole scene."

Probably the best Thelma Todd–Patsy Kelly short was their next-to-last one, *Top Flat* (1935). Its contagious sense of fun and gentle poke at pretentiousness keep it as fresh today as when it first came out. Thelma and Patsy break up because Thelma's insulted that her roommate doesn't appreciate her abstract poetry. She vows that some day she'll be living in a Park Avenue penthouse, and her books will be best sellers. The next time Patsy sees her old pal, she's emerging from a limousine, about to go into an exclusive store—she's the French maid to a couple on Park Avenue, but Patsy naturally thinks that Thelma has struck it rich. So that night she brings her two rowdy boyfriends (Fuzzy Knight and Garry Owen) to "Thelma's" apartment, where havoc reigns supreme until the real owners come home; there is much confusion, but finally the girls and their boyfriends make a hasty exit. Patsy's awed reaction to the ritzy apartment (the bathroom is so deluxe she can't resist taking a bath), the antics of the boyfriends, and the comedy of errors when the owners return make *Top Flat* a delight.

Alas, after one more two-reeler, the series came to an abrupt end with the tragic death of Thelma Todd—a death that remains to this day one of Hollywood's great unsolved mysteries. Even sadder is the fact that most people today know Thelma Todd only because of her death and not because of her beauty, vivacity, and great comic skill. These survive in her many films and overshadow any talk of scandal that has persisted over the years.

With one half of his starring team gone, Hal Roach sought to continue the series by first pairing Pert Kelton with Patsy in a comedy called *Pan Handlers*. Although Miss Kelton was a wonderful comedienne, she was forced to play it straight for the most part in this short, and the teaming didn't have the spark to make it a success. Then Roach teamed Patsy with the delightful Lyda Roberti—a teaming that *did* have some possibilities. These are shown to some extent in the two shorts they made, but much more so in the feature comedy *Nobody's Baby*. Sadly, Lyda Roberti also died very young, in 1938.

Patsy Kelly achieved lasting fame for her supporting roles in dozens of sprightly feature films of the 1930s and early 1940s. She was fortunate in having many fine showcases for her comic talent. But she has a special place in her heart for the two-reel comedies she did with Thelma Todd. "We all had such a good time I didn't feel right taking the money for them," she says.

This sense of fun always came across to the audience, and it carried even the lesser shorts in the series. It was a classic case of skilled performers overcoming weak material, and it was responsible for making the Thelma Todd–ZaSu Pitts and Thelma Todd–Patsy Kelly shorts something special in the 1930s.

The Thelma Todd–ZaSu Pitts Shorts

All the following were produced by Hal Roach and released by MGM; they are all two-reelers, except No. 1.

1. *Let's Do Things* (6/6/31). Hal Roach. George Byron, Jerry Mandy, Charlie Hall. In New York, ZaSu falls for a lunkhead, and drags Thelma on a double date to a nightclub. Three reels.

2. *Catch As Catch Can* (8/22/31). Marshall Neilan. Guinn "Big Boy" Williams, Reed Howes, Billy Gilbert. ZaSu falls in love with a prizefighter, and promises to be present at the arena that night wearing the hat he's given her.

An enticing production number cut from *Slightly Static*.

The girls, fleeing from a turkish bath, have hijacked Billy Gilbert's coat in *Red Noses*.

3. *The Pajama Party* (10/3/31). Hal Roach. Elizabeth Forrester, Eddie Dunn, Donald Novis, Billy Gilbert, Lucien Prival, Charlie Hall. After running the girls' car off the road, a society matron insists that the girls stay at her mansion for the evening.

4. *War Mamas* (11/14/31), Marshall Neilan. Charles Judels, Allan Lane, Guinn "Big Boy" Williams, Stuart Holmes, Carrie Daumery, Harry Schultz, Charlie Hall. During World War One, the girls become spies when they spend the evening with two German officers.

5. *On the Loose* (12/26/31). Hal Roach. John Loder, Claud Allister, William (Billy) Gilbert, Laurel and Hardy. Sick to death of Coney Island, the girls meet two young Britishers who take them out—to Coney Island.

6. *Seal Skins* (2/6/32). Gil Pratt, Morey Lightfoot. Charlie Hall, Leo Willis, Billy Gilbert. The girls hear that a Royal Seal has been stolen from a foreign country—and they go after a sea lion.

7. *Red Noses* (3/19/32), James W. Horne. Blanche Payson, Wilfred Lucas, Billy Gilbert. The girls go to a Turkish bath to work off a cold.

8. *Strictly Unreliable* (4/30/32). George Marshall. Billy Gilbert, Charlie Hall, Charlotte Nemo, Bud Jamison, Symona Boniface. ZaSu inadvertently stumbles onto the stage at the vaudeville theatre where Thelma is performing.

9. *The Old Bull* (6/4/32). George Marshall. Otto Fries, Robert Burns. The girls are stranded out in the country, where a lion is on the loose.

10. *Show Business* (8/20/32). Jules White. Anita Garvin, Monty Collins, Charlie Hall. The girls join a vaudeville troupe en route by train, and proceed (with their pet monkey) to disrupt everything. Remade with the Three Stooges as *A Pain in the Pullman*.

11. *Alum and Eve* (9/24/32). George Marshall. James C. Morton, Almeda Fowler. When the girls are stopped for speeding, Thelma says they're on their way to the hospital—and then has to prove it.

12. *The Soilers* (10/29/32) George Marshall. Bud Jamison, James C. Morton, Charlie Hall, George Marshall. The girls try selling magazine subscriptions door-to-door, but somehow get mistaken as anarchists in a judge's chambers.

13. *Sneak Easily* (12/10/32). Gus Meins. Robert Burns, James C. Morton, Billy Gilbert, Rolfe Sedan, Harry Bernard, Charlie Hall. While serving on a jury, ZaSu swallows Exhibit A— a time bomb.

14. *Asleep in the Fleet* (1/21/33). Gus Meins. Billy Gilbert, Eddie Dunn, Anita Garvin. To earn some money, the girls become taxi dancers for a night.

15. *Maids a la Mode* (3/4/33), Gus Meins. Billy Gilbert, Harry Bernard, Kay Deslys, Charlie Hall. The girls are supposed to deliver some dresses to a customer; instead, they wear them to a party.

16. *The Bargain of the Century* (4/9/33). Charley Chase. Billy Gilbert, James Burtis, Harry Bernard. The girls cost a cop his job; he moves in with them, and to get rid of him they try to get him rehired.

Temperamental actress Anita Garvin makes life miserable for ZaSu and Thelma in *Show Business*.

17. *One Track Minds* (5/20/33). Gus Meins. Billy Gilbert, Lucien Prival, Jack Clifford, Sterling Holloway, Charlie Hall, Spanky McFarland. Thelma wins a screen test with director Von Sternheim at Roaring Lion Studios, but the train ride out west finishes her career.

The Thelma Todd–Patsy Kelly Shorts

1. *Beauty and the Bus* (9/16/33). Gus Meins. Don Barclay, Charlie Hall, Tiny Sandford, Tommy Bond, Eddie Baker, Ernie Alexander, Robert McKenzie. The girls win a car at a movie raffle.

2. *Backs to Nature* (11/14/33). Gus Meins. Don Barclay, Charlie Hall. Patsy convinces Thelma that they should camp out in the woods for their vacation.

3. *Air Fright* (12/23/33). Gus Meins. Don Barclay, Billy Bletcher, Charlie Hall. The girls are stewardesses on an experimental flight.

4. *Babes in the Goods* (2/10/34). Gus Meins. Jack Barty,

ZaSu and Thelma hear the landlady approaching in *Asleep in the Feet.*

Arthur Housman, Charlie Hall, Fay Holderness. Demonstrating washing machines in a department store window, the girls get locked in for the night.

5. *Soup and Fish* (3/31/34). Gus Meins. Gladys Gale, Billy Gilbert, Don Barclay, Charlie Hall. The girls think they've been invited to a society party, which they proceed to disrupt.

6. *Maid in Hollywood* (5/19/34), Gus Meins. Eddie Foy, Jr., Don Barclay, Alphonse Martell, Charlie Hall, James C. Morton, Charles Rogers, Billy Bletcher, Ted Stroback, Carlton E. Griffin, Constance Bergen, Jack Barty, Billy Nelson. Patsy wrecks Thelma's screen test.

7. *I'll Be Suing You* (6/23/34). Gus Meins. Eddie Foy, Jr., Douglas Wakefield, Billy Nelson, Benny Baker, Charles Rogers, Charles McAvoy, William Wagner, Fred Kelsey, Mr. Miffin. After a slight auto accident, Patsy pretends to have a broken leg in order to collect insurance.

8. *Three Chumps Ahead* (7/14/34), Gus Meins. Benny Baker,

Charley Chase entertains Thelma between scenes on the Hal Roach lot.

Frank Moran, Eddie Phillips, Harry Bernard. Patsy keeps annoying Thelma and her boyfriend, so he gets his brother to escort Patsy when they all go out to dinner.

9. *One Horse Farmers* (9/1/34), Gus Meins. James C. Morton, Charlie Hall, Fred Holmes, Nora Cecil, Billy Bletcher, Jack "Tiny" Lipson. The girls buy a country home that turns out to be a sand trap.

10. *Opened by Mistake* (10/6/34). James Parrott. William Burress, Nora Cecil, Fanny Cossar, Charlie Hall, Ronald Rondell, Allen Caven, James Eagles, Rose Plummer, Virginia Crawford, Mary Egan, Robert McKenzie. Patsy tries to stay with Thelma at the hospital where she works, but Thelma is forced to pretend that Patsy is a patient.

11. *Done in Oil* (11/10/34). Gus Meins. Arthur Housman, Eddy Conrad, Leo White, William Wagner, Rolfe Sedan. Thelma tries to pass herself off as Madame LeTodd, a famous French painter.

12. *Bum Voyage* (12/15/34). Nick Grinde. Adrian Rosley, Constance Franke, Albert Petit, Germaine De Neel, Francis Sayles, Noah Young, Charles Gamorra. The girls find steamship tickets, not knowing that their cabin is also inhabited by a gorilla.

13. *Treasure Blues* (1/26/35). James Parrott. Sam Adams, Arthur Housman, Tiny Sandford, Charlie Hall, photo of James Finlayson. Patsy inherits a treasure map, so the girls go out to sea to claim the loot.

14. *Sing, Sister, Sing* (3/2/35). James Parrott. Arthur Housman, Harry Bowen, Charlie Hall, Barbara Webster. As the girls become roommates, they agree to sing a song every time one of them gets angry.

15. *The Tin Man* (3/30/35). James Parrott. Matthew Betz, Clarence Wilson, voice of Billy Bletcher. Thelma and Patsy wander into a spooky old house inhabited by a crazy man and his woman-hating robot.

16. *The Misses Stooge* (4/20/35). James Parrott. Herman Bing, Esther Howard, Rafael Storm, Adrian Rosley, Harry Bayfield, Harry Bowen, Henry Roquemore, James C. Morton, Ward Shattuck. Patsy gets a job as assistant to magician Professor Zazarak, and Thelma is hired as his "stooge."

17. *Slightly Static* (9/7/35). William Terhune. Harold Waldridge, Dell Henderson, Ben Taggart, Louis Natheaux, Sydney de Grey, Eddie Craven, Kay Hughes, Aileen Carlyle, Dorothy Francis, Harry Bowen, Nora Cecil, Carlton E. Griffin, Bobby Burns, Elinor Vandivere, Lorene Carr, Carl Le Viness, Brooks Benedict, Randall Sisters, The Vitaphone Four, Sons of the Pioneers (including Roy Rogers). The girls get their chance to work at radio station LOCO when the regular stock company refuses to perform a sickly play the president's son has written.

18. *Twin Triplets* (10/12/35). William Terhune. John Dilson, Greta Meyer, Bess Flowers, Billy Bletcher, Charlie Hall. The girls, reporters in search of a story, hear that a woman has given birth to sextuplets at the local hospital.

19. *Hot Money* (11/16/35). James W. Horne. James Burke, Fred Kelsey, Hooper Atchley, Louis Natheaux, Brooks Benedict, Charlie Hall, Sherry Hall, Anya Tiranda, Lee Prather, Lee Phelps,

Patsy is an unwilling model for artist Thelma in *Done in Oil*.

Thelma and Patsy strike a pose from *Maid in Hollywood*.

Monty Vandegrift. A thief dumps his stolen money in the girls' apartment.

20. *Top Flat* (12/21/35). William Terhune and Jack Jevne. Grace Goodall, Fuzzy Knight, Ferdinand Munier, Gary Owen, Harry Bernard. Patsy and her boyfriends come to visit Thelma in the penthouse apartment where she works as a maid.

21. *All-American Toothache* (1/25/36). Gus Meins. Mickey Daniels, Johnny Arthur, Duke York, Dave Sharpe, Charlie Hall, Ben Hall, Bud Jamison, Billy Bletcher, Ernie Alexander, Ray Cooke, Si Jenks, Sue Gomes, Manny Vezie, Buddy Messinger. Thelma volunteers Patsy as a subject for dental-student Mickey.

After Thelma Todd's death, she was replaced by Pert Kelton, then Lyda Roberti, for three final shorts:

1. *Pan Handlers* (2/29/36). William Terhune. Grace Goodall, Rosina Lawrence, David Sharpe, Harry Bowen, Willie Fung, Larry Steers. Pert and Patsy try selling aluminum ware door to door.

2. *At Sea Ashore* (4/4/36). William Terhune. Al Shean, Robert Emmet O'Connor, Joe Twerp, The Avalon Boys (including Chill Wills), Harry Bowen, Fred Kelsey. Patsy goes to meet Lyda at the dock, and is mistaken for an immigrant herself.

3. *Hill Tillies* (4/24/36), Gus Meins. Toby Wing, Harry Bowen, Jim Thorpe, Sam Adams, James C. Morton. Lyda and Patsy try to camp out in the woods for several weeks as a publicity stunt.

Andy Clyde

You don't think of Andy Clyde when the topic of great comedians comes up. To be sure, he doesn't rate next to Keaton or Chaplin in terms of artistry or creativity. But Andy Clyde was a talented, versatile comedian whose popularity endured over four decades and who was as well liked by his colleagues as he was by his audiences.

Born in Blairgowrie, Scotland, Andy grew up in a show-business atmosphere. His father was a producer and manager, and Andy went into the theatre when he was quite young. There he met another young Scotsman named James Finlayson who, the story goes, was responsible for getting Andy into the movies. Finlayson emigrated to America, and, by 1919, was working for Mack Sennett. He encouraged his old friend to join him in California and set him up at the Sennett studios. Clyde started out playing bit roles, but his uncanny talent for makeup made him a natural for any supporting part in need of an actor.

Through the 1920s, Clyde became one of the mainstays on the Sennett lot, playing everything from young slickers to old geezers—each equally unrecognizable as Andy Clyde. He hit his stride in a series of two-reelers costarring Billy Bevan; these lightning-paced sight-gag comedies (*Whispering Whiskers, Circus Today, Ice Cold Cocos*) are among the finest and fastest silent comedies of all time.

In the late 1920s, Andy developed the makeup for which he is best remembered. It was described by Sam Gill and Kalton Lahue as "tousled hair and stubble of a beard-to-be (typically the product of absentmindedness), a large 'gay nineties' mustache, and a pair of bifocals that emphasized both his age and embarrassment as he raised his eyebrows, peering sheepishly over the rims."

The amiable hayseed characterization that went along with the makeup came into full flower with Sennett's first talking pictures in 1929. With the coming of sound, Andy became Sennett's top star, and although he was required to do double duty by playing supporting roles in other comedies, he was finally given star billing in his own series of two-reelers.

Andy's character was named Ed "Pop" Martin, and although he was technically the star, he seldom carried the weight of the comedies alone. "Pop" was almost always having trouble with a daughter who wanted to elope, so the footage alternated between the young couple and the concerned father. But Andy had all the footage he needed to do his stuff. His sequences as a dean being seduced in *College Vamp,* a would-be inventor who goes cross-country on a rocket locomotive in *The Cannonball,* a veterinarian who tries to crash society in *The Dog Doctor,* a theatre manager in *A Hollywood Star,* and half of the Hollywood producing team of McIntosh and Horowitz in *In Conference* ànd *Monkey Business in Africa* were proof of his comic skill.

Some of the Sennett two-reelers were considered first-rate by most of the contemporary reviewers, for various reasons. *Hello Television* (1930) wowed everyone at the time because of its ingenious gimmick of a boy-meets-girl story told with the twist of having them meet via television. Andy, of course, played the irate father. *Don't Bite Your Dentist* (1930) was hailed as a return to the old-time Sennett slapstick—something of a puzzlement, since Sennett was using such slapstick all through his talkie comedies. In *In Conference,* producers McIntosh and Horowitz sign the romantic star Romaine Salisbury (Harry Gribbon) for a whopping one million dollars, only to discover that his voice sounds like "an asthmatic frog." In *Monkey Business in Africa,* the producing team is called McIntosh and Gonzola (the latter played by Luis Alberni), and the duo film their picture, *Gorilla Love,* in "the wilds of Africa."

Andy was easily the busiest man on the Sennett lot, making approximately seventeen comedies a year during the early sound years. The quality, of course, varied, not only because of the pace, but because various directors and writers took turns preparing the films. Andy had the good fortune to work not only with Sennett, but with two of his best comic directors, Eddie Cline and Del Lord. Lord continued to work with Andy through the late 1940s at Columbia, where both found it helpful to hark back to the Sennett days for ideas.

Although Sennett was fond of Clyde, the two were frequently embroiled in disputes over working conditions and contracts, and finally, at the end of 1932, Clyde walked out. His latest comedies, such as *Shopping with Wifie* and *Speed in the Gay '90s,* had been very good, and his popularity was at a peak, so Andy had no trouble moving over to Educational Pictures, where he continued to make two-reelers without interruption.

One of Andy's Educational two-reelers is a delightful film called *Dora's Dunkin' Donuts.* It occupies a special niche in film history because it costars little Shirley Temple, just on the threshold of her biggest success. The plot has schoolteacher Andy and his musical students going on the radio to promote the doughnuts made by Andy's sweetheart, Dora. Andy even sings a commercial jingle, accompanied by the class: "Dora's Dunkin' Donuts/Dora's Dunkin' Donuts/We'll have you know/They float!" Naturally, Shirley is the most precocious youngster in the class, and when Andy tries to tell a children's story as part of the radio broadcast, she continually interrupts to ask questions.

Andy's stay at Educational was brief; in 1934 he moved to the newly formed Columbia Pictures comedy unit and remained with it for more than twenty years. At Columbia he was no longer supporting anyone; he was the focus of attention in the comedies, and he was invariably good. The beauty of his characterization (and makeup), of course, was that he was able to use it for such a long time. He started to play an old man when he was young and just grew into the role, until, near the end of the series, he was using hardly any makeup at all.

Andy and Dorothy Granger are like two lovebirds in *Shopping with Wifie.*

Nothing ever topped the initial comedies Andy made for Columbia. His two-reelers from the mid-1930s are unquestionably his best, and while there were some good ones later, they never reached this level on a regular basis. For the most part, they were much more standardized than his earlier, fast-paced, freewheeling efforts.

In the Dog House (1934) has Andy married to battle-axe Vivien Oakland, who fawns over her poodle ChiChi but can't stand Andy's grandson, who's come to live with them. When she catches him trying to steal a pie, she whips him, and the pie is hurled up in the air, where it sticks to the ceiling. Andy comes in and the boy runs out; then Vivien begins to tell him how sad she is because he isn't romantic any more. He protests that he loves her as much as ever, and he takes her in his arms, throwing her head back dramatically to kiss her. Just then the pie falls down from the ceiling and lands smack in her face!

In *Alimony Aches* (1935), Vivien is back, this time as Andy's *ex*-wife. She's remarried, but when she sees that Andy's also taken a new bride (Jan Duggan), she decides to gouge him for back alimony—failing to inform him that she's got a new husband. She moves in on Andy and spouse during their honeymoon, and, with the help of her bratty son (Tommy Bond), makes herself as obnoxious as possible. The battle between the wives reaches a climax when Andy is taken ill, and the two of them nearly tear him apart trying to nurse him, each in her own way.

As explained before, part of the beauty of 1930s comedies is that the companies still shot on location and went to a lot of trouble for a good sight gag—qualities that were abandoned for the most part in the 1940s. *Peppery Salt* (1936) is not an especially good comedy, but it does contain one of the funniest sight gags ever seen. In it, Andy is told that he's inherited the *Admiral Dewey*. Yearning for a life at sea, he buys himself a full admiral's regalia to take command. The *Admiral Dewey* turns out to be a lunch counter by the dock. He goes into business and, the first day, decides to nail a sign reading "Andy Clyde, Skipper" to the rear wall of his diner. But he unwittingly drives his long nails through the wall of his diner and into a ship docked along the pier. The ship soon pulls out and takes the lunch stand and its foundation with it! One customer pays for his lunch, and says good-bye. "Drop in again soon," calls Andy as the fellow steps off the counter platform and falls into the water below. It's a fantastically elaborate gag—and what is best, it's *real*.

Caught in the Act and *It Always Happens* maintain a brisk pace full of outstanding gags throughout; both were directed by Del Lord. In *Caught in the Act,* Andy gets tangled up with the notorious Jack the Kisser (John T. Murray). The two are accidentally handcuffed together, and, as Murray tries to escape (on motorcycle, through buildings, sliding on telephone wires and such) Andy is obliged to go with him. *It Always Happens* is a remake of a Sennett comedy Andy made called *Taxi Troubles.* There's nothing special in the plot—Andy's suspicious wife and sister-in-law trail him on a business trip, where he becomes innocently involved with the pretty wife of

his new client, who is insanely jealous. But the pacing is so fast, the gags so neat, and the cast so exuberant that it all seems fresh. At one point Andy closes his car door on the client's wife's dress and begins to drive away, leaving her (Geneva Mitchell) standing on the sidewalk in her lingerie. She hops into the back seat of his car and, before either of them know what's happening, her husband (Bud Jamison) has invited himself for a ride with Andy and sits in the front seat.

To confuse matters more, Andy doesn't know that the two are man and wife until Geneva writes a note to him and holds it up to the rearview mirror. Andy sees it and nearly faints; then he hits upon a scheme. He pretends to be drunk, and drives crazily around street corners, narrowly missing other cars, the sidewalk, lampposts, etcetera, to force Bud to bail out at the first opportunity (which he does). Del Lord was known for his prowess with car scenes, and this comedy bears out that reputation.

Without a doubt, Andy's most disappointing Columbia shorts were a pair directed by Charley Chase in the late 1930s. *Ankles Away* is a remake of Chase's classic silent comedy *His Wooden Wedding,* about a bridegroom who is told by a rival, just before the wedding, that his wife-to-be has a wooden leg. In the Chase silent, it was hilarious material, but somehow, in the remake, it seemed oddly tasteless and unfunny. The second Chase-directed short, *The Old Raid Mule,* was supposedly based on an *Esquire* story, although one wonders how. It's a plotless two reels built around the rivalry of Andy and Olin Howland out in hill country. It's the type of comedy in which, as one observer put it, "it seems they expected to get laughs with the makeup."

The 1940s saw Andy's comedies becoming more standardized. His most frequent screen wife was shrewish Esther Howard, and for a while Shemp Howard was cast as his despicable brother-in-law. The results, in such films as *Boobs in the Woods,* were predictable.

One of Andy's best comedies from 1940 was one of his most atypical. Called *Andy Clyde Gets Spring Chicken* (after the popular feature *Andy Hardy Gets Spring Fever*), it cast Andy as a young-at-heart millionaire who goes girl crazy every spring. Luck of luck, a bevy of beauties has moved in next door and Andy goes over and tries to get somewhere with them. They get a kick out of the old guy, but, one by one, give him the brush-off. Then someone tells the girls that they've been talking to a millionaire, and they start to pounce on him, literally fighting over which one will accept his marriage proposal! (One of the film's more offbeat ideas has an Amazonian girl in the group who speaks with a deep bass voice.)

Unfortunately, such breezy comedies were the excep-

Andy is a would-be playboy in *Andy Clyde Gets Spring Chicken*. The den mother is Eva McKenzie, the brunette on his left is Dorothy Appleby.

Andy clobbers Bud Jamison, but he meant the punch for Shemp Howard.

tion rather than the rule in Andy Clyde's 1940s output. The gags and plots got more repetitious and the humor more physical—especially in the violence-prone comedies directed by Jules White.

Some of the repetition was literal, for, like the other Columbia comics from the late 1940s onward, Clyde was forced to do remakes and patchwork films using stock footage. One film, *A Blissful Blunder* (1952), is an outrageous "remake" of *A Bundle of Bliss* (1940) with a ratio of about nine to one of old footage to new. Jules White went so far as to hire Fred Kelsey, who had been in the 1940 film, to do a few new scenes—but very few. Still, one can only marvel at the ingenuity that went into putting these crazy quilts together.

Andy Clyde continued to make two-reelers into the late 1950s, including a pair of comedies with Gil Lamb at RKO, after which he found a welcome spot in television as a regular on "The Real McCoys," with Walter Brennan, and, later on, "No Time for Sergeants." He remained active until his death in 1967.

A thorough professional, Andy always did the best job possible, and he earned the respect of all his coworkers. Ed Bernds, who directed him in the 1940s, called him "a delight," echoing the sentiments of many others. And perhaps the secret of Andy Clyde's success, a formula followed by so many other comedians of this era, was that he truly loved his work.

Andy Clyde's Talkie Shorts

This list is complete as far as Andy Clyde's two-reelers are concerned. It does not include his guest appearances in such shorts as "The Voice of Hollywood" and "Screen Snapshots." It is worth noting that while Educational Pictures was releasing Mack Sennett's talking comedies in 1929, Pathé was still issuing new silent shorts that Sennett had made before leaving the company; this index includes only the talkies. To distinguish between the Sennett shorts released by Educational and those actually produced by Educational, the former group will be identified only as "Sennett." David Turconi's excellent Sennett filmography in his book *Mack Sennett* lists Andy Clyde as being in the cast of the first Sennett talkie short, *The Lion's Roar,* but it seems that he juxtaposed the cast of the second short, *The Bride's Relations,* by accident, for Clyde appears only in the latter. Turconi also lists some shorts that do not exist—apparently using working titles or different translations.

1. *The Bride's Relations.* Sennett (1/13/29), Mack Sennett. Johnny Burke, Harry Gribbon, Thelma Hill, Louise Carver, Sunshine Hart, Ruth Kane. Johnny and Thelma spend their honeymoon with their country cousins.

2. *The Old Barn*. Sennett (2/16/29), Mack Sennett. Johnny Burke, Daphne Pollard, Thelma Hill, Vernon Dent, Irving Bacon, Dave Morris, Ruth Kane. The folks encounter what appears to be a haunted barn.

3. *Whirls and Girls*. Sennett (2/24/29), Mack Sennett. Harry Gribbon, Dot Farley, Ruth Kane. Harry and Andy get involved with a group of flappers.

4. *The Bee's Buzz*. Sennett (4/7/29), Mack Sennett. Harry Gribbon, Thelma Hill, Dot Farley. Harry and Andy get tangled up in a hornet's nest while trying to thwart Andy's daughter's marriage.

5. *The Big Palooka*. Sennett (5/12/29), Mack Sennett. Harry Gribbon, Thelma Hill, Addie McPhail. A shotgun wedding takes place.

6. *Girl Crazy*. Sennett (6/9/29), Mack Sennett. Vernon Dent, Alma Bennett, Thelma Hill. Aging Andy goes after a young girl and gets quite a run for his money.

7. *The Barber's Daughter*. Sennett (7/21/29), Mack Sennett. Thelma Hill, Vernon Dent. Keeping track of his daughter's romances has Andy on his toes.

8. *The Constabule*. Sennett (8/11/29), Mack Sennett. Thelma Hill, Harry Gribbon. Harry, a cop, wrongly accuses Andy and Thelma's fiancé of robbery.

9. *The Lunkhead*. Sennett (9/1/29), Mack Sennett. Harry Gribbon, Thelma Hill, Addie McPhail, Patsy O'Leary. Thelma tries to get rid of Harry, who's in love with her.

10. *The Golfers*. Sennett (9/22/29), Mack Sennett. Harry Gribbon, Thelma Hill, Patsy O'Leary, Bert Swor, Charlie Guest. Professional golfer Guest shows the others the right way to play golf.

11. *A Hollywood Star*. Sennett (10/13/29), Mack Sennett. Harry Gribbon, Marjorie Beebe, Patsy O'Leary, Bert Swor. A ham cowboy star comes to a premiere of his first talking picture—a total disaster.

12. *Clancy at the Bat*. Sennett (11/3/29), Earle Rodney. Harry Gribbon, Patsy O'Leary. Harry is a baseball star much in need of practice.

13. *The New Halfback*. Sennett (11/24/29), Mack Sennett. Harry Gribbon, Marjorie Beebe, Bert Swor, Wade Boteler, Patsy O'Leary. College dean Andy is forced to put Harry on his football team.

14. *Uppercut O'Brien*. Sennett (12/5/29), Earle Rodney. Harry Gribbon, Marjorie Beebe, Bert Swor, James Leong. Andy's star fighter Harry walks out on him, returns later as a self-proclaimed champ.

15. *Scotch*. Sennett (1/19/30), Mack Sennett. Billy Bevan,

Movie magic at work: Andy, Fred Kelsey, and Dorothy Appleby in the 1940 comedy *A Bundle of Bliss* . . .

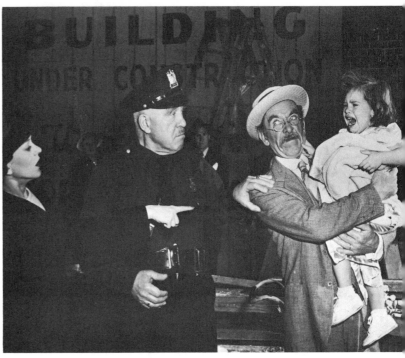

. . . and a re-creation of the same scene twelve years later, with Ruth Godfrey replacing Dorothy Appleby, Fred Kelsey in his old role. The new title: *A Blissful Blunder*.

Addie McPhail, Ernie Wood. Andy and Billy sample too much bathtub booze.

16. *Sugar Plum Papa.* Sennett (2/16/30), Mack Sennett. Harry Gribbon, Daphne Pollard, Marjorie Beebe, Bud Jamison, Rosemary Theby, Bert Swor, Charles Darvis. Daphne marries wealthy Andy with an ulterior motive.

17. *Bulls and Bears.* Sennett (3/2/30), Mack Sennett. Marjorie Beebe, Daphne Pollard, Bud Jamison, Rosemary Theby. Seeing Bud's success, Andy's wife Daphne decides to invest in the stock market.

18. *Match Play.* Sennett (3/16/30), Mack Sennett. Walter Hagen, Leo Diegel, Marjorie Beebe, Bud Jamison. Golf pros Hagen and Diegel match their expertise against the antics of Andy and Marjorie.

19. *Radio Kisses.* Sennett (5/4/30), Leslie Pearce. Marjorie Beebe, Nick Stuart, George Duryea, Rita Carewe, Tom Keene. Marjorie does an advice-to-the-lovelorn radio show, but needs help herself. In color.

20. *Fat Wives for Thin.* Sennett (5/25/30), Mack Sennett. Marjorie Beebe, George Barraud, Aggie Herring, William Davidson, Patsy O'Leary. Marjorie gains so much weight that her husband starts paying more attention to other girls.

21. *Campus Crushes.* Sennett (6/15/30), Mack Sennett. Marjorie Beebe, Nick Stuart, Patsy O'Leary. Andy disapproves of Marjorie's crush on Nick, but he proves himself worthy.

22. *The Chumps.* Sennett (7/6/30), Mack Sennett. Marjorie Beebe, Franklin Pangborn, Bud Jamison, Miami Alvarez, Lew Kelly, Patsy O'Leary, Maurice Black. Newlyweds Marjorie and Franklin fall into the hands of crooks.

23. *Goodbye Legs.* Sennett (7/27/30), Mack Sennett. Nick Stuart, Daphne Pollard, Ann Christy, Will Hays, Vernon Dent, Tom Dempsey, Patsy O'Leary. Producer Andy's son Nick hires a girl for their show, falls in love with her; Andy mistakenly thinks she has bad legs and fires her.

24. *Hello, Television.* Sennett (8/17/30), Leslie Pearce. Ann Christy, Nick Stuart, Julia Griffith. In this futuristic comedy, Andy's daughter meets her boyfriend via a television-telephone.

25. *Average Husband.* Sennett (9/7/30), Mack Sennett. Natalie Moorehead, Albert Conti, Pat O'Malley, Patsy O'Leary. Natalie tries to make her husband look impressive to her ex-boyfriend.

26. *Vacation Loves.* Sennett (9/28/30), Mack Sennett. Betty Boyd, Ben Bard, Patsy O'Leary, John Darrow. While vacationing at the shore, Andy falls prey to man-chasing Mrs. Smith-Brown-Jones.

27. *The Bluffer.* Sennett (9/28/30), No director credited. Patsy O'Leary, Lincoln Stedman, Gaylord Pendleton. Andy insists that his daughter's husband must be brave—and is taken in by a phony. Color: one reel.

28. *Grandma's Girl.* Sennett (10/12/30), Mack Sennett. Florence Roberts, Margie "Babe" Kane, Nick Stuart, Lincoln Stedman, Patsy O'Leary. Old-fashioned Andy is knocked for a loop when his modern-thinking mother moves in and sides with his daughter on her love life.

29. *Take Your Medicine.* Sennett (10/26/30), Edward Cline. Patsy O'Leary, Vernon Dent, Frank Eastman. Andy can't escape The California Crooner, especially when he falls in love with Andy's daughter. One reel: color.

30. *Don't Bite Your Dentist.* Sennett (11/9/30), Edward Cline. Daphne Pollard, Patsy O'Leary, Lincoln Stedman, Julia Griffith, Don Rader, Jerry Ziers. Dentist Andy's daughter wants to elope.

31. *Racket Cheers.* Sennett (11/23/30), Mack Sennett. Daphne Pollard, Charles Irwin, Marjorie Beebe, Patsy O'Leary, Cyril Chadwick, Julia Griffith. Mr. and Mrs. Clyde are newly rich, and try to marry their daughter into society, before discovering their neighbors are rumrunners.

32. *No, No, Lady.* Sennett (1/4/31), Edward Cline. Dorothy Christy, Frank Eastman, Cyril Chadwick, Bud Jamison. Andy's actress wife tests him for his reaction when she say she's got a lover.

33. *The College Vamp.* Sennett (2/15/31), William Beaudine. Yola D'Arvil, Patsy O'Leary. The college kids put their fuddy-duddy dean Andy into a compromising position with their alluring drama coach.

34. *The Dog Doctor.* Sennett (3/15/31), Phil Whitman. Patsy O'Leary, Dot Farley, Will Stanton, Billy Barty. Andy's wife convinces him to give up his veterinary practice so she can crash society.

35. *Just a Bear.* Sennett (3/29/31), Babe Stafford. Harry Gribbon, Patsy O'Leary. To win over his prospective father-in-law, Harry takes Andy to the woods for a hunting trip.

36. *In Conference.* Sennett (4/26/31), Edward Cline. Harry Gribbon, George Wilson, Marion Sayers, Patsy O'Leary. Producers McIntosh and Horowitz sign romantic Romaine Salisbury for one million dollars, then find out his voice is terrible.

37. *The Cow-Catcher's Daughter.* Sennett (5/10/31), Babe Stafford. Harry Gribbon, Marjorie Beebe, Frank Eastman. Rancher Andy can't control his capricious daughter.

38. *Ghost Parade.* Sennett (5/24/31), Mack Sennett. Harry Gribbon, Marjorie Beebe, Frank Eastman, Marion Sayers. Andy owns a haunted house, and is exposed to its spooks while showing it to some buyers.

39. *Monkey Business in Africa.* Sennett (6/21/31), Mack Sennett. Marjorie Beebe, Frank Eastman, Luis Alberni. McIntosh and Gonzola go to Africa to film "Gorilla Love," their latest epic.

40. *Fainting Lover.* Sennett (8/16/31), Mack Sennett. Vernon Dent, Addie McPhail, Ann Hernandez, Wade Boteler. Andy tries to help Boteler woo his daughter, but she's not interested.

41. *Too Many Husbands.* Sennett (8/30/31), Leslie Pearce. Irene Thompson, Joe [E.] Lewis, Jimmy Harrison, Patsy O'Leary. Andy's honeymoon is upset by the appearance of Andy's son, with his fiancée and her uncle—who turns out to be his bride's first husband.

42. *The Cannonball.* Sennett (9/6/31), Del Lord. Ann Hernandez, Irene Thompson, Lew Sargent, George Grey, Vernon Dent. Andy attaches his rocket invention to a locomotive in order to win a race with a bus. Remade as *Fireman, Save My Choo Choo.*

43. *Speed.* Sennett (9/27/31), Mack Sennett. Marjorie Beebe, Alberta Vaughn, Frank Eastman, Walter Weems, Cyril Chadwick, Marion Sayers. If Andy's flivver can go coast to coast faster than a plane, his daughter will get to marry a gridiron star.

44. *Taxi Troubles.* Sennett (10/18/31), Del Lord. Ruth Hiatt, Rosemary Theby, Walter Long, Blanche Payson. Cabbie Andy inadvertently gets mixed up with the wife of a gangster. Partially remade as *It Always Happens.*

45. *All-American Kickback.* Sennett (11/29/31), Del Lord. Harry Gribbon, Marjorie Beebe. Harry is a would-be football star.

46. *Half Holiday.* Sennett (12/13/31), Babe Stafford. Alice Ward, Patsy O'Leary, William Davidson, Dorothy Granger. Hopelessly henpecked Andy decides to "step out," but the consequences are disastrous.

47. *Shopping with Wifie.* Sennett (2/7/32), Babe Stafford. Dorothy Granger, Fred Kelsey, Arthur Stone, Snowflake, Blackie Whiteford, Ethel LaBlanche, Marvin Lobach. Andy is supposed to go on a fishing trip, but he encounters endless delays with his lovey-dovey wife.

48. *Heavens! My Husband.* Sennett (3/6/32), Babe Stafford. Dorothy Granger, George Byron, Bud Jamison, Ward Cawlfield, Allan Lane, Opal Gangle. Andy and Dorothy's Niagara Falls honeymoon is disrupted by a kibitzer.

49. *Speed in the Gay '90s.* Sennett (4/3/32), Del Lord. Barney Oldfield, Helen Mann, Joe Young, Anna Hernandez, Delmar Watson, Marvin Loback. Inventor Andy tries to win a State-Fair race with his tin lizzie.

50. *The Boudoir Butler.* Sennett (5/28/32), Leslie Pearce. Irene Thompson, Joe Donohue, Tom Kennedy. Andy's wife is playing up to her new employers, unaware that they are crooks.

51. *Alaska Love.* Sennett (7/17/32), Babe Stafford. Matt McHugh, Irene Thompson, James Murray, Pat Wing. Andy sends his wife to Alaska on vacation, then finds that her former boyfriend is also going there!

52. *For the Love of Ludwig.* Sennett (7/24/32), Emil Harberger. Wade Boteler, Addie McPhail, Vernon Dent. Andy tries to help a rejected suitor when the man's girl marries her music teacher.

53. *His Royal Shyness.* Sennett (7/28/32), Leslie Pearce. Dorothy Granger, Richard Cramer, Knute Ericson. A spoof of *The Prisoner of Zenda,* with Andy recruited to take the place of his lookalike, the kidnapped King of Bullgravia.

54. *The Giddy Age.* Sennett (9/25/32), Babe Stafford. Dorothy Granger, Franklin Pangborn, Albert Conti, Bud Jamison. Sharpsters use an alluring girl to get Andy in a compromising position so they can blackmail him.

55. *Sunkissed Sweeties.* Educational (10/30/32), Harry Edwards. Vernon Dent, Faye Pierre, Monty Collins, Thelma Hill, Stanley Blystone. Judge Andy is appointed bathing-suit censor in town.

56. *A Fool About Women.* Educational (11/27/32), Harry Edwards. Faye Pierre, Vernon Dent, Fern Emmett, Tom Dempsey, Melbourne McDowell. Andy visits an old friend, who remembers him as a ladies' man; to be safe, the friend sends his wife away —but Andy meets her en route.

57. *Boy, Oh, Boy.* Educational (12/25/32), Harry Edwards. Gwen Lee, James Finlayson, Gertie Messinger, Ted O'Shea, Fern Emmett, Charles K. French, Edward LeSaint. During Father-and-Son Week, Andy cuts loose to show up an old rival.

58. *Artists Muddles.* Educational (1/29/33), Harry Edwards. Vernon Dent, Luis Alberni, Faye Pierre. Andy is mistaken for an artist by Mr. and Mrs. Cellini, who have commissioned her portrait.

59. *Feeling Rosy.* Educational (4/30/33), Harry Edwards. Lita Chevret, Faye Pierre, Les Goodwin, Edward LeSaint, Eddie Baker, Richard Powell. Andy, thinking he's inherited fifty-thousand dollars, becomes a new man.

60. *Loose Relations.* Educational (6/11/33), Harry Edwards. Lita Chevret, Blanche Payson, Bud Jamison, Lee Auburn, Bobby Dunn, "Prince Barry." Andy's mother-in-law visits for the first time, and it becomes a battle royal.

61. *Big Squeal.* Educational (7/9/33), Charles Lamont. Billy Bevan, Ethel Sykes, Dorothy Christy, Bud Jamison, Charles K. French. Andy thinks an old friend has married his ex-sweetheart.

62. *Dora's Dunkin' Donuts.* Educational (9/1/33), Harry Edwards. Shirley Temple, Ethel Sykes, Bud Jamison, Florence Gill, Meglin Kiddies Band. Andy and his musically minded school class go on the radio to promote his sweetheart's donut business.

63. *His Weak Moment.* Educational (10/13/33), Harry Edwards. Cecelia Parker, Bruce Riley, Fern Emmett, Esther Muir, Spec O'Donnell, Bud Jamison. Andy, entrusted with a lot of money, is wooed by the town vamp.

64. *Frozen Assets.* Educational (11/17/33), Harry Edwards. Eddie Phillips, Harry Bradley, Cecelia Parker, Fern Emmett, Josephine Hall, Spec O'Donnell. Andy gives money to a bogus director to film his screenplay.

65. *An Old Gypsy Custom.* Educational (1/12/34), Harry Edwards. John Sheehan, Addie McPhail, Lloyd Hamilton, Cecelia Parker, Fern Emmett, Spec O'Donnell, Betty Boyd, Chiquita de Montes. A gypsy caravan comes to town and sweeps Andy off his feet.

66. *Super Snooper.* Educational (2/9/34), Harry Edwards. Jason Robards, Dorothy Dix, Arthur Hoyt, Addie McPhail, Jack Norton, Broderick O'Farrell, Harold Berquist. Andy decides to investigate his daughter's prospective husband.

67. *Hello, Prosperity.* Educational (4/30/34), Charles Lamont. Ethel Sykes, Jack Shutta, Josef Swickard. After fifteen years, Andy decides to marry an old sweetheart—who is about to be wed to Andy's new boss.

68. *Half-Baked Relations.* Educational (6/1/34), Charles Lamont. Jack Shutta, Ethel Sykes, Ed LeSaint, Broderick O'Farrell. Andy is on trial for striking his brother-in-law with a wrench, and he explains how it came about. Remade as *Not Guilty Enough.*

69. *It's the Cat's.* Columbia (10/11/34), Al Ray. Dorothy Granger, Inez Courtney, Kay Hughes, Ceil Duncan, Frances Morris, Mary Foy, Bill Irving, Raymond Brown. Andy has to take his boss's place as guest speaker for a woman's cat-fanciers group.

70. *In the Dog House.* Columbia (12/1/34), Arthur Ripley. Vivien Oakland, Delmar Watson. Andy's grandson gets even with Andy's new wife by sending her dog to the dog pound.

71. *I'm a Father.* Columbia (2/7/35), James Horne. Lillian Elliott, Geneva Mitchell, Ferdinand Munier, Robert Allen, Inez Courtney, Allyn Drake, Mary Gordon, Grace Goodall, Phil Dunham, Louise Carver, Bess Flowers, Frank Yaconelli, Billy Engle, Charles Dorety, Evelyn Pierce, Phyllis Crane, Beulah Hutton, Sally Tead, Jack Kenney. Andy hates kids, until he thinks his wife is pregnant.

72. *Old Sawbones.* Columbia (4/11/35), Del Lord. Lucille Ward, James C. Morton, Wes Warner, Marie Wells, Phyllis Crane, Ford West, Lou Archer, John Rand, Si Jenks, Val Harris, Marvin Lobach, Charles Dorety, Hubert Diltz, Billy Franey, George Ovey, Heinie Conklin, Harry Semels, George Gray, Bud Jamison, Eugene Anderson, Helen Dickson, Rudolf Chavers. Andy and another town doctor are competing for post as county physician; whoever treats the most patients one day wins.

73. *Tramp Tramp Tramp.* Columbia (5/22/35), Charles Lamont. Dot Farley, Heinie Conklin, Robert "Bobby" Burns. Andy's wife decides to make their home a haven for the town's derelicts.

74. *Alimony Aches.* Columbia (6/29/35), Charles Lamont. Jan Duggan, Vivien Oakland, Tommy Bond, Bud Jamison. When Andy remarries, his ex-wife tries to chisel money out of him—not telling him that she's remarried too.

75. *It Always Happens.* Columbia (9/15/35), Del Lord. Geneva Mitchell, Esther Muir, Bud Jamison, Esther Howard, Arthur Housman, Robert McKenzie, Sam Lufkin. Andy gets innocently involved with the wife of a jealous client. A partial remake of *Taxi Troubles;* remade as *His Tale Is Told* and, later, with Bert Wheeler, as *Innocently Guilty.*

76. *Hot Paprika.* Columbia (12/12/35), Preston Black (Jack White). Thinking he has three months to live, Andy runs away to the revolution-ridden Republic of Paprika.

77. *Caught in the Act.* Columbia (3/5/36), Del Lord. Anne O'Neal, John T. Murray, Bud Jamison, James C. Morton, William Irving. Andy tangles with the notorious Jack the Kisser.

78. *Share the Wealth.* Columbia (3/16/36), Del Lord. Mary Gordon, Vernon Dent, Bob Barry, Blackie Whiteford, James C. Morton, Tom Dempsey, Bobby Barber, Fay Holderness. Andy is elected mayor on a "share-the-wealth" platform, after which the townspeople divvy up everything he owns!

Vernon Dent has brought good news to Andy and Mary Gordon in *Share the Wealth.*

79. *Peppery Salt.* Columbia (5/15/36), Del Lord. Mary Lou Dix, Warner Richmond, Harry Keaton, Bert Young, Blackie Whiteford, Tom Dempsey, John Ince, Charlie Phillips. Andy inherits the "Admiral Dewey," thinking it's a ship; it turns out to be a lunch counter. Remade as *Marinated Mariner.*

80. *Mister Smarty.* Columbia (7/15/36), Preston Black. Andy criticizes his wife's slowness in cleaning house, and says he can do the spring cleaning, top to bottom, in one day.

81. *Am I Having Fun.* Columbia (9/18/36), Preston Black. Arthur Housman, Harry Semels, Lou Davis, Gale Arnold, Helen Martinez, C. L. Sherwood, Sam Lufkin. Cab driver Andy gets involved in a publicity stunt with his inebriated passenger, a press agent. Remade with Billy Gilbert and Jack Norton as *Crazy Like a Fox.*

82. *Love Comes to Mooneyville.* Columbia (11/14/36), Preston Black. Esther Howard, Bob McKenzie. Postmaster-sheriff-merchant Andy and fire chief Ruggles vie for the affections of the town's new arrival, Widow Flower.

83. *Knee Action.* Columbia (1/9/37), Charles Lamont. Vivien Oakland, Tommy Bond. Andy marries, not knowing the woman has a bratty ten-year-old son.

84. *Stuck in the Sticks.* Columbia (3/26/37), Preston Black. Esther Howard, Bob McKenzie, Tom Dempsey, Robert Burns, Jack Evans, Jack Hendricks, Eva McKenzie. Andy and his rival compete, rough and ready, for the hand of Widow Flower, only to discover later that she's a notorious swindler.

85. *My Little Feller.* Columbia (5/21/37), Charles Lamont. Andy is unknowingly taking care of a kidnapped baby.

86. *Lodge Night*. Columbia (6/11/37), Preston Black. Joan Woodbury, Nick Copeland, Bonita Weber, Doodles Weaver, Sammy Blum, Penny Parker, Louise Carver, Billy McCall, Antrim Short, Georgia Dell, Eva McKenzie. Andy gets in hot water because of his fraternal lodge meetings.

87. *Gracie at the Bat*. Columbia (10/29/37), Del Lord. Louise Stanley, Leora Thatcher, Ann Doran, Bud Jamison, Vernon Dent, Eddie Fetherstone, Bess Flowers, William Irving. Veteran baseball man Andy is assigned the manager's position on a girl's softball team.

88. *He Done His Duty*. Columbia (12/10/37), Charles Lamont. Bob McKenzie, Dorothy Granger. Andy and his rival in Mooneyville are both taken in by a wily female crook and her female-impersonator husband.

89. *The Old Raid Mule*. Columbia (3/4/38), Charley Chase. Olin Howland, Ann Doran, Bud Jamison, Vernon Dent, Robert McKenzie. Andy has a heated feud with a hillbilly neighbor who continually trades him things that are no good.

90. *Jump, Chump, Jump*. Columbia (4/15/38), Del Lord. Gertrude Sutton, Bud Jamison, George Ovey, Snowflake. Andy and the schoolmarm expose some crooked politicians.

91. *Ankles Away*. Columbia (5/13/38), Charley Chase. Ann Doran, Gene Morgan, Gino Corrado, Bess Flowers, Grace Goodall, Vernon Dent, Symona Boniface, John T. Murray. Andy's rival convinces him that his bride-to-be has a wooden leg. A remake of the Charley Chase silent *His Wooden Wedding*.

92. *Soul of a Heel*. Columbia (6/4/38), Del Lord. Gertrude Sutton, Bud Jamison, Eva McKenzie, James C. Morton, Cy Schindell, Frank Mann. Andy wants to marry Gertie, but her father disapproves.

93. *Not Guilty Enough*. Columbia (7/30/38), Del Lord. Andy tells a judge why he struck his brother-in-law. Remake of *Half-Baked Relations*.

94. *Home on the Rage*. Columbia (12/9/38), Del Lord. Lela Bliss, Shemp Howard, Gene Morgan, Vernon Dent. Andy thinks his wife and brother-in-law are trying to kill him.

95. *Swing, You Swingers*. Columbia (1/29/39), Jules White. Andy is now in charge of three orphans, who change him from a conservative to a jitterbugger.

96. *Boom Goes the Groom*. Columbia (3/24/39), Charley Chase. Vivien Oakland, Dick Curtis, Monty Collins. Just as Andy is to be married, a gold mine he partly owns pays off.

97. *Now It Can Be Sold*. Columbia (6/2/39), Del Lord. Anita Garvin, Tommy Bond, Dick Curtis. Andy and his junior-G-man nephew go on the trail of some bank robbers.

98. *Trouble Finds Andy Clyde*. Columbia (7/28/39), Jules White. Dick Curtis. The presence of Andy's twin brother leads to suspicions on Mrs. Clyde's part.

99. *All-American Blondes*. Columbia (10/20/39), Del Lord. Dick Curtis. Andy gets a job as basketball coach at a girl's school.

100. *Andy Clyde Gets Spring Chicken*. Columbia (12/15/39), Jules White. Richard Fiske, Beatrice Blinn, Don Beddoe, Eva McKenzie, Dorothy Appleby, John Tyrrell, Kay Vallon. Playboy Andy gets the love bug when a group of girls move in next door.

101. *Mr. Clyde Goes to Broadway*. Columbia (2/2/40), Del Lord. Vivien Oakland, John T. Murray, Dorothy Vaughn, Vernon Dent, Don Beddoe. Andy invests in a local show; when the actors skip town with the money, and he and his wife are forced to perform.

102. *Money Squawks*. Columbia (4/5/40), Jules White. Shemp Howard. Andy get nervous when he has to hold onto a ten-thousand-dollar payroll for a local mine.

103. *Boobs in the Woods*. Columbia (5/31/40), Del Lord. Esther Howard, Shemp Howard, Bud Jamison, Bruce Bennett, Jack Lipson. Andy goes on a trouble-prone trip to the woods with his wife and obnoxious brother-in-law.

104. *Fireman, Save My Choo Choo*. Columbia (8/9/40), Del Lord. Esther Howard, Roscoe Ates, Richard Fiske, John Tyrrell. Andy has to race his train against a modern bus to see who'll get a government franchise. A remake of *The Cannonball*.

105. *A Bundle of Bliss*. Columbia (11/1/40), Jules White. Esther Howard, Vernon Dent, Fred Kelsey, Bruce Bennett, Dorothy Appleby. Andy gets mixed up with an abandoned baby he thinks is his own. Remade, with stock footage, as *A Blissful Blunder*.

Tommy Bond looks cynical about this domestic scene between Andy and Anita Garvin in *Now It Can Be Sold*.

106. *The Watchman Takes a Wife.* Columbia (1/10/41), Del Lord. Night-watchman Andy thinks his wife is seeing another man while he's working.

107. *Ring and the Belle.* Columbia (5/2/41), Del Lord. Vivien Oakland, Jack Roper, Dudley Dickerson, Vernon Dent. Andy is a fight manager whose fighter leaves town.

108. *Yankee Doodle Andy.* Columbia (6/13/41), Jules White. Dorothy Appleby, Tom Kennedy, Vernon Dent. Airplane-factory-worker Andy falls into the hands of saboteurs.

109. *Host to a Ghost.* Columbia (8/8/41), Del Lord. Andy, in the demolition business, gets involved with a haunted house.

110. *Lovable Trouble.* Columbia (10/23/41), Del Lord. Esther Howard, Ann Doran, Luana Walters, Vernon Dent. Andy coaches

Barbara Pepper, Vivien Oakland, Vernon Dent, Marjorie Deanne, Julie Duncan, Bertha Priestly, Lois James, Dorothy O'Kelly. Andy, proprietor of a bicycle shop, gets innocently involved with a pretty customer and her jealous husband.

115. *Wolf in Thief's Clothing.* Columbia (2/12/43), Jules White. Andy and Slim try to top each other in courting the town widow.

116. *A Maid Made Mad.* Columbia (3/19/43), Del Lord. Barbara Pepper, Gwen Kenyon, Mabel Forrest, Vernon Dent, Blanche Payson. Andy's wife misunderstands his entanglement with a female customer in their store and walks out on him.

117. *Farmer for a Day.* Columbia (8/20/43), Jules White. Betty Blythe, Douglas Leavitt, Shemp Howard, Adele St. Maur, Bud Jamison. Andy plants a Victory Garden.

Vivien Oakland's flirting seems to be having an effect on Andy in *Mr. Clyde Goes to Broadway*.

Forest ranger Bruce Bennett has had enough of Shemp Howard and Andy in *Boobs in the Woods*.

a troupe of show girls to form a baseball team; his wife misunderstands.

111. *Sappy Birthday.* Columbia (2/5/42), Harry Edwards. Esther Howard, Matt McHugh, Olin Howland, Vernon Dent. Andy wants to play golf, but wife and brother-in-law want to have a picnic instead.

112. *How Spry I Am.* Columbia (5/7/42), Jules White. Mary Dawn, Nat Bunker, Paul Clayton, Daisy. A kiddie musical.

113. *All Work and No Pay.* Columbia (7/16/42), Del Lord. Frank Lackteen, Duke York, Eddie Laughton, Vernon Dent, Bud Jamison. Watchman Andy has a vault full of gems stolen from under his nose, and follows the crooks in hot pursuit onto a ship.

114. *Sappy Pappy.* Columbia (10/30/42), Harry Edwards.

118. *He Was Only Feudin'.* Columbia (12/3/43), Harry Edwards. Bill Henry, Barbara Pepper. Bill hires a pretty girl to flirt with Andy so he'll be more receptive to his daughter marrying him.

119. *His Tale Is Told.* Columbia (3/4/44), Harry Edwards. Christine McIntyre, Ann Doran, Mabel Forrest, Vernon Dent, Snub Pollard, Heinie Conklin, Jack Norton, Bud Jamison. Andy goes to the city to sell an invention. Remake of *It Always Happens;* remade with Bert Wheeler as *Innocently Guilty*.

120. *You Were Never Uglier.* Columbia (6/2/44), Jules White. Emmett Lynn. Andy and his seafaring pal leave the sailor's life to settle down and get married, but it's not what they bargained for. Remake of the Tom Kennedy–Monty Collins short *Gobs of Trouble.* Remade as *Hooked and Rooked,* with stock footage.

Between takes, during the 1940s: director Del Lord, producer Hugh McCollum, script-girl Josephine Aleman, and Andy. Behind the camera, L. W. O'Connell (in hat) and his first assistant.

121. *Gold Is Where You Lose It*. Columbia (9/1/44), Jules White. Emmet Lynn, Gertrude Sutton, Hank Mann, Eva McKenzie, Bud Jamison, James C. Morton, Frank Mills, Cy Schindell. When robbers pass some gold in Andy's store, he and Emmett think there's been a strike and set off to do some prospecting. Footage used in *Pleasure Treasure*.

122. *Heather and Yon*. Columbia (12/8/44), Harry Edwards. Andy agrees to pose as a killer while his reporter friend tracks down the real culprit. A remake of Buster Keaton's *Jail Bait*.

123. *Two Local Yokels*. Columbia (3/23/45), Jules White. Charles Judels. Andy and Charlie each considers himself the local Don Juan—until Andy's wife decides to divorce him.

124. *A Miner Affair*. Columbia (11/1/45), Jules White. Charles Rogers, Gloria Marlen, Charles Bates, Jack Lipson, Al Thompson, Robert Williams. Andy and his pal try to get money to pay for an operation for a crippled boy; they dig for gold—right into

a bank vault. Remake of the Three Stooges' *Cash and Carry*. Footage used in *Two April Fools*.

125. *The Blonde Stayed On*. Columbia (1/24/46), Harry Edwards. Christine McIntyre, Gladys Blake, Vernon Dent, John Tyrrell. Every time Andy manages to convince his wife that he's faithful, something else goes wrong.

126. *Spook to Me*. Columbia (12/27/45), Jules White. Vi Barlow, Frank Hagney, Dick Botiller, Wally Rose, Dudley Dickerson, Lulu Mae Bohrman. Andy and his "Bloodhounds" boys group investigate a haunted house.

127. *Andy Plays Hooky.* Columbia (12/19/46), Edward Bernds. Andy goes to incredible lengths to attend a prizefight—and everything backfires.

128. *Two Jills and a Jack.* Columbia (4/14/47), Jules White. Dorothy Granger, Christine McIntyre, Vernon Dent. Mistaken identity and mix-ups abound as Andy, in search of his wife, meets an old friend and his sweetheart.

129. *Wife to Spare.* Columbia (11/20/47), Edward Bernds. Christine McIntyre, Lucille Browne, Dick Wessel, Vera Lewis, Murray Alper, Heinie Conklin. Andy tries to help his brother-in-law out of a jam with a blonde, but only gets into the thick of it himself.

130. *Eight-Ball Andy.* Columbia (3/11/48), Edward Bernds. Dick Wessel, Maudie Prickett, Florence Auer, Vernon Dent. Andy's brother-in-law, who's gadget crazy, makes life miserable for Andy and family.

131. *Go Chase Yourself.* Columbia (10/14/48), Jules White. Florence Auer, Dudley Dickerson. The campus where Andy teaches is plagued by a nightshirt bandit. A remake of Charley Chase's *The Nightshirt Bandit,* remade by Andy as *Pardon my Nightshirt.*

132. *Sunk in the Sink.* Columbia (3/10/49), Jules White. Inventor Andy tries out various household devices while the wife is away.

One of the last Andy Clyde comedies, from the 1950s, *Andy Goes Wild,* with Dick Wessel.

133. *Marinated Mariner.* Columbia (3/30/50), Hugh Mc-Collum. Jean Willes, John Merton, Blackie Whiteford. A remake of *Peppery Salt.*

134. *A Blunderful Time.* Columbia (9/7/50), Jules White. Margie Liszt, Christine McIntyre. Andy's drunken twin brother creates havoc when his wife thinks he's in love with his sister-in-law.

135. *Blonde Atom Bomb.* Columbia (3/8/51), Jules White. Jean Willes, Emil Sitka, George Chesebro, Minerva Urecal, Billy Frandes, Clay Anderson. Andy tries to rescue his nephew from the clutches of a gold-digging nightclub singer, and gets entwined himself.

136. *A Blissful Blunder.* Columbia (5/8/52), Jules White. Ruth Godfrey, Fred Kelsey, Bonnie Bennett, Barbara Lande; in stock footage, Esther Howard. A remake, with stock footage, of *A Bundle of Bliss.*

137. *Hooked and Rooked.* Columbia (9/11/52), Jules White. Emmett Lynn. A remake, with stock footage, of *You Were Never Uglier.*

138. *Fresh Painter.* RKO (1/16/53), Hal Yates. Gil Lamb, Carol Hughes, Dick Wessel, Florence Lake. Under a hypnotic spell, Gil thinks he's a great painter, and proceeds to paint his fiancée's house.

139. *Pardon My Wrench.* RKO (3/13/53), Hal Yates. Gil Lamb, Carol Hughes, Lyle Latell, George Wallace, Emil Sitka. Gil tries to impress prospective father-in-law Andy with his mechanical ability.

140. *Love's A-Poppin.* Columbia (6/11/53), Jules White. Phil Van Zandt, Margia Dean. Andy's got the love bug, and an actress, thinking he's wealthy, accepts his marriage proposal.

141. *Oh, Say, Can You Sue.* Columbia (9/10/53), Jules White. Andy thinks his best friend has married his sweetheart.

142. *Two April Fools.* Columbia (6/17/54), Jules White. Charles Rogers. Andy and his pal buy a treasure map and dig right into a bank vault. A reworking, with stock footage, of *A Miner Affair.*

143. *Scratch Scratch Scratch.* Columbia (4/28/55), Jules White. Dorothy Granger, Eric Lamond. Andy's nephew's rival uses practical jokes to call off an engagement—then the tables are turned.

144. *One Spooky Night.* Columbia (9/15/55), Jules White. Barbara Bartay, Norman Ollestad, Carol Coombs, Doyle Baker. Andy attempts to prove his bravery by going to a haunted house.

145. *Andy Goes Wild.* Columbia (4/26/56), Jules White. Dick Wessel, Florence Auer, Maudie Prickett, Vernon Dent. Andy's brother-in-law drives him crazy with his inventions. A remake, with stock footage, of *Eight-Ball Andy.*

146. *Pardon My Nightshirt.* Columbia (11/22/56), Jules White. Ferris Taylor, Florence Auer, Dudley Dickerson, Patricia White, Gay Nelson, Joe Palma. A remake, with stock footage, of *Go Chase Yourself.*

Edgar Kennedy

The Edgar Kennedy series was one of the most durable in the field of short subjects. It lasted seventeen years, from 1931 to 1948, and even after it had ceased production, RKO continued to release shorts from its backlog for the next seven years.

What made the comedies so popular? The Kennedy series had the secret ingredient fo all good comedy: it was basically real, no matter how far out the gags became. The foundation was always based on a situation with which the audience could identify—adding a room to the house, going on vacation, running a store, trying to borrow money, etcetera. The players managed to become real people to the audience; the continuity of the films enabled moviegoers to regard the Kenney family as the people next door (although one would hate to think of living next door to such a screwy household). The rapport between Edgar and his most frequent screen wife, Florence Lake, was marvelous, so marvelous that it was impossible to picture anyone else in the role of Mrs. Kennedy.

Where the series often failed, however, was in straying too far from credibility, usually in the antics of Edgar's meddlesome mother-in-law, played by Dot Farley, and his no-account brother-in-law, first played by William Eugene and then by Jack Rice. In most cases, one could accept their obnoxious nature, and the fact that Edgar was forced to live with it since his wife was devoted to them; but when they blithely wreck a car in *Quiet Please,* "borrow" Edgar's life savings in *Brother Knows Best,* or engage in one of the sundry get-rich-quick schemes in which Edgar always loses, it's a bit hard to take.

Not that Edgar would let them get away with it. One of the most satisfying sequences in the series comes in *Do or Diet,* when the family starts to give Ed trouble just as he's about to start two weeks off from work. As Edgar is about to sock Jack Rice in the nose, Florence says, "Now, Edgar, hitting Brother is no way to start your vacation." Edgar growls, "You have your fun your way, I'll have my fun my way!"

Edgar Kennedy's own starring series was the culmination of a career in film comedy that dated back to 1914. Born in Monterey, California, in 1890, young Kennedy was bitten with wanderlust in his youth, and traveled around the country working at various jobs. He had a robust singing voice, which got him several jobs in stage shows along the way. By 1914 he was back in California, and, like so many other out-of-work actors and vaudevillians, he wandered into the Mack Sennett studio looking for a job. He was hired, and remained at the Sennett studio for several years as a Keystone Kop and supporting player.

By the 1920s he was well enough established to freelance in feature films and short subjects, and appeared in scores of films throughout the decade. In 1928, Kennedy joined the Hall Roach studio, where he did much of his finest work with Laurel and Hardy, Charley Chase, and Our Gang, among others. He also starred in some of his own comedies, notably a classic silent two-reeler called *A Pair of Tights,* with Stu Erwin, Anita Garvin, and Marion Byron and directed by Hal Yates, who was to do much more work with Edgar many years later. Kennedy also tried his hand at directing. Billed as E. Livingston Kennedy, he piloted several Laurel and Hardy, Charley Chase, and "Boy Friends" shorts before deciding to remain a performer.

At Roach's he matured into a first-rate comedian with his own distinctive style. He also developed his trademark, the slow burn. Edgar became the perfect mirror of frustration—frustration not with complicated machinery, or great disaster, but with little annoyances of life. When confronted with such a trifle, he would screw up his face, as if to say, "I'm determined not to let this bother me." There would be a delayed reaction as he absorbed the situation. Then, as a finishing touch, he would slowly rub his hand over his face in a gesture of exasperation. So closely was he linked with this trademark that, before long, in his own RKO series, the face-rub became the punch line on many of his shorts, a neat way of concluding one of many disastrous denouements.

In late 1930, Edgar left the Roach studio to free-lance again. He appeared in an increasing number of feature films, and starred or costarred in a variety of short subjects for Educational, Pathé, and Universal, including a short-lived series at Pathé costarring perennial drunk Arthur Housman. At Educational he starred in a two-reeler called *All Gummed Up,* with Florence Lake as his wife and Louise Carver as his aunt. This short was a forerunner of his soon-to-be-born starring series at RKO.

The "Average Man" series, as it was originally called, was developed by Harry Sweet, a director, supervisor, and sometimes actor in the RKO comedy department. His script supervisor, Gloria Morgan, remembers his gentle nature and recalls, "He was always playing the piano while waiting for the lighting. He directed most of the Kennedy shows in a very nonchalant style." The first two-reeler, *Rough House Rhythm,* was released on April 5, 1931, from that time on, the series released an episode once every other month for the next seventeen years.

The cast (Florence Lake as the wife, Dot Farley as

Director George Stevens helps Florence Lake and Edgar celebrate the second anniversary of their short-subject series at RKO.

the mother-in-law, William Eugene as the brother-in-law) and format (Edgar as the harried head of a nutty household) were established immediately. Sweet favored visual slapstick comedy (pie-throwing was frequent) and tried to keep the pacing of the comedies very tight. He was also fortunate in that he had flexibility at this time with regard to location shooting and use of sets. One of the best early comedies, *Fish Feathers* (1932), was shot at a lakeside resort, with Edgar and the family going fishing on Tom Kennedy's group-fishing boat. Their first problem is a temperamental outboard motor on the dinghy they hire to take them out to the yacht. When Edgar tries to fix it, he falls overboard, and, holding onto the motor, is propelled around the lake! Similar catastrophes abound, climaxing in a wild ride in the runaway boat, all shot without the aid of process screens or photographic

trickery—adding, naturally, to the believability and enjoyment of the scene.

Harry Sweet's association with the series ended abruptly in 1933. Gloria Morgan recalls, "I never hear the tune 'Stormy Weather' now but I don't think of him with sadness as, after a long Friday's shooting and much clowning on the piano while playing that number (it was raining), he took off for his mountain cabin in a small plane he flew himself, and was killed. It was a dreadful shock to all of us."

From that time on, a handful of directors took turns directing the Kennedy series. One of them was George Stevens, just before he got the OK to progress to feature films at RKO. He collaborated on the script of his three two-reelers, and still remembers with fondness the final gag of *Quiet Please*. Set on a cross-country train called "The Happy Valley Express," Edgar inadvertently shoots a hole in the ceiling of his car, and sits dejectedly as it starts to snow through the roof.

Many other directors and writers worked on the shorts, with extremely erratic results. Alf Goulding, who had a long but basically unimpressive comedy career, helmed one of the most unusual, and pleasing, early shorts, *Wrong Direction,* in which Edgar is (incredibly enough) an assistant director at Magnet Pictures, the logo of which is a nice spoof of RKO's. The director of an important picture on which Ed has been working walks off the set one morning, and the studio boss (Nat Carr) asks Edgar if he thinks he can finish the picture in one day. There are just two scenes left. Edgar assures him he can, and is told that if he can surmount the major obstacle—a temperamental star (Jean Fontaine)—a plum career is waiting for him.

Edgar arrives on the set (a surprisingly faithful depiction of a movie set) and calmly takes charge. The scene to be shot takes place in the lady's boudoir, and is basically very simple. But just as things seem to be progressing smoothly, Ed's family arrives to watch him work. They come during shooting, and argue with a studio guard (Bud Jamison) about getting onto the set. As they fight with him, they pound on the door to the sound stage, ruining three or four takes. Once inside, they make a shambles of the operation: Mother interrupts a scene to get the star's autograph, Brother turns on the wind machine, etcetera. Before long, Edgar is shooting the fifty-second take of this same scene! When the studio boss arrives on the set and sees what's going on, the filming turns into a shoutfest. As the picture fades, we know that Edgar's career as a director has little chance for survival.

In 1936, Leslie Goodwins tried his hand at directing the shorts, with delightful results. *Will Power* is one of the strangest comedies in the series. In it, Edgar pretends to have a heart attack so Brother will be forced to go to work. Once the family is out of the house, Edgar exercises "mind over matter," and puts himself into a trancelike state. With the rest of the room darkened, the camera focuses in on his eyes as he solemnly repeats, "Brother . . . get . . . a . . . job. . . . Brother . . . get . . . a . . . job. . . ." Unfortunately, the scheme backfires, as Brother returns home to announce that he's employed—he's taken over Edgar's job!!!

Two other Goodwins entries from 1936 are among the series' all-time best. In *Dummy Ache,* Edgar misunderstands Florence's sneaking about, not realizing that she's just rehearsing for a local play. Edgar spies on a rehearsal, and watches as Florence and her leading man, George Lewis, kill an unwanted husband and dump his body into a laundry basket. Naturally, it's just a dummy, but Edgar, convinced that he's witnessed a murder, decides to dispose of the body and protect his wife. As he carries the basket down the city's main street,

Florence and Jack Rice are planning something behind Edgar's back—literally.

a hand protrudes through a hole in the container, making Edgar quite a sight to the local citizenry! In *High Beer Pressure,* the family decides to build Kennedy's Canteen, a quaint little tavern. Absolutely nothing goes right as the four novices decide to fix up the place themselves. The climax comes when beer deliveryman Tiny Sandford, parked on a steep hill, unlatches twenty barrels of beer, which tumble down the hill and crash into the canteen, demolishing it instantly. Amid the rubble, Florence starts to chatter (in her inimitable mile-a-minute voice) about rebuilding, but all Edgar can do is rub his face in defeat.

For reasons unknown, Florence Lake left the series in the late 1930s. She came back and appeared occasionally during the rest of the decade, and returned to the series for good in the early 1940s. During her absence, Edgar played opposite a number of leading ladies, none of whom managed to capture the same spirit as Miss Lake, whose disarming dizziness made her unique among the many comic wives in two-reelers at this time. Indeed, one of her replacements, Sally Payne, was obviously shown a bunch of Miss Lake's comedies, for she mimicked her to the letter, with only fair results.

Vivien Oakland, a fine comedienne in her own right,

Two Kennedys, Tom and Edgar, meet head-on.

going on. Edgar explains and, as he does, Vivien goes to a closet door to put away her coat. When she opens the door, she is deluged with a ton of dirt that pours into the living room, revealing Franey's hiding place for the remnants of the tunnel.

What the Edgar Kennedy series lacked, from around 1938 to 1944, was consistency. The change of screen wives was a major upset to the continuity of the series, and the lack of a single director, or even one writer, made the quality of the films fluctuate like a stock-market report. Directors at this time included Ben Holmes, a former vaudeville straight man to Chic Sale, who had turned to directing in the early 1930s; Charles E. Roberts, who wrote many of the best RKO shorts; Lloyd French, a talented comedy writer-director; and Clem Beauchamp, an assistant director in feature films who got his first step up when assigned these two-reelers. Besides Sally Payne, Edgar had several other screen mates, including Irene Ryan, later known as Granny on the "Beverly Hillbillies" television show.

The series benefited greatly from some of the players who participated in the films. Billy Franey, the house painter in *Dumb's the Word,* played Edgar's father-in-law in several shorts from the late 1930s. Lucy Beaumont contributed a hilarious, and surprising, characterization in *Parlor, Bedroom, and Wrath* (1932) as an apparently sweet little old lady who is leasing an apartment. Florence feels sorry for her and convinces Edgar that they should move in; the minute they do, they discover that the sweet old lady is an incredible pest! James Finlayson played an uncle in *False Roomers;* Iris Adrian, a maid in *How to Clean House;* Tom Kennedy, a variety of roles in such films as *Fish Feathers, Sock Me to Sleep,* and *Love Your Landlord;* Darryl Hickman, a bratty nephew in *Heart Burn;* and, perhaps best of all, in *Bad Housekeeping,* Franklin Pangborn, a piano tuner who goes to work on the baby grand, and when he's finished, all the keys are the same!

The comedies continued to come out six times a year, alternating between hits and misses. Finally, in 1944, a strong hand took over both the writing and the directing of the films, and the improvement was remarkable. The man in question was Hal Yates, who came to the series after twenty years with Hal Roach and managed to breathe new life into the shorts by both writing the screenplays and directing the films (a task he also performed at this time on the Leon Errol series). Yates quickly developed a surefire formula that had already been applied by Columbia producer Jules White: make the comedies move so fast that if they aren't funny, no one will have time to notice. For the most part, Yates's entries in the series *were* funny, and they all were marked

was rather subdued as Edgar's wife. She participated, however, in one of the series' all-time best gags, in *Dumb's the Word* (1937). In this comedy, Edgar has found what he believes to be actual gold coins, and he hides them in a flowerpot on the side of his house. But, at the same time, his irate neighbor (Eddie Dunn), reexamines his property line, and builds a fence at the point he determines to be the edge of his land—just over the spot where Edgar has buried the gold! There is no way to get to the plant, for Dunn is primed, with shotgun in hand. So Edgar and his wily house painter (Billy Franey) decide to tunnel underground to reach the site. As they tunnel further and further along, Edgar inquires what Franey is doing with all the dirt. The oldster tells him not to worry. Their work is all for naught, however; they spring a water main, and, in the excitement, it turns out that Edgar had dropped the goldfilled flowerpot next to his house long ago, and it was another one he buried in the yard. His wife has been away during all this. When she returns home, she demands to know what's been by tight, rapid pacing. His screenplays tended to repeat themselves, especially in the Errol comedies, but the brisk pace overcame even that.

While most short-subject series declined as the 1940s progressed, the RKO series, both Errol and Kennedy, improved. They moved, they were funny, and, most of all, they were consistent. Yates relied on situations more than slapstick, and his pattern for two-reel comedies became the blueprint for television's staple, the situation comedy. (Not coincidentally, Yates directed several of TV's pioneer series, such as "My Little Margie".) He also gave the series more organization, cutting down the shooting time from five days to three.

Some of Yates's comedies were among the best entries in the Edgar Kennedy series. In *Sleepless Tuesday* (1945), Edgar walks around half-asleep during the day because he's kept up every night by the radio, which Mother insists on playing at full volume into the wee hours. His attempts to sabotage the radio, however, are constantly thwarted. Finally, after succeeding in getting rid of the radio one night, he's led to believe that Florence had tucked their nest egg away in the back of the set! After retrieving it, he learns that it was the kitchen radio she had used. At this point, Edgar takes axe in hand and proceeds to smash the radio into little bits while it plays the "Stars and Stripes Forever." But the song continues until he smashes each of the tubes individually, each one shutting out another instrument, until only a piccolo remains. The film also features an ingenious device during the titles: Over the "End" title, Edgar irises in and says, "The End—I hope." Just below him, Mother irises in. She is on the telephone to the store, ordering a new radio.

In *Do or Diet* (1947) the family is convinced that Edgar will be fired if he doesn't lose weight to keep in step with his younger colleagues. To goad him into dieting, Mother invites Florence's old boyfriend (Dick Wessel) over one evening to show off his physical dexterity. Edgar takes the bait, going through a rigorous exercise program (as Brother coaches him, sitting on the sideline eating a banana). But the morning after, when Edgar tries to get up, he can't move a muscle without having his bones sound like crackling peanut brittle. At this point, he abandons the exercise program and decides to take reducing pills instead. After taking a pill, Florence mixes up the pillbox with a box of insecticide tablets she's spreading around the house. Edgar looks at the box and thinks he's taken poison! The family goes crazy trying to find a cure. After misreading the first-aid manual, they send him into a bathtub full of ice water. When a doctor arrives and declares Edgar normal, Florence explains the whole scheme; Edgar realizes it was Broth-er's brainstorm, and he dunks *him* in the icy bathtub for retribution.

Home Canning (1948), the next-to-last comedy in the series, has the family economizing by putting up their own fruit preserves. Ed buys a bushel of fruit downtown, and the girls dig up a lot of empty jars. While they're at work, housepainter Charlie Hall arrives to do the kitchen and tells them it must be done that afternoon. Meanwhile, chic next-door neighbor Vivien Oakland has asked Florence to keep an eye on her kitchen, which is to be photographed that afternoon for *House Beautiful* magazine. The family decides to use Vivien's kitchen to do their chores. Mother, however, is worried about ruining the luxurious kitchen. "What could happen?" laughs Edgar. Everything does. He swats a fly, which leaves a stain on one wall. When he tries to remove the stain, he removes the paint as well. Then Ed brings in the pressure cooker to prepare the fruit and leaves it unattended for a few minutes. The result is a tremendous explosion which makes a shambles of the kitchen, not to mention the family. Just then, Vivien returns home and sees the mess. She demands that they pay for a complete redecorating job, and decides to keep the 150 jars of fruit on account. Then Florence discovers that she's lost her wedding ring. After searching around a bit, she concludes that it must be in one of the fruit jars. Vivien, however, won't let them go through the jars unless they buy them back. She mentions a round sum, but Edgar asks if he can buy the jars back one by one until they find the ring. Vivien agrees—for five dollars a jar! Naturally, they go through 149 of the 150 jars before finding the ring. By that time, they've emptied all the fruit into big bowls and spent a fortune. Vivien just stands by keeping count, with a sly smile on her face. As they are about to leave, Vivien asks what they're going to do with the fruit. "We were going to leave it," says Florence, "but you've given me a better idea." She takes one of the bowls and dumps it on Vivien's head, as the family, thoroughly satisfied, returns home.

Contest Crazy was the 103rd short in the highly successful RKO series. It followed the same formula as the first, starring two of the original cast members, Florence Lake and Dot Farley, as well as Jack Rice, who had been with the series for over ten years. The theme song was still the same—"Chopsticks"—and the comic expertise of Edgar and company had, if anything, sharpened over the years.

Since making the shorts took up an average of only twenty shooting days a year, Edgar was free to work in feature films as well, which he did, amassing an imposing list of credits. He usually had small roles in feature films, but his footage, no matter how small, was always a highlight. Among his best films were *Duck Soup, Twentieth Century, San Francisco, A Star Is Born, True Confession, It Happened Tomorrow,* and *Unfaithfully Yours.* By 1948, Edgar was one of the movies' best-liked comedians and a veteran of forty-five years in the business. A testimonial dinner was planned in his honor, but on November 9, 1948, thirty-six hours before it was to take place, he died of throat cancer.

Edgar once said of himself, "I overact. I know I overact. But at least I do try to act, and it's easy enough for a director to say 'Easy now,' and I know what he means and calm it down." He never encountered that problem in his two-reel series, where he was the star, and where the films were tailor-made for his talents. As the Average Man whose attempts to rise above it all were usually frustrated, Edgar delighted movie audiences of five decades. Today, his comedies continue to entertain many people who find themselves as fond of him as moviegoers were when the films were new. Edgar Kennedy and the comedies in which he starred had heart, and it's that very special quality that set them apart from their competitors.

The Edgar Kennedy Short Subjects

This list comprises all the titles in Kennedy's starring series for RKO, originally titled "Mr. Average Man." Over the years Kennedy appeared in innumerable other shorts wtih Our Gang, Laurel and Hardy, Charley Chase, Roscoe Ates, and others for virtually every studio in Hollywood. All the following shorts were released by RKO, and were two reels in length.

1. *Rough House Rhythm* (4/5/31). Harry Sweet. Franklin Pangborn, Florence Lake, Claud Allister. The Kennedys move into a "modern bungalow" which turns out to be one big pain in the neck.

2. *Lemon Meringue* (8/3/31). Harry Sweet. Florence Lake, Dot Farley, William Eugene. The family decides to open a luncheonette, the opening day climaxing in a pie-throwing melee.

Vivien Oakland is not too happy with what the family has done to her kitchen in *Home Canning*.

3. *Thanks Again* (10/5/31. Harry Sweet. Florence Lake, Dot Farley, William Eugene, Jerry Drew. Edgar tries to build himself an airplane.

4. *Camping Out* (12/14/31). Harry Sweet. Florence Lake, Dot Farley, William Eugene, Walter Catlett. What was intended as a simple camping trip turns into a major production.

5. *Bon Voyage* (2/22/32). Harry Sweet. Florence Lake, Dot Farley, William Eugene, Jerry Mandy, Renée Torres, Charlie Hall. A steward who's heard of the Kennedy family lets them on his cruise ship only when they promise not to fight.

6. *Mother-In-Law's Day* (4/25/32). Harry Sweet. Florence Lake, Dot Farley, William Eugene, Isabelle Withers, Eddie Boland, Georgie Billings, André Cheron. Mother and brother think Edgar has gone crazy; he's only acting suspicious to surprise Mother on her birthday.

7. *Giggle Water* (6/27/32). Harry Sweet. Florence Lake, Dot Farley, William Eugene, Eddie Boland. Finding a bottle of champagne, the family deems it logical to build a boat so they can christen it.

8. *The Golf Chump* (8/5/32). Harry Sweet. Florence Lake, Dot Farley, William Eugene. Ed and the family make a shambles of an exclusive country club.

9. *Parlor, Bedroom, and Wrath* (10/14/32). Harry Sweet. Florence Lake, Dot Farley, William Eugene, Lucy Beaumont, Arthur Housman. The family rents an apartment from a "sweet old lady" who turns out to be an obnoxious pest.

10. *Fish Feathers* (12/16/32). Harry Sweet. Florence Lake, Dot Farley, William Eugene, Maude Truax, Tom Kennedy. The family goes on a fishing expedition, with disastrous results.

11. *Art in the Raw* (2/24/33). Harry Sweet. Florence Lake, Dot Farley, William Eugene, Franklin Pangborn, Mona Ray. Ed becomes an artist, and is convinced that he ought to move to Greenwich Village.

12. *The Merchant of Menace* (4/21/33). Harry Sweet. Florence Lake, Dot Farley, William Eugene, Nat Carr, Dorothy Granger. Brother gets a job as salesclerk in a department store.

13. *Good Housewrecking* (6/16/33). Harry Sweet. Florence Lake, Dot Farley, William Eugene, Arthur Housman, Jane Darwell, Bud Jamison. The family goes into the interior-decorating business. Remade as *Inferior Decorators,* and originally titled *Interior Decorations.*

14. *Quiet, Please* (8/11/33). George Stevens. Florence Lake, Dot Farley, William Eugene, Charles Dow Clark, Al Hill, Fred Kelsey, Bud Jamison. Ed has taken Florence with him on a business trip, but their train ride is disrupted by the appearance of Mother and Brother.

15. *What Fur* (11/3/33). George Stevens. Florence Lake, Dot Farley, William Eugene, Treva Lawler, Nat Carr, Charlie Hall. Florence buys an expensive fur coat, while Ed has troubles of his own with a blackmail photo.

16. *Grin and Bear It* (12/29/33). George Stevens. Florence Lake, Dot Farley, William Eugene, Fred Kelsey. The family confronts an irate landlord on Ed's birthday.

Edgar and Dorothy Granger in *The Merchant of Menace.*

17. *Love on a Ladder* (3/2/34). Sam White. Florence Lake, Dot Farley, William Eugene, Jean Fontaine. Florence says that Ed isn't romantic anymore, and persuades him to climb to her window one night to serenade her.

18. *Wrong Direction* (5/18/34). Alf Goulding. Florence Lake, Dot Farley, William Eugene, Nat Carr, Jean Fontaine, Bud Jamison. Ed, an assistant director, gets his big break to direct a film—then the family decides to visit the set.

19. *In-Laws Are Out* (6/29/34). Sam White. Florence Lake, Dot Farley, William Eugene, Jean Fontaine. Florence says she'll divorce Edgar the very next time he loses his temper.

20. *A Blasted Event* (9/7/34). Alf Goulding. Florence Lake, Dot Farley, Jack Rice. The family tries to adopt a baby, over Edgar's protests.

21. *Poisoned Ivory* (11/16/34). Alf Goulding. Florence Lake, Dot Farley, Jack Rice, William Augustine. The family thinks they've accidentally given Ed poison.

22. *Bric-a-Brac* (1/18/35). Sam White. Florence Lake, Dot Farley, Jack Rice, Walter Brennan. The family tries to build a cabin in the mountains.

23. *South Seasickness* (3/29/35). Arthur Ripley. Florence Lake, Dot Farley, Jack Rice, Adrian Rosley. Ed plans to sail to the South Seas to escape from his family.

24. *Sock Me to Sleep* (5/17/35). Ben Holmes. Florence Lake, Dot Farley, Jack Rice, Tom Kennedy. Brother becomes a fight manager—using Edgar's money.

25. *Edgar Hamlet* (7/5/35). Arthur Ripley. Florence Lake, Dot Farley, Jack Rice. A quiet day is disrupted by arguments over Shakespearian speeches.

26. *In Love at 40* (8/30/35). Arthur Ripley. Florence Lake, Dot Farley, Jack Rice, Curley Wright. Edgar falls in love with another woman.

27. *Happy Tho Married* (11/1/35). Arthur Ripley. Florence Lake, Dot Farley, Jack Rice. Edgar hires a double to pose as himself with the family at night. Remade by Leon Errol as *Double Up.*

28. *Gasoloons* (1/3/36). Arthur Ripley. Florence Lake, Dot Farley, Jack Rice, Charles Withers, Dickie Jones, Brandon Hurst, Pearl Eaton. On their way to a vacation, the family decides to buy a gas station.

29. *Will Power* (3/6/36). Arthur Ripley. Florence Lake, Dot Farley, Jack Rice, Kitty McHugh, Harrison Green, Harry Bowen. Edgar pretends to have a heart attack, so Brother will have to go to work.

30. *High Beer Pressure* (5/8/36). Leslie Goodwins. Florence Lake, Dot Farley, Jack Rice, Tiny Sandford. Over Edgar's objections, the family decided to build a tavern called Kennedy's Canteen.

31. *Dummy Ache* (7/10/36). Leslie Goodwins. Florence Lake, Dot Farley, Jack Rice, Harry Bowen, George Lewis, Lucille Ball, Bobby Burns. Ed thinks Florence is an adulteress and a murderess—not knowing she's just rehearsing for a play. Nominated for an Academy Award. Remade by Leon Errol as *Who's a Dummy?*

32. *Vocalizing* (10/23/36). Leslie Goodwins. Edgar takes a singer home from her concert, and before long he's become a chauffeur. Remade by Leon Errol as *Seeing Nellie Home.*

33. *Hillbilly Goat* (1/15/37). Leslie Goodwins. Si Jenks, Fern Emmett. When salesman Ed goes into Ozark country, he accidentally comes between two sweethearts.

34. *Bad Housekeeping* (3/5/37). Leslie Goodwins. Vivien Oakland, Franklin Pangborn. Edgar and his wife switch places for a day.

35. *Locks and Bonds* (4/15/37). Leslie Goodwins. Bill Franey, Eddie Dunn. Ed has used supposedly worthless stock certificates for wallpaper, and now is told they're worth $25 a share. Remade as *Wall Street Blues.*

36. *Dumb's the Word* (6/11/37). Leslie Goodwins. Vivien Oakland, Billy Franey, Eddie Dunn. Ed finds a cache of gold, buries it, then realizes he's buried it on his neighbor's property.

37. *Tramp Trouble* (8/7/37). Leslie Goodwins. Vivien Oakland, Billy Franey, Bill Benedict, Lloyd Ingraham, Ed Dunn. Ed "adopts" a troublesome young boy.

38. *Morning, Judge* (9/24/37). Leslie Goodwins. Agnes Ayres, Billy Franey, George Irving, Harry Bowen, Bud Jamison. Ed is brought into court for trying to break into jail. Remade by Leon Errol as *Hold 'em Jail.*

39. *Edgar and Goliath* (11/19/37). Leslie Goodwins. Florence Lake, Billy Franey, Frank O'Connor, Dick Rush, Stanley Blystone. Edgar wins a Goliath automobile in a contest.

Edgar and another frequent screen wife, Vivien Oakland.

40. *Ears of Experience* (1/28/38). Leslie Goodwins. Florence Lake, Billy Franey, Richard Lane, Jack Rice, Landers Stevens. Ed consults with famed counselor "Ears of Experience," who gets him into nothing but trouble.

41. *False Roomers* (3/26/38). Leslie Goodwins. Constance Bergen, Billy Franey, James Finlayson, Jack Rice. A screwy roomer, and a visit from Ed's uncle, make havoc of life.

42. *Kennedy's Castle* (5/28/38). Leslie Goodwins. Vivian Tobin, Ed Dunn, Billy Franey, J. P. McGowan, Bud Jamison. Three social events at the same time turn the Kennedy household into a madhouse.

43. *Fool Coverage* (7/15/38). Leslie Goodwins. Vivien Oakland, Billy Franey, Robert E. Keane, Max Wagner. Trouble starts when Pop wants to get a driver's license.

44. *Beaux and Errors* (10/7/38). Charles E. Roberts. Vivien Oakland, Billy Franey, Ed Dunn, Eva McKenzie. Vivien complains that Ed is looking old before his time, unlike some of her former beaux.

45. *A Clean Sweep* (12/2/38). Charles E. Roberts. Vivien Oakland, Ed Dunn, Billy Franey, John Dilson, Tiny Sandford, Lillian Miles. Ed becomes a vacuum-cleaner salesman.

46. *Maid to Order* (1/27/39). Charles E. Roberts. Vivien Oakland, Billy Franey, Minerva Urecal, Tom Dempsey. Edgar, in a scheme to get rid of his father-in-law, sends for a mail-order bride.

47. *Clock Wise* (3/24/39). Charles E. Roberts. Vivien Oakland, Billy Franey, Fred Kelsey, Harry Harvey, James Morton. Pop's noisy mechanical clock drives Edgar crazy.

48. *Baby Daze* (5/19/39). Charles E. Roberts. Vivien Oakland, Billy Franey, Don Brodie, Lillian Miles. Ed thinks (incorrectly) that Vivien is going to have a baby.

49. *Feathered Pests* (7/14/39). Charles E. Roberts. Vivien Oakland, Billy Franey, Eva McKenzie, Dix Davis, Tim Davis, Derry Deane, Sonnie Bupp. Ed is trapped into baby-sitting for some kids one afternoon.

50. *Act Your Age* (10/6/39). Charles E. Roberts. Vivien Oakland, Billy Franey, Robert Graves, Larry Steers. Ed thinks he's being eased out of his job because he's getting old.

51. *Kennedy the Great* (12/8/39). Charles E. Roberts. Vivien Oakland, Billy Franey, Robert Graves, Barbara Jo Allen, Keith Kenneth. Ed tries to become a magician.

52. *Slightly at Sea* (2/9/40). Harry D'Arcy. Vivien Oakland, Billy Franey, Jack Rice, Robert Graves, Charlie Hall, Tiny Sandford. Nothing goes right as the family travels to Paradise Lodge for a vacation.

53. *Mutiny in the County* (5/3/40). Harry D'Arcy. Vivien Oakland, Billy Franey, James Morton, Fred Kelsey. Edgar has to go to court the one day of the year when the city is run by youngsters.

54. *'Taint Legal* (5/25/40). Harry D'Arcy. Vivien Oakland, Billy Franey, Arthur O'Connell, Robert Graves. The Kennedys have reason to believe that they're not legally married. Remade by Leon Errol as *Bachelor Blues.*

Edgar and Brother have used worthless stock certificates as wallpaper in *Wall Street Blues.*

Brother is behind bars, at least temporarily, and Edgar laughs triumphantly.

55. *Sunk by the Census* (9/6/40). Harry D'Arcy. Vivien Oakland, Billy Franey, Anita Garvin, Jody Gilbert, Clara Blore. Ed tries to marry off Pop, but the whole thing backfires.

56. *Trailer Tragedy* (10/18/40). Harry D'Arcy. Vivien Oakland, Billy Franey, Tiny Sandford, Charlie Hall, Tom Dempsey. The family goes on vacation in their trailer, but it's one calamity after another.

57. *Drafted in the Depot* (12/20/40). Lloyd French. Vivien Oakland, Billy Franey, Phil Arnold, Ralph Dunn, Frank O'Connor, Warren Jackson. Edgar pretends to be in the National Guard so he can sneak away from the wife and go on a hunting trip.

58. *Mad About Moonshine* (2/21/41). Harry D'Arcy. Vivien Oakland, Billy Franey, Fran O'Connor, Kay Vallon. Pop thinks he's inherited a luxurious Southern manor, but it's just a dust-laden dump.

59. *It Happened All Night* (4/4/41). Charles E. Roberts. Vivien Oakland, Billy Franey, Ernie Adams, Donald Kerr, Ed Foster. Edgar unwittingly gets involved with two escaped convicts.

60. *An Apple in His Eye* (6/6/41). Harry D'Arcy. Vivien Oakland, Charlie Hall, Harry Harvey. Ed tries making pies for Vivien's charity bazaar.

61. *Westward Ho-Hum* (9/15/41). Clem Beauchamp. Sally Payne, Jack Rice, Glenn Strange, Ernie Adams, Ethan Laidlaw. The family has bought a hotel in a ghost town.

62. *I'll Fix That* (10/7/41). Charles E. Roberts. Sally Payne, Jack Rice, John Dilson, Harry Harvey, Ken Christy, Charlie Hall, Curly Wright, Charlie Delaney. Ed decides to do a plumbing job himself.

63. *A Quiet Fourth* (12/19/41). Harry D'Arcy. Sally Payne, Jack Rice, Pat Taylor, Frankie Ward, Charlie Hall. The family is unaware that their picnic grounds are being used for army target practice. A remake of an earlier RKO all-star comedy of the same name.

64. *Heart Burn* (2/20/42). Harry D'Arcy. Sally Payne, Jack Rice, Dot Farley, Archie Twitchell, Darryl Hickman, Roy Butler. A neighbor tells Ed that if he feigns heart trouble, the family will have to do all his household chores.

65. *Interior Decorator* (4/13/42). Clem Beauchamp. Sally Payne, Dot Farley, Jack Rice, Eddie Kane, Keith Hitchcock, Isabel LeMal. The family goes into the interor-decorating business. Remake of *Good Housewrecking*.

66. *Cooks and Crooks* (6/5/42). Henry James. Sally Payne, Dot Farley, Jack Rice, Ann Summers, Marten Lamont, John Maguire, Lew Kelly, Lillian Randolph. Edgar is a would-be detective whose client wants him to find a hidden cache of gold in his old mansion.

67. *Two for the Money* (8/14/42). Lloyd French. Florence Lake, Dot Farley, Jack Rice, Bryant Washburn, Mary Halsey, Gertrude Short, Johnny Berkes, Charlie Hall. Two shady characters and Florence's dumb-cluck relatives spend the night at the Kennedys'. A remake of Leon Errol's *Crime Rave*.

68. *Rough on Rents* (10/30/42). Ben Holmes. Florence Lake, Dot Farley, Jack Rice, Bud Jamison, Dorothy Granger, Martin Lamont, Charlie Hall, Gertrude Astor, Max Wagner, Kernan Cripps. Ed takes in a boarder so he can pay off a gambling debt.

69. *Duck Soup* (12/18/42). Ben Holmes. Florence Lake, Dot

Florence, Paul Maxey, Dot Farley, Jack Rice, Harry Strang, and Edgar in *Brother Knows Best.*

Farley, Jack Rice. Edgar thinks Brother and Mother are trying to kill him so they can collect on his insurance policy.

70. *Hold Your Temper* (2/5/43). Lloyd French. Irene Ryan, Dot Farley, Jack Rice, Isabel LeMal, Eddie Dew, Marte Faust, Casey Johnson. A remake of *In-Laws Are Out*.

71. *Indian Signs* (3/26/43). Charles E. Roberts. Irene Ryan, Dot Farley, Jack Rice. Irene becomes interested in the occult, and Brother claims he is a medium.

72. *Hot Foot* (5/14/43). Ben Holmes. Pauline Drake, Dot Farley, Jack Rice, Bud Jamison, Jimmy Farley. A pal of Ed's schemes to get him out of the house so he can attend a prize-fight.

73. *Not on My Account* (9/17/43). Charles E. Roberts. Pauline Drake, Dot Farley, Jack Rice. Edgar tries to return an expensive coat to a department store.

74. *Unlucky Dog* (11/12/43). Ben Holmes. Pauline Drake, Dot Farley, Jack Rice, Harrison Green, Mary Jane Halsey, Eddie Borden. Brother, now a ventriloquist, sells Edgar a "talking" dog.

75. *Prunes and Politics* (1/7/44). Ben Holmes. Pauline Drake, Dot Farley, Jack Rice, Hugh Beaumont, Harrison Green, Barbara Hale, Russell Wade. Ed and Mother are rival candidates for the office of County Supervisor.

76. *Love Your Landlord* (3/3/44). Charles E. Roberts. Florence Lake, Claire Carleton, Tom Kennedy, Russell Hopton, Lloyd Ingraham, Harry Harvey, Harry Tyler, Emory Parnell, Bud Jamison. Ed and Florence get caught up in the insanity of moving from one house to another. A remake of Leon Errol's *Moving Vanities*.

77. *Radio Rampage* (3/28/44). Charles E. Roberts. Florence Lake, Dot Farley, Jack Rice, Tom Kennedy, Russell Hopton, Charlie Hall, Mary Van Halsey, Emory Parnell, Lee Trent. Edgar tries to fix the family radio.

78. *The Kitchen Cynic* (6/25/44). Hal Yates. Florence Lake, Jack Rice, Sarah Edwards, Emory Parnell, Teddy Infuhr, Bert Moorehouse. Edgar tries to fix up the kitchen.

79. *Feather Your Nest* (10/23/44). Hal Yates. Florence Lake, Dot Farley, Jack Rice, Emory Parnell, Maxine Semon, Lee Trent, Bryant Washburn. Edgar tries to get Brother married, to get rid of him.

80. *Alibi Baby* (1/5/45). Hal Yates. Florence Lake, Elaine Riley, Emory Parnell, Mierva Urecal, Jim Jordan, Jr., Sammy Blum, Baby Dickie. Florence "borrows" a friend's baby to see how Edgar would react to having a child.

81. *Sleepless Tuesday* (2/23/45). Hal Yates. Florence Lake, Dot Farley, Jack Rice, Edmund Glover, Carl Kent, Sam Blum. Mother's insistence on playing the radio full blast all night is driving Edgar crazy.

82. *What, No Cigarettes?* (7/13/45). Hal Yates. Florence Lake, Dot Farley, Jack Rice, Jimmy Conlin, Tom Noonan, Jason Robards, Emory Parnell, Paul Brooks, Gwen Crawford, Robert Andersen, Sam Blum, George Holmes. The family caters to Brother's uncle's every whim, hoping he'll set Brother up in business.

83. *It's Your Move* (8/10/45). Hal Yates. Florence Lake, Dot Farley, Jack Rice, Maxine Semon, Larry Wheat, Gwen Crawford, Edmund Glover, Sam Blum. Ed has two weeks to buy his house before the landlord sells it out from under him.

84. *You Drive Me Crazy* (9/7/45). Hal Yates. Florence Lake, Jack Rice, Emory Parnell, Eddie Kane, Dick Elliott, Betty Gillette, Jack Wheat. Brother gets on Edgar's nerves, and the result is no less than three demolished cars.

85. *The Big Beef* (10/19/45). Charles E. Roberts. Florence Lake, Dot Farley, Jack Rice, Emory Parnell, Harry Harvey, Eddie Kane, Tom Noonan, Bob Manning, Paul Brooks. Ed has invited his boss to dinner, but the wrong party gets served.

86. *Mother-in-Law's Day* (12/7/45). Hal Yates. Florence Lake, Jack Rice, Dot Farley, Dick Elliott, Sarah Edwards, Bess Flowers. Ed is forced to play up to Mother because his boss believes one should be kind to mothers-in-law.

87. *Trouble or Nothing* (1/25/46). Hal Yates. Florence Lake, Dot Farley, Jack Rice, Dick Elliott, Harry Woods, Joe Devlin, Harry Harvey. The family gets involved in betting on horses.

88. *Wall Street Blues* (7/12/46). Hal Yates. Florence Lake, Dot Farley, Jack Rice, Robert Smith, Charlie Hall, Ralph Dunn, Harry Strang. Remake of *Locks and Bonds*.

89. *Motor Maniacs* (7/26/46). Wallace Grissell. Florence Lake, Dot Farley, Jack Rice, Tom Kennedy, Robert Smith. Brother uses Ed's money to buy a new outboard-motor contraption.

90. *Noisy Neighbors* (9/20/46). Hal Yates. Florence Lake, Dot Farley, Jack Rice, Dick Wessel, Harry Harvey. Brother tries to fix up Ed's old car, to the annoyance of a neighbor who's trying to sleep.

91. *I'll Build It Myself* (10/18/46). Hal Yates. Florence Lake, Dot Farley, Jack Rice, Jason Robards, Harry Strang, Robert Bray. Rather than pay a contractor, Ed decides the family can add a room to the house.

92. *Social Terrors* (12/18/46). Charles E. Roberts. Florence Lake, Jack Rice, Dot Farley, Chester Clute, Phyllis Kennedy, Paul Maxey, Vivien Oakland. Ed is trying to marry Brother off, but when the family meets the prospective bride's family, all goes haywire.

93. *Do or Diet* (2/10/47). Hal Yates. Florence Lake, Dot Farley, Jack Rice, Dick Wessel, Cy Ring, Bryant Washburn, Jason Robards. The family is worried about Ed losing his job because he's getting too old and fat.

94. *Heading for Trouble* (6/20/47). Hal Yates. Florence Lake, Dot Farley, Jack Rice, Lee Frederick, Robert Bray. The family goes on vacation in their new trailer.

95. *Host to a Ghost* (7/18/47). Hal Yates. Florence Lake, Jack Rice, Dot Farley, Chester Clute, Ida Moore. Brother sells the family house, and they all move into a creepy old mansion.

The film is called *How to Clean House*. This picture tells the whole story.

Edgar on the set with writer-director Hal Yates.

96. *Television Turmoil* (8/15/47). Hal Yates. Florence Lake, Dot Farley, Jack Rice, Eddie Dunn, Hal K. Dawson, Dick Elliott. Ed decides to save money by buying a build-it-yourself TV set.

97. *Mind over Mouse* (11/21/47). Hal Yates. Florence Lake, Dot Farley, Jack Rice, Max the Mouse. Edgar declares war on a mouse that's running around the house.

98. *Brother Knows Best* (1/2/48). Hal Yates. Florence Lake, Dot Farley, Jack Rice, Paul Maxey, Harold Strang. Edgar is forced to lend Brother a thousand dollars so he'll look good in front of his boss.

99. *No More Relatives* (2/6/48). Hal Yates. Florence Lake, Dot Farley, Jack Rice, Walter Long. Brother hires someone to pose as Ed's long-lost uncle, to influence Ed's feelings toward him and Mother.

100. *How to Clean House* (5/14/48). Charles E. Roberts. Florence Lake, Jack Rice, Dot Farley, Iris Adrian, Harry Harvey, Anne O'Neal, Charlie Hall. Ed bets the family he can clean the house thoroughly in three hours, saving the cost of a maid.

101. *Dig That Gold* (6/25/48). Hal Yates. Florence Lake, Jack Rice, Dick Wessel, Robert Bray. Remake of *Dumb's the Word*.

102. *Home Canning* (8/16/48). Hal Yates. Florence Lake, Jack Rice, Dot Farley, Vivien Oakland, Charlie Hall. The family decides to jar their own fruit preserves.

103. *Contest Crazy* (10/1/48). Hal Yates. Florence Lake, Jack Rice, Dot Farley, Paul Maxey. Florence wins a radio contest, but can't collect her prize because Ed has just become an employee of the sponsoring company.

Leon Errol

Leon Errol was one of that rare breed, the funnyman. There are comedians, comics, and a few clowns still around, but funnymen are hard to find. A funnyman can be amusing under any circumstances; he doesn't need stories to support him, as comedians do; he doesn't need jokes, as comics do; and he doesn't need particular settings, as clowns do. He is funny in himself.

Most funnymen have trademarks which make them

Harry Harvey, Florence, and Edgar in the last comedy of the series, *Contest Crazy*.

unique. Leon Errol is still remembered as the man with the rubber legs. When he portrayed drunks, Errol continually fractured audiences with his outrageously flexible limbs, which always looked as if they were going to give way, but never quite did. Although the rubber legs were Errol's pièce de résistance, they were actually only part of his comic equipment; he knew how to use his entire body to get laughs, in an explosive double take or a funny walk.

Years of training on the stage made him a compleat entertainer, and like most of his colleagues, he was a truly versatile performer. His ability to depict various comic characters went beyond an affinity for makeup and dialects, it consumed him, and, like any good actor, he became the person he was playing. His fondness for adopting disguises and playing contrasting dual roles bears this out.

What is even more amazing is that the Leon Errol most of us know, from movies of the 1930s and 1940s, was hardly a young man. At the height of his film success, in the 1940s, he was already past the age of sixty.

The two-reel comedy was the ideal vehicle for Errol's talents. Like many stage performers of the early twentieth century, Errol had perfected certain staple routines that helped to make him a star. He used these routines in a succession of hit Broadway shows, including the *Ziegfeld Follies,* and on tour in the top vaudeville theatres of the country. A performer like Errol could have built an entire career on just a few acts, which could be repeated for years for different audiences. When vaudeville began to expire, and movies became the prime medium for mass entertainment, many comics and entertainers found themselves in trouble, for once they used their treasured bag of tricks they had to search for new material. When formerly they may have spent twenty years perfecting one routine for the stage, now they had to come up with fresh ideas every month.

Leon Errol's Hollywood career had been very spotty during the 1920s and early 1930s. He starred in a few silent features and landed supporting roles in several talkies, but, for all his talent, he was having trouble finding himself, establishing an effective movie characterization that could carry him through film after film. The two-reel comedy saved him. It was short and sweet. A twenty-minute comedy was the ideal outlet for his talent.

Right from the start, at Paramount in 1933, the basic theme for his later series came into focus: the henpecked husband, given to imbibing, who is always having girl trouble. One interesting aspect of Errol's comedies, especially true of the later RKO shorts, is that Leon's wife actually had something to be suspicious about. In the films of Laurel and Hardy, Hugh Herbert, and most other comics, the wives would misinterpret some totally innocent gesture as a sign that their husbands were philandering, thus providing the basis for a comedy of errors. With Leon Errol, it was made quite clear many times that he really *was* "making whoopee" when his wife's back was turned. *Variety* reviewed *Three Little Swigs* thus: "Long on laughs and well produced, with more than the customary attention apparent. . . . The

dialog is crisp and witty, Errol doing the rest." Another Paramount effort, *No More Bridge,* featured a young comedy actress named Dorothy Granger, whose major association with Errol was not to come for another ten years.

Errol was free-lancing at this time, appearing in some features like *We're Not Dressing* and *The Notorious Sophie Lang,* and starring in two-reelers for The Lambs Club, Paramount, Vitaphone, and finally Columbia. At Vitaphone he filmed a wild two-reeler in Technicolor called *Service with a Smile.* An engagingly absurd short, it centers around a fictitious super-duper gas station, fully equipped with modern gadgets and a chorusful of shapely attendants. Another musical two-reeler for Vitaphone, *Good Morning, Eve,* was a farcical variation on the Adam and Eve story.

Leon's first starring comedy series for Columbia was short-lived. These shorts are a strange lot. *Hold Your Temper,* the first, has Dorothy Granger as Leon's wife, with an engaging premise that just misses the mark. Leon and Dorothy are newlyweds just home from their honeymoon; at breakast, they are perfect lovebirds and begin to giggle quietly. Soon, they burst into laughter, and every time one of them tries to speak, the intended phrase is submerged in another spurt of raucous laughter. In this cheerful state of mind, Leon starts off for work at the Kiwanisy Novelty Company (he's Mr. Kiwanisy). On his way, absolutely everything goes wrong, causing him to lose his perennially sunny disposition and become grouchy and irritable. The fever spreads around his normally happy office and is carried, like a disease, from person to person, weaving its way back to his wife at home, so that by the time he arrives for dinner—calm and composed again—*she* is out of control.

Perfectly Mismated has Vivien Oakland as Leon's wife and Dorothy Granger as the "other woman," plus Lucille Ball in a walk-on as a secretary. *One Too Many* again features Vivien as the wife, and probably the most brutal screen wife Leon ever had. In one prolonged scene, she engages him in an alarmingly real fistfight and beats the daylights out of him! The film also includes Leon's classic stage routine, "Mailing a Letter," the effect of which is completely lost because of director Robert McGowan's attempt to make it more cinematic. Designed for the stage, the routine should be seen from the vantage point of a theatre audience, and not from the top of a mailbox, as it is in this short. The two-reeler is also noteworthy for casting movie souse Jack Norton as a judge sentencing Leon for drunken disorder!

Honeymoon Bridge is one of the most bizarre two-reelers of all time. Leon's honeymoon and subsequent marriage are ruined by his wife's passion for playing bridge.

116

Instead of having dinner on his first anniversary, he ends up waiting for wifie (Geneva Mitchell) at a friend's bridge game. When he can stand it no more, Leon finds a gun and shoots everyone in the room, including himself. As he lies on the floor, his spirit ascends to heaven. We see Leon entering the pearly gates, only to discover the whole group of card players continuing their game, as angels, as if nothing had happened. Leon screams and runs off, passing an elevator to Hades with a leering devil inside. "Do they play bridge down there?" he asks excitedly. "They never heard of it!" shouts the devil, flames flashing around him. "Good," says Leon as he dives into the elevator. The atmosphere is then broken by revealing the episode to be a nightmare, dreamed by Errol on his wedding day.

In 1934, Leon went to RKO, where he continued to make two-reel comedies for the next sixteen years. Initially, his shorts were written and directed by Al Boasberg, one of the top vaudeville and radio comedy writers. These films took on the aura of vaudeville sketches, and, indeed, many of them were expansions of famous comedy acts (*Counselitis* was inspired by "Pay the Two Dollars"). While most of these films were uncinematic, to say the least, they all had one asset—great dialogue. In *Down the Ribber,* Leon is about to join a practical jokers' club; as the initiation, they abduct his car and pose as the staff of his insurance company, the Motor Joy Auto Club. The exchanges are fast and furious, as Leon tries to get some-

In *Perfectly Mismated,* an early Errol comedy, Dorothy Granger is the "other woman" who gets Leon in trouble.

where with the curiously uncooperative staff. "I'd like to see someone about a stolen car," he says for openers. "Certainly," a clerk replies. "What kind of car would you like stolen?"

After Al Boasberg left RKO, Leon's comedies fell into the hands of the short-subject staff that had been working with Edgar Kennedy, Walter Catlett, Clark and McCullough, and RKO's other two-reeler stars. The shorts became more standardized, and Leon's familiar problems —a suspicious wife, oodles of blondes, too much booze, quack business schemes—became regular fare in his fast-paced comedies. His screen wives included Vivian Tobin, Maxine Jennings, Dorothy Christy, and Barbara Jo Allen (later known as Vera Vague). Comedy regulars Bud Jamison, Tom Kennedy, Eddie Gribbon, Jack Rice, and Harry Harvey populated these films, along with such occasional visitors as Lucille Ball (*One Live Ghost*), Irene Ryan (*Tattle Television*), and Lona Andre (*Ring Madness*). While he made many mediocre shorts during this period, Leon always tried his best, and managed to get laughs with his own bits of business even when the gags themselves were weak. One two-reeler, *Should Wives Work?* was nominated for an Academy Award in 1937, but lost to an MGM *Crime Does Not Pay* subject.

Two comedies stand out from this group. The first is *The Jitters* (1938), in which Leon, with too much to drink, decides to enroll at a dancing school. While he waits in one room, the head of the studio is telling a group of chorus girls that he is expecting one of the world's great dance artistes to arrive at any minute. When he comes, the chorus girls are informed, they are not to question him, but follow his every move. Moments later, Leon stumbles in, and, in time to the music, goes into his rubber-legs routine. The girls are a bit perplexed, but, following orders, mimic Leon's every move. The resulting sequence, with Leon in the foreground, and twenty girls behind him determinedly stumbling into each other, is hilarious.

The other outstanding short is *Truth Aches* (1939), in which Leon suffers from being too honest and too talkative. When he goes to see his boss about a raise, friends advise him to keep his mouth shut, but to Leon's consternation, the boss simply stares at him, not saying a word. Trying to make small talk, Leon digs himself into a sizeable hole. "Was that your son who came through the office the other day?" he asks. "Yes," says his taciturn boss. "Well, that's why Mrs. Errol and I have never had any children," Leon says amiably. "They grow up so homely." Needless to say, Leon is fired, and his pal (Harry Harvey) persuades him to get drunk that night and forget his troubles. When Leon still isn't home at 6 A.M.,

Leon Errol and Geneva Mitchell in *Honeymoon Bridge.*

his wife (Anita Garvin) becomes distraught and calls for her parents to comfort her. Harry and Leon have run out of gas on a lonely country road, and it has taken two hours to hike back to town and get a container of fuel. "What are you going to tell your wife?" asks Harry as they drive home. "I'm going to tell her the truth," says Leon. Harry tells him that no one would believe such a hoary tale, and advises him to invent a story about being kidnapped by gangsters. Leon tells him the truth is always best.

When he walks into his home early that morning, his wife and in-laws are waiting, demanding a good story. Leon starts to tell the truth, but he can see that his

Leon has been imbibing, and now he thinks he's making a new acquaintance in *The Jitters.*

Contrary to type in the Errol comedies, Claire Carleton looks rather friendly here.

Lloyd Ingraham and Anita Garvin are waiting for Leon's alibi in _Truth Aches._

skeptical audience will never swallow it, so he reels off Harry's yarn about being kidnapped, and they fall for it completely. Mother-in-law shows Leon pictures in the paper of two crooks who are on the loose, and Leon tells her that they were the ones. He ends up at the police station describing the criminals, and is proclaimed a town hero for his bravery in escaping from their clutches. That evening, while driving along the same road, Leon and Harry pick up two hitchhikers who turn out to be the very same crooks! They spend the night getting a going-over, and when Leon returns home at six the next morning, he is a mess. To his anxious wife, mother-in-law, and father-in-law he confesses, "You know the story I told you last night? Well, it wasn't true." They gasp, as he quickly adds, "It wasn't true last night, but _tonight_ it's true." When they begin to question him, he gets flustered, and finally loses his patience. "You want to know what happened? I RAN OUT OF GAS!!!" he shouts, as his wife hurls a flowerpot at his head.

Leon's comedies at this time had more in common with the Edgar Kennedy shorts than just the same roof over their heads. Errol's shorts suffered, as did Kennedy's, from a lack of consistency in quality and comic management. On the whole, they seemed to hit the bull's-eye, in this period, more often than did the Kennedy shorts. Directors

Leslie Goodwins, Harry D'Arcy, Ben Holmes, Jean Yarbrough, and Lambert Hillyer seemed to fare better with the farcial nature of Leon's comedies than with the situation-comedy flavor of Edgar's. Interestingly enough, Errol remade several of Kennedy's shorts in the 1940s, and vice versa.

In 1942, Dorothy Granger returned to the series, at first as the other woman (in the excellent _Gem Jams_), but then as Leon's wife. She and Errol worked so well together that the constant shift of actresses in the role of Mrs. E. finally came to an end; Dorothy remained his screen wife for the duration of the series. As they got into the groove of making the two-reelers, shooting time was cut down to three days. Says Miss Granger today, "Leon was a real craftsman, very serious about his work. Once we'd get going on a short, he wouldn't let anything interfere with him—it was strictly business."

She goes on to explain, "But he had quite a sense of humor. When you're working in three days, and we were in every scene, and you had a long script, you didn't have time to chase around. But he was a joy to work with. I remember a funny incident on a film which was called _I'll Take Milk_. He keeps having his little nips all the time, in the film, and I'm very annoyed and I'm going to break him. He promises not to have any more, so at the tail end of the film I come into him and he says, 'Honey, I need a drink.' I hand him a glass of milk, and, without looking at it, he takes a swig of it, realizes it's milk, and spits it out. Well, the camera is dollying up for a big close-up as he tastes it, and as he spits it out, to get his reaction. We shot it, but we didn't rehearse it. So he takes this big swig of milk, and he spits out false teeth and everything right into the camera! I think he laughed harder than anyone."

The Errol shorts improved as the 1940s wore on. Although their plots lacked great variety, each one was so fast-paced and professionally done that it hardly mattered. It is a tribute to Errol, Dorothy Granger, director-writer Hal Yates, and the supporting casts that each two-reeler seemed fresh and original. The casts of these shorts included such fine comedy players as Claire Carleton, Wally Brown, Charles Halton, Jack Norton, Vince Barnett, Paul Maxey, Vivien Oakland (much more matronly than she had been in earlier two-reelers), Emory Parnell, Jason Robards, Chester Clute, Russell Hopton, and Harry Harvey, as well as newcomers like Lawrence Tierney, Noel Neill, and Suzi Crandall (who went on to star in her own RKO series, "The Newlyweds").

The typical Errol short at this time had him mixed up with some girl, either innocently (*Girls, Girls, Girls,* with Claire Carleton as a fan dancer named Windermere) or not so innocently (*One Wild Night*). In either case, Dorothy would be suspicious and Leon would have to wriggle out of the situation by one scheme or another. This could involve disguises (*Punchy Pancho*), taking advantage of a lookalike (*Let's Go Stepping*), or simply escaping by climbing out on the apartment ledge (*High and Dizzy*).

Perhaps the archetypical Leon Errol comedy is *Blondes Away* (1947), which contains virtually every element. Leon and Dorothy are celebrating their fifteenth anni-

Dorothy listens in as Leon lets Arthur Loft in on a secret.

versary in the same hotel where they spent their honeymoon. The state of bliss is interrupted when Lulu (Claire Carleton) calls Leon on the phone from the lobby, saying she's got to see him. He meets her in the hall, where she shows him a photo taken of the two of them at a nightclub the previous weekend; she wants $10,000 for the negative, and, generously, gives him a few hours to think it over. House detective Dick Wessel overhears, and offers to help Leon out of the mess. He suggests hiring a girl to pose as Mrs. Errol, letting Lulu show her the photo, and calling her bluff. Leon sends Dorothy out to buy herself a present, and gets to work finding a girl; he winds up with the pretty hotel stenographer (Peggy Maley) and coaches her on her dialogue ("*I* am Mrs. Errol; I *am* Mrs. Errol; I am Mrs. *Errol*"). Meanwhile, Dorothy overhears Dick on the lobby telephone looking for a girl, and volunteers for the job. He sends her up to Leon's room; when she arrives, Leon frantically pushes Peggy into a closet. Dorothy demands to know what's going on. When she goes to hang up her coat, Leon thinks he's sunk—but Peggy isn't there. She's ducked into the shower, which Leon had turned on as *his* alibi. Then house dick Wessel arrives with Lulu, who shows the photograph to Dorothy. Leon climbs out of his bedroom window and along the ledge into the neighboring room, where a British fellow who looks exactly like him is shaving. Unnoticed, Leon borrows his monocle and clothes and goes through the front door down the hall. When he reaches Dorothy and friends, he greets Lulu warmly in his British accent, and manages to convince Dorothy that he's the one in the photo. She angrily sends Lulu on her way, and goes back inside to apologize to Leon. She thinks he's in the shower, and waits patiently as the real Leon climbs back along the ledge into his room, in time to accept Dorothy's apology for being so suspicious. He magnanimously tells her it's all right, and makes her promise never to be suspicious again. Just then, Peggy, still in the bathroom, sneezes. Dorothy stalks inside, and finds the soaking secretary, who musters up her dignity and announces, "I am Mrs. Errol!" Leon makes a hasty retreat, but not hasty enough to duck a flying vase that crashes over his head.

While at RKO in the late 1930s, Leon Errol had co-starred in a film called *The Girl from Mexico* with Lupe Velez. It was a surprising success and led to the popular "Mexican Spitfire" series, in which Leon played a dual role as Uncle Matt, Lupe's benevolent cohort, and as Lord Basil Epping, the amiably bumbling president of the House of Parliament Scotch Whisky Company. The series continued through the mid-1940s and helped to rejuvenate Leon's movie career. He was featured in

Leon, posing as a bandit, runs into the *real* bandit in *Punchy Pancho*.

countless Universal B pictures, providing comic relief for musical stars like Jane Frazee and Johnny Downs. With his old Ziegfeld Follies colleague W. C. Fields he appeared in *Never Give a Sucker an Even Break,* worked occasionally in musicals like *Higher and Higher* at RKO, and finally played Knobby Walsh in the popular Monogram "Joe Palooka" series. On top of all this, he continued to turn out six two-reel comedies every year, hardly showing his age, and indulging in as much physical comedy as ever.

One of his best shorts of the late 1940s was *The Spook Speaks* (1947), in which Dorothy decides to teach her imbibing husband a lesson. The Errols' nephew, lost in an airplane accident and thought dead, is actually alive and well. When he comes to visit Dorothy, she plans to use him in a bizarre scheme to bring Leon to his senses. Leon arrives home practically unconscious, and is put to sleep. When he awakes, his nephew is by his side. "But you're dead!" Leon exclaims. "Yes," says the nephew calmly, "and so are you." He convinces Leon that they are both on probation from heaven, and that no one else can see or hear them. Dorothy then goes through a charade of marrying Leon's best pal and makes many insulting remarks about him, to make him appreciate how much he has neglected her. The scheme works *too* well, however; Leon decides to shoot Dorothy so they can be together again! He is stopped by a vase on the head, and, when he wakes up again, everything has returned to normal. Although laced with oddball black humor, *The Spook Speaks* is one of the most entertaining, offbeat entries in the Errol series.

The two-reelers remained consistently fast and funny at this period, and the comedy unit turned them out like a well-oiled machine. Miss Granger says of working with Errol at this time, "We just rolled it off like nothing. We'd have visitors come on the set and they would think we were really married. And some of them would say, 'Gee, he sure married a young gal!' There *was* quite a difference in our ages at that time." Of Hal Yates, she recalls, "You'd break up if you watched him. To show you how he'd lose himself, we did one short (*High and Dizzy*) with a trained chicken. They had it up on the piano, and Hal was getting a shot of it, and he was saying, 'Look, do this, do this!' He's talking and getting very upset because the chicken won't do what he says!"

The Errol series continued into the 1950s, long after most short-subject series had expired. RKO continued to use the shorts as a training ground for young talent, although Dorothy Granger comments, "The trouble with these youngsters who they would send over to showcase in these films was that they didn't realize they could have learned so much by just watching. They resented the fact that they had been put into a two-reeler. They were above that."

In one particularly amusing short from 1951, *Lord Epping Returns,* Leon revived his hilarious characterization from the "Mexican Spitfire" films, with gratifying results. He might have used the character again in further comedies had *Lord Epping Returns* not been his next-to-last film. After a weekend hunting trip with his good friend Harry Shannon, he suffered a heart attack and died on October 12, 1951, a few months past his seventieth birthday.

At the time of Leon Errol's death, the Errol series was still going strong, and there was definite talk of expanding it into a television series. RKO continued to reissue old shorts for the next few years, however, and included them in short-subject melanges such as "Footlight Varieties."

Errol's fine costar Dorothy Granger has fond memories of the Leon Errol comedy unit. "We were sort of big fish in a little pond. We had our own little group. We had our rotation of two or three cameramen, we had our own hairdressers, we had our own wardrobe mistress, our own make-up man, our own stand-ins. We had a little clique, and we enjoyed it. It was fun. It was hard work, but it was fun." And that hard work and fun are what come across on the screen, and what made the Leon Errol comedies so good.

The Leon Errol Shorts

Following is a complete list of Leon Errol's starring two-reelers; unless otherwise noted, they were released by RKO. In 1931, Warner Brothers filmed *Partners,* a sketch Leon had written for William Gargan, in which he did not appear. He did appear in one of the Bobby Jones golf shorts. During World War Two, he starred in two government shorts which are not on this list: *A Family Feud* (Columbia, 1943), with Jane Darwell, and *Prices Unlimited* (O.W.I., 1944), with Martha O'Driscoll.

1. *Poor Fish.* Columbia (4/27/33), Joseph Santley. Luella Gear, Lynn Overman, Harry Tyler, Harry Short, Harry Shannon. A Lambs Club short in which Leon's wife catches him with an actor in drag and misunderstands.

2. *Three Little Swigs.* Paramount (11/10/33), Arvid E. Gillstrom. Vernon Dent, Lita Chevret. Leon tries to stay sober at his own anniversary party.

3. *Hold Your Temper.* Columbia (12/15/33), Sam White. Dorothy Granger, Arthur Hoyt, James C. Morton, Gertrude Sutton, Phil Dunham, Charlie Hall, Bud Jamison, Robert Burns, Spec O'Donnell. A series of calamities destroys Leon's perennially sunny disposition.

4. *No More Bridge.* Paramount (3/16/34), Arvid E. Gillstrom. Dorothy Granger, Cyril Ring, Ethel Sykes, Francis McDonald, Cupid Ainsworth. Leon and Cyril pretend to go away on business to avoid entering a bridge tournament with their wives.

While Leon disguises himself, Claire Carleton and Harry Harvey look on, in Leon's last short, *Lord Epping Returns.*

Vivien Oakland is about to let Leon have it in *One Too Many;* Bud Jamison holds him back, and Judge Jack Norton tries to interfere.

5. *Autobuyography* (3/16/34). Al Boasberg. Eddie Kane. Edward Keane, Dorothy Wolbert, George Billings. Leon trades in his old car for an expensive new one which proceeds to fall apart.

6. *Service with a Smile.* Warner Brothers (7/28/34), Roy Mack. Maxine Doyle, Herbert Evans, Marie Wells, Harry Seymour, Frank Darien. Leon spins a tall tale about his super-deluxe gas station, run by chorus girls. Filmed in color.

7. *Good Morning, Eve.* Warner Brothers (9/27/34), Roy Mack. June MacCloy, Vernon Dent, Maxine Doyle. The adventures of Adam and Eve over the centuries.

8. *Perfectly Mismated.* Columbia (11/1/34), James Horne. Dorothy Granger, Vivien Oakland, Fred Malatesta, Phil Dunham, Lucille Ball, James Blakely, Arthur Rankin, Allyn Drake, Frank Yaconelli, Ruth Brooks, Billy West, Charles King. Leon has trouble with his bride when his ex-wife turns up next door. Originally titled *Scrambled Wives.*

9. *Fixing a Stew* (11/2/34). Al Boasberg. Eddie Kane, Jack Norton, Lew Kelly, Dot Farley, Pearl Eaton. Leon's wife and mother take drastic action to stop him from his excessive drinking.

10. *One Too Many.* Columbia (12/28/34), Robert McGowan. Vivien Oakland, William Irving, Bud Jamison, Jack Norton. Nothing his wife can do can stop Leon from imbibing after work each day.

11. *Hit and Rum* (4/26/35). Ben Holmes. Edward Kane, Lew Kelly. Leon has an auto accident and gets involved with a genial lunatic.

12. *Salesmanship Ahoy* (7/19/35). Al Boasberg. Lew Kelly, Edward Keene, Marion Lord. Door-to-door salesman Leon uses incredible cunning to get into a house where no peddlers are allowed.

13. *Home Work* (9/20/35). Alf Goulding. Barbara Pepper, Bud Jamison, Edith Craig. Leon, an ''answer man'' at the newspaper where he works, doesn't do so well at home.

14. *Honeymoon Bridge.* Columbia (10/3/35), Del Lord. Geneva Mitchell, Bud Jamison, Bobby Burns, Bess Flowers. Leon's honeymoon, and subsequent marriage, are ruined by his wife's bridge mania.

15. *Counselitis* (11/22/35). Al Boasberg. Edward Kane, Landers Stevens, Ralph Graves, Maxine Jennings. Leon, suspected of shoplifting, has the book thrown at him in court.

16. *Down the Ribber* (3/27/36). Al Boasberg. Kitty McHugh, Edgar Dearing, Ed Keene, Jack Norton, Arthur Aylesworth. Leon is unwittingly initiated into the Loyal Order of Ribbers.

17. *Wholesailing Along* (5/29/36). Al Boasberg. Kitty McHugh, Don Brodie, Robert Graves, Billy Franey, Curly Wright. Rather than pay a plumber, Leon decides to install a bathtub himself.

18. *One Live Ghost* (11/6/36). Leslie Goodwins. Vivien Oakland, Robert Graves, Delmar Watson, Lucille Ball. Leon pretends to commit suicide, to see how his family will react.

19. *Wrong Romance* (5/14/37). Leslie Goodwins. Vivien Oakland, Barbara Pepper, Maxine Jennings, Diana Gibson, Harry Bowen. Leon's wife, entering a story-writing contest, writes to a lonely-hearts columnist. Leon reads the letter and misunderstands.

20. *Should Wives Work?* (9/10/37). Leslie Goodwins. Vivien Oakland, Richard Lane, William Brisbane, Lauretta Puck, Isabel LeMal, Harry Bowen. Leon's boss, who opposes wives working, doesn't know that his secretary is Leon's spouse. Nominated for an Academy Award.

21. *A Rented Riot* (11/7/37). Jean Yarbrough. Jack Carson, Lorraine McLane, Dot Farley, Marjorie Beebe. Leon sublets his apartment while the wife's away, to pay off a debt; a wild party ensues.

22. *Dummy Owner* (1/7/38). Jean Yarbrough. Billy Franey, Maxine Jennings, Frank O'Connor, Edward Keane, Harry Bowen, Eddie Kane, Larry Steers, Donald Kerr, voice of Richard Lane. The boss buys a racehorse in Leon's name.

23. *His Pest Friend* (3/11/38). Leslie Goodwins. Vivien Oakland, William Brisbane, Ed Dunn, Leotta Lorraine. Leon's friend makes his wife appear guilty of two-timing him.

24. *Berth Quakes* (5/6/38). Jean Yarbrough. Benny Bartlett, Vivien Oakland, Joe Dougherty, Landers Stevens, Fred Kelsey. Child psychologist Leon contends with a bratty stepson when he marries a widow.

25. *The Jitters* (7/1/38). Leslie Goodwins. Vivian Tobin, Richard Lane, Alfonso Martell, Jack Rice. Leon drunkenly stumbles into a dancing class.

26. *Stage Fright* (9/23/38). Charles Roberts. Vivian Tobin, Paul Guilfoyle, Eva McKenzie, Don Brodie, Bud Jamison, George Volk. Leon's amateur-actress wife and her colleagues decide to play a joke on Leon, which backfires when he doesn't realize that they're acting.

27. *Major Difficulties* (11/18/38). Lou Brock. Vivian Tobin, Jeffrey Sayre, Barbara Jo Allen, John Dilson, Jack Smart, Dorothy Granger. Leon poses as a noted British explorer to bamboozle a judge who's trying him on a gambling charge.

28. *Crime Rave* (1/13/39). Jean Yarbrough. Vivian Tobin, Ed Kane, Frank Faylen, Louise Squire, Fred Santley, Netta Packer, Bud Jamison. Leon unwittingly brings home two crooks for dinner. Remade by Edgar Kennedy as *Two for the Money*.

29. *Home Boner* (3/10/39). Harry D'Arcy. Muriel Evans, Ed Kane, Lloyd Ingraham, Katherine Sheldon, Dick Elliott, Anita Garvin, Lew Kelly. Leon pretends to his bride and family that a model home is his.

30. *Moving Vanities* (5/5/39). Lou Brock. Barbara Jo Allen, Eddie Gribbon, Bud Jamison, Fred Kelsey, James C. Morton. Leon stalks out when his landlord imposes a 10 percent rent raise, but finds that getting another apartment isn't easy. Remade with Edgar Kennedy as *Love Your Landlord*.

31. *Ring Madness* (6/30/39). Harry D'Arcy. Barbara Jo Allen, Lona Andre, Harry Harvey, John Dilson, Bud Jamison. Leon buys a ring for a pal's girl friend, but Mrs. Errol misunderstands. Partially reworked as *Punchy Pancho*.

32. *Wrong Room* (9/22/39). Lou Brock. Ed Dunn, Connie Keane (Veronica Lake), Charlotte Treadway, John Laing. Professor Errol is an authority on charm—until he gets drunk in a hotel.

33. *Truth Aches* (11/3/39). Charles Roberts. Anita Garvin, Lloyd Ingraham, Katherine Sheldon, Dick Elliott, Harry Harvey. Always-honest Leon has to explain to his wife why he's been out all night.

34. *Scrappily Married* (1/12/40). Arthur Ripley. George Meeker, Lona Andre, Adele Pearce, Katherine Sheldon. Leon, as lawyer to a potential bigamist, gets in plenty of hot water himself.

35. *Bested by a Beard* (7/16/40). Charles Roberts. Anita Garvin, Sally Payne, Arthur O'Connell, Mervin Williams. Leon tries to get himself out of a jam by posing as a noted medium.

36. *He Asked for It* (9/27/40). Harry D'Arcy. Anita Garvin, Harry Harvey, Ken Christy, Arthur O'Connell, Dave Oliver. A judge decides to teach a lesson to Leon, who stands on "constitutional rights" every time he's caught for some misdemeanor.

37. *Tattle Television* (11/29/40). Harry D'Arcy. Lulu Mae Hubbard, Irene Ryan, Ken Christy, Ethel Levey. Mrs. Errol suspects Leon of philandering, when he's only trying to buy her a television set.

38. *The Fired Man* (1/10/41). Charles Roberts. Virginia Vale, James Forte, Nondas Metcalf, Joe Greene, Alaine Brandes. Leon works in a department store's complaint department.

39. *When Wifie's Away* (3/14/41). Harry D'Arcy. Sally Payne, Geraldine Ross, Jean Fontaine, Kenneth Keith. Leon has been rehearsing to appear in vaudeville with Mademoiselle Fifi, but the wife misunderstands.

40. *A Polo Phony* (5/16/41). Harry D'Arcy. Bob Graves, James C. Morton, Keith Hitchcock, Warren Jackson, Bud Jamison, Jack Rice, Charlie Hall. Leon masquerades as an Australian polo star to get through to an important client.

41. *A Panic in the Parlor* (6/27/41). Charles Roberts. Virginia Vale, Josef Forte, Ken Christy, Frank O'Connor. Leon's wife tries to teach him a lesson by pretending to have several lovers.

42. *Man I Cured* (9/26/41). Harry D'Arcy. Eva Puck, Dorothy Granger, Tom Kennedy, Bob Smith, Joan Barclay, Donald Kerr. At a honeymoon lodge, Leon gets involved with a pretty manicurist.

43. *Who's a Dummy?* (11/28/41). Harry D'Arcy. Vivian Tobin, Herbert Vigran, Dorothy Granger, Eddie Kane, Ralph Sanford, Harry Harvey. Leon finds his wife's actions suspicious, not knowing she's rehearsing for a play. A remake of Edgar Kennedy's *Dummy Ache*.

44. *Home Work* (1/9/42). Harry D'Arcy. Vivian Tobin, Tom Kennedy, Dorothy Granger, Harry Harvey, Archie Twitchell. Leon stays home from the office one day to avoid a process server.

45. *Wedded Blitz* (3/13/42). Henry James. Marion Martin, Harry Tyler, Anne O'Neal, Hallene Hill, Polly Bailey, John Maguire, Renée Haal, Lee Bonnell. Neighbors misunderstand when Leon wears various makeups and costumes home. Remade by Gil Lamb as *Hollywood Honeymoon*.

46. *Framing Father* (5/15/42). Charles Roberts. Frances Carson, Walter Reed, Charlie Hall, Dick Martin. Leon's son is seen with a torch singer, but word gets around that it's Dad she's seeing. A remake of the 1936 Ford Sterling comedy of the same name.

48. *Mail Trouble* (9/4/42). Lloyd French. Vivian Tobin, George Cleveland, Tom Kennedy, Isabel LeMal, Heinie Conklin, Pat O'Malley, Lee Shumway, Marten Lamont. Leon explains to a judge why he was trying to break into jail. A remake of Edgar Kennedy's *Morning, Judge*.

48. *Mail Trouble* (9/4/42). Lloyd French. Vivian Tobin, George Cleveland, Anne O'Neal, Mary Halsey. Leon tries to marry off his obnoxious father-in-law. A remake of Edgar Kennedy's *Maid to Order*.

49. *Dear! Deer!* (10/23/42). Ben Holmes. Lydia Bilbrook, Harry Harvey, Bud Jamison, Ann Summers, Russell Wade, Dorothy Granger, Fred Kelsey, Ken Christy, Mary Halsey. Leon tells his wife he's been on a deer-hunting trip, when actually he's gone to a convention.

50. *Pretty Dolly* (12/11/42). Ben Holmes. Carmel Myers, Thelma White, Tom Kennedy, Gerald Hamer, Alfred Hall, Joan

Barclay, Ann Summers, William Gould, Jack Arnold. Leon buys his wife a doll for her birthday, then accidentally burns it.

51. *Double Up* (1/29/43). Ben Holmes. Dorothy Christy, Constance Purdy, Bud Jamison, Myrtle Anderson, Pat O'Malley. Leon hires a lookalike to take his place at home every night while he goes out. A remake of Edgar Kennedy's *Happy Tho Married.*

52. *Gem Jams* (3/19/43). Lambert Hillyer. Dorothy Christy, Dorothy Granger, William Gould, Al Hill, Mary Halsey, Isabel LeMal, Charlie Hall. Leon truthfully tells his wife that he's going out that night to meet a client—then the client turns out to be a woman.

53. *Radio Runaround* (5/7/43). Lambert Hillyer. Dorothy Christy, Wally Brown, Kathryn Keys, Eddie Gribbon, Ann Summers, Isabel LeMal. Operating a radio station has disrupted Leon's marriage.

54. *Seeing Nellie Home* (9/3/43). Ben Holmes. Dorothy Christy, Almira Sessions, Juanita Alvarez, Kate McKenna, Bud Jamison, Earl Dewey, Al Bridge. After taking a lady home from her vocal concert, Leon unwittingly becomes a chauffeur. A remake of Edgar Kennedy's *Vocalizing.*

55. *Cutie on Duty* (10/29/43). Ben Holmes. Dorothy Christy, Claire Carleton, Tom Kennedy, Ida Moore, Isabel LeMal. A blonde who's sold Leon some pots and pans offers to cook a demonstration dinner.

56. *Wedtime Stories* (12/24/43). Ben Holmes. Barbara Brown, Claire Carleton, Sharon Douglas, Larry Lund, Tom Kennedy, Jack Mulhall. Two Leon Errols—Junior and Senior—get married without telling each other, and end up at the same Niagara Falls hotel.

57. *Say Uncle* (2/8/44). Ben Holmes. Claire Carleton, Joan Blair, Bud Jamison, Bob Homans, Earl Dewey, Ken Christy. When the wife catches Leon with a blonde, he tells her that she's a long-lost cousin from Australia.

58. *Poppa Knows Worst* (4/14/44). Ben Holmes. Claire Carleton, Joan Blair. Leon doesn't realize that the woman he's taking to a costume party is his wife.

59. *Girls, Girls, Girls* (6/9/44). Harry D'Arcy. Dorothy Granger, Claire Carleton, Tom Kennedy, Charlie Hall, Russ Hopton, Joan Barclay, Lee Trent, Isabel LeMal. Leon unwittingly buys a burlesque show and gets mixed up with a fan dancer.

60. *Triple Trouble* (9/1/44). Harry D'Arcy. Claire Carleton, Lee Trent, Dorothy Granger, Harry Harvey, Emory Parnell. Leon can't understand his secretary's husband being jealous—until he begins getting suspicious of his *own* wife.

61. *He Forgot to Remember* (10/27/44). Hal Yates. Dorothy Granger, Patti Brill, Emory Parnell, Elaine Riley, Byron Foulger, Harry Harvey. Leon feigns amnesia when the wife starts to suspect that his recent fishing trip was not as advertised. Later used in the 1951 omnibus feature, *Footlight Varieties.*

62. *Birthday Blues* (2/16/45). Hal Yates. Dorothy Granger, Elaine Riley, Larry Tierney, Harry Harvey, Harry Strang, Russ

Hopton, Edmund Glover. Leon unknowingly buys a stolen fur coat for Dorothy's birthday.

63. *Let's Go Stepping* (5/4/45). Hal Yates. Dorothy Granger, Maxine Semon, Chester Clute, Harry Harvey, Jason Robards, Sam Blum, Johnny Strong. Homebody Leon disguises as his gay-blade twin brother to test his wife's loyalty. A remake of Charley Chase's *Vamp Till Ready.*

64. *It Shouldn't Happen to a Dog* (6/15/48). Hal Yates. Dorothy Granger, Emory Parnell, Tom Kennedy, George Holmes, Jason Robards. Dorothy wants to get rid of Leon's dog, but he thinks she's plotting to do away with *him*.

65. *Double Honeymoon* (8/3/45). Hal Yates. Dorothy Granger, Myrna Dell, Marc Cramer, Jack Norton, Paul Brooks, James Jordan, Jr. After a night on a bender, Leon has reason to believe he's married a second wife.

66. *Beware of Redheads* (9/14/45). Hal Yates. Dorothy Granger, Myrna Dell, Arthur Loft, Marc Cramer, Cyril Ring, Tanis Chandler, Tom Noonan. When Leon finds a lady's compact in his pocket, he gives it to Dorothy as a present; then the owner shows up and wants it back.

67. *Maid Trouble* (2/2/46). Harry Edwards. Dorothy Granger, Myrna Dell, Claire Carleton, Harry Hayden, Robert Bray, Phil Warren. Leon's wife and maid are forced to switch places when Leon's boss comes home for dinner.

68. *Oh, Professor, Behave* (3/1/46). Hal Yates. Dorothy Granger, Amelita Ward, Charles Coleman, Joe Devlin, Phil Warren, Myrna Dell, Betty Gillette, Daisy. Leon rents a room to a professor, unaware that the prof is a pretty blonde.

69. *Twin Husbands* (5/10/46). Hal Yates. Dorothy Granger, Marian Carr, Jason Robards, Myrna Dell. Dorothy gets a new hairdo, and Leon's twin brother comes to town, leading to multiple mistaken identity.

70. *I'll Take Milk* (7/19/46). Hal Yates. Dorothy Granger, Myrna Dell, Phil Warren, Claire Carleton, Jason Robards, Lee Frederick. Leon thinks he's stolen a bracelet while drunk at a party, and Dorothy gives it to her newly married niece.

71. *Follow That Blonde* (9/27/46). Hal Yates. Harry Harvey, Claire Carleton, Phil Warren, Marian Carr, Dick Elliott, Carol Forman, Teddy Infuhr. Trouble begins when Leon agrees to drive a friend's car home from a fishing trip.

72. *Borrowed Blonde* (3/7/47). Hal Yates. Dorothy Granger, Peggy Maley, Paul Maxey, Vivien Oakland, Phil Warren. Leon's boss mistakes his pretty blonde neighbor for Leon's wife.

73. *Wife Tames Wolf* (4/25/47). Hal Yates. Dorothy Granger, Eddie Kane, Carol Forman, Phil Warren, Peggy Maley, Barbara Smith. Leon's partner cooks up a scheme to cure him of his flirtations.

74. *In Room 303* (4/25/47). Hal Yates. Harry Harvey, Robert Clarke, Paul Maxey, Gail Davis, Peggy Maley, Jay Norris, Dick Wessel. Leon thinks his son, who's about to be married, is seeing another woman, and tries to straighten it out.

75. *Hired Husband* (5/9/47). Hal Yates. Dorothy Granger,

Jack Norton, Minerva Urecal. Dorothy's aunt is coming to visit, and to please her, Dorothy pretends to be married to her old boyfriend. Used in the compilation feature *Variety Time*.

76. *Blondes Away* (7/11/47). Hal Yates. Dorothy Granger, Claire Carleton, Dick Wessel, Peggy Maley. A tough cookie tries to blackmail Leon while he's on his second honeymoon with Dorothy.

77. *The Spook Speaks* (12/5/47). Hal Yates. Dorothy Granger, Steven Flagg, Harry Harvey, Suzi Crandall, Phil Warren, Donald Kerr, Mickey Simpson. The Errol household conspires to shock Leon out of drinking by pretending that he's dead.

78. *Bet Your Life* (1/16/48). Hal Yates. Dorothy Granger, Suzi Crandall, Charles Halton, Phil Warren. Leon bought a sweepstakes ticket in a friend's name; now he's won, and he has to pretend to be his friend.

79. *Don't Fool Your Wife* (3/5/48). Charles Roberts. Dorothy Granger, Steven Flagg, Suzi Crandall, Lotte Stein. Leon thinks his family only likes him for his money, so he decides to put them to a test.

80. *Secretary Trouble* (4/9/48). Hal Yates. Dorothy Granger, Amelita Ward, Michael Harvey. Leon has trouble with his secretary's jealous husband.

81. *Bachelor Blues* (9/17/48). Leslie Goodwins. Dorothy Granger, Wally Brown, Betty Underwood, Grandon Rhodes. Leon and Dorothy discover that they aren't legally married.

82. *Uninvited Blonde* (11/12/48). Hal Yates. Dorothy Granger, Myrna Dell, Steven Flagg, Marc Logan, Harry Harvey. The

Now Dorothy Granger is Leon's wife, and Peggy Maley is the other woman, in *Borrowed Blonde*.

morning after a wild party, Leon sends a stray blonde home—with Dorothy's fur coat.

83. *Backstage Follies* (12/24/48). Hal Yates. Dorothy Granger, Wally Brown, Betty Underwood, Steven Flagg, Anne O'Neal, Dan Foster. Dorothy is part of a women's group trying to close down the local burlesque theatre; its owner tries to get to her through Leon.

84. *Dad Always Pays* (2/18/49). Hal Yates. Dorothy Granger, Suzi Crandall, Scott Elliott, Judy Clark. Dorothy thinks Leon is setting up a mistress; actually he's preparing for his daughter's marriage.

85. *Cactus Cut-Up* (4/15/49). Charles Roberts. Dorothy Granger, Noel Neill, Roland Morris, Ralph Peters. Leon's daughter's fiancé, a westerner, doesn't want to destroy Leon's illusions about the West.

86. *I Can't Remember* (6/10/49). Hal Yates. Dorothy Granger, Chris Patterson, Robert Bray, Jack Overman, Ralph Dunn, Wheaton Chambers. Leon accidentally takes home a briefcase full of stolen money.

87. *Oil's Well That Ends Well* (8/5/49). Hal Yates. Dorothy Granger, Betty Underwood, Paul Maxey, Charles Coleman. Leon gets tangled up with some oil stocks and his son's boss and fiancée.

88. *Sweet Cheat* (10/28/49). Hal Yates. Dorothy Granger, Vince Barnett, Jack Rice, Robert Gellison, George Chandler. Dorothy dons a blonde wig and disguises as a Southern belle to see if Leon will fall for her.

89. *Shocking Affair* (12/23/49). Hal Yates. Dorothy Granger, Russell Hicks, Raymond Roe, Jack Overman, Christine Larson. One of Leon's screwy inventions almost ruins his son's engagement to a banker's daughter.

90. *High and Dizzy* (2/17/50). Hal Yates. Dorothy Granger, Betty Underwood, Willie Best, Marlo Dwyer, Irmatrude. After

Leon, as a ham actor, tries to make love to Dorothy Christy in *Double Up*.

having one too many, Leon brings home a live chicken which belongs to a blonde nightclub singer.

91. *Texas Tough Guy* (9/15/50). Hal Yates. Dorothy Granger, Wendy Waldron, Robert Neil, Charles Smith, Charles Coleman. Leon poses as his cousin Tex to call off a marriage his daughter has been forced into.

92. *Spooky Wooky* (12/1/50). Hal Yates. Dorothy Granger, Wendy Waldron, Ralph Hodges, Edward Gargan, Charlie Hall. Leon's daughter's friends try to make his new country house seem haunted so he'll move back to the city.

93. *Chinatown Chump* (1/26/51). Hal Yates. Dorothy Granger, Richard Loo, Henry Kulky, Ray Walker. Leon tells Dorothy he's got business with a Chinese importer (he's going to play poker)—then has to prove it.

94. *Punchy Pancho* (3/20/51). Leslie Goodwins. Dorothy Granger, Patricia Michon, James Dobson, Chester Clute, Vivien Oakland, Emil Sitka. Leon disguises as a Mexican bandit to retrieve an expensive ring he inadvertently bought for Dorothy.

95. *One Wild Night* (5/25/51). Hal Yates. Dorothy Granger, Jack Kirkwood, Perry Sheehan, Karen Randle, Judith Allen. Leon's determination not to go out while Dorothy is away is spoiled when a friend brings a party right to Leon's apartment.

96. *Deal Me In* (8/3/51). Hal Yates. Wendy Waldron, Harry Harvey, Emory Parnell, Harry Hayden, Lyle Latell, Ralph Hodges. Leon wants to let an important client win a poker game, but nothing goes right.

97. *Lord Epping Returns* (9/21/51). Leslie Goodwins. Dorothy Granger, Claire Carleton, Harry Harvey. Leon disguises as Lord Epping for an alibi, which works until the real Lord Epping shows up.

98. *Too Many Wives* (12/21/51). Hal Yates. Dorothy Granger, Harry Harvey, Joanne Jordan, Paul Maxey, Sam McDaniel. When Leon's wife walks out, he has a neighbor pose as Mrs. Errol to keep up appearances when his boss comes to dinner.

"The Three Stooges"

In the sound era, no one topped the Three Stooges for longevity and productivity in the two-reeler field. From 1934 to 1958 they starred in 190 comedies for Columbia Pictures; and their shorts continue to be shown today on television stations around the world, capturing the fancy of a whole new generation of fans.

The Stooges' appeal, then and now, is basic. Their humor is built on slapstick and violence, two commodities of universal appeal, and few comics could ever bring off this kind of low comedy as well as the Stooges.

Moe Howard recently explained the formula for their two-reelers: when it came time to fashion a new story, they would think, "Where would we be most out of place?" and on that premise a comedy would be developed. The great part of this was that the Stooges seemed out of place *anywhere,* for their characterizations were, from the very beginning, never quite real.

Moe was, of course, the domineering member of the trio, always barking orders and usually being the butt of their subsequent backfire. Jerry "Curly" Howard (later Sam "Shemp" Howard, still later Joe Besser, and finally Joe DeRita) was the patsy of the group, the fall guy who usually had more going on in his head than anyone would ever suspect. Like Harpo in the Marx Brothers, Curly was slightly surreal, and his bizarre little quirks were never questioned. In *In the Sweet Pie and Pie,* for instance, the threesome are in jail, bemoaning their fate, and Moe mutters, "If we only had some tools." Curly turns to him and asks, "How about these?" He lifts up his shirt and there, tucked into his pants, are a dozen shop utensils of various kinds—saws, files, and so forth. Larry usually got caught in the middle of his two compatriots' schemes, generally going along with the ideas and then sharing in the consequences.

If there is an art to violence, then the Three Stooges were among the few to master it. Over the years they devised seemingly endless variations on ways to slap, poke, and hit one another and somehow make it funny. The trick to the humor was to eliminate the pain; when this failed, the action would become vulgar instead of funny—a mishap that occurred all too often.

The Stooges' basic formula was developed while they were working with comedian Ted Healy in vaudeville. Healy was a boyhood friend of Moe Howard, and later, when both were working in vaudeville, they teamed up and worked out an act; Moe would heckle Healy from the audience. One day when Moe's older brother, Shemp, was watching the performance, they brought him into the action, and he decided to stay. In 1925, they met Larry Fine, who had been with an odd musical act called Haney Sisters and Fine. From there, Ted Healy and his Stooges (also known as Ted Healy and his Gang, Ted Healy and His Southern Gentlemen, and Ted Healy and his Racketeers) became a staple on the top vaudeville circuits around the country. They played on Broadway, and even did a film in 1930 called *Soup to Nuts.*

When Healy accepted a more substantial offer from MGM several years later, the act had taken on a new member, Moe's younger brother Jerry, who became known as "Curly." Shemp left the act when he got a promising offer from Vitaphone in New York. Curly made an ideal stooge, and the team spent a happy year at MGM doing small parts in feature films like *Dancing Lady,* with Clark Gable and Joan Crawford, and starring

Something's bound to happen in this scene from *Three Little Beers*.

in five two-reelers on their own, some of which were filmed in Technicolor.

There was a young director at MGM during this period who got the chance to start his own comedy department at Columbia in 1934. His name was Jules White. One of the first acts he hired to star in his films was the Three Stooges; their mentor, Ted Healy, remained at MGM. White recalls, "I met the Stooges when we were all at MGM. They were funny, no question about that. Once they were on their own, it didn't take us long to prove it. I made sure they had good material, good directors, good casts."

It took a little while for the Stooges to hit their stride at Columbia, even though their second short, *Men in Black,* was nominated for an Academy Award. They first hit the bull's-eye when they were given a new director, Del Lord. Lord was trained in the Mack Sennett school of comedy, and he was the perfect director for the Stooges; he brought a fast pace and a wealth of gag material with him and, before long, was making a string of hilarious comedies.

Lord took one of his all-time best gags, used in a silent short with Billy Bevan, and gave it to Curly in *Dutiful But Dumb* (1942). Curly is trying to eat a bowl of soup, but instead has to do battle with an ornery clam which is apparently very much alive and determined to turn the soup into a battleground. The clam steals Curly's crackers, squirts him, and in general makes things difficult. As funny as the gag was when Billy Bevan did it, it worked twice as well for Curly, whose portrayal of frustration was unequaled by any other screen comic.

Another good director who worked with the Stooges was Charley Chase. He too had a storehouse of material to draw upon, and made good use of it. A key sequence in *Tassels in the Air* (1938), in which the Stooges try to paint a kitchen table, but paint one another more than anything else, was reworked from Chase's own comedy *Luncheon at Twelve* (1933). Done with a careful, deliberate pacing, the sequence was one of the Stooges' all-time best.

Good directors weren't everything to the Stooges, of course; if the material wasn't there, there was only so much a director could do. Del Lord had his misfires, as did Charley Chase. Lord's *Movie Maniacs* (1935), with the irresistible premise of the Stooges running a movie studio, promised much more than it delivered. *Cash and Carry* (1937) was an oddly sentimental venture for three comics who depended heavily on knockabout farce.

Once they had a good story idea with built-in gags in it, the Stooges were home free; if the director on that particular short knew how to make the most of this mate-rial, it turned out even better. Del Lord's *An Ache in Every Stake* (1941), written by veteran comedy director Lloyd French, doesn't have a wasted frame from beginning to end. It opens with the boys as icemen, forced to deliver to a home situated on top of a tremendous flight of steps (not unlike Laurel and Hardy's situation in *The Music Box*). By the time Curly climbs up the steps, his block of ice has melted to the size of an ice cube! The first solution that Moe proposes is to take up *two* blocks of ice, so that, allowing for shrinkage, he will end up with one at the end of his trip. This time, of course, Curly has *two* ice cubes.

After conquering the ice problem, the boys offer their services to the lady of the house as cooks par excellence, to prepare food for her husband's birthday party. This leads into another set of gags in the kitchen, including a wonderful scene in which Curly is told to "shave some ice." He treats the block of ice like a human being and launches into a stream of typical barber patter. Finally, at the party itself, the boys horn in on the guests and generally make a mess of things.

One is left breathless at the end of the short; it moves about as quickly as humanly possible, yet none of the gags seems rushed or abrupt. The continuity flows, and the transitions, from delivering ice to cooking dinner to attending the party, seem perfectly natural—qualities often lacking from the best two-reel comedies.

Director Edward Bernds, who joined the Stooges in 1945, explained how a typical short would come into being. "We'd usually have kind of a bull session in which the boys would wander all over the place, ad-libbing routines, reminiscing, and I would make notes. I would borrow from old scripts too, but mostly I listened. I would stockpile routines, devise some sort of a framework for them to hang onto. I would then write a rough-draft script and call them in. They would go through the first draft; it would give them other notions, and I would make cuts and additions, and somehow hammer out a further draft so that it was pretty much agreed upon by the time it got into final draft."

The Stooges were aided and abetted by a fine group of character comics who comprised a stock company at Columbia. Either Bud Jamison or Vernon Dent was in every film they made; these veteran actors made every scene count, and their presence was of inestimable value. Symona Boniface, the perfect dowager, was a superb foil for the Stooges in slapstick situations, where she invariably wound up with a pie in the face. Christine McIntyre made dozens of shorts with the team, as either heroine or villainess; as often as possible, it was contrived to make use of her fine singing voice (most notably

Curly is passing himself off as a prima donna, with Moe and Larry as his accompanists. Dowager Symona Boniface falls for it completely in *Micro-Phonies*.

in the delightful short *Micro-Phonies*). Dorothy Appleby, Emil Sitka, Kenneth MacDonald, Gene Roth, Phil Van Zandt, Gino Corrado, Fred Kelsey, Dick Curtis, and Bruce Bennett were among the many other supporting players who brought their comic know-how to the Stooges' comedies.

In the mid-1940s Curly became very ill. He tried to remain active, but by 1946 it was evident from his screen appearances that he was not well; his actions were slower and his youthful vitality practically gone. He retired in 1946, returning just once to make an amusing cameo appearance in *Hold That Lion* (1947).

The original "third stooge," Shemp, was rerecruited for the trio, and made himself at home quite easily. An undisputably talented comic, Shemp held his own in the Stooges shorts, but he simply could not take the place of Curly, upon whom so much of the comedy depended. When one thinks of the best Three Stooges shorts, almost all of them are those that featured Curly: *Pardon My Scotch, Healthy, Wealthy, and Dumb, In the Sweet Pie and Pie, An Ache in Every Stake, Micro-Phonies, A-Plumbing We Will Go*, and so forth.

Moreover, at the time Shemp joined the Stooges, Columbia was tightening its belt when it came to making the two-reelers. Remakes and stock footage abounded; very elaborate sight gags were pretty much out of the

question. The best craftsmen in shorts were no longer active, although some of the younger breed, like Ed Bernds, carried on their tradition. Using every means to overcome budgetary restrictions, Bernds even wrote stories to fit available sets.

He explains, "I recall the day I walked in on Stage 7 at Columbia and saw them building this beautiful castle. I immediately went to Hugh McCollum (the producer) and got an OK to do two stories. I wrote one, *Squareheads of the Round Table,* and Elwood Ullman wrote one called *Hot Scots,* both of them shot on those sets. We started writing the scripts while the sets were being built. We put the scripts aside until the picture (I think it was *Lorna Doone*) was all shot, and then we could use pretty much any set that was still standing."

One of Curly's best shorts, *A-Plumbing We Will Go,* was remade as *Vagabond Loafers,* and turned out to be one of Shemp's best as well. In it, he tries to fix a leaky bathtub by adding one pipe after another, eventually trapping himself inside a maze of metal, the water still shooting out of the open end he has not been able to plug! Not content simply to reshoot this old footage, director Jules White also added a new subplot to the film that enabled him to splice in stock footage of the Stooges' mammoth pie fight from *Half-Wits Holiday* (footage that found its way into innumerable two-reelers). In

Curly has his hands full in this scene from *A-Plumbing We Will Go.*

1956, the entire film was re-used as *Scheming Schemers.*

From the early 1950s onward, Jules White took over as producer-director of all the Three Stooges shorts. A competent director with plenty of comedy background, White nevertheless did not have the sense of timing many of his colleagues possessed, nor did he have good taste. Sight gags were fewer and the violence greater in his shorts, and, through the 1950s, he missed his mark more often than he hit it.

The Stooges experimented with different kinds of comedy, with varying degrees of success. Some of their shorts tackled political satire, adult situations, and situation comedy, but, oddly enough, only in the first category did the team succeed. The film in question was *Three Dark Horses,* released during the 1952 presidential campaign.

Jules White also experimented wtih the 3-D rage, testing it out on a short called *Spooks* (1953). As comedy it was fair, but the 3-D gimmick turned out to be just that, and White and Columbia decided to drop the whole idea.

In 1955, Shemp Howard died; he was replaced by veteran comic Joe Besser. The shorts that followed are probably the worst comedies the Stooges ever made, but they do have one saving grace—Besser's comedic talent. It was his vitality that gave those two-reelers what life they had. Several of the shorts made liberal use of stock footage, *Pies and Guys* harking back to *Half-Wits Holiday,* and *Rusty Romeos* repeating *Corny Casanovas* from several years before. Some of these shorts were filmed in exactly *one day.* In fact, they were shot so quickly, and so close together, that although the Stooges stopped working for Columbia in January of 1958, the studio had enough material to release new shorts into early 1959.

Since that time, the Stooges have taken on a new partner, Joe DeRita, known as Curly Joe, and have starred in a handful of compactly made feature films and a series of animated cartoons for television. While they received no residuals from the shorts, the constant telecast of the two-reelers on television stations was responsible for returning the Three Stooges to the limelight. It is these comedies, more than anything else, that keep their names alive.

Just as it is impossible for a television series to maintain consistently superior quality on a week-to-week basis, so it was with the prolific Three Stooges. In twenty-four years of two-reelers, they certainly had their ups and downs. But when there was a spark, when a combination of juices flowed from director, writer, cast, and the Stooges themselves, the results were superb. The best of the Three Stooges shorts can hold their own against any other shorts made during Hollywood's golden age of comedy.

"The Three Stooges" Shorts

Following is a complete list of the Stooges' starring shorts for Columbia. Prior to these, they appeared with Ted Healy in one of Paramount's "Hollywood on Parade" reels, a "Screen Snapshots," and a handful of shorts for MGM, some of them filmed in color (titles include *Hello Pop, The Big Idea, Beer and Pretzels,* and *Plane Nuts*). Later, they appeared in several other "Screen Snapshots" entries for their home stuido, Columbia, which released all the following two-reelers:

1. *Woman Haters* (5/5/34). Archie Gottler. Marjorie White, A. R. Haysel, Monty Collins, Bud Jamison, Snowflake, Jack Norton, Don Roberts, Tiny Sandford, Dorothy Vernon, Les Goodwin, Charles Richman, George Gray, Gilbert C. Emery, Walter Brennan. The story of three woman haters, with the dialogue spoken in rhyme.

2. *Punch Drunks* (7/13/34). Lou Breslow. Dorothy Granger, Arthur Housman, William Irving, Jack "Tiny" Lipson, Billy Bletcher, Al Hill. Curly gets fighting mad every time he hears "Pop Goes the Weasel."

3. *Men in Black* (9/28/34). Raymond McCarey. Dell Henderson, Jeanie Roberts, Ruth Hiatt, Irene Coleman, Billy Gilbert, Little Billy, Arthur West, Bud Jamison, Hank Mann, Joe Mills, Bob Callahan, Phyllis Crane, Carmen André, Helen Splane, Kay Hughes, Eve Reynolds, Eve Kimberly, Lucile Watson, Billie Stockton, Betty André, Arthur Rankin, Neal Burns, Joe Fine, Charles Dorety, Charles King. Doctors Fine, Howard, and Howard dedicate themselves "to duty and humanity" as they systematically wreck a hospital's decorum. Nominated for an Academy Award.

4. *Three Little Pigskins* (12/8/34). Raymond McCarey. Lucille Ball, Gertie Green, Phyllis Crane, Walter Long, Joseph Young, Milton Douglas, Harry Bowen, Lynton Brent, Bud Jamison, Dutch O. G. Hendrian, Charles Dorety, William Irving, Joe Levine, Alex Hirschfield, Billy Wolfstone, Bobby Burns, Jimmie Phillips, Johnny Kascier. A gambler mistakes the Stooges for three ace football players.

5. *Horses Collars* (1/10/35). Clyde Bruckman. Dorothy Kent, Fred Kohler, Fred Kelsey. The Stooges are sent out West by detective Hyden Seek to help a young girl being victimized by a local villain.

6. *Restless Knights* (2/20/35). Charles Lamont. Geneva Mitchell, Walter Brennan, Chris Franke, George Baxter, James Howard, Bud O'Neill, Stanley Blystone, Jack Duffy, Ernie Young, Lynton Brent, Bobby Burns, William Irving, Joe Perry, Al Thompson, Bert Young, Dutch Hendrian, George Speer, Billy Franey. To uphold their royal heritage (their father married the royal chambermaid) the Stooges protect their queen.

7. *Pop Goes the Easel* (3/29/35). Del Lord. Leo White, Bobby Burns, Jack Duffy, Elinor Vandivere, Geneva Mitchell (?). The Stooges run amuck in an artists' studio, climaxing in a clay-throwing melee.

8. *Uncivil Warriors* (4/26/35). Del Lord. Theodore Lorch, Lew Davis, Marvin Loback, Billy Engle, Ford West, Si Jenks, Charles Dorety, Jack Kenny, Bud Jamison, Phyllis Crane, Jennifer Gray, Celeste Edwards, Wes Warner, Lew Archer, Hubert Diltz, Charles Cross, George Gray, Jack Rand, Harry Keaton, James C. Morton. The boys are Duck, Dodge, and Hide, Union spies sent to the South to get enemy secrets during the Civil War.

9. *Pardon My Scotch* (8/1/35). Del Lord. Nat Carr, James C. Morton, Billy Gilbert, Grace Goodall. The boys unwittingly become bootleggers.

10. *Hoi Polloi* (8/29/35). Del Lord. Harry Holmes, Robert Graves, Bud Jamison, Grace Goodall, Betty McMahon, Phyllis Crane, Geneva Mitchell, Kathryn Kitty McHugh, James C. Morton, William Irving, Arthur Rankin, Robert McKenzie, Celeste Edwards, Harriett De Bussman, Mary Dees, Blanche Payson, George B. French, Gail Arnold, Don Roberts, Billy Mann. A professor bets a colleague that he can turn the Stooges into gentlemen. Remade as *Half-Wits Holiday* and *Pies and Guys;* stock footage used in *In the Sweet Pie and Pie.*

11. *Three Little Beers* (11/28/35). Del Lord. Bud Jamison. The boys decide to enter a golf tournament sponsored by their beer company.

12. *Ants in the Pantry* (2/6/36). Preston Black (Jack White). Clara Kimball Young, Harrison Green, Bud Jamison, Isabelle LeMal, Vesey O'Davoren, Douglas Gerrard, Anne O'Neal, James C. Morton, Arthur Rowlands, Phyllis Crane, Al Thompson, Helen Martinez, Charles Dorety, Hilda Title, Bert Young, Lew Davis, Ron Wilson, Bobby Burns, Lynton Brent, Arthur Thalasso, Elaine Waters, Althea Henly, Idalyn Dupré, Stella LeSaint, Flo Promise, Gay Waters. The boys are exterminators who create their own business at a swanky party. Remade as *The Pest Man Wins.*

13. *Movie Maniacs* (2/20/36). Del Lord. Bud Jamison, Lois Lindsey, Arthur Henly, Eve Reynolds, Kenneth Harlan, Mildred Harris, Harry Semels, Antrim Short, Jack Kenney, Charles Dorety, Elaine Waters, Bert Young. The Stooges are mistaken for three New York experts who have taken charge of a Hollywood studio.

14. *Half-Shot Shooters* (4/30/36). Preston Black. Stanley Blystone, Vernon Dent, Harry Semels, John Kascier. Even when they're discharged, the Stooges can't seem to escape their ornery top sergeant.

15. *Disorder in the Court* (5/30/36). Preston Black. Susan Karaan, Dan Brady, Tiny Jones, Bill O'Brien, Bud Jamison, Harry Semels, Edward LeSaint, Hank Bell, James C. Morton. The boys are star witnesses in a murder case.

16. *A Pain in the Pullman* (6/27/36). Preston Black. Bud Jamison, James C. Morton. The Stooges join a vaudeville troupe traveling by train, and make life hectic for their colleagues. A remake of the Thelma Todd–ZaSu Pitts *Show Business.*

17. *False Alarms* (8/16/36). Del Lord. Stanley Blystone. The boys would rather attend a birthday party than fight fires.

18. *Whoops I'm an Indan* (9/11/36). Del Lord. Bud Jamison.

The Stooges with former silent-screen star Clara Kimball Young in *Ants in the Pantry.*

Our con-men heroes have been found out, and in fleeing a lynch mob, take refuge on an Indian reservation.

19. *Slippery Silks* (12/27/36). Preston Black. Vernon Dent, Robert Williams. The Stooges wreck a valuable Chinese cabinet and tangle with its owner.

20. *Grips, Grunts, and Groans* (1/13/37). Preston Black. Harrison Greene, Casey Colombo, Herb Stagman, Chuck Callahan, Blackie Whiteford, Tony Chavez, Elaine Waters, Budd Fine, Sam Lufkin, Everett Sullivan, Bill Irvng, Cy Schindell, Harry Wilson. The Stooges are to guard a wrestler; when he gets away, Curly has to take his place in the ring.

21. *Dizzy Doctors* (3/19/37). Del Lord. June Gittelson, Eva Murray, Ione Leslie, Vernon Dent, Wilfred Lucas, Betty MacMahon, Louise Carver, Bud Jamison, Eric Bunn, Frank Mills, Harley Wood, James C. Morton, A. R. Haysel, Ella McKenzie. The boys go to a local hospital to sell their wonder medicine, "Brighto."

22. *Three Dumb Clucks* (4/17/37). Del Lord. Lynton Brent, Frank Austin. The boys' father wants to leave their mother to marry a gold-digging blonde. Curly plays himself and Father. Remade as *Up in Daisy's Penthouse.*

23. *Back to the Woods* (5/14/37). Preston Black. Bud Jamison, Vernon Dent. In Colonial days, the Stooges are banished into the American wilderness, for a series of encounters with Indians.

24. *Goofs and Saddles* (7/2/37). Del Lord. Ethan Laidlaw, Ted Lorch, Hank Mann, Stanley Blystone, George Gray, Sam

The Stooges enthusiastically take direction from Charley Chase during the filming of *Violent Is the Word for Curly*. Cameraman Lucien Ballard is seated behind Chase. (Notice how the director's chair was originally labeled for Ray McCarey.)

Lufkin, Hank Bell. Moe is Wild Bill Hiccup, Curly is Buffalo Billious, and Larry is Just Plain Bill; they disguise as gamblers to bring in a pack of cattle rustlers.

25. *Cash and Carry* (9/3/37). Del Lord. Lester Dorr. The boys try to help a girl and her crippled brother by buying a house with supposed buried treasure in it. Remade by Andy Clyde.

26. *Playing the Ponies* (10/15/37). Charles Lamont. William Irving, Jack "Tiny" Lipson. The Stooges buy a broken-down race horse called Thunderbolt.

27. *The Sitter-Downers* (11/26/37). Del Lord. Marcia Healey, Betty Mack, June Gittelson, James C. Morton, Bob McKenzie, Jack Long. When the father of the boys' sweethearts refuses to let them marry, the Stooges go on a sit-down strike.

28. *Termites of 1938* (1/7/38). Del Lord. Dorothy Granger, Bud Jamison, Bess Flowers. The Stooges are mistaken for professional escorts and invited to a society party.

29. *Wee Wee, Monsieur* (2/18/38). Del Lord. Bud Jamison, Vernon Dent. The Stooges accidentally join the French army and encounter problems in the land of Tsimmis.

30. *Tassels in the Air* (4/1/38). Charley Chase. Bess Flowers, Vernon Dent, Bud Jamison. The boys are hired as interior decorators. A partial reworking of Chase's *Luncheon at Twelve*.

31. *Flat Foot Stooges* (5/13/38). Charley Chase. Chester Conklin, Dick Curtis, Lola Jensen. Firemen Moe, Larry, and Curly don't realize that it's their own fire house which is ablaze.

32. *Healthy, Wealthy, and Dumb* (5/20/38). Del Lord. Lucille Lund, James C. Morton, Bud Jamison, Bobby Burns. Curly wins a fortune in a radio contest, and three gold-digging girls move in and try to collect. Remade as *A Missed Fortune*.

33. *Violent Is the Word for Curly* (7/2/38). Charley Chase. Eddie Fetherstone, Gladys Gale, Marjorie Dean, Bud Jamison, John T. Murray, Pat Gleason. The Stooges are mistaken for visiting professors at a girls' school, and teach the girls a nonsense song.

34. *Three Missing Links* (7/29/38). Jules White. Monty Collins, Jane Hamilton, James C. Morton, Naba. The only way the boys can get into the movies is to have Curly don a gorilla suit.

35. *Mutts to You* (10/14/38). Charley Chase. Bess Flowers, Lane Chandler, Vernon Dent, Bud Jamison. The Stooges, professional dog-washers, take home an abandoned baby, which is thought to have been kidnapped.

36. *Three Little Sew and Sews* (1/6/39). Del Lord. Harry Semels, Phyllis Barry, James C. Morton, Vernon Dent, Bud Jamison. The boys are mistaken for sailors, Curly for an admiral,

Ann Doran has been accidentally sprayed with powder by Curly in *Three Sappy People*; Moe and hostess Lorna Gray disapprove.

as they become involved with an espionage ring. Original title: *Three Goofy Gobs*.

37. *We Want Our Mummy* (2/24/39). Del Lord. Bud Jamison, Jame C. Morton, Dick Curtis, Robert Williams. The Stooges are hired to find an archaeologist who disappeared while seeking the mummy of King Rutentuton.

38. *A-Ducking They Did Go* (4/7/39). Del Lord. Vernon Dent, Bud Jamison. The boys sell memberships in a duck-hunting club on a lake that hasn't seen a duck in years.

39. *Yes, We Have No Bonanza* (5/19/39). Del Lord. Dick

Curtis, Lynton Brent, Vernon Dent. The boys abandon their jobs as singing waiters in a saloon to dig for gold.

40. *Saved by the Belle* (6/30/39). Charley Chase. Carmen LaRue, Leroy Mason. While in the tropical region of the globe, the Stooges go into business selling earthquake shock-absorbers.

41. *Calling All Curs* (8/25/39). Jules White. Lynton Brent. A prize pooch is stolen from the Stooges' dog hospital.

42. *Oily to Bed, Oily to Rise* (10/6/39). Jules White. Dick Curtis, Richard Fiske, Eddie Laughton, Eva McKenzie. The boys discover that crooks have swindled a kindly widow out of a flourishing oil well. Remade as *Oil's Well That Ends Well.*

43. *Three Sappy People* (12/1/39). Jules White. Lorna Gray, Don Beddoe, Bud Jamison, Ann Doran, Richard Fiske. The Stooges, thought to be psychiatrists, are hired by Beddoe to examine his nutty wife.

An unorthodox summit meeting in *I'll Never Heil Again.*

44. *You Nazty Spy* (1/19/40). Jules White. Dick Curtis, Don Beddoe. A spoof of Hitler and company, with Moe made the dictator of Moronica. Introduction reads, ''Any resemblance between the characters in this picture and any persons, living or dead, is a miracle.''

45. *Rockin' Through the Rockies* (3/8/40). Jules White. Linda Winters (Dorothy Comingore), Dorothy Appleby, Lorna Gray, Kathryn Sheldon. As medicine show entrepreneurs, the Stooges and their troupe face trouble from Indians and wild bears as they travel west.

46. *A-Plumbing We Will Go* (4/19/40). Del Lord. Symona Boniface, Bud Jamison, Bess Flowers, Eddie Laughton. The Stooges try to fix the plumbing in a society mansion, with disastrous results. Remade by El Brendel as *Pick a Peck of Plumbers,* then by the Stooges, using stock footage, as *Vagabond Loafers* and *Scheming Schemers.*

47. *Nutty but Nice* (6/14/40). Jules White. Vernon Dent. The Stooges work to reunite a hospitalized young girl with her father.

48. *How High Is Up?* (7/26/40). Del Lord. Bruce Bennett, Vernon Dent, Edmund Cobb. The boys work as riveters on the 97th story of a building under construction.

49. *From Nurse to Worse* (8/23/40). Jules White. Vernon Dent, Dorothy Appleby. The boys take health insurance on Curly, then try to collect by convincing a doctor that he's crazy.

50. *No Census, No Feeling* (10/4/40). Del Lord. Vernon Dent, Symona Boniface, Max Davidson, Bruce Bennett, Elinor Vandivere. As census takers, the boys go from a bridge party to a football game, all supposedly in the line of duty.

51. *Cuckoo Cavaliers* (11/15/40). Jules White. Dorothy Appleby, Jack O'Shea. The boys buy what they think is a Mexican saloon; it turns out to be a beauty salon.

52. *Boobs in Arms* (12/27/40). Jules White. Richard Fiske, Evelyn Young. The Stooges, working as greeting-card salesmen, accidentally enlist in the Army and wind up behind enemy lines. Opening sequence is a reworking of Laurel and Hardy's *Fixer-Uppers.*

53. *So Long, Mr. Chumps* (2/7/41). Jules White. Vernon Dent, Bruce Bennett, Robert Williams. The Stooges try to get an ''innocent'' man out of prison. Footage used in *Beer Barrel Polecats.*

54. *Dutiful but Dumb* (3/21/41). Del Lord. Vernon Dent, Bud Jamison, James C. Morton, Bruce Bennett, Chester Conklin. The Stooges, as photographers Click, Clack, and Cluck, go to the kingdom of Vulgaria.

55. *All the World's a Stooge* (5/16/41). Del Lord. Lelah Tyler, Emory Parnell, Bud Jamison, Symona Boniface, Olaf Hytten, Richard Fiske. A man tries to pass off the Stooges to his wife as ''refugee children.''

56. *I'll Never Heil Again* (7/11/41). Jules White. Mary Ainslee, John Kascier, Vernon Dent, Bud Jamison. Another Hitler spoof set in Moronica, with a Mata Hari type planting a bomb inside headquarters.

57. *An Ache in Every Stake* (8/22/41). Del Lord. Vernon Dent, Bud Jamison, Gino Corrado, Bess Flowers, Symona Boniface. The Stooges, as icemen, are hired to prepare a fancy birthday dinner.

58. *In the Sweet Pie and Pie* (10/16/41). Jules White. Dorothy Appleby, Mary Ainslee, Ethelreda Leopold, Symona Boniface, Vernon Dent, John Tyrrell, Eddie Laughton. Three society girls marry the Stooges, who are about to be hanged; when they're pardoned, the girls are stuck with them. Includes stock footage

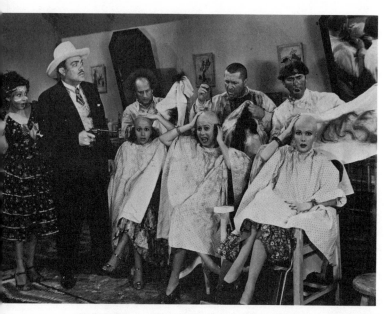

Voila! The results of the boys' beauty treatment in *Cuckoo Cavaliers*. Dorothy Appleby at extreme left, with Bob O'Conor.

with Geneva Mitchell from *Hoi Polloi*. Footage used in *Beer Barrel Polecats*.

59. *Some More of Samoa* (12/4/41). Del Lord. Louise Carver. The boys journey to the island of Rhum Boogie in search of a persimmon tree.

60. *Loco Boy Makes Good* (1/8/42). Jules White. Dorothy Appleby, Vernon Dent, Bud Jamison, Robert Williams. The boys try to save an ailing hotel and its widowed owner, with the help of columnist Waldo Finchell.

61. *Cactus Makes Perfect* (2/26/42). Del Lord. Monty Collins, Vernon Dent, Ernie Adams. The Stooges invent a device that sniffs out gold.

62. *What's the Matador?* (4/23/42). Jules White. Suzanne Kaaren, Harry Burns, Dorothy Appleby, Eddie Laughton. The boys run afoul of a jealous husband just before they are to do a comedy bullfight. Reworked, with stock footage, as *Sappy Bullfighters*.

63. *Matri-Phony* (7/2/42). Harry Edwards. Vernon Dent, Marjorie Deanne. In ancient Erysipelas, the Stooges incur the wrath of their emperor, Octopus Grabus.

64. *Three Smart Saps* (7/30/42). Jules White. Bud Jamison, Barbara Slater, John Tyrrell. The Stooges' fiancées, Stella, Della, and Bella, won't marry them until their father is released from jail.

65. *Even As I.O.U.* (9/18/42). Del Lord. Ruth Skinner, Stanley Blystone, Wheaton Chambers, Vernon Dent, Bud Jamison,

Heinie Conklin, Jack Gardner, Billy Bletcher. The boys progress from bookmakers to race-horse owners.

66. *Sock-a-Bye Baby* (11/13/42). Jules White. Bud Jamison, Julie Gibson, Clarence Straight. The boys take in an abandoned baby and then are accused of kidnapping.

67. *They Stooge to Conga* (1/1/43). Del Lord. Vernon Dent. The Stooges, as repairmen, get mixed up with a gang of saboteurs.

68. *Dizzy Detectives* (2/5/43). Jules White. Bud Jamison. The Stooges, as policemen, are assigned to track down a missing gorilla.

69. *Spook Louder* (4/2/43). Del Lord. Stanley Blystone, William Kelly, Symona Boniface. A reporter hears a wild story about the Stooges' adventures while guarding an inventor's eerie house. A remake of Mack Sennett's *The Great Pie Mystery.*

70. *Back from the Front* (5/28/43). Jules White. Vernon Dent, Bud Jamison. During the war, the Stooges (in the Merchant Marine) encounter two Nazis.

71. *Three Little Twerps* (7/9/43). Harry Edwards. Chester Conklin, Heinie Conklin, Stanley Blystone, Bud Jamison, Duke York. The Stooges barge into a local circus and try to work their way into the proceedings unnoticed.

72. *Higher Than a Kite* (7/30/43). Del Lord. Dick Curtis, Vernon Dent. The Stooges miraculously get inside a bomb which is dropped over Germany; behind German lines, they don disguises and try to get out.

73. *I Can Hardly Wait* (8/13/43). Jules White. Bud Jamison. Curly gets a toothache, and has to visit the dentist.

74. *Dizzy Pilots* (9/24/43). Jules White. Richard Fiske. The Stooges are trying to invent a new plane, but Curly is the one who gets up in the air.

75. *Phony Express* (11/18/43). Del Lord, Shirley Patterson, Chester Conklin, Snub Pollard, Bud Jamison. A Western bandit gang mistakes the Stooges for detectives. Footage used in *Merry Mavericks.*

76. *A Gem of a Jam* (12/30/43). Del Lord. Bud Jamison. The Stooges are janitors in the office of Drs. Harts, Burns, and Belcher, but a trio of crooks think they're the doctors.

77. *Crash Goes the Hash* (2/5/44). Jules White. Vernon Dent, Bud Jamison, Dick Curtis, Symona Boniface. Our three ace reporters act as servants to get the lowdown on a phony nobleman who's going to marry Mrs. Van Bustle.

78. *Busy Buddies* (3/18/44). Del Lord. Vernon Dent, Fred Kelsey. Their short-order restaurant isn't making much money, so the Stooges enter Curly in a cow-milking contest at the State Fair.

79. *The Yoke's on Me* (5/26/44). Jules White. Bob McKenzie. Rejected by the armed services, the boys do their bit in the war by farming.

80. *Idle Roomers* (7/16/44). Del Lord. Christine McIntyre, Duke York, Vernon Dent. The Stooges, as hotel bellboys, are

attracted by a pretty blonde, unaware that she's in vaudeville, and there's also a wild gorilla in her room.

81. *Gents Without Cents* (9/22/44). Jules White. Lindsay, Laverne, and Betty. A musical short as the Stooges pair up with a female trio to do a benefit show at a local shipyard.

82. *No Dough, Boys* (11/24/44). Jules White. Vernon Dent, Christine McIntyre. The Stooges, disguised as Japanese, are believed to be the real thing by an underground Nazi group.

83. *Three Pests in a Mess* (1/9/45). Del Lord. Vernon Dent, Vic Travers, Snub Pollard, Christine McIntyre, Brian O'Hara. A gang moves in on the Stooges when it's thought that they've won a sweepstakes.

84. *Booby Dupes* (3/17/45). Del Lord. Rebel Randall, Vernon Dent. With Curly dressed in a navy captain's uniform, the boys go fishing.

85. *Idiots Deluxe* (7/20/45). Jules White. Vernon Dent, Paul Kruger, Gwen Seager, Eddie Laughton. The boys go on a disaster-prone hunting trip; told in flashback, it explains why Moe is on trial for assaulting Larry and Curly.

86. *If a Body Meets a Body* (8/30/45). Jules White. Theodore Lorch, Fred Kelsey. To claim an inheritance, the boys have to spend a night in a creepy old house. Remake of *Laurel-Hardy Murder Case*.

87. *Micro-Phonies* (11/15/45). Edward Bernds. Christine McIntyre, Gino Corrado, Symona Boniface, Fred Kelsey, Sam Flint, Chester Conklin. A society dowager sees the boys pantomiming to one of Christine's records, and hires them to entertain at her party.

88. *Beer Barrel Polecats* (1/10/46). Jules White. Robert Williams, Vernon Dent, Bruce Bennett. The Stooges go to jail for bootlegging, and do their best to escape.

89. *A Bird in the Head* (2/28/46). Edward Bernds. Vernon Dent, Robert Williams, Frank Lackteen. A mad scientist wants to use Curly's "brain" for an experiment.

90. *Uncivil Warbirds* (3/29/46). Jules White. Faye Williams, Eleanor Counts, Marilyn Johnson, Maury Dexter, Ted Lorch, Al Rosen, Blackie Whiteford. The Stooges get caught between both sides in the Civil War.

91. *Three Troubledoers* (4/25/46). Edward Bernds. Christine McIntyre, Dick Curtis, Bud Fine, Hank Bell, Steve Clarke, Ethan Laidlaw, Joe Garcio, Blackie Whiteford. Curly becomes sheriff, Moe and Larry deputies, in a rough western town.

92. *Monkey Businessmen* (6/20/46). Edward Bernds. Kenneth MacDonald, Fred Kelsey, Snub Pollard, Jean Donahue, Cy Schindell, Rocky Woods. The Stooges find themselves in a very shady sanitarium. Remake of a Smith and Dale two-reeler, *Mutiny on the Body*.

93. *Three Loan Wolves* (7/4/46). Jules White. Beverly Warren, Harold Brauer, Wally Rose, Joe Palma. The Stooges, as pawnbrokers ("Here Today, Pawn Tomorrow"), adopt an infant boy.

94. *G.I. Wanna Go Home* (9/5/46). Jules White. Judy Malcolm, Ethelreda Leopold, Doris Houck, Symona Boniface. The Stooges, ex-G.I.s, face the postwar housing shortage when they want to get married.

95. *Rhythm and Weep* (10/3/46). Jules White. Jack Norton, Doria Patrice, Ruth Godfrey. Just as they are about to end it all, the Stooges and three girl entertainers are hired for a musical show.

96. *Three Little Pirates* (12/5/46). Edward Bernds. Christine McIntyre. The Stooges, shipwrecked on Dead Man's Island, try to escape from the clutches of The Governor.

97. *Half-Wits Holiday* (1/9/47). Jules White. Vernon Dent, Barbara Slater, Ted Lorch, Emil Sitka, Symona Boniface, Helen Dickson. A professor tries to turn the boys into gentlemen—which results in a pie-throwing melee. A remake of *Hoi Polloi*; stock footage from this film used several times in the future. Curly's last starring film with the Stooges.

98. *Fright Night* (3/6/47). Edward Bernds. Cy Schindell, Dick Wessel, Harold Brauer, Claire Carleton. The Stooges, fight managers, are warned by a gangster that if their man wins, it's curtains for them. Film used almost intact as *Fling in the Ring* several years later. This was Shemp's first short as part of the Stooges.

99. *Out West* (4/24/47). Edward Bernds. Jack Norman (Norman Willis), Jacques (Jock) O'Mahoney, Christine McIntyre,

The Stooges try to diagnose Snub Pollard's problem in
Monkey Businessmen.

Vernon Dent, Stanley Blystone, George Chesebro, Frank Ellis. The Stooges do their best to foil a dastardly villain, with the help of the Arizona Kid. Final gag repeated years later in the Stooges' feature *The Outlaws Is Coming.*

100. *Hold That Lion* (7/17/47). Jules White. Kenneth Mac-Donald, Emil Sitka, Dudley Dickerson. The boys board a train going after the man who cheated them out of their inheritance. Curly makes a brief gag appearance on the train. Footage used in *Booty and the Beast.*

101. *Brideless Groom* (9/11/47). Edward Bernds. Dee Green, Christine McIntyre, Doris Colleen. Shemp will inherit half a million dollars if he is married within twenty-four hours.

102. *Sing a Song of Six Pants* (10/30/47). Jules White. Dee Green, Harold Brauer, Virginia Hunter. In need of money, the boys try to capture a wanted criminal to get the reward.

103. *All Gummed Up* (12/18/47). Jules White. Christine McIntyre, Emil Sitka. The Stooges invent a youth serum—and it works!

104. *Shivering Sherlocks* (1/8/48). Del Lord. The Stooges accompany a girl to the spooky old mansion she's inherited.

105. *Pardon My Clutch* (2/26/48). Edward Bernds. Matt McHugh, Emil Sitka. The boys want to go on vacation for the benefit of Shemp's frazzled nerves, but all their plans go amuck.

106. *Squareheads of the Round Table* (3/4/48). Edward Bernds. Phil Van Zandt, Vernon Dent, Jacques O'Mahoney, Christine McIntyre, Harold Brauer, Joe Garcia. The boys, troubadors in King Arthur's Court, help their friend the blacksmith foil the evil Black Prince. Remade, with stock footage, as *Knutzy Knights.*

107. *Fiddlers Three* (5/6/48). Jules White. Vernon Dent, Phil Van Zandt, Virginia Hunter. As Old King Cole's fiddlers, the Stooges come to the aid of their kingdom when the Princess is kidnapped.

108. *Heavenly Daze* (9/2/48). Jules White. Vernon Dent, Sam McDaniel. Shemp dies, but he can't enter Heaven until he goes back to earth and reforms Moe and Larry. Remade, using stock footage, as *Bedlam in Paradise.*

109. *Hot Scots* (7/8/48). Edward Bernds. Herbert Evans, Christine McIntyre, Ted Lorch, Charles Knight. Passing themselves off as detectives, the Stooges guard a "haunted" castle in Scotland. Remade, with stock footage, as *Scotched in Scotland.*

110. *I'm a Monkey's Uncle* (10/7/48). Jules White. Dee Green, Virginia Hunter. In caveman days, the Stooges pursue three lovelies named Aggie, Maggie, and Baggie. Remade with stock footage as *Stone Age Romeos.*

111. *Mummy's Dummies* (11/4/48). Edward Bernds. Dee Green, Phil Van Zandt, Ralph Dunn, Vernon Dent. The Stooges are used-chariot dealers in ancient Egypt.

112. *Crime on Their Hands* (12/9/48). Edward Bernds. Kenneth MacDonald, Christine McIntyre, Charles C. Wilson, Lester

Kenneth McDonald is about to let Shemp have it in *Crime on Their Hands;* **Larry is no help at all.**

Allen. In trying to track down a stolen diamond, Shemp accidentally swallows it.

113. *The Ghost Talks* (2/3/49). Jules White. The Stooges are moving men assigned to an ancient castle where they meet the ghost of Peeping Tom. Footage used in *Creeps.*

114. *Who Done It?* (3/3/49). Edward Bernds. Christine McIntyre, Kenneth MacDonald, Symona Boniface, Emil Sitka, Dudley Dickerson, Herbert Evans. The Stooges, as private detectives, are supposed to protect a millionaire from the clutches of a gang.

115. *Hocus Pocus* (5/5/49). Jules White. Mary Ainslee, Vernon Dent, Jimmy Lloyd. The boys become flagpole-walkers under the influence of Svengarlic, the Magician.

116. *Fuelin' Around* (7/7/49). Edward Bernds. Jacques O'Mahoney, Christine McIntyre, Emil Sitka, Vernon Dent, Phil Van Zandt. Spies mistake Larry for a scientist who's developed a secret rocket fuel, and kidnap him and the Stooges.

117. *Malice in the Palace* (9/1/49). Jules White. George Lewis, Frank Lackteen, Vernon Dent. The boys set out to recover a famous diamond that rests somewhere in Egypt.

118. *Vagabond Loafers* (10/6/49). Edward Bernds. Christine McIntyre, Kenneth MacDonald, Symona Boniface, Emil Sitka, Dudley Dickerson, Herbert Evans. While fixing the plumbing in a society mansion, the Stooges get involved with some clever thieves. A reworking of *A-Plumbing We Will Go,* with some stock footage from *Half-Wits Holiday.* Used almost intact several years later as *Scheming Schemers.*

119. *Dunked in the Deep* (11/3/49). Jules White. Gene Stutenroth (Roth). The Stooges get involved in a spy hunt involving some microfilm.

120. *Punchy Cowpunchers* (1/5/50). Edward Bernds. Jacques O'Mahoney, Christine McIntyre, Dick Wessel, Kenneth MacDonald, Vernon Dent, Emil Sitka. The Stooges work incognito for the United States Cavalry. Note: This and several

subsequent shorts have been incorrectly credited to Hugh Mc-Collum, who produced them.

121. *Hugs and Mugs* (2/2/50). Jules White. Christine McIntyre, Nanette Bordeaux, Kathleen O'Malley, Emil Sitka. The Stooges go on a frantic search for some missing pearls.

122. *Dopey Dicks* (3/2/50). Edward Bernds. Christine McIntyre, Stanley Price, Phil Van Zandt. The Stooges encounter a scientist on the lookout for a brain he can use for his experimental robot.

123. *Love at First Bite* (5/4/50). Jules White. Christine McIntyre, Yvette Reynard, Marie Montiel. The Stooges are awaiting the arrival of the sweethearts they met during the war in France.

124. *Self-Made Maids* (7/6/50). Hugh McCollum. Each Stooge plays four parts in this film, depicting blossoming romance between three artists and their models.

125. *Three Hams on Rye* (9/7/50). Jules White. Nanette Boardman, Emil Sitka, Christine McIntyre. The Stooges, propmen in a theatre, finally get a chance to go on stage.

126. *Studio Stoops* (10/5/50). Edward Bernds. Kenneth MacDonald, Stanley Price, Vernon Dent. Publicists for the B.O. Movie Studio, the Stooges try to foil the kidnapping of one of their stars.

127. *Slap Happy Sleuths* (11/9/50). Hugh McCollum. Stanley Blystone, Emil Sitka, Gene Roth. The Stooges investigate the Great Onion Oil Company robbery.

The Stooges are eyeing Christine McIntyre in this scene from *Who Done It?*

128. *A Snitch in Time* (12/7/50). Edward Bernds. Jean Willes. Furniture dealers, the Stooges get tangled up with jewel thieves.

129. *Three Arabian Nuts* (1/4/51). Edward Bernds. Vernon Dent, Phil Van Zandt, Dick Curtis, Wesley Bly. The Stooges acquire a lamp with an obliging genie inside.

130. *Baby Sitters Jitters* (2/1/51). Jules White. Lynn Davis, David Windsor, Margie Liszt, Myron Healey. A baby is snatched from under the Stooges' noses as they're supposed to be baby-sitting.

131. *Don't Throw That Knife* (5/3/51). Jules White. Dick Curtis, Jean Willes. The Stooges are census takers who just seem to get tangled up more than they should with their interviewees.

132. *Scrambled Brains* (7/7/51). Jules White. Babe London, Emil Sitka, Vernon Dent. Shemp is suffering from hallucinations.

133. *Merry Mavericks* (9/6/51). Edward Bernds. Dan Harvey, Mary Martin, Paul Campbell. The Stooges are medicine-show con men mistaken for fearless lawmen by a gang of toughs. Uses footage from *Phony Express*.

134. *The Tooth Will Out* (10/4/51). Edward Bernds. Margie Liszt, Vernon Dent. The Stooges are none-too-efficient dentists. Original title: *A Yank at the Dentist*.

135. *Hula La La* (11/1/51). Hugh McCollum. Jean Willes, Joy Windsor, Kenneth MacDonald, Emil Sitka. The boys are dancing teachers sent to a South Sea island on assignment.

136. *The Pest Man Wins* (12/6/51). Jules White. Margie Liszt, Nanette Bordeaux, Emil Sitka, Vernon Dent, Helen Dickson, Symona Boniface. The Stooges as exterminators who

Moe lets Shemp know what he thinks of his speech.

bring their own insects with them. A remake of *Ants in the Pantry,* with stock footage from *Half-Wits' Holiday.*

137. *A Missed Fortune* (1/3/52). Jules White. Nanette Bordeaux, Vivian Mason, Vernon Dent. Three gold-digging girls pounce on Shemp when they learn he's won a radio contest. Remake of *Healthy, Wealthy, and Dumb.*

138. *Listen, Judge* (3/6/52). Edward Bernds. Emil Sitka, Vernon Dent, Kitty McHugh. The Stooges are short-order cooks in trouble with the law.

139. *Corny Casanovas* (5/1/52). Jules White. Connie Cezan. Moe, Larry, and Shemp are all in love with the same girl, but they don't know it. Remade, with stock footage, as *Rusty Romeos.*

140. *He Cooked His Goose* (7/3/52). Jules White. Mary Ainslee, Angela Stevens. Larry is two-timing Moe's wife and Shemp's fiancée at the same time. Remade, with stock footage, as *Triple Crossed.*

141. *Gents in a Jam* (7/4/52). Edward Bernds. David Bond, Mary Ainslee, Vernon Dent, Emil Sitka, Kitty McHugh, Mickey Simpson, Dany Sue Nolan. The Stooges try to collect a legacy.

142. *Three Dark Horses* (10/16/52). Jules White. Kenneth MacDonald, Ben Welden. The Stooges get involved with crooked politics.

143. *Cuckoo on a Choo Choo* (12/4/52). Jules White. Patricia Wright, Victoria Horne. The Stooges are stuck on an abandoned train car.

144. *Up in Daisy's Penthouse* (2/5/53). Jules White. Connie Cezan, John Merton, Jack Kenny. The boys' pa wants to marry a young girl—who turns out to be a gun moll. Shemp plays himself and Pa. A remake of *Three Dumb Clucks.*

145. *Booty and the Beast* (3/5/53). Jules White. Kenneth MacDonald, Vernon Dent. The boys unintentionally help a man commit a robbery.

146. *Loose Loot* (4/2/53). Jules White. Kenneth MacDonald, Tom Kennedy, Emil Sitka. Their lawyer, from Cess, Poole, and Drayne, tells the boys they will have to subpeona MacDonald to get their inheritance from him.

147. *Tricky Dicks* (5/7/53). Jules White. Benny Rubin, Connie Cezan, Ferris Taylor, Phil Arnold, Murray Alper. The Stooges go to jail to find their man.

148. *Spooks* (6/15/53). Jules White. Phil Van Zandt, Tom Kennedy, Norma Randall. Posing as pie salesmen, the detective Stooges invade a mad scientist's spooky hideout. Filmed in 3-D.

149. *Pardon My Backfire* (8/15/53). Jules White. Benny Rubin, Frank Sully, Phil Arnold, Fred Kelsey. The Stooges, proprietors of a garage, encounter three crooks on the lam. Filmed in 3-D.

150. *Rip Sew and Stitch* (9/3/53). Jules White. Vernon Dent, Phil Arnold. The boys are tailors who find one of their mannequins has come to life—or so it seems, with a criminal on the loose.

151. *Bubble Trouble* (10/8/53). Jules White. Emil Sitka, Christine McIntyre. A youth serum that works for an old woman backfires on her husband. Overlapping from *All Gummed Up,* using some footage.

152. *Goof on the Roof* (12/3/53). Jules White. The Stooges try to install a television aerial.

153. *Income Tax Sappy* (2/4/54). Jules White. Benny Rubin, Margie Liszt, Nanette Bordeaux. The boys do so well cheating on their income tax that they decide to go into business doing it.

154. *Musty Musketeers* (5/13/54). Jules White. Vernon Dent, Phil Van Zandt. The boys help rescue an abducted princess.

155. *Pal and Gals* (6/3/54). Jules White. Christine McIntyre, George Chesebro. Norman Willis, Heinie Conklin, Vernon Dent. The Stooges go west, and come to the aid of defenseless Little Nell.

156. *Knutzy Knights* (9/2/54). Jules White. Jacques O'Mahoney, Christine McIntyre, Phil Van Zandt. A remake, with stock footage, of *Squareheads of the Round Table.*

157. *Shot in the Frontier* (10/7/54). Jules White. Rivalry over women brings the Stooges to a shoot-out in the old West.

158. *Scotched in Scotland* (11/4/54). Jules White. Phil Van Zandt, Christine McIntyre, Charles Knight. The Stooges are assigned to detective work in a haunted castle. Remake, with stock footage, of *Hot Scots.*

159. *Fling in the Ring* (1/6/55). Jules White. Richard Wessel, Claire Carleton, Frank Sully. The Stooges, as fight managers, are warned against success by the head man in the racket. Remake with much footage from *Fright Night.*

160. *Of Cash and Hash* (2/3/55). Jules White. Kenneth MacDonald, Christine McIntyre, Frank Lackteen. Restaurant owners Moe, Larry, and Shemp get involved with gangsters.

161. *Gypped in the Penthouse* (3/10/55). Jules White. Jean Willes, Emil Sitka. The boys fall for a gold digger.

162. *Bedlam in Paradise* (4/14/55). Jules White. Phil Van Zandt, Sylvia Lewis, Vernon Dent, Symona Boniface. Shemp dies, goes to Heaven, but can't be admitted until he reforms Moe and Larry. Virtually the same film, with most of the footage, as *Heavenly Daze*.

163. *Stone Age Romeos* (6/2/55). Jules White. Emil Sitka, Dee Green, Nancy Saunders, Virginia Hunter. A new framework for footage from *I'm a Monkey's Uncle*.

164. *Wham Bam Slam* (9/1/55). Jules White. Matt McHugh, Alyn Loar, Dora Revier, Wanda Perry. The boys and their family go on a camping trip. Overlapping *Pardon My Clutch*, using some of its footage.

165. *Hot Ice* (10/6/55). Jules White. Kenneth MacDonald, Christine McIntyre. The Stooges are Scotland Yard detectives after the Punjab diamond.

166. *Blunder Boys* (11/3/55). Jules White. Benny Rubin, Angela Stevens, Kenneth MacDonald. The Stooges, as police sergeants Holiday, Tarraday, and Labor Day, track down a gunman disguised as a woman. A spoof of *Dragnet*.

167. *Husbands Beware* (1/5/56). Jules White. Emil Sitka, Christine McIntyre. Moe and Larry, both henpecked, don't see why Shemp shouldn't be in the same boat.

168. *Creeps* (2/2/56). Jules White. The Stooges play their own sons. They relate to the kids their adventures in a haunted castle. Includes stock footage from *The Ghost Talks*.

Joe Besser is obviously a very mature youngster in *Quiz Whiz*. Gene Roth looks impressed.

169. *Flagpole Jitters* (4/5/56). Jules White. Beverly Thomas, Barbara Bartay, Mary Ainslee, Bonnie Menjum, Don Harvey, David Bond, Frank Sully, Dick Alexander. Remake, with stock footage, of *Hocus Pocus*.

170. *For Crimin' Out Loud* (5/3/56). Jules White. Barbara Bartay, Emil Sitka, Christine McIntyre, Duke York, Charles Knight. The boys try to rescue a kidnapped politician.

171. *Rumpus in the Harem* (6/21/56). Jules White. Harriette Tarler, Diana Darrin, Helen Jay, Ruth Godfrey White, Suzanne Ridgeway. The Stooges dare to protect three lovelies from servitude under the Sultan.

172. *Hot Stuff* (9/6/56). Jules White. Emil Sitka, Christine McIntyre, Connie Cezan, Evelyn Lovequist, Andri Pola, Vernon Dent, Harold Brauer. The Stooges try to protect a professor (who has a top-secret rocket fuel formula) and his daughter.

173. *Scheming Schemers* (10/4/56). Jules White. Christine McIntyre, Kenneth MacDonald, Symona Boniface, Emil Sitka, Dudley Dickerson, H. Coons. Virtually the same film as *Vagabond Loafers*, which itself was a remake of *A-Plumbing We Will Go*, with stock footage from *Half-Wits Holiday*.

174. *Commotion on the Ocean* (11/8/56). Jules White. Gene Roth, Harriette Tarler. The Stooges go to sea to track down a spy ring. Shemp's last film with the Stooges.

175. *Hoofs and Goofs* (1/31/57). Jules White. Benny Rubin, Harriette Tarler. The Stooges' sister is reincarnated as a horse! This was Joe Besser's first short with the Stooges.

176. *Muscle Up a Little Closer* (2/28/57). Jules White. Maxine Gates, Ruth Godfrey White, Matt Murphy, Harriette Tarler. The Stooges resort to wrestling to recover an engagement ring stolen from Joe's girlfriend.

177. *A Merry Mix-Up* (3/28/57). Jules White. Nanette Bordeaux, Jeanne Carmen, Ruth Godfrey White, Suzanne Ridgeway, Harriette Tarler, Diana Darrin. The Stooges play identical triplets.

178. *Space Ship Sappy* (4/18/57). Jules White. Benny Rubin, Emil Sitka, Lorraine Crawford, Harriette Tarler, Marilyn Hanold, Doreen Woodbury. The boys travel to a strange planet inhabited by beautiful Amazons.

179. *Guns A-Poppin* (6/13/57). Jules White. Frank Sully, Joe Palma, Vernon Dent. Vacationing in a cabin in the woods, the Stooges get involved with a bandit, a sheriff, and a grizzly bear.

180. *Horsing Around* (9/12/57). Jules White. Emil Sitka, Tony the Wonder Horse, Harriette Tarler. A sequel to *Hoofs and Goofs* with their sister-horse trying to save her husband from the glue factory.

181. *Rusty Romeos* (10/17/57). Jules White. Connie Cezan. The Stooges are all in love with the same girl, only they don't know it. A remake of *Corny Casanovas,* with stock footage.

182. *Outer Space Jitters* (12/5/57). Jules White. Emil Sitka, Gene Roth, Phil Van Zandt, Joe Palma, Dan Blocker, Harriette Tarler, Diana Darrin, Arline Hunter. The boys fly to the planet Sunev and meet some girls with electricity in their veins.

183. *Quiz Whiz* (2/13/58). Jules White. Greta Thyssen, Gene Roth, Milton Frome, Bill Brauer, Emil Sitka. Joe wins a big TV jackpot, then loses it to a gang of swindlers.

184. *Fifi Blows Her Top* (4/10/58). Jules White. Vanda Dupre, Phil Van Zandt, Harriette Tarler, Joe Palma. Joe discovers that his old heart throb, Fifi, is now married and living across the hall.

185. *Pies and Guys* (6/12/58). Jules White. Greta Thyssen, Gene Roth, Milton Frome, Helen Dickson, John Kascier, Harriette Tarler, Symona Boniface. A remake of *Half-Wits' Holiday,* using stock footage.

186. *Sweet and Hot* (9/4/58). Jules White. Muriel Landers. A musical short featuring Muriel as Joe's sister and Moe as a psychiatrist who tries to help her.

187. *Flying Saucer Daffy* (10/9/58). Jules White. Harriette Tarler, Emil Sitka, Gail Bonney, Bek Nelson, Diana Darrin. Joe wins a contest taking a photo of a phony flying saucer—and then encounters a real one.

188. *Oil's Well That Ends Well* (12/4/58). Jules White. A remake, with stock footage, of *Oily to Bed, Oily to Rise.*

189. *Triple Crossed* (2/2/59). Jules White. Angela Stevens, Mary Ainsley, Diana Darrin. Larry tries to cross up Moe and

Phil Van Zandt, Gene Roth, Emil Sitka, and the Stooges in *Outer Space Jitters.*

Joe with their girl friends. A remake, with stock footage, of *He Cooked His Goose.*

190. *Sappy Bullfighters* (6/4/59). Jules White. Greta Thyssen, George Lewis. The boys do their comedy bullfight act in Mexico, and run afoul of a beautiful blonde's husband. A remake, with stock footage, of *What's the Matador.*

"The Pete Smith Specialties"

One of the longest-running, most prolific, and most successful short-subject series of all time was "The Pete Smith Specialties." Viewing some of the shorts today, one often finds it hard to appreciate what made them so popular; many of them seem stilted, and hampered by a gee-whiz, obvious narration.

To understand the success of the Pete Smith shorts, one must put them into their proper context. Smith, born in 1892 in New York City, got into show business as secretary to the general manager of a vaudeville performers' union, and gravitated to the weekly magazine the union published. When it folded, he landed a job on *Billboard,* the trade magazine, as movie editor and critic. Moving into press agentry, he worked for such luminaries as Douglas Fairbanks and Samuel Goldwyn, and eventually became the head of MGM's publicity department, later moving to the advertising branch. When, in 1931, someone was needed to write and narrate Metro's factual short subjects, Smith was nominated, and took on the job as a sideline to his advertising duties. Before long, however, the shorts became his full-time occupation.

Smith's first shorts were part of two current MGM series, "Fisherman's Paradise," and "Sports Champions." His first short, *Wild and Woolly,* featured rodeo footage. Pete took one look at it and decided that instead of treating it factually (rodeo footage was not very unusual anyway), he would "trick it up" by running footage backward, stop-printing, even showing scenes upside down, and adding his wry narration and funny sound effects. This became his standard style.

Right from the start, Smith created a rapport with his audience. His voice was not that of a professional announcer, and that, combined with his perpetual "this-is-only-a-movie-folks" attitude, ingratiated him with the American moviegoing public. The narration device, of course, was also an economic factor, since most of Smith's shorts were shot silent, a great time- and money-saver.

Smith scholar D. Victorek has described the Pete Smith style as a "facility with puns ('a wolf in cheap clothing'), new twists for verbal clichés ('Minnie was poor but particular'), odd but meaningful names for characters ('Lawyer Hightonsil'), and a forthright, and winningly Irish, exploitation of his—and the public's—unfamiliarity with any subject."

As Smith's popularity grew, and MGM saw his potential, he expanded from sports films to a broader range of material. Some of the Smith shorts were instructional. *Inflation* (1933), which explained the economic crisis facing the country, was sugar-coated with the unique Smith treatment, and retained its first-rate entertainment value.

He did ten films in a series called "Goofy Movies," using silent film and newsreel material hoked up via new titles and narration. Each one opened with "Wotaphony Newsreel," and continued with a "Super-Stupid Pictures" presentation, such as *Mad Mike: Archfiend of the Universe.* Some of these were overdone—laden with backward-motion sequences and other gimmicks—but the tedium was usually relieved by Smith's amusing narration. In Number 3 of the series, an actor falls in the water and Smith comments, "His suit is ruined! And he was to speak at the Actors Equity that night!"

In 1935 MGM finally gave Smith his own series, "Pete Smith Specialties," which released from ten to eighteen shorts a year for the next twenty years, uninterrupted. More than twenty of the Specialties were nominated for Academy Awards, with two winning the citation.

Says Smith today, "These shorts were a highly personalized undertaking. In other words, I was in on every phase of production starting with the idea, writing of scripts (our story conferences went on for hours; everyone took a turn at acting out sequences); frequently I sat down at a typewriter and rewrote sequences rather than go into long meetings with the writer and director when the rush was on. In fact, we were a team and no one felt offended when someone else came up with an idea in his or her department and helped out."

Smith had a fixed budget from MGM every year, and it was his to spend as he saw fit. In the 1940s each short averaged $20,000, but when one could be made more cheaply, say by using stock footage, Smith could be more elaborate with another film during the season. Some shorts, for instance, were shot in Technicolor.

One of Smith's directors, George Sidney, explains: "Some shorts were shot in a day, others in a week. Writing, preparation, budgeting, shooting, and editing were done with the same thoroughness as for a feature. From the idea to the answer print would be several months.

A sketch of Pete Smith.

We had access to most (MGM) facilities so long as we did not get in the way." Sidney was a teen-ager, shooting MGM's screen tests, when he submitted a script called "Polo" to Smith in 1936. Smith liked it, and, since Sidney was the only one on the staff who actually played polo, he was asked to direct it as well. Others who started their directing careers doing Pete Smith shorts included Jack Cummings, David Miller, Jules White, Jacques Tourneur, Fred Zinnemann, Edward Cahn, Felix Feist, Joseph Newman, and Roy Rowland.

Ironically, one of Smith's most successful shorts was comprised of footage he bought from some free-lancers named Jack Norling and Jack Leventhal. Together with a young man named Robert Neuschotz, they had filmed some 3-D footage that intrigued Smith. He bought it for $11,000 and molded the footage into a short called *Audioscopiks,* which reportedly grossed an amazing $300,000 in the United States and Canada. In 1938, a sequel, called *New Audioscopiks,* was released to similar acclaim; in 1941 a third subject, *The Third-Dimensional Murder,* was made. Says George Sidney, who directed this last film, "No one knew how to do 3-D. There was no book from which to get answers and there was no equipment. I suppose I got the assignment because of my being a photographer and an experimenter. We built a track and had two Bells [Bell and Howell] facing each other. Then we made a trap, or matte box, which accepted the lens of each camera focusing on a 90° prism. We had no finder, so we had to guess by eye if the object was in the frame. We lined up the shot by the cameraman, Walter Lundin, looking in one camera and me in the other simultaneously and then we would tell each other our framing. We then would change positions and repeat the information. My eyes were 20-20 +20, Walter's minus 4½, so every time we would change cameras our eyes would get knocked out of our heads until we readjusted the eye piece. By trial and error, we had to make our own parallax table, as well as figure out the inner ocular response."

All the trouble was worthwhile, however, for Pete Smith's 3-D shorts were unique and fantastically successful. When 3-D was booming in the 1950s, MGM released a composite of the shorts, called *Metroscopiks,* overseas and grossed one million dollars with it.

Typical Smith shorts of the 1930s covered such topics as women's makeup (*Gilding the Lily*), bounced checks (*The Grand Bounce*), mountain climbing (*Three on a Rope*), cooking (a series with *The Los Angeles Examiner*'s Prudence Penny, the first of which, *Penny Wisdom,* won an Academy Award), and archery (*Follow the Arrow*).

In 1935, Smith made a short on the Virginia Military Academy. He asked the academy for someone to act as technical adviser, and they appointed a young cadet for the job. The cadet was Frank McCarthy, who later became a film producer and crowned his career in 1970 with *Patton.*

In 1937 the Smith crew became the first to photograph radium, at the California Institute of Technology, for *The Romance of Radium.* The year before, two young men named Arthur Ornitz and Gunther von Fritsch brought Smith a 16mm film they had made about a stray dog. Pete liked it, and hired them to expand and refilm it, as *Wanted: A Master.* Von Fritsch continued to make dog stories for the Smith series into the 1940s, including the excellent *Fala* (1943), which remains one of Smith's favorites.

Sports films were always popular, but Pete struck a special chord with *Football Thrills of 1937* (1938), which proved so popular that he continued to do the short on an annual basis, releasing one at the start of every football season. Another series-within-the-series was *What's Your I.Q.?,* a sure-fire quiz device first used in a 1940 short of that title and continued, covering everything from music to world travel in an audience-quiz format, for the duration of the series.

Pete and Dr. Harold Eggerton of M.I.T. take a stroboscopic shot of an egg dropping into a fan, for their Academy-Award-winning short, *Quicker 'n a Wink.*

Pete signs Dave O'Brien to a long-term contract as actor, writer, and director in 1945.

In 1940 Pete topped his 3-D series with another unique reel called *Quicker 'n a Wink,* which won an Academy Award. The short was a collaboration among director George Sidney, writer Buddy Adler (later the head of 20th Century Fox), and Dr. Harold Eggerton of the Massachusetts Institute of Technology, and was the first time the stroboscope was used to film fleeting actions which we all take for granted, to show what actually happens in that split second (a bubble bursting, and so forth). It is one of the best shorts ever made in the series, and remains a special favorite of both Smith and Sidney. Sidney enjoyed working with Eggerton, but added, "Of course, he only thought of the technical use of the stroboscope, and my thinking was visual entertainment and informational. We ended up using the lens from my Leica."

In 1942 one of Smith's best directors, Will Jason, recommended a young actor-stuntman with wide experience to star in one of the series' domestic comedies. Dave O'Brien became a fixture in the "Pete Smith Specialties" of the 1940s, and, before long, was directing and writing (under the pseudonym of David Barclay) the shorts, as well as starring in them.

As the 1940s progressed, the Pete Smith team concentrated more and more on the O'Brien shorts, which explored various common human foibles, using visual humor (emphasizing O'Brien's prowess as a stuntman) rather than verbal humor (as Robert Benchley did with the same kind of material). In fact, it was in these shorts that Smith's narration first seemed at times to be genuinely intrusive. Many of the ingenious sight gags his team dreamed up were dissipated by Smith's narrative anticipation of the gags. Apparently aware of this hazard, Smith started to use this handicap to his own ends, virtually satirizing his own narration.

In *Let's Cogitate,* Dave is playing with a boomerang. At one point it fires back; he ducks as the object flies through a windowpane behind him, missing his head. Smith comments that we were probably expecting it to hit Dave on the noggin, and he adds, "Folks, I wouldn't disappoint you for the world," as the boomerang suddenly reappears and knocks Dave out cold.

Dave O'Brien later told D. Victorek that working for Pete was "very educational, comedy-wise," and that Smith had "a great sense of humor and would never accept a comedy gag without a good switch at the end." Indeed, this kind of gag became a staple in the O'Brien shorts.

Smith recalls, "Sometimes, developing laugh situations had its complications, as for instance the time we needed a real live bumblebee (the prop ones looked too phony) to crawl up Dave O'Brien's naked back and up under his toupee while he was sunning himself on the patio couch. It just happened that bumblebees were out of season at the time. I reached the nearest beekeeper who could produce a bumblebee at Indio, a few hundred miles away in the desert. I needed such a bee and several stand-in bees the following day, or hold up a whole sequence. It was too good to drop. So I dispatched a driver and a studio limousine to the desert at midnight (studios always transported important passengers in limos). Our bumblebee, and stand-ins, arrived on the set the following morning just in time for Dave's big scene. No, the bumblebees were not trained to take direction. The action was started with the bee under Dave's hairpiece. To escape, it crawled out and down his back. The film was then reversed when cut into the picture.

"The topper came a week later. As I looked out of my office window there, sitting peacefully on the pane, was a nice fat bumblebee. His season in Culver City had arrived, and like most everyone else, he was trying to get into the movies."

Some of the best O'Brien comedies were based on various "pests." The first in this series, *Movie Pests,* was nominated for an Academy Award as Best One-reel Short Subject of 1944. It depicts what is unfortunately a typical movie audience: a lady who insists on wearing her hat while sitting in front of another hapless patron; a guy who cracks peanuts throughout the show, and throws the empty shells at random; a long-legged patron who keeps his foot out in the aisle for people to trip over, and so forth. The short is very funny, but the key to its enjoyment is that, at the end, Pete says, "Don't you sometimes wish . . ." and shows deliriously happy moviegoers taking revenge on all those obnoxious pests: a fellow cuts the feathers off the hat of the lady in front of him, another stomps on the toe of the jerk with his foot in the aisle, and so on.

Pests became a fixture in the O'Brien shorts, with felicitous results in *Bus Pests* (1945), where Dave has to contend with men who read his newspaper, stare at him, hold up the bus while searching for the correct fare, only to come up with a twenty-dollar bill, etcetera; *Guest Pests* (1945), showing annoying houseguests; and *Neighbor Pests* (1948), in which Dave's neighbors use his phone, borrow his lawn mower, throw wild parties late at night, and, worst of all, harbor a vicious police dog.

Pete's assistant was Phil Anderson, who had originally been an assistant cutter at MGM. He later acted as O'Brien's assistant director on most of the shorts, although Pete recalls, "At times I went on the set when Dave was in trouble directing and acting a tricky gag at the same time, and took a hand at directing." He adds that in story conferences, Dave would always demonstrate his spectacular falls, which very often "shook the building."

But as a director Dave was equally skillful. One beautiful visual gag from *I Love My Wife But* . . . comes to mind. Whenever a husband accompanies his wife on a shopping trip, hubby invariably catches the eye of an embarrassed female shopper in the vicinity. In this case, it's an older woman buying a girdle. By using the sundry mirrors that fill the salesroom (and O'Brien's ingenious camera angles) he makes it impossible for their eyes *not* to meet, in mutual embarrassment.

Of course, the O'Brien comedies were not the only ingredient in Pete Smith's bag of tricks during the 1940s. During the war, he made morale-building and instructional films, although these were usually presented in a lighthearted manner. *Fixin' Tricks* (1943), for instance, stars Dave O'Brien and has many of the markings of a typical comedy reel. But there's an object lesson behind each of the household gadgets that backfires in the short: Pete tells the viewer how to do his own repairs. Safety-instructional films included *First Aid, Seventh Column, Water Wisdom,* and *Safety Sleuth.* War-oriented shorts included *Aeronautics, Army Champions, Victory Quiz, Self-Defense, Victory Vittles, Marines in the Making,* and *Scrap Happy.*

One of the best wartime shorts was *Fala* (1943), an "autobiographical" short of President Roosevelt's popular dog, who (in Pete's voice) tells us about a typical day in his life. The short combines newsreel and stock footage

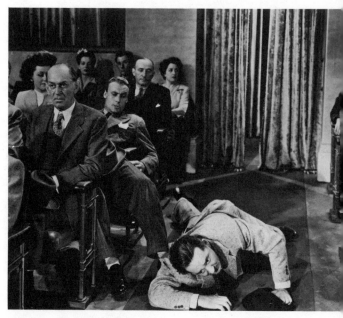

A movie customer trips over the foot of Dave O'Brien, one of the typical *Movie Pests*.

with new material actually filmed at the White House, including some charming scenes of Fala playing with "the Chief." A Technicolor sequel, *Fala at Hyde Park,* was made several years later, with a script approved and slightly revised by FDR.

When one of Lena Horne's musical numbers, "Ain't It the Truth," was cut from *Cabin in the Sky,* Pete grabbed it and later made use of it in *Studio Visit* (1946), a short that ostensibly showed moviegoers how movies were made. It was actually a showcase for sequences from earlier Specialties, along with the musical number, and a new connecting thread showing Dave O'Brien on the set of one of the Pete Smith shorts.

The postwar period brought many changes to Hollywood and wreaked havoc at some studios, notably MGM. But nothing seemed to affect the "Pete Smith Specialties," which continued uninterrupted, with the same ingenuity and production values as always. In fact, some of the best shorts from the series were done in the late 1940s and 1950s, including *Those Good Old Days,* a hilarious O'Brien comedy comparing modern times to the gay nineties, featuring Dave as incongruously funny gentleman in days of yore. The film also includes one of the series' all-time wildest gags: after proposing marriage, and having his proposal accepted, Dave leaves his sweetheart's home "walking on air"—literally! (Dave's leading lady in this, and all his shorts since 1946, was his real-life wife, Dorothy Short). Another winner was *Things We Can Do Without* (1954), an especially elaborate short showing modern inventions for the home—furniture that comes out of the wall when a button is pressed, and the like. Needless to say, before the short is over, everything backfires.

In 1954, the victim of heart trouble, Pete Smith announced his impending retirement later that year, after completing enough films to last through the 1955 season. The final short in the durable series was a tribute to Dave O'Brien called *The Fall Guy*, in which Pete introduced Dave as "the number one fall guy of the movies," and went on to prove it with clips from *Let's Cogitate, You Can't Win, Wrong-Way Butch, Pet Peeves,* and *We Can Dream, Can't We?* showing some of O'Brien's most awesome stunts (which were often more breathtaking than amusing).

In 1955, the Academy of Motion Picture Arts and Sciences presented Pete with a special award reading, "To Pete Smith for his witty and pungent observations of the

Dorothy Short has an "I-told-you-so" look on her face; all Dave has on his face is soot in this scene from *I Love My Wife, But . . .*

Later in the film, the victim gets an opportunity for revenge.

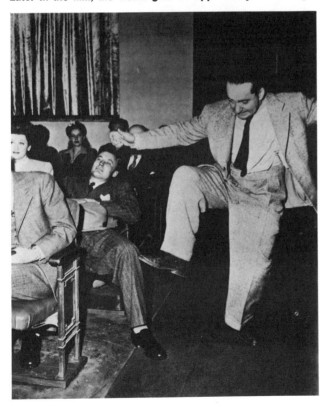

American scene in his series of 'Pete Smith Specialties.'" It was an award well deserved, for, over the past twenty-odd years, Pete Smith himself had become part of the national scene—an institution, an indelible part of the movie program, as much as a newsreel and a cartoon. Yet his billing, "A Smith named Pete," and his familiar sign-off, "G'bye now," always kept the films down to earth, so that moviegoers came to regard him as a friend, and the films as friendly visits rather than movies.

The enduring popularity of the shorts is a testament to Pete Smith's success.

The Pete Smith Shorts

Pete Smith was making his own distinctive shorts for five years at MGM before they officially became "Pete Smith Specialties." Therefore, this list includes all his shorts, separated into the various series on which he worked. The list does not include such wartime government shorts as *Tree in a Test Tube* (1943), which Smith narrated and which featured Laurel and Hardy. All the following were released by MGM, and were one reel in length.

"Fisherman's Paradise"

1. *Fisherman's Paradise* (8/15/31). No director credited. The initial short in this series.

2. *Pearls and Devil-Fish* (9/19/31). Harold Austin. Depicting the dangers pearl divers face in the South Seas, especially from the huge devil-fish.

3. *Sharks and Swordfish* (10/24/31). No director credited. More underwater views.

4. *Piscatorial Pleasures* (11/28/31). Harold Austin.

5. *Trout Fishing* (4/2/32). Irving Reis.

6. *Color Scales* (4/23/32). Zion Myers. Filmed in color, this short shows various species of fish at the San Francisco aquarium.

"Sports Champions"

1. *Splash!* (10/3/31). Zion Myers, Jules White. The art of diving.

2. *Wild and Woolly* (11/7/31). Charles Dorian. Action galore at a Wild West rodeo.

3. *Whippet Racing* (12/12/31). Ward Wing. Training whippets for racing; the reel concludes with an actual race.

4. *Lesson in Golf* (1/16/32). Dudley Murphy. A how-to session.

5. *Dive In* (2/21/32). Ray McCarey. Well-known swimmers and divers doing difficult water tricks with apparent ease; slow motion shows how it's done.

6. *Olympic Events* (3/5/32). Ray McCarey. Pole vaulting, hurdle topping, relay racing, and the hammer throw at the 1932 Olympic Games.

7. *Athletic Daze* (3/26/32). Ray McCarey. The history and background of various events to take place at the 1932 Olympic Games in Los Angeles.

8. *Flying Spikes* (4/16/32). Ray McCarey. Track and field sports.

9. *Timber Toppers* (5/7/32). Ray McCarey. More track and field footage.

10. *Snow Birds* (8/20/32). Jules White. 1931 skiing champions show their stuff on the world's longest ski jump, in Norway.

11. *Desert Regatta* (9/17/32). Jules White. The world's leading outboard motorists compete on the Salton Sea.

12. *Pigskin* (10/22/32). Ray McCarey. Dick Hanley. The rigors of preseason football training are shown and explained.

13. *Block and Tackle* (11/5/32). Dick Hanley, Northwestern University football team, "Pug" Rentner. With the aid of slow motion, the intricacies of modern football line work and trick plays are revealed.

14. *Swing High* (11/12/32). Jack Cummings. The slow-motion camera shows the skill and precision needed to perform aerial acts. Nominated for an Academy Award.

15. *Football Footwork* (11/19/32). Felix E. Feist. Dick Hanley, "Pug" Rentner. Shows the training necessary for a player to hold his feet in quick runs and shifts, and the hip work required when he is in a broken field. Illustrated with the help of slow motion.

16. *Chalk Up* (12/10/32). Zion Myers. Willie Hoppe. The world's champion billiard player demonstrates his remarkable skill.

17. *Motorcycle Mania* (1/28/33). Jack Cummings. A session with motorcycle stunt riders.

18. *Bone Crushers* (2/8/33). Ward Wing. The art of wrestling, depicted with the aid of slow motion.

19. *Allez Oop* (3/11/33). Jack Cummings. The Five Maxellos. Expert tumbling and balancing tricks by an ace acrobatic act.

20. *Throttle Pushers* (4/1/33). Jules White. The thrills of auto racing.

"Goofy Movies"

1. *Goofy Movies #1* (12/23/33).
2. *Goofy Movies #2* (2/24/34).
3. *Goofy Movies #3* (3/24/34).
4. *Goofy Movies #4* (5/5/34).
5. *Goofy Movies #5* (6/6/34).
6. *Goofy Movies #6* (7/28/34).
7. *Goofy Movies #7* (9/18/34).
8. *Goofy Movies #8* (10/6/34).
9. *Goofy Movies #9* (11/3/34).
10. *Goofy Movies #10* (12/1/34).

"MGM Oddities"

1. *Handlebars* (8/26/33). Jules White. The history of bicycling from the nineteenth century to date.

2. *Microscopic Mysteries* (10/18/32). Hugo Lund. The microscope reveals the activities and battles of insect life.

3. *Menu* (9/23/33). Nick Grinde. A colorful look at food written by Thorne "Topper" Smith. Filmed in color. Nominated for an Academy Award.

4. *Happy Warriors* (10/21/33). Jules White. The unusual Indian ball game is shown.

5. *Fine Feathers* (11/18/33). Jules White. Shows various species of birds. Filmed in color.

6. *Roping Wild Bears* (2/10/34). W. Earle Frank. Forest Rangers lasso wild bears that have been killing livestock, and send them off to zoos.

7. *Vital Victuals* (3/3/34). Nick Grinde. A cooking demonstration for the ladies, filmed in color.

8. *Trick Golf* (3/24/34). No director credited. Trick golf shots are performed by experts.

9. *Nipups* (4/28/34). Marty Brooks. More acrobatic feats.

10. *Flying Hunters* (5/12/34). Lauron A. Draper. Hunting coyote by airplane over the snow-covered fields of Montana.

11. *Attention, Suckers* (6/19/34). Jack Cummings. Luis Zingone, Irene Hervey, Muriel Evans, Harrison Greene. Expert Zingone gives away gambling tricks that most often baffle people. Footage later used in *Studio Visit*.

12. *Taking Care of Baby* (8/25/34). Jack Cummings. Irene Hervey. A domestic comedy that illustrates how to care for a newborn child.

13. *Pro Football* (9/22/34). Ray McCarey. Chicago Bears, Red Grange, Bronko Nagurski, Carl Brombaugh, Ookie Miller. Top football stars caught by the slow-motion camera.

14. *Pichianni Troupe* (9/22/34). No director credited. The acrobatic Pichianni Troupe goes through its paces.

15. *Strikes and Spares* (10/20/34). Felix E. Feist. Andy Varipapa. The world's champion bowler demonstrates proper form and technique. Nominated for an Academy Award.

16. *Dartmouth Days* (11/17/34). Maurice Rapf. A tour of the Dartmouth campus, highlighting the famous winter sports there.

17. *Rugby* (12/15/34). Ray McCarey. A look at the game which is the father of modern American football.

18. *Motorcycle Cossacks* (1/12/35). Antonio Samaniego. The crack motorcycle corps of the Mexico City Police Department is shown in action.

19. *Donkey Baseball* (3/2/35). John Waters. Showing one of the 1930s wackier fads—playing baseball while riding donkeys.

20. *Sporting Nuts* (3/23/35). No director credited. More action footage.

21. *Fightin' Fish* (4/6/35). No director credited. The thrill of battling with a fish from the end of a line.

22. *Chain Letter Dimes* (4/20/35). Al Ray. A burlesque on the chain-letter craze sweeping the country.

23. *Prince, King of Dogs* (7/6/35). Felix E. Feist. The only German shepherd that can jump rope, leap through a hoop, and walk a high wire.

"Sports Parade"

1. *Basketball Technique* (8/31/35). Ray McCarey. A demonstration of proper form in playing basketball.

2. *Football Teamwork* (9/8/35). Felix E. Feist. How a team coordinates its actions in a game of football.

3. *Gymnastics* (10/26/35). Charles T. Trego. A demonstration by experts.

4. *Water Sports* (10/26/35). Ray McCarey. Covering sailboat racing and surfboard riding.

5. *Crew Racing* (12/21/35). David Miller. Showing one of America's most time-honored sports.

6. *Air Hoppers* (1/18/36). Joseph Boyle. The story of glider planes.

7. *Table Tennis* (2/15/36). David Miller. Coleman Clark, Ping-Pong champ, demonstrates some delightful trick plays. Color sequences.

8. *Racing Canines* (3/14/36). David Miller. How hounds are raised and trained for racing purposes.

9. *Aquatic Artistry* (4/11/36). David Miller. Gus Smith, Olympic diving champion, demonstrates springboard diving par excellence.

10. *Polo* (5/9/36). George Sidney. The many factors that combine to make polo one of the most exciting of all sports.

11. *Harnessed Rhythm* (6/6/36). Jacques Tourneur. The education and training of a trotting horse from the time of birth to the age of three, when racing begins.

12. *Dare-Deviltry* (6/27/36). David Miller. Such daredevils as aerialists, flagpole sitters, and high divers are shown.

"MGM Miniatures"

1. *Trained Hoofs* (10/12/35). David Miller. The training and racing of horses.

2. *Let's Dance* (1/4/36). David Miller. Demonstration of tap and ballroom dancing.

3. *West Point of the South* (2/1/36). Richard Rosson. The history and present-day life at Virginia Military Institute. In bit roles are Douglas Smith (Pete's son) and director George Sidney.

4. *Jonker Diamond* (3/28/36). Jacques Tourneur. The history of this famous gem, from the beginning of Jonker's search for the stone to its successful conclusion eighteen years later, including cutting the original into twenty separate stones.

"MGM Specials"

1. *Inflation* (6/15/33). Zion Myers. An economic history of the depression and its cycle of inflation and reemployment.

2. *Audioscopiks* (12/26/35). No director credited. An adventure in three-dimensional photography. A man throws a baseball toward the audience, a pistol is fired, a trombone player works his slide, someone squirts seltzer, etcetera. Nominated for an Academy Award. [Note: This film was not given a release date; date provided above is copyright date.]

3. *New Audioscopiks* (1/15/38). No director credited. A sequel to *Audioscopiks*, using the same devices.

4. *Third-Dimensional Murder* (3/1/41). George Sidney. Ed Peyser. An eerie whodunit using the 3-D process. Color; green sequences.

"MGM Musical Revue"

1. *La Fiesta de Santa Barbara* (12/7/35). Louis Lewyn. A boating party, filmed in color, with glimpses of such stars as

Gary Cooper, Harpo Marx, Maria Gambarelli, Warner Baxter, Leo Carrillo, Adrienne Ames, Robert Taylor, Mary Carlisle, Edmund Lowe, Toby Wing, Buster Keaton, Ida Lupino, Irvin S. Cobb, and Ted Healy. Two reels.

"Pete Smith Specialties"

1. *Killer Dog* (8/29/36). Jacques Tourneur. Babs Nelson. A police dog accused of murdering sheep is brought to trial, and establishes its innocence by proving itself a hero.

2. *Behind the Headlines* (9/12/36). Edward Cahn. How a newspaper operates, from the inception of a story to the time the paper hits the street. Filmed at the *Los Angeles Times.*

3. *Olympic Ski Champions* (10/3/36). No director credited. Highlights of the Winter Olympics in the Bavarian Alps. Also known as *Ski Champions.*

4. *Sports on Ice* (10/10/36). No director credited. Many world champions competing in various events; shows bobsled racing at eighty-five miles per hour.

5. *Hurling* (11/14/36). David Miller. Showing Ireland's athletic sport that makes American football look like child's play.

6. *Wanted: A Master* (12/26/36). Gunther Von Fritsch, Arthur Ornitz. A day in the life of a homeless mongrel in a busy city. Nominated for an Academy Award.

7. *Dexterity* (1/16/37). David Miller. Charles Carrer, Harry Jackson, Vyrl Jackson, Mrs. Vyrl Jackson, Paul Sydell. Various kinds of expert skills are shown, including horseshoe pitching, axe slinging, and dog acrobatics.

8. *Gilding the Lily* (2/6/37). David Miller. Jack Dawn, Monya André, André Beranger. The history of feminine makeup, to the present day.

9. *Bar-Rac's Night Out* (2/27/37). Earl Frank. A raccoon, hunting for food for his family, is menaced by a bobcat, among other adventures.

10. *Penny Wisdom* (4/10/37). David Miller. Prudence Penny, Gertrude Short, William Newell. Homemaking expert Penny comes to the aid of a desperate housewife with cooking hints. Filmed in color, winner of an Academy Award.

11. *Tennis Tactics* (5/1/37). David Miller. Fred Perry. Demonstration of the artistry that won Perry almost every world championship.

12. *Grand Bounce* (5/22/37). Jacques Tourneur. Following a thousand-dollar check for several days, as it pays several debts and returns to its owner—worthless.

13. *Golf Mistakes* (6/12/37). Felix E. Feist. Horton Smith, Lawson Little, Harry Cooper, Jimmy Thompson. Famous golf pros show what to do and what not to do in playing golf, and perform several trick shots.

14. *Pigskin Champions* (8/14/37). Charles Clarke. Football demonstration by the Green Bay Packers team.

15. *Equestrian Acrobatics* (8/14/37). David Miller. The Christiani Family, horseback performers, work with trained equines.

16. *Jungle Juveniles* (10/21/37). John A. Haeseler. Peter Behn, Shorty and Ditto (chimps). Adventures of a youngster who meets two monkeys.

17. *Ski Skill* (10/23/37). No director credited. Demonstration of the art of skiing includes a game of tag at fifty miles an hour.

18. *The Romance of Radium* (10/23/37). Jacques Tourneur. The history of radium and its scientific importance. Nominated for an Academy Award.

19. *Candid Cameramaniacs* (12/11/37). Hal Yates. Gwen Lee, Leonid Kinskey, Bobby Caldwell. A capsule history of photography from the fourth century B.C. to the present, focusing on today's camera bugs.

20. *Decathlon Champion* (11/20/37). Felix E. Feist. Glenn Morris. The story of the farm boy who worked his way to the 1936 Olympics and the title of "World's Greatest Athlete."

21. *Friend Indeed* (1/1/38). Fred Zinnemann. The story of a blind man and his dog.

22. *Jungle Juveniles #2* (1/29/38). John A. Haeseler. Peter Behn, Shorty and Toughy (chimps), Mickey (elephant). Further adventures of the boy and his animal friends.

23. *Three on a Rope* (2/19/38). Willard Vander Veer. Arthur Johnson, Bill Rice, Jim Smith. Experts demonstrate the art of mountain climbing on Mount Baldy.

24. *La Savate* (3/12/38). David Miller. Professor Charles Charlemont. The French method of boxing, in which the feet as well as the fists are used. Filmed in color.

25. *Penny's Party* (4/9/38). David Miller. Prudence Penny, Gwen Lee. More mouth-watering food ideas. Filmed in color.

26. *Modeling for Money* (4/30/38). David Miller. Dorothy Belle Dugan, Lois Ward, Diane Rochelle, Frances McInerny, Louise Small, Sally Payne. Behind the scenes of the modeling profession. Released in sepia.

27. *Surf Heroes* (5/28/38). Charles T. Trego. Personnel of the Santa Monica life-saving department are shown in action.

28. *The Story of Dr. Carver* (6/18/38). Fred Zinnemann. Clinton Rosemond, Walter Soderling, Frank McGlynn, Jr., William Royle, Forrest Taylor, Ferris Taylor, John Lester Johnson, Bernice Pylet, Fred Warren. The amazing life of George Washington Carver, a slave child who grew up to be an outstanding scientist.

29. *Anesthesia* (7/9/38). Will Jason. Ed Gribbon, William Stanton, Tom Rutherford, Phillip Terry, Mitchell Lewis, Albert Morin, George Du Count, Beverly Wills. Tracing anesthesia from ancient Egypt, where a man was hit on the head, to modern methods.

30. *Follow the Arrow* (7/30/38). Felix E. Feist. Howard Hill, Captain Fred G. Somers, Sally Payne, Diane Cooke, Monica Bannister, Diana Marshall. The world's greatest archer demonstrates his ability.

31. *Fisticuffs* (8/27/38). David Miller. Max Baer, Hank Hankinson, Mickey McAvoy, Al Morro, Bob Evans, Jack Roper, Ancil Hoffman, Sally Payne. Baer, ex-world's champion and

Pete poses with "Miss Perfection of 1938," Dorothy Belle Dugan, who appears in *Modeling for Money*.

contender for the heavyweight title, demonstrates fight technique. Released in sepia.

32. *Football Thrills of 1937* (9/10/38). No director credited. Highlights of the previous season's games.

33. *Grid Rules* (10/15/38). Edward Cahn. Development of the game of football, and how the current rules came to be. Released in sepia.

34. *Hot on Ice* (10/22/38). Willard Vander Veer, in cooperation with Tom Lieb. Loyola University's hockey team shows the ins and outs of this exciting sport. Released in sepia.

35. *Man's Greatest Friend* (11/19/38). Joe Newman. The role of animals in scientific research on man's health over the years. Released in sepia.

36. *Penny's Picnic* (12/17/38). Will Jason. Prudence Penny, Sally Payne, Phillip Terry, Harry Tyler, Hooper Atchley. With the barest cooking essentials, Penny whips up a deluxe meal. Filmed in color.

37. *Double Diving* (1/14/39). Felix E. Feist. Dutch Smith, Farid Sumaika, Ethelreda Leopold, Mitzie Uehlein. Diving champions float through the air in perfect synchronization. Released in sepia.

38. *Heroes at Leisure* (2/1/39). Charles T. Trego. What lifeguards do in the off-season.

39. *Marine Circus* (3/11/39). James A. FitzPatrick. A fish-eyed view of a thousand and one species of sea life, filmed in color at Florida's Marine Studios.

40. *Weather Wizards* (4/8/39). Fred Zinnemann. Alonzo Price, Ruth Robinson, Will Stanton, John Dilson, Bobby Winkler. A tribute to weathermen.

41. *Radio Hams* (5/20/39). Felix E. Feist. Jack Carleton, Eleanor Counts, Phillip Terry, Barbara Bedford. A tribute to amateur broadcasters.

42. *Poetry of Nature* (6/17/39). Mervyn Freeman. Flora and fauna of California's famed redwood forests. Released in sepia.

43. *Culinary Carving* (7/1/39). Felix E. Feist. Max O. Cullen, Sally Payne, Phillip Terry, Billy Newell, Jane Barnes, Ann Morriss. A dissertation on the art of carving.

44. *Take a Cue* (8/12/39). Felix E. Feist. Charles Peterson, billiard expert, shows how it's done. Released in sepia.

45. *Football Thrills of 1938* (9/16/39). Highlights of the previous season's games. Released in sepia.

46. *Set 'em Up* (10/7/39). Felix E. Feist. Andy Varipapa, Ned Day, Sally Payne, Ann Morriss. Expert bowlers Day and Varipapa demonstrate proper bowling technique. Released in sepia.

47. *Let's Talk Turkey* (10/28/39). Felix E. Feist. Max O. Cullen, Billy Newell. A how-to guide for serving a turkey.

48. *Ski Birds* (12/18/39). Charles T. Trego. History of skiing, from the days when it was just plain hard work, to the present.

49. *Romance of the Potato* (12/9/39). Sammy Lee. Albert Morin, Emmet Vogan, Buck Russell, Fern Emmett, Irene Coleman, Judith Allen. A history of the potato. Released in sepia.

50. *Maintain the Right* (1/13/40). Joe Newman, Willard Vander Veer. The life of the Canadian Northwest Mounted Police, from initial training to going out on the job.

51. *What's Your I.Q., #1* (2/10/41). No director credited. An audience-participation quiz on various and sundry topics. Released in sepia.

52. *Stuffie* (3/2/40). Fred Zinnemann. Nancy Long, Buck, Jr., Fluffy. Stirring tale of a dog that sacrifices its life. Released in sepia.

53. *The Domineering Male* (3/30/40). John Hines. Johnny Hines. A study of women's tactics in pursuing men, and advice on how to parry.

54. *Spots before Your Eyes* (5/4/40). John Hines. Ernest P. Jones, Jr., Gertrude Short, Emmet Vogan, Mickey Gubitosi, Leon Tyler. Expert Jones shows how to remove spots from various objects.

55. *What's Your I.Q., #2* (6/8/40). George Sidney. More questions, on everything from Lady Godiva to the Panama Canal. Released in sepia.

56. *Cat College* (6/29/40). Joe Newman. Clyde Beatty, Harriet Beatty, Patricia English. Clyde Beatty conducts a course for coeds in the care and training of lions. Released in sepia.

57. *Social Sea Lions* (7/20/40). John Hines. A family of sea lions deserts its habitat to see how others live. Released in sepia.

58. *Please Answer* (8/24/40). Roy Rowland. Interesting questions and answers on Portuguese man-of-war fish, the Rosetta stone, etcetera. Released in sepia.

59. *Football Thrills of 1939* (9/21/40). Highlights of the previous season's games. Released in sepia.

60. *Quicker 'n a Wink* (10/12/40). George Sidney. Tex Harris, Charles Lacey, Clarence Curtis, June Preisser. Stroboscopic photography reveals the intricacies of the simplest actions. Released in sepia. Academy Award winner.

61. *Wedding Bills* (11/30/40). Roy Mack. Sally Payne, Billy Newell. A look at newlyweds and what happens when the bills begin to arrive.

62. *Sea for Yourself* (12/21/40). Charles T. Trego. A look at a new sport—spearing fish underwater.

63. *Penny to the Rescue* (1/25/41). Will Jason. Prudence Penny, Sally Payne, Billy Newell. Prudence Penny provides more cooking hints. Filmed in color.

64. *Quiz Biz* (2/8/41). Will Jason. Questions on onions, the origins of words, etcetera. Released in sepia.

65. *Memory Tricks* (3/15/41). Will Jason. Methods of improving the memory through the use of nursery rhymes. Released in sepia.

66. *Aeronautics* (4/26/41). Francis Corby, S. B. Harrison. A flight with a student pilot, with tips on how to operate an airplane. Released in sepia.

67. *Lions on the Loose* (5/24/41). Marjorie Freeman. A record of the daily pursuits of two lion cubs at a California zoo.

68. *Cuban Rhythm* (6/14/41). Will Jason. Mickey Alvarez, Madeline Pollard. Lessons in dancing the rhumba and La Conga. Released in sepia.

69. *Water Bugs* (8/16/41). Will Jason. Water-minded athletes perform the latest fads in water sports.

70. *Football Thrills of 1940* (9/20/41). Highlights of the previous season's games. Released in sepia.

71. *Flicker Memories* (10/4/41). George Sidney. A look at the good old days of the nickelodeon. Released in sepia.

72. *Army Champions* (10/11/41). Paul Vogel. A survey of the United States Army, and how its military muscle is getting stronger every day. Nominated for an Academy Award. Released in sepia.

73. *Fancy Answers* (11/1/41). Basil Wrangell. Christiani Family. More questions and answers on various subjects. Released in sepia.

74. *How to Hold Your Husband—Back* (12/13/41). John Hines. Vera Smart. How marriages can start to crumble.

75. *Aqua Antics* (1/24/42). Louis Lewyn. Pete Peterson, Bot Butts, Windy MacDonald, Carey Loftin. Water skiers have fun with various tricks. Released in sepia.

76. *What About Daddy?* (2/28/42). Will Jason. Dave O'Brien, Mary Shepherd. The expectant father becomes a nervous wreck by the time his wife gives birth.

77. *Acro-Batty* (3/28/42). Louis Lewyn. Rich Sisters, Jay Trio, Apollos, Cameron Troupe, The Ericksons. How circus performers spend their winters keeping in practice.

78. *Victory Quiz* (5/9/42). Will Jason. Dave O'Brien. Questions and answers dealing with the armed forces. Released in sepia.

79. *Pete Smith's Scrapbook* (5/23/42). No director credited. Highlights from earlier sports films, including *Take a Cue, Table Tennis,* and *Follow the Arrow,* among others. Released in sepia.

80. *Barbee-Cues* (5/30/42). Will Jason. Max O. Cullen, Dorothy Morris. Max comes to the rescue of a floundering barbecue.

81. *Self-Defense* (7/25/42). Philip Anderson. Samuel B. Cummings, Hazel Smith. How a woman can protect herself against a man twice her height.

82. *It's a Dog's Life* (8/22/42). Robert Wilmot. A dog's life depends on its master.

83. *Victory Vittles* (9/19/42). Will Jason. Dave O'Brien, Polly Patterson, Gertrude Short. Home-economics expert Patterson shows how to prepare interesting meals inexpensively. Filmed in color.

84. *Football Thrills of 1941* (9/26/42). Highlights of the previous season's games. Released in sepia.

85. *Calling All Pa's* (10/24/42). Will Jason. Dave O'Brien, Dorothy Morris. A sequel to *What About Daddy,* showing the father's problems with a newborn baby.

86. *Marines in the Making* (12/26/42). Herbert Polesie. Showing Major Hanley's new physical fitness program for aviation cadets in the war. Nominated for an Academy Award.

87. *First Aid* (1/2/43). Will Jason. Dave O'Brien, Eileen Percy, Sally Eilers, Leila Hyams, Edna Harris. Both serious and lighthearted looks at proper administration of first aid.

88. *Hollywood Daredevils* (3/20/43). Louis Lewyn. Harry Woolman. A day in the life of one of Hollywood's most successful stunt men.

89. *Fala* (4/10/43). Gunther V. Fritsch. Fala, Franklin D. Roosevelt, Diana Hopkins, Sir Winston Churchill, General J. H. Doolittle, Lieutenant Commander Edward H. O'Hare. A day in the life of the President's dog.

90. *Wild Horses* (4/17/43). No director credited. Prospectors

of the old West often abandoned their animals. This is the story of one such family of horses.

91. *Sky Science* (5/23/43). Will Jason. The laboratory ingenuity that goes into the design and creation of our fighter planes.

92. *Dog House* (6/12/43). Robert Wilmot. A dog's-eye view of a pooch who is picked up by the dog catcher.

93. *Seeing Hands* (7/3/43). Gunther V. Fritsch. Ben Helwig. How a man, blind from birth, developed into a self-reliant citizen. Nominated for an Academy Award.

94. *Seventh Column* (7/31/43). Will Jason. Dave O'Brien. Accidents and carelessness, particularly in wartime production, their cause and cure.

95. *Scrap Happy* (9/4/43). Will Jason. The history of odd bits of metal that have found their way to the victory scrap pile.

96. *Fixin' Tricks* (9/18/43). Will Jason. Dave O'Brien, Dorothy Hoffman. Helpful household hints on window shades, leaky faucets, stuck doors.

97. *Football Thrills of 1942* (9/25/43). Highlights of the previous season's games. Released in sepia.

98. *Tips on Trips* (11/13/43). Will Jason. Dave O'Brien. What a soldier might expect when he is sent to foreign countries.

99. *Water Wisdom* (11/27/43). No director credited. The American Red Cross's water-safety course for experienced swimmers.

100. *Practical Joker* (1/8/44). Will Jason. Harry Barris, Don DeFore, Suzanne Kaaren. A look at the self-styled trickster.

101. *Home Maid* (2/19/44). Will Jason. Polly Patterson, Aina Constant, Rod Rogers. Polly does household chores with ease and grace.

102. *Groovie Movie* (2/19/44). Will Jason. Arthur Walch. The background of the jitterbug, followed by a demonstration by some energetic dancers.

103. *Sportsman's Memories* (4/22/44). No director credited. Fishing from a blimp for marlin, shooting coyotes from a speeding plane, catching giant devil fish from a small boat, and lassoing a wild bear. Comprised of stock footage from earlier Smith shorts.

104. *Movie Pests* (7/8/44). Will Jason. Dave O'Brien, Harry O. Tyler, Ben Hall, Heinie Conklin, William Norton Bailey. Exposing the various pests one encounters at the movie theatre. Nominated for an Academy Award.

105. *Sports Quiz* (9/2/44). No director credited. Carl Hubbell, Lawson Little, Fred Perry, Harold "Dutch" Smith, Alf Engen. Demonstrating the techniques of several sports masters.

106. *Football Thrills of 1943* (9/23/44). No director credited. Highlights of the previous season's games.

107. *Safety Sleuth* (11/25/44). Will Jason. David O'Brien. How accidents happen when proper safety devices are neglected.

A story conference, with writer Joe Ansen, Smith, O'Brien, and Pete's assistant, Phil Anderson.

108. *Track and Field Quiz* (3/3/45). No director credited. Audience quiz on hurdle running, broad and high jumping, and other field sports.

109. *Hollywood Scout* (4/14/45). Phil Anderson. Paul Sydell, Celia Travers. A typical day with a Hollywood animal talent scout.

110. *Football Thrills of 1944* (9/8/45). No director credited. Highlights of the previous season's games.

111. *Guest Pests* (10/20/45). Will Jason. Anthony Hugh Rogell, Gertrude Short. A look at the unwelcome guests who have a knack for ruining socal gatherings.

112. *Bus Pests* (12/1/45). Chuck Riesner. Dave O'Brien, Guy Wilkerson, Sam Edwards, Kay Deslys. Showing the nuisances you meet on a typical bus ride.

113. *Badminton* (12/8/45). Philip Anderson. Ben Blue, Ken Davidson. How badminton is played, and how not to build your own backyard court.

114. *Sports Sticklers* (1/5/46). No director credited. Another audience quiz on various sports topics.

115. *Fala at Hyde Park* (1/29/46). Gunther V. Fritsch. Fala, Franklin D. Roosevelt. Another visit with the President's scottie dog. Filmed in color.

116. *Gettin' Glamor* (2/2/46). Philip Anderson. The ordeal a lady goes through to maintain her glamor, and a few of her special tricks.

117. *Studio Visit* (5/11/46). No director credited. Dave O'Brien. In stock footage, Lena Horne, Luis Zingone, Muriel Evans, Irene Hervey, Harrison Greene, Helen Sue Goldy. Behind the scenes at a Hollywood studio; most of the film is comprised of footage from earlier shorts.

118. *Equestrian Quiz* (5/18/46). No director credited. Dave O'Brien, Christiani Brothers. Another quiz reel centered around horses.

119. *Treasures from Trash* (6/8/46). David Barclay. Dave O'Brien, Harry Lachman. A trip to Beverly Hills's unusual Patio Shop, run by former film director Lachman.

120. *Football Thrills #9* (9/7/46). No director credited. Highlights of the previous season's games.

121. *Sure Cures* (11/2/46). David Barclay. Dave O'Brien. A look at some old-fashioned home remedies for various ills. Nominated for an Academy Award.

122. *I Love My Husband, But!* (12/7/46). David Barclay. Dave O'Brien, Dorothy Short, Veda Ann Borg. A husband's annoying habits.

123. *Playing by Ear* (12/28/46). David Barclay. Bob Anderson, Al Schmid. Blind athletes who perform amazing feats.

124. *Athletiquiz* (1/11/47). David Barclay. Audience quiz on such subjects as swimming, wrestling, golf, and midget auto racing.

Dave O'Brien seems relaxed in this pose from *What I Want Next*.

125. *Diamond Demon* (2/1/47). David Barclay. Johnny Price, the world's greatest trick baseball player, shows his stuff.

126. *Early Sports Quiz* (3/1/47). David Barclay. Dave O'Brien. Questions on various primitive versions of now-popular sports.

127. *I Love My Wife, But!* (4/5/47). David Barclay. Dave O'Brien, Dorothy Short, Marie Windsor. A wife's annoying habits.

128. *Neighbor Pests* (5/3/47). David Barclay. Dave O'Brien. How nextdoor neighbors can make themselves obnoxious.

129. *Pet Peeves* (7/5/47). David Barclay. Dave O'Brien, Margaret Hamilton, Harry Barris. Irritating habits that become someone's pet peeves.

130. *Football Thrills #10* (9/6/47). No director credited. Highlights of the previous season's games.

131. *Surfboard Rhythm* (10/18/47). David Barclay, Charles T. Trego. Bathing beauties perform on surfboards, displaying grace and dexterity. Filmed in color.

132. *What D'Ya Know* (11/8/47). David Barclay. A quiz based on wheels, showing some very unusual wheeled vehicles.

133. *Have You Ever Wondered* (12/13/47). David Barclay. Dave O'Brien. Looking at some commonplace oddities of life that always seem to happen.

134. *Bowling Tricks* (1/10/48). David Barclay. Andy Varipapa demonstrates some impressive bowling feats.

135. *I Love My Mother-in-Law, But!* (2/7/48). David Barclay. Dave O'Brien. Trials and tribulations of living with one's mother-in-law.

136. *Now You See It* (3/20/48). Richard L. Cassell. Wonders of the world revealed by filming through a microscope. Nominated for an Academy Award. Filmed in color.

137. *You Can't Win* (5/29/48). David Barclay. Dave O'Brien. Proving that everything always goes wrong when you want it to go smoothly. Nominated for an Academy Award.

138. *Just Suppose* (7/17/48). David Barclay. Dave O'Brien, Dorothy Short, Don Brodie. Just suppose men had women's traits.

139. *Football Thrills #11* (8/21/48). No director credited. Highlights of the previous season's games.

140. *Why Is It?* (9/11/48). David Barclay. Dave O'Brien. Life's minor annoyances—shoelaces that break, alarm clocks that don't go off, pests in the public library, etcetera.

141. *Pigskin Skill* (9/18/48). Carl Dudley. Showing the Los Angeles Rams football team in practice. Filmed in color.

142. *Ice Aces* (11/6/48). David Barclay. Stars of the Ice Capades of 1949 rehearsing new stunts.

143. *Let's Cogitate* (12/25/48). David Barclay. Dave O'Brien, Dorothy Short. Another "Have you ever wondered?" short covering such subjects as why a boomerang returns and how many miles an elevator boy travels in a day.

144. *Super Cue Men* (1/29/49). David Barclay. Jimmie

Caras, Willie Mosconi. Demonstrations of skill in pocket billiards.

145. *What I Want Next* (2/12/49). David Barclay. Dave O'Brien. Suggestions for new inventions, such as a spaghetti fork and a nontilting chair.

146. *Scientifiquiz* (4/2/49). No director credited. Questions on everything from insects to newspapers.

147. *Those Good Old Days* (4/16/49). David Barclay. Dave O'Brien, Dorothy Short. Compares present-day living with grandpa's time.

148. *Fishing for Fun* (4/23/49). Lewis Ossi. Gene Beilharz. An outstanding angler hooks a mighty sailfish using a thin line. Filmed in color.

149. *Football Thrills #12* (8/27/49). No director credited. Highlights from the previous season's games.

150. *Water Trix* (11/5/49). Charles T. Trego. Unusual water-skiing tricks, filmed from a helicopter. Nominated for an Academy Award.

151. *How Come?* (4/19/49). David Barclay. Dave O'Brien, Dorothy Short, Pam Barclay. Why is it that people are deliberately careless—standing on a pile of boxes instead of a ladder, etcetera.

152. *We Can Dream, Can't We?* (12/3/49). David Barclay. Dave O'Brien, Don Brodie. Gadgets we'd like to see, such as catsup in a tube, tilting book shelves, nonlocking car bumbers, etcetera.

153. *Sports Oddities* (12/31/49). No director credited. Experts doing unusual feats in the field of diving, bowling, ice skating, etcetera.

154. *Pest Control* (1/14/50). David Barclay. Showing everyday pests—the kid who can't leave things alone in a store, the careless parking lot attendant, etcetera.

155. *Crashing the Movies* (1/28/50). No director credited. Collection of footage showing what lengths people go to in order to get into a newsreel.

156. *Wrong Son* (4/8/50). Gunther V. Fritsch. Story of an orphan boy who has to fill another boy's boots.

157. *Did 'Ja Know* (5/6/50). David Barclay. Third in the "Have You Ever Wondered?" series.

158. *That's His Story* (6/17/50). David Barclay. Dave O'Brien. This guy will tell you he can do everything.

159. *A Wife's Life* (7/8/50). David Barclay. Dave O'Brien. Problems in a housewife's typical day.

160. *Wrong Way Butch* (9/2/50). David Barclay. Dave O'Brien. How accidents happen in industry through careless and improper safety devices. Nominated for an Academy Award.

161. *Football Thrills #13* (9/9/50). No director credited. Highlights of the previous season's games.

162. *Table Toppers* (10/21/50). David Barclay. Willie Mosconi, Charles Peterson, Jimmie Caris. Pool and billiards experts at work.

On the set of *Kiss Me Kate,* Pete joins two alumnae, Jack Cummings and George Sidney, along with Dave O'Brien.

163. *Curious Contests* (11/11/50). No director credited. A newsreel compilation of crazy contests.

164. *Wanted: One Egg* (12/16/50). David Barclay. Dave O'Brien, Dorothy Short. What a wife goes through to get one egg to bake a cake.

165. *Sky Skiers* (2/17/51). Charles T. Trego. Carl Easterly, Preston Peterson. Water-skiing stunts involving ski planes, kites, and helicopters.

166. *Fixin' Fool* (3/24/51). David Barclay. Dave O'Brien. The would-be handyman who makes things worse around the house.

167. *Camera Sleuth* (4/28/51). David Barclay. Bill Goggin. The amazing things an insurance investigator discovers.

168. *Bandage Bait* (6/16/51). David Barclay. Dave O'Brien. A sequel to *Wrong Way Butch* about a careless worker in an industrial plant.

169. *Football Thrills #14* (9/1/51). No director credited. Highlights of the previous season's games.

170. *That's What YOU Think* (10/13/51). David Barclay. Dave O'Brien. Never judge a book by its cover; a man poses as an executive, screen lover, TV repairman, and a patient in a doctor's office.

171. *In Case You're Curious* (11/17/51). David Barclay. Curious facts about baseball, beverages, and broken glass.

172. *Fishing Feats* (12/22/51). Charles T. Trego. Big-game fishing technique for baiting marlin, shark, tuna, and salmon.

173. *Musiquiz* (2/16/52). David Barclay. A musical quiz, plus a survey of some unusual musical instruments.

174. *Reducing* (3/22/52). David Barclay. Dave O'Brien, Maxine Gates. The problems facing an obese woman trying to reduce.

175. *Mealtime Magic* (5/3/52). Will Jason. How to make a quick meal, easily and with impressive results. Filmed in color.

176. *Gymnastic Rhythm* (5/24/52). No director credited. The teen-age Sofia girls of Sweden in a series of gymnastic routines. Filmed in color.

177. *It Could Happen to You* (6/28/52). David Barclay. Dave O'Brien, Anne O'Neal. Foibles of everyday living, including the typical obnoxious dinner guest.

178. *Pedestrian Safety* (7/12/52). David Barclay. Dave O'Brien. The cause and prevention of pedestrian accidents.

179. *Football Thrills #15* (9/16/52). No director credited. Highlights of the previous season's games.

180. *Sweet Memories* (11/4/52). David Barclay. Dave O'Brien, Dorothy Short. Memories are inspired by a family album.

181. *Keep It Clean*. Not released. David Barclay. Dave O'Brien, Benny Rubin. Cleanliness in restaurants is the topic. Not released, although approved by a national restaurant association.

182. *I Love Children, But!* (12/27/52). David Barclay. Dave O'Brien, Don Brodie. Focus on bratty children, and worse, permissive parents.

183. *Aquatic Kids* (2/14/53). No director credited. A group of youngsters demonstrate water-skiing tricks at Florida's Cypress Gardens.

184. *The Mosconi Story* (2/7/53). David Barclay. Willie Mosconi. The story of the world's billiard champ.

185. *Travel Quiz* (4/25/53). No director credited. Questions on travel and faraway places. Filmed in color.

186. *The Postman* (5/30/53). No director credited. Dave O'Brien. What the average mailman has to go through every day.

187. *Dogs 'n Ducks* (6/27/53). No director credited. A boy learns that animals have feelings when he favors one pet over another.

188. *Ancient Cures* (7/11/53). No director credited. How medicine was practiced in the Middle Ages and as far back as the Stone Age.

189. *Cash Stashers* (8/29/53). David Barclay. Dave O'Brien, Frank Yaconelli. People who stuff their money into strange places around the house suffer the consequences.

190. *It Would Serve 'em Right* (9/12/53). David Barclay. Dave O'Brien. Everyday pests—show-off neighbor, boring proud

parents, destructive drunk—and the satisfaction of seeing them get their comeuppance.

191. *This Is a Living* (10/10/53). No director credited. The differences between ordinary workers and highly skilled professionals.

192. *Landlording It* (11/7/53). David Barclay. Dave O'Brien. What a landlord has to endure from his tenants.

193. *Things We Can Do Without* (12/5/53). David Barclay. Dave O'Brien. Ultramodern home inventions that cause more trouble than they're worth.

194. *Film Antics* (1/2/54). David Barclay. Children and animals displaying their capacity for tantrums.

195. *Ain't It Aggravatin'* (2/6/54). David Barclay. Dave O'Brien. Things—both people and inanimate objects—that get on our nerves.

196. *Fish Tales* (3/13/54). No director credited. Various views of fishing, highlighted by an attempt to catch salmon in the treacherous rapids of the Rogue River. Filmed in color.

197. *Do Someone a Favor* (4/10/54). David Barclay. Dave O'Brien. Lending a helping hand, a husband incurs his wife's wrath.

198. *Out for Fun* (5/8/54). David Barclay. Dave O'Brien. An office worker nearly goes crazy trying to relax on his day off.

199. *Safe at Home* (6/12/54). David Barclay. Dave O'Brien. A house can be an obstacle course when things are left out of their proper places.

200. *The Camera Caught It* (10/9/54). No director credited. A collection of unusual and amusing newsreel clips.

201. *Rough Riding* (12/11/54). No director credited. Cowboys really rough it up at a Wyoming rodeo. Filmed in color.

202. *The Man Around the House* (1/1/55). David Barclay. Dave O'Brien. Our hero tries to do some handiwork around the house, but everything backfires.

203. *Keep Young* (2/5/55). No director credited. Dave O'Brien. Trying to keep fit and active without breaking your neck.

204. *Sports Trix* (3/5/55). No director credited. Sports experts have fun with skiing, skating, golf, and billiards.

205. *Just What I Needed* (4/16/55). David Barclay. Dave O'Brien. The complications that arise from receiving useless gifts.

206. *Global Quiz* (5/14/55). No director credited. Questions on lakes, bridges, caves, and cattle. Filmed in color.

207. *Animals in Action* (5/21/55). No director credited. Action shots of monkeys, greyhounds, reindeer, and other animals.

208. *Historical Oddities* (5/28/55). No director credited. A closer look at historical legends. Several sequences from earlier "Passing Parade" shorts.

209. *Fall Guy* (6/4/55). No director credited. A tribute to Dave O'Brien and his athletic prowess, with scenes from *You*

Can't Win, Wrong Way Butch, Pet Peeves, We Can Dream, Can't We?, Let's Cogitate.

Buster Keaton

Legend has it that Buster Keaton's career started sliding downhill in 1930 and never stopped—that his talkie films are unspeakable horrors. Keaton himself perpetuated this myth, and there are many who believe it.

The talking films, however, still exist, and they disprove what has been said for so many years. To be sure, they are not in the same league as Keaton's silents, but they show a comic talent very much alive, and, in some cases, they compare favorably to other comedies being made at the same time.

Keaton, of course, was a great artist, and in the 1920s he fulfilled an artist's dream. He was able to make films the way he wanted, with whom he wanted, at the pace he desired. No effort was too great to achieve the desired effect on the screen, and Keaton's team of gag writers was probably the best in the business, as were his co-directors, Mal St. Clair and Eddie Cline, and his camera-man, Elgin Lessley.

In the late 1920s, Buster signed with MGM, unaware that the studio expected him to conform to studio policies. The metamorphosis was gradual, but by the early talkie era Keaton was no longer making *his* films; they were MGM's.

Personal problems crept up on him. MGM fired him, and for a while it looked as though he was finished. In 1934, E. W. Hammons of Educational Pictures gave Keaton a chance for a comeback by starring him in a series of two-reel comedies. The sixteen shorts that he made over the next few years ranged from excellent to awful, but even in the worst, Buster tried his best. He was too dedicated a comedian to give anything less than his all, so he swallowed his pride and tried to make the most of some hopeless situations.

For his second short, *Allez Oop,* Educational hired Dorothy Sebastian, who had been Buster's leading lady in his last silent film, *Spite Marriage,* in 1929. Miss Sebastian's stock in the movie world had also slipped, although she was still beautiful and a delightful vis-a-vis as the girl Buster tries to impress by taking up acrobatics.

Most of the Educationals were simple comedies built around a boy-meets-girl theme, with another man usually completing the triangle and causing Buster to fight for his woman. As such, they were pleasant, and not pushy, but they lacked the inventive sight gags that had marked Keaton's earlier work.

Buster Keaton and lovely Dorothy Sebastian in *Spite Marriage,* 1929; they were re-teamed five years later for Buster's Educational short, *Allez Oop*.

The *Gold Ghost* comes closest to being a ''silent'' comedy, with practically no dialogue. Buster, dejected when his girl friend jilts him, goes away to forget her and winds up in a western ghost town. He makes himself at home there, and fantasizes himself as sheriff. Trouble begins when gold is discovered nearby and a horde of people—including a robber (Leo Willis) and Buster's girl (Dorothy Dix)—invade the one-horse town. The film gives Buster an excellent vehicle for pantomime and some good sight gags; for once, the cheapness of the Educational product works in the film's favor.

One-Run Elmer was likewise conceived to be shot as economically as possible, but the concepton is logical and the short turns out to be quite pleasant. Buster runs a gas station in the middle of the desert, and, before long, he faces competition from a young go-getter (Harold Goodwin) who builds a similar station across the road. The plot thickens when a pretty young girl (Lona Andre) drives through and announces that she's come

156

to live in the nearby town. Buster and Harold set out to impress her at the next local baseball game, which provides the basis for a string of good gags and enables Buster to win the girl in the end.

Buster was directed in one short by none other than Mack Sennett, temporarily out of retirement and working at Educational; the result, *The Timid Young Man,* was hardly evocative of either Keaton or Sennett at his best, but it was an adequate entry in the two-reeler series. More felicitous was the casting of Buster's performing family in two of his shorts. His father, mother, and sister (Joe, Myra, and Louise Keaton) appeared in *Palooka from Paducah,* and Louise and younger brother Harry appeared in *Love Nest on Wheels,* along with Buster's old friend and colleague Al St. John. The entire Keaton family was a joy to behold, and Myra and Louise fitted in so well to comic hillbilly characterizations that Mack Sennett used both of them in another short he made for Educational at the time, *Way up Thar,* starring Joan Davis.

Some of the Educationals were embarrassingly bad, notably *Ditto,* a film that starts off promisingly with Buster as an iceman, but quickly deteriorates. The final gag is not to be believed. Throughout the film, Buster has been plagued by twin girls, one of whom likes him and one of whom does not. He becomes so nervous that he runs away and spends the next few years living as a hermit in the woods. One day he chances to meet a pretty young girl who invites him to visit her campsite around the bend. He goes back to his quarters, spruces up, and runs to join the girl, only to find out that she is one of seven identical sisters. And how is this shown? From the rear! On this lamentably unfunny shot the film ends.

Only once did Buster actually write one of his shorts, and the result, appropriately, was the best film he made for Educational, *Grand Slam Opera.* A hilarious spoof of the Major Bowes amateur-hour radio show, it opens with Buster leaving his home town via train to crash the Big Time in New York. As he leaves, the townspeople sing a farewell song ("So Long, Elmer/Gee we're glad to see you go. . . ." Rudi Blesh reports in his book *Keaton* that Buster paid three hundred dollars out of his own pocket to buy the rights to George M. Cohan's "So Long, Mary" to parody in this short; he took the initiative rather than have the short go over-budget).

Buster manages to get on Colonel Crow's Amateur Hour (the Colonel does nothing but sit at a microphone and repeat genially, "All right, all right"), where he proceeds to do magic and juggling tricks the radio audience can't possibly appreciate. He makes a shambles of the broadcast, and spends that evening in his apartment

trying to brush up on various tricks (balancing a bowling ball on a bililard cue, for instance), much to the chagrin of the girl who lives below him (Diana Lewis). Once he meets the girl he's hooked and tries to woo her, but without success. Defeated, he returns home, but chances to hear a radio show announcing that Colonel Crow is looking for him—he's won the weekly prize, apparently in the comedy category. Buster rushes back to New York to get his prize, and wins the girl at the same time.

Grand Slam Opera contains one belly laugh after another, and Keaton's guiding hand is felt in the number of visual gags the short carries out. His trip home, after he thinks he's lost everything, is shown via a montage of train wheels, car wheels, and bicycle wheels. It concludes with Buster walking along a lonely road hitching a ride. The short shows what Keaton was capable of doing at this time—if someone had only given him a chance.

Buster made his last short for Educational in 1937, at which time he got a job as gag writer at MGM. While there, he directed three one-reel shorts. Two years later, he returned to the screen in a series of two-reel comedies made at Columbia Pictures. The Columbia series reunited him with Clyde Bruckman, who had been one of Buster's

Gino Corrado challenges Buster to a duel in *Pest from the West;* they're fighting over Senorita Lorna Gray.

Buster's in hot water with officer Bud Jamison in *Nothing But Pleasure;* Dorothy Appleby looks helpless. (Note: This is a posed shot—there is no such action in the film.)

Dorothy Appleby is fed up with Buster in *His Ex Marks the Spot,* and lets him know it.

closest associates on the silent classics. Bruckman wrote some top-notch strips for Keaton, and his first film was directed by the top comedy man on the lot, Del Lord. The triple-threat combination was unbeatable, and *The Pest from the West* was one of Keaton's funniest films. It borrowed heavily from Buster's mid-'30s feature *An Old Spanish Custom,* but Keaton, Bruckman, and Lord pulled out everything they had from their considerable bag of tricks and filled the two-reeler with bright bits of business.

The climax is worthy of Keaton's best silent films. Having pursued a lovely senorita, he finds himself confronted by her jealous employer, who challenges him to a duel at sunrise in the nearby forest. "You come from the north, and I will come from the south," instructs the adversary. "And come shooting, because I am going to kill you!" No sooner does Buster digest this than the girl's lover appears, demanding satisfaction. Buster thinks quickly and tells him that they will fight a duel the next morning. "You come from the south, and I will come from the north. And come shooting, because I am going to kill you!" Satisfied, Buster walks away and bumps into a paunchy native whom he has been annoying all day. Buster slaps him and tells the dazed fellow, "You come from the east."

Next morning, lover and employer spy each other, shoot, and fall to the ground in comic-opera fashion. From behind a bush Buster, in World-War-One army regalia, and the senorita, dressed as a Red Cross nurse, appear. Buster surveys the situation and concludes, "Finis la guerre!" tossing away his gun. Just then, the local opponent appears, guns loaded. "My husband!" shrieks the girl, and Buster takes off amid a flurry of bullets.

Few of the other Columbia comedies reached this level of quality, although some have their moments. *The Spook Speaks* is one of the worst; although co-written by Bruckman, its gags are stale and the haunted-house gimmicks are predictable. *The Taming of the Snood* is saved by Buster's acrobatics with Elsie Ames (a raucous comic dancer whom Columbia was trying to build up as a comedienne), and includes his famous feat of putting one leg and then the other up on a table without falling. *His Ex Marks the Spot* is almost entirely slapstick. It isn't bad, but it isn't really Buster's cup of tea.

The other gem in the Columbia series is *Nothing But Pleasure,* directed by Jules White and written by Bruckman. It is a funny and beautifully constructed comedy built around the idea of Buster and his wife deciding to save money by buying their new car in Detroit. With what they save in shipping fees, Buster figures, they can enjoy a vacation to and from the motor city. The trip turns into a nightmare, from the time Buster drives the car through the showroom window to the night they spend in a bungalow colony where Buster has to swipe some food (they've run out of money).

The film reprises two classic routines. The first is a parking-space sequence which Bruckman originally wrote

Keaton poses with producer-director Jules White and a visitor to the set of Buster's Columbia comedy, *Mooching Through Georgia*.

for W. C. Fields in *The Man on the Flying Trapeze*. In it, Buster is hemmed in between two cars on the street. He works like crazy to get out of the tight space, and gets so involved that he doesn't notice when the car behind him drives away, leaving him unlimited space. The other routine involves putting a drunken woman to bed. This originated in Buster's 1929 feature *Spite Marriage* and became one of his classic routines, performed with his wife when he went on tour in the 1940s and 1950s. The film is also aided by the vivacious Dorothy Appleby, who was Buster's leading lady in most of his Columbia shorts.

After completing ten two-reelers, Keaton left Columbia in 1941 and worked on a steadily uphill climb to renewed fame in the later years of his life. His silent films have now been revived, and people who had nearly forgotten him have begun to appreciate again his magnificent talent.

His talkie shorts, however, remained obscure, partly because most people believe the myths about their consistently poor quality, and partly because every time one is shown, it seems to be one of the worst of the batch.

The films do not deserve to be dismissed; the best of them show a true professional, still creating great comedy. Even in the weakest films, one can always spot the special something that made Keaton the comic artist he was.

Buster Keaton's Talkie Shorts

All are two reels (approximately twenty minutes in length. These are only Keaton's starring shorts; the list does not include guest appearances, such as those made in "Screen Snapshots" and *La Fiesta de Santa Barbara*, nor does it include Keaton's three directorial efforts for Carey Wilson's short-subject series at MGM.

1. *The Gold Ghost*. Educational (3/16/34), Charles Lamont. Dorothy Dix, William Worthington, Lloyd Ingraham, Warren Hymer, Leo Willis, Joe Young. Jilted by his fiancée in Boston, Buster dejectedly drives out to Vulture City, Nevada, a ghost town, where he appoints himself sheriff.

2. *Allez Oop*. Educational (5/25/34), Charles Lamont. Dorothy Sebastian, George Lewis, Harry Myers, The Flying Escalantes. When Buster's girl friend falls for a trapeze artist, Buster tries to beat him at his own game.

3. *Palooka from Paducah*. Educational (1/11/35), Charles Lamont. Joe, Myra, and Louise Keaton, Dewey Robinson, Bull Montana. The repeal of prohibition cuts off the family's source of income, so Pa decides to go into the prizefight game.

4. *One Run Elmer*. Educational (2/22/35), Charles Lamont. Lona André, Dewey Robinson, Harold Goodwin. Buster and Goodwin run rival gas stations in the middle of the desert; when a pretty girl comes along, they do battle for her on the baseball diamond.

5. *Hayseed Romance*. Educational (3/15/35), Charles Lamont. Jane Jones, Dorothea Kent. Buster answers an "object matrimony" ad, finds the lady in question to be an old bag, but falls in love with her niece.

6. *Tars and Stripes*. Educational (5/3/35), Charles Lamont. Vernon Dent, Dorothea Kent, Jack Shutta. Rookie Buster's relationship with a tough petty officer isn't improved when he falls for his girl.

7. *The E-Flat Man*. Educational (8/9/35), Charles Lamont. Dorothea Kent, Broderick O'Farrell, Charles McAvoy, Si Jenks, Fern Emmett, Jack Shutta. Runaway bandits foil Buster's plan to elope.

8. *The Timid Young Man*. Educational (10/25/35), Mack Sennett. Lona André, Tiny Sandford, Kitty McHugh, Harry Bowen. Buster is set to marry one girl, proposes to another the night before, and in running away, meets and falls in love with another.

9. *Grand Slam Opera*. Educational (2/21/36), Charles Lamont. Diana Lewis, Harold Goodwin, John Ince, Melrose Coakley, Bud Jamison, Eddie Fetherstone. Buster comes to New York to appear on Colonel Crow's Amateur Hour on the radio.

10. *Three on a Limb*. Educational (3/3/36), Charles Lamont. Lona André, Harold Goodwin, Grant Withers, Barbara Bedford, John Ince, Fern Emmett, Phyllis Crane. Boy-Scout leader Buster unwittingly walks into a triangle situation when he falls in love with carhop Molly.

11. *Blue Blazes*. Educational (8/21/36), Raymond Kane. Arthur Jarrett, Rose Kessner, Patty Wilson, Marlyn Stuart. Buster is an inept fireman who in the end becomes a hero, saving three women from a blazing building.

12. *The Chemist*. Educational (10/9/36), Al Christie. Marlyn Stuart, Earl Gilbert, Donald MacBride, Herman Lieb. Buster, a chemist's assistant, gets mixed up with gangsters.

13. *Mixed Magic*. Educational (11/20/36), Raymond Kane.

Buster tries to blot up the mess he's made of Elsie Ames in *General Nuisance*.

Eddie Lambert, Marlyn Stuart, Eddie Hall, Jimmy Fox, Walter Fenner, Pass Le Noir. Buster falls in love with a magician's beautiful assistant.

14. *Jail Bait*. Educational (1/8/37), Charles Lamont. Harold Goodwin, Bud Jamison, Mathew Betz, Betty Andre. Buster agrees to pose as a murderer to throw off the police while his reporter pal searches for the real killer. Remade as *Heather and Yon* by Andy Clyde.

15. *Ditto*. Educational (2/12/37), Charles Lamont. Gloria Brewster, Barbara Brewster, Harold Goodwin, Lynton Brent, Al Thompson, Bob Ellsworth. Iceman Buster has a crush on one of his customers, not knowing she has a twin who lives next door.

16. *Love Nest on Wheels*. Educational (3/26/37), Charles Lamont. Myra Keaton, Al St. John, Lynton Brent, Diana Lewis,

Bud Jamison, Louise Keaton, Harry Keaton. A hillbilly family is in danger of losing their rural hotel.

17. *Pest from the West*. Columbia (6/16/39), Del Lord. Lorna Gray, Gino Corrado, Richard Fiske, Bud Jamison, Eddie Laughton, Ned Glass, Forbes Murray. International traveler Buster falls in love with fickle senorita Lorna in Mexico.

18. *Mooching Through Georgia*. Columbia (8/11/39), Jules White. Monty Collins, Bud Jamison, Jill Martin, Lynton Brent, Jack Hill, Stanley Mack, Ned Glass. Aging Confederate soldier Buster reminiscences about his so-called bravery during the Civil War.

19. *Nothing But Pleasure*. Columbia (1/19/40), Jules White. Dorothy Appleby, Beatrice Blinn, Bud Jamison, Richard Fiske, Robert Sterling, Jack Randall. Buster and his spouse decide to buy their new car in Detroit and drive it home.

20. *Pardon My Berth Marks*. Columbia (3/22/40), Jules White. Dorothy Appleby, Vernon Dent, Richard Fiske. Bumbling reporter Buster ends up on a train with the wife of a public enemy.

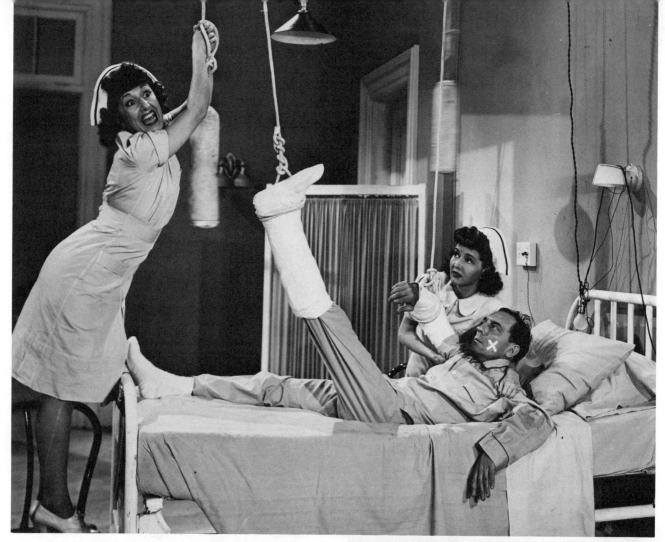

Elsie Ames and Dorothy Appleby with Buster in *General Nuisance.* With nurses like these, he'd be better off alone.

21. *The Taming of the Snood.* Columbia (6/28/40), Jules White. Dorothy Appleby, Elsie Ames, Richard Fiske, Bruce Bennett. A jewel thief uses Buster as an unsuspecting pawn.

22. *The Spook Speaks.* Columbia (9/20/40), Jules White. Elsie Ames, Don Beddoe, Dorothy Appleby, Bruce Bennett. A magician hires Buster and Elsie as housekeepers while he's away.

23. *His Ex Marks the Spot.* Columbia (12/13/40), Jules White. Elsie Ames, Dorothy Appleby, Matt McHugh. Buster's happy home is upset when his ex-wife and her boyfriend move in.

24. *So You Won't Squawk.* Columbia (2/21/41), Del Lord. Eddie Fetherstone, Matt McHugh, Bud Jamison, Hank Mann, Vernon Dent, Edmund Cobb. Buster is mistaken for a mobster who's supposed to be bumped off.

Buster and Eddie Laughton engage in gunplay for the hand of Elsie Ames in *She's Oil Mine.* Monty Collins is referee; Bud Jamison is over Buster's shoulder.

26. *She's Oil Mine.* Columbia (11/20/41), Jules White. Elsie Ames, Monty Collins, Eddie Laughton, Bud Jamison. Buster is forced to fight a duel over oil-heiress Elsie.

25. *General Nuisance.* Columbia (9/18/41), Jules White. Elsie Ames, Dorothy Appleby, Monty Collins, Bud Jamison, Lynton Brent, Nick Arno, Harry Semels. Buster gets himself injured so he can go into the army hospital and be cared for by a pretty nurse.

"Crime Does Not Pay"

One of the most fascinating of all short subject series was MGM's "Crime Does Not Pay." Releasing a maximum of five or six shorts per year, from 1935 to 1947, the series maintained an extremely high standard of quality, won two Academy Awards, and gave impressive starts to numerous actors and directors. The very first short, made in 1935 by George B. Seitz, gave a break to a handsome young lad named Robert Taylor.

Film historian Don Miller has theorized that had the series concentrated on cops-and-robbers type of material, as it did in its initial short, *Buried Loot,* it would never have achieved the success it did. But instead, "Crime Does Not Pay" turned to exposing injustices which affected the public—"you, the public," as the narration was fond of saying.

The uncovering of various rackets was more indigenous to Warner Brothers than to MGM, yet the series did some admirable muckraking, much more so than any Metro features, although John Baxter has written that "the political climate of the time sometimes led to excesses in which union leaders were depicted as seditious gangsters and many basic human rights viewed as less important than a well-ordered community."

Viewing some of the films today, one finds a naïve and right-handed outlook on the American way of life, although many of the targets of attack—the smuggling of aliens, retail stores selling stolen goods, undercover employment agencies that demand a kickback, shoplifting, evading United States Customs duties, and so on—are just as real, and just as scurrilous, today as they were then.

These topics also provide the series with perfect fodder for large-scale publicity campaigns. Local police departments and civic-minded organizations were only too glad to cooperate in promoting the shorts, reaching a zenith with *Drunk Driving* in 1939.

Many of the shorts were written by a former police reporter, Karl Kamb, and the series won plaudits from

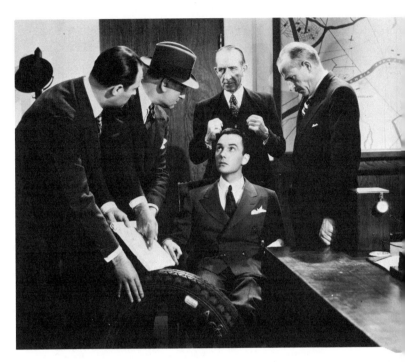

Morgan Wallace, Carl Stockdale, and Jonathan Hale put the heat on a young player in *Hit and Run Driver*.

respected officials throughout the country, including the attorney general, and even J. Edgar Hoover himself, who wrote in a testimonial letter, "I have personally viewed several of these pictures and feel that they are performing a most worthwhile purpose in helping to curb crime."

The trade papers were even more enthusiastic. *Motion Picture Herald* said *Hit-and-Run Driver* was "superbly staged, intelligently conceived, and purposefully produced."

MGM, of course, was the most exultant of all in its press releases and advertising material, even defending itself against possible criticism for *You the People,* a short on election racketeering, by proclaiming, "Only a democracy dares to examine its political processes."

The 1930s format of the series was fairly standard. An opening montage would show a police badge, a gunshot, car chase, etcetera, and would dissolve into a close-up of "your MGM crime reporter," played at various times by Reed Hadley, William Tannen, and Mark Daniels, among others. He in turn would introduce some official—a police captain, FBI man, or the like—who would relate the film's story in flashback form.

The Academy Award–winning short *The Public Pays*

Unidentified player, William Pawley, Paul Stanton, and Cy Kendall prove that *The Public Pays* in this Academy Award winner.

(1936) opens with a talk by one John Alworth of the Federal Department of Justice. Speaking in a clipped, authoritative style, he talks directly to the camera and says, "The problem that I have to present to you is not a nice one nor an amusing one. I am not going to quote figures and let it go at that. I am not going to lay the problem in your lap—I intend throwing it full in your faces!" He turns to a map and continues, "Here is our country, perhaps the richest nation of all. But also a country that feeds a hideous cancer. The problem is this: the robbery of our nation, the systematic and organized plundering of your country, of yourselves.

"Our department estimates that many industries are paying tribute to racketeers who have formed fake protective associations and fake unions. Businessmen and workers are frightened into joining, and once they do the prices go up, and the consumer pays—which means *everybody in this audience.* Ten cents of every dollar you spend goes into the pockets of crime, and that's a dime for which you get absolutely nothing. Those dimes add up to two thousand million dollars a year to criminals."

Then Mr. Alworth introduces a police chief from a small town (Cy Kendall) who relates the story of a group of racketeers who moved into the community and set up a dairymen's association, and through strong-arm persuasion eventually got all the companies in town to sign with

them and pay them a percentage of their intake. But the police are helpless without concrete evidence. Finally, the last holdout in town, when about to give in, agrees to help the police trap the criminals by sending cops out to operate the milk wagons, which are certain to be attacked. The scheme works, and when the gang's triggerman uses his gun once too often, evidence based on the identification of his bullets nails the gang for good.

We return to Alworth, who speaks rapidly as the camera moves in to a tight shot of his face. "Extortion demands good organization, clever brains, and much money—but extortion cannot operate against a brave man who faces down these parasites and goes to the police for help. *He cannot be robbed!"* Alworth concludes, and the music swells for a fadeout.

In most cases, these speeches were not the most effective way of getting across a message. One of the most hard-hitting entries in the series was *Drunk Driving* (1939), directed by David Miller, with Dick Purcell as a man who refuses to heed warnings and stops at a bar before going out on the road. In the climactic sequence, he drives while intoxicated and plows into a car coming in the opposite direction. The victim of the crash turns out to be his wife (Jo Ann Sayers), and the frantic Purcell follows the ambulance to the hospital, where, after an agonizing wait, he asks a doctor if his wife will live. "Yes," says the doctor solemnly, "She'll live." He looks down at his wife on the hospital cart, and the camera slowly pans from her face down, until the bed sheet is suddenly shown lying empty: both her legs have been amputated.

Call it phony melodramatics, but the avowed purpose of the series was to shake audiences out of their apathy, to shock them into a recognition of the serious problems facing them in everyday life. By making the people in the stories, and the settings, as believable as possible, the filmmakers hoped to get across some vital points. Judging from audience reaction, they succeeded with flying colors, proving anew that film is probably the strongest propaganda medium known to man.

In the 1940s, the series turned its attention more and more to war-oriented subjects, particularly Nazi spies and fifth columnists, without whom screenwriting might have come to a complete standstill in the early part of that decade. One short, *Plan for Destruction* (1943), dealt with Karl Haushofer, who introduced Adolf Hitler to the science of geopolitics during the 1930s and led Hitler on his mass-brainwashing campaign throughout Germany.

"The purpose of this short," an MGM release explained, "is to give the John Joneses of America a better understanding of the local character of this war, to help them understand why it is necessary to send our troops to all parts of the world in defensive maneuvers and at the same time prepare for the offensive thrust which must be delivered at the fascist monster's heart."

MGM's contract directors, including such "reliables" as Edward Cahn, Felix Feist, Harold Bucquet, Leslie Fenton, and Basil Wrangell, and such novices as Jacques Tourneur, David Miller, Fred Zinnemann, Joe Newman, and Joseph Losey, did some of their most interesting work on this series. Postwar episodes in the series spotlighted two young actors, Barry Nelson and Cameron Mitchell, both on the thresholds of successful careers.

But acting and directing are not really what stay in the mind when one thinks of "Crime Does Not Pay"; rather, the various topics covered in the course of the forty-eight two-reelers are what remain vivid in most people's memories. At a time when most short subjects were pure escapism, "Crime Does Not Pay" tackled some very meaty subjects, no less biting because they were presented in an entertaining fashion.

The "Crime Does Not Pay" Shorts

All the following were two reels in length and released by MGM. The initial series was produced by Jack Chertok. Two 1940s shorts, *Eyes of the Navy* (an Academy Award winner) and *Don't Talk,* are often listed as being part of this series; they were "MGM Special" shorts, released in the same package as "Crime" for the studio's convenience.

1. *Buried Loot* (1/19/35). George B. Seitz. Robert Taylor, Robert Livingston, Richard Tucker, George Irving, Al Hill. A bank cashier steals money, "loses" it, serves a jail sentence knowing he can reclaim the so-called lost loot when he's freed.

2. *Alibi Racket* (9/14/35). George B. Seitz. How police crack the "airtight" alibi of a criminal.

3. *Desert Death* (10/19/35). George B. Seitz. Raymond Hatton, Harvey Stephens. A man kills his cousin in the desert, then assumes his identity and tries to collect insurance on himself!

4. *A Thrill for Thelma* (11/23/35). Edward Cahn. Irene Hervey, Robert Warwick, Robert Livingston, William Tannen. A girl takes the "easy route" to a life of luxury, and ends up in jail.

5. *Hit and Run Driver* (12/28/35). Edward Cahn. Morgan Wallace, Carl Stockdale, Jonathan Hale. A man runs over a young man and woman on a deserted country road, drives off, and tries to cover up the incident.

6. *Perfect Set-Up* (2/1/36). Edward Cahn. A bright but frustrated young man uses his electrical ingenuity to foil a burglar alarm for a friend, which snowballs into deeper involvement with crime.

7. *Foolproof* (3/7/36). Edward Cahn. Niles Welch, Alonzo Price, Donrue Leighton, Wiliam Tannen, John Marsden, Alden Chase, Harry Hayden, Esther Howard, Stanley Andrews, George Cleveland. An apparently foolproof murder is revealed as a plot between a wife and her lover.

8. *The Public Pays* (10/10/36). Errol Taggart. Paul Stanton, Cy Kendall, William Pawley, Emmet Vogan, Frank Puglia, Edwin Stanley, Wan Miller, Frederik Vogeding, George Humbert, John Dilson, Carl Hackett, Russ Clark, Don Taggart, Philip Trent. Extortionists move in on all the dairy companies in a small town and demand kickbacks. Academy Award winner.

9. *Torture Money* (1/2/37). Harold S. Bucquet. A reporter

Women's prison is the setting for *A Thrill for Thelma*, with Irene Hervey (center).

tests out an accident racket that takes advantage of insurance companies. Academy Award winner.

10. *It May Happen to You* (6/5/37). Harold S. Bucquet. Emmett Vogan, Clarence Wilson. Exposé of the racket of putting stolen and/or spoiled meat into butcher shops.

11. *Soak the Poor* (8/21/37). Harold S. Bucquet. Racketeers force grocers to turn over relief tickets to them, so the grocers must charge poor people more.

12. *Give Till It Hurts* (9/18/37). Felix Feist. Janet Beecher, Clay Clement, Howard Hickman. Exposé of fake charity rackets, where professionals offer to raise money for worthy causes.

13. *Behind the Criminal* (10/30/37). Harold S. Bucquet. Ed-

164

ward Emerson, Walter Kingsford, Joe Sawyer, Anna Q. Nilsson. Exposing the unscrupulous criminal lawyer who gets guilty men off scot-free.

14. *What Price Safety* (2/5/38). Harold S. Bucquet. John Wray, George Huston, Lionel Royce, Anthony Warde, Leonard Penn, Mitchell Lewis, Phillip Terry, Joe Downing, Harvey Clark, Ben Welden, Emmet Vogan, Johnny Butler, G. Pat Collins, Harold Lang, Sherry Hall, Gordon Hart, Harry Holden, Johnny Fitzgerald. Story of racketeers who muscle in on contracting business, substitute inferior materials, and make large profits.

15. *Miracle Money* (3/26/38). Leslie Fenton. John Miljan, Claire DuBrey, Frederik Vogeding, Robert Middlemass, Boyd Crawford, Fred Warren, Victor Kilian, Barbara Bedford, Ruth Robinson, Clem Bevans, Eleanor Wesselhoeft, Wally Maher. A clever quack doctor convinces people that his Volta Ray cures cancer, and he makes a fortune.

16. *Come Across* (5/14/38). Harold S. Bucquet. Bernard Nedell, Donald Douglas, Bernardene Hayes, Rita LeRoy. After a bank robbery, gangster spends all his money for protection from G-Men, but finds his "friends" unwilling to help when his money runs out.

17. *A Criminal Is Born* (6/5/38). Leslie Fenton. George Breakston, David Durand, Norman Phillips, Warren McCollum, Joseph Crehan, Dorothy Vaughn, Eddy Waller, Ben Taggart, Harry Strang, Rex Lease, Tom Kennedy. Case history of the making of three juvenile delinquents, and how one escapade snowballs into a life of crime.

18. *They're Always Caught* (7/3/38). Harold S. Bucquet. Stanley Ridges, John Eldredge, Charles Waldron, Louis Jean Heydt. The role of the laboratory in catching crooks, and how the tiniest detail can lead to a capture. Nominated for an Academy Award.

19. *Think It Over* (7/24/38). Jacques Tourneur. Lester Matthews, Dwight Frye, Donald Barry, Robert Emmet Keane, Frank Orth, Charles D. Brown. A gang moves in to help a businessman collect on fire insurance.

20. *The Wrong Way Out* (12/24/38). Gustav Machaty. Linda Terry, Kenneth Howell. A couple marries young, runs away from home, and turns to crime, on impulse.

21. *Money to Loan* (3/11/39). Joe Newman. Alan Dinehart, Paul Guilfoyle, Truman Bradley, Tom Collins, Warren McCollum, Christina Welles, John Butler, Tom Neal, Phil Terry. The activities of a crooked loan shark.

22. *While America Sleeps* (4/15/39). Fred Zinnemann. Dick Purcell, Roland Varno, Frederik Vogeding, Egon Brecher, Lenita Lane, Bobby Winkler, Paul Stanton, Richard Tucker, Charles Trowbridge, Richard Lane, Gaylord Pendleton, Phil Terry. How spies operate within the United States.

23. *Help Wanted* (6/10/39). Fred Zinnemann. Tom Neal, Jo Ann Sayers, Arthur Hohl, Truman Bradley, Clem Bevans, Edward Pawley, Eddy Chandler, Arthur Loft, Cliff Clark, Leon Ames, Phillip Terry, Eddie Acuff, Lester Dorr. Crime moves in on the employment field, trapping innocent people into giving kickbacks.

Political problems come between Paul Everton and Neil Hamilton in *Pound Foolish*. Former silent-screen star Barbara Bedford can be seen in the background.

24. *Think First* (9/9/39). Roy Rowland. Laraine Day, Ann Morriss, Jo Ann Sayers, Marc Lawrence, Sara Haden, John Butler, Ann Shoemaker, Hooper Atchley. The story of girls who are lured into the shoplifting racket.

25. *Drunk Driving* (10/28/39). David Miller. Dick Purcell, Jo Ann Sayers. The tragedy that can result from mixing alcohol and gasoline. Nominated for an Academy Award.

26. *Pound Foolish* (1/27/40). Felix Feist. Neil Hamilton, Lynne Carver, Victor Varconi, Gertrude Michael, John Hamilton, Wally Maher, Egon Brecher, Roy Gordon, Edwin Maxwell, William Tannen, Charles Wagenheim, Paul Everton, Barbara Bedford. Exposing the "better people" who try to evade customs duties.

27. *Know Your Money* (1/27/40). Joe Newman. Dennis Moore, Noel Madison, Adrian Morriss, John Wray, William Edmunds, Charles D. Brown. Exposing the counterfeiting racket.

28. *Jack Pot* (3/9/40). Roy Rowland. Tom Neal, Ann Morriss, Jean Rouverol, Edwin Maxwell, Joe Downing, Paul Phillips, Donald Barry, Reed Hadley, Lloyd Corrigan, Cliff Clark, Joseph Crehan, William Tannen, Charles Wagenheim, Hal Price, Guy Kingsford. How slot machines feed the nationwide crime network.

29. *Women in Hiding* (6/22/40). Joe Newman. Marsha Hunt, C. Henry Gordon, Jane Drummond, Mary Bovart, Charles Middleton. Exposes phony and unsafe maternity clinics.

30. *Buyer Beware* (8/17/40). Joe Newman. Charles Arnt. Exposing retail merchants who deal in stolen goods.

31. *Soak the Old* (8/24/40). Sammy Lee. Ralph Morgan, Kenneth Christy, George Lessey, George Lloyd, Charles Wagenheim, Guy Kingsford, Hugh Beaumont. Exposing pension-plan racketeers.

32. *You the People* (11/30/40). Roy Rowland. C. Henry Gordon, Paul Everton, Byron Shores, Matt McHugh, Norman

Willis, Dick Rich, Ken Christy. Behind the scenes in election racketeering.

33. *Respect the Law* (1/4/41). Joe Newman. Moroni Olsen, Richard Lane, William Forrest. Shows how so-called minor law-breakers can do more damage than criminals.

34. *Forbidden Passage* (2/8/41). Fred Zinnemann. Harry Woods. During wartime the government cracks down on the alien-smuggling racket. Nominated for an Academy Award.

35. *Coffins on Wheels* (6/7/41). Joe Newman. Cy Kendall, Larry Nunn, Darryl Hickman. Unscrupulous used-car dealers who sell faulty cars.

36. *Sucker List* (9/27/41). Roy Rowland. Lynne Carver, John Archer, Noel Madison, George Cleveland, Norman Willis. Exposing crooked racetrack touts.

37. *For the Common Defense* (6/20/42). Allan Kenward. Van Johnson. Douglas Fowley, Jacqueline Dalya, Egon Brecher, Horace McNally. Story of spy ring headquartered in South America that blackmails an American gangster into helping their cause.

38. *Keep 'em Sailing* (11/28/42). Basil Wrangell. Jim Davis, Lou Smith, Byron Foulger, Ian Wolfe. An FBI man goes undercover to investigate sabotage of American cargo ships during World War Two.

39. *Plan for Destruction* (4/22/43). Edward Cahn. Narrated by Lewis Stone. The origin of the geopolitics theory in Germany, and how it was introduced to Adolf Hitler.

40. *Patrolling the Ether* (4/22/44). Paul Burnford. The radio intelligence division of the F.C.C. and radio "hams" join forces to track down enemy radio transmissions.

41. *Easy Life* (5/20/44). Walter Hart. Bernard Thomas, Steve Geray. How a seventeen-year-old becomes a hardened criminal.

42. *Dark Shadows* (12/16/44). Paul Burnford. Arthur Space, John Vosper, Morris Ankrum, Henry O'Neill, Jacqueline White, Paul Guilfoyle, William Tannen. A man is proven guilty of a criminal charge, but he can't explain why he did it.

43. *Fall Guy* (4/14/45). Paul Burnford. Leon Ames. A bank teller is made the patsy for one of his colleague's crime.

44. *The Last Installment* (5/5/45). Walter Hart. Cameron Mitchell, Walter Sande, George Lynn, Herbert Lytton, William "Bill" Phillips, Jack Carr, Anthony Caruso, Dick Curtis, Dick Rich, Garry Owen, Robert Lewis, Charles Wagenheim, Harry Strang, Paul Newlan, Frank Darien, Addison Richards. A young criminal is fascinated by the magazine account of the life of a 1920s racketeer.

45. *Phantoms, Inc.* (6/9/45). Harold Young. Frank Reicher, Ann Shoemaker, Arthur Shields, Dorothy Adams. Phony spiritualists help people "communicate" with lost loved ones.

46. *A Gun in His Hand* (9/15/45). Joseph Losey. Anthony Caruso, Richard Gaines, Ray Teal. A man joins the police force, thinking that now he has the perfect alibi for a life of crime. Nominated for an Academy Award.

Barry Nelson is *The Luckiest Guy in the World* in the final "Crime Does Not Pay" short; the girl is Eloise Hardt.

47. *Purity Squad* (11/3/45). Harold Kress. Byron Foulger, Dick Elliott. Two con men promote a wonder-drug substitute for insulin.

48. *Luckiest Guy in the World* (1/25/47). Joe Newman. Barry Nelson, Eloise Hardt, Milton Kibbee, Harry Cheshire, George Travell, Robert B. Williams, voice of Red Skelton on the radio. Fate dictates life of man who gets caught up in several crimes, then is given a perfect alibi that leaves him free and untouched. Nominated for an Academy Award.

Robert Benchley

One night in 1922, Robert Benchley, drama critic for the old *Life* magazine, walked out on a Broadway stage to make his contribution to *No Siree,* a one-performance show assembled by a group of New York critics, including Benchley's friends Dorothy Parker, Marc Connelly, and Alexander Woollcott.

Legend has it that Benchley neglected to prepare anything for the show and came up with a last-minute idea in a cab on the way to the theatre. He walked out on stage, cleared his throat, and began to read a dry financial statement—or so it seemed. It soon became evident that he was engaging in a brilliant parody of just such speeches, and the routine became world famous as *The Treasurer's Report.*

The humorist's son, author Nathaniel Benchley, refutes the idea that the *Report* was a last-minute inspiration. "The whole routine of the after-dinner speaker was a thing he'd done in college; he did it after that, anytime. He'd improvise speeches just by putting a napkin on the wall and pretending it was a chart. It was a routine he'd perfected a long time, so *The Treasurer's Report* was, as far as he was concerned, nothing new."

In 1928, Fox Films, anxious to show off its new Movietone talking-picture process, searched for interesting subjects to film. The result was reels on everything from George Bernard Shaw to the West Point Marching Band. They also filmed Benchley reading *The Treasurer's Report,* after which the humorist commented, "I guess that no one ever got so sick of a thing as I, and all my friends, have grown of this treasurer's report. I did it every night and two matinees a week in the third *Music Box Revue.* Following that, I did it for ten weeks in vaudeville around the country. I did it at banquets and teas, at friends' houses and in my own house, and finally went to Hollywood and made a talking movie of it. In fact, I have inflicted it upon the public in every conceivable way except over the radio and dropping it from airplanes."

Nevertheless, the short was so successful that Fox signed him to do five more. The second, *The Sex Life of the Polyp,* is an acknowledged motion-picture classic, and is included in the collection of the Museum of Modern Art. The Museum's Eileen Bowser has written, "While filmed in an entirely static manner, Benchley's natural and intimate manner of speaking could have taught much to the actors from Hollywood and from the stage who had to learn the techniques of speaking before a microphone."

Indeed, but for the early-talkie clumsiness of the camera, it is hard to believe the short is over forty years old. The film—Dr. Benchley lecturing to a ladies' luncheon club on his scientific research concerning the polyp, aided by some nonsensical slides—is a fresh and delightful experience even today. The absurdity of the lecture reaches a climactic peak when Benchley explains that the male polyp glows brightly when displaying sexual attraction toward a female of the species, but just for experiment's sake he substituted a collar button, and then a piece of corn bread, for the female polyp, which didn't seem to have any effect on the male's reactions. The doctor then explains that he and his assistant reluctantly abandoned their experimentation at this point to examine some other creature that takes its sex life "a little more seriously."

After these initial shorts, Benchley devoted himself to

Robert Benchley, behind his traditional desk, enlightens us on something-or-other.

other activities—continuing his writing, and occasionally working on film scripts—through the early 1930s. He made one short for Universal in 1933 (*Your Technocracy and Mine*) and one for RKO in 1935 (*How to Break 90 at Croquet*), neither of which seems to have survived. He began spending more time in Hollywood, however, and appeared in more and more feature films, in which he was generally allowed to contribute his own dialogue. Most of his time was spent at MGM, and it was there that he made his next great short subject.

Nathaniel Benchley recalls, "*How to Sleep* started because he was out doing dialogue for some picture. *How to Sleep* was supposed to be a Pete Smith short, but Pete Smith was sick. It was going to be a thing on Simmons mattresses; they had this film of quick shots showing how many positions you take during an evening's sleep. They tried to have somebody else do it, who couldn't make it, and they finally came to my father, and asked if he would try to do it. That was what finally wound up being *How to Sleep.*"

How to Sleep set the pattern for most subsequent Benchley shorts. It opened with him sitting behind a desk, addressing the audience directly: "If you remember in our last lecture we took up the subject of 'how to stay awake' . . . and on looking about me I notice that many of you did not seem to catch the idea. Today, therefore, we are taking up the subject of 'how to sleep.' And I am hoping for a little better response." During the rest of the short, Benchley narrated various sequences showing aspects of sleeping; he himself appeared in each sequence to illustrate each idea.

The short was a tremendous success, partly because of Benchley's superb delivery and his natural acting sense, and partly because its humor was based on a subject with which everyone could identify. To those who find it hard to understand how someone as subtle and sophisticated as Benchley could succeed at a time when most screen humor was of a broader nature, Nathaniel Benchley explains, "In Hollywood, nothing succeeds like box-office success, and *How to Sleep* won an Oscar; therefore, they let him do pretty much as he wanted."

Not wishing to tamper with a successful formula, MGM asked for more "how to" reels, and Benchley obliged with *How to Behave, How to Train a Dog, How to Vote,* and *How to Be a Detective* over the next year. Then the shorts became more diverse, although they usually kept the lecture format which had proved so successful.

Though Benchley's lectures sounded spontaneous, he had written each one out beforehand in the form of a

Benchley lectures on *How to Vote*.

script. In 1937 he was assigned a director named Roy Rowland, with whom he hit it off immediately. The two were kindred souls and became friends; it made shooting the one-reelers a very relaxed and enjoyable experience for everyone concerned.

"There was always some kind of theme to each short," says Nathaniel Benchley. "In *How to Read,* for instance, the theme underneath was avoiding eyestrain. *How to Eat*

This is, obviously, *How to Be a Detective*.

was avoiding indigestion. A lot of people didn't realize this and they'd send suggestions in, like 'How to Open a Can of Sardines,' which obviously doesn't make a ten-minute short. 'How to Open a Can of Sardines' would have possibly fitted into *How to Get Along Without the Cook,* but there had to be a bigger theme than just the one incident."

Occasionally, Benchley fell into the trap of becoming too formularized. *How to Vote* had him speaking before a political club, and while it is amusing, in typical Benchley style, it is too similar to other Benchley endeavors to stand out. Occasionally, the material was so good that it hardly mattered whether one had heard it before or not. *The Courtship of the Newt* was clearly a reworking of *The Sex Life of the Polyp,* with some of the same dialogue. The newt's courting season, Benchley explained, "opens on the 10th of March and extends on through the following February—leaving about ten days for general over-hauling and redecoration."

Generally, however, the Benchley charm was able to put over *any* kind of material, and much of the laughter came in *anticipation* of what was going to happen as much as from the outcome. It is possible, for instance, to go into hysterics just looking at stills from some of the shorts, as one's mind pictures Benchley explaining income tax forms, or editing his home movies.

The MGM shorts had another plus factor in the latter part of the decade: good supporting casts. Little Ricardo Cezon was perfect as the youngster who doggedly stares at Benchley throughout the evening in *A Night at the Movies;* Ruth Lee was a perfect wife in numerous shorts; and such familiar character actors as Hobart Cavanaugh provided Benchley with exactly the ordinary everyday types he sought to satirize.

In 1941, for reasons unknown, Benchley left MGM to make his shorts for Paramount. What is even more curious is how the quality of the one-reelers plummeted after this move. The Paramount shorts, are not only generally unfunny, but they miss out on surefire ideas. *The Witness,* for instance, is based on one of Benchley's best essays, *Take the Witness!,* yet it falls flat. In *Crime Control,* he draws on another standard ploy, the idea that inanimate objects can only get the upper hand if they know what you intend to do with them. Thus, trying to read a newspaper on top of a double-decker bus, the wind makes it impossible for him to turn the page the way he wants. He concludes that the way to get to page seven is to make the newspaper think he wants to turn to page fourteen. "Well," he says out loud, "I guess I'll turn to page fourteen." The plan succeeds. While the ingredients are there, the sequence just doesn't come off as well as it should.

One must presumably place part of the blame on Leslie Roush, who directed all nine Paramount shorts with very little distinction. Perhaps it was just that Benchley got along so well with the crew at MGM that the switch threw him off pace. In any event, the best of the group is the last, *The Man's Angle,* in which Benchley details wives' annoying habits. (It is worth noting, incidentally, that the same actress, Ruth Lee, played Benchley's wife from the late 1930s at MGM through this series at Paramount and then later again at Metro.)

In 1943 Benchley returned to MGM for a final group of shorts, of which one stands out. *No News Is Good News* is an exercise in double-talk, pure and simple, as Benchley offers to answer questions from the audience. His responses are of this order: "I'm glad this question came up in a way, because there are so many different ways to answer it that one of them is bound to be right."

The short also does something unique in the Benchley series: it makes fun of the idea of a static camera always filming Benchley head-on at his desk. During one answer, the camera slowly starts to move around to the right of the desk. When Benchley looks up, he can't find it at first, then, spotting it, he says with relief, "Oh, there you are." During the next answer, the camera moves back again and circles slowly around to the other side. Benchley looks up again, hesitates once more, and finally says, "Well really, if you're going to keep moving around like that . . ."

Benchley's last MGM short, in 1944, was a so-so entry called *Why, Daddy?* The following year he appeared in a film for the navy called *I'm a Civilian Here Myself,* and in a two-reel Technicolor musical at Paramount called *Boogie Woogie,* as one Frederick Stumplefinger.

Robert Benchley died in 1945, at a time when he had given up writing and was devoting himself almost entirely to movies. By the 1940s he was tired of dealing with many of the people in Hollywood. In deference to the large salary they paid him, he stopped being a creator to a large degree and merely did as he was told in feature films. Occasionally, as in Hitchcock's *Foreign Correspondent,* where he wrote the dialogue, or *The Sky's the Limit,* where he interpolated a variation on *The Treasurer's Report,* he would shine.

Fortunately, he left behind him a treasure trove of wonderful essays as well as his delightful short subjects, which still amuse today because they deal with timeless things; they poke fun at the absurdities of life and the quirks of human nature. Nathaniel Benchley cringes when people try to analyze his father's humor, and is fond of quoting from E. B. White's introduction to *A Subtreasury of American Humor:* "Humor can be dissected like a frog, but the thing dies in the process, and the results are discouraging to any but the purely scientific mind."

Not being purely scientific, we will let it suffice to say that the Benchley shorts were unique because his humor was unique—a rare combination of witty mind and an empathy for the little man who is confounded by society. These films, like all Benchley's work, will never date; as long as human foibles exist, his humor will seem fresh and new to countless generations to come.

The Robert Benchley Shorts

Following is a complete list of Robert Benchley's short subjects, which are one reel in length unless otherwise noted. Since the format in most of them was essentially the same—Benchley giving a lecture to illustrate a certain topic—the titles are most often self-explanatory. Therefore, plotlines are provided only where the title does not already make this clear. The early Fox shorts apparently had no release dates, so copyright dates are given instead.

1. *The Treasurer's Report.* Fox (3/12/28), Thomas Chalmers.

2. *The Sex Life of the Polyp.* Fox (7/25/28), Thomas Chalmers.

3. *The Spellbinder.* Fox (12/13/28), Thomas Chalmers.

4. *Lesson No. 1.* Fox (2/4/29), James Parrott. Two reels.

5. *Furnace Trouble.* Fox (2/4/29), James Parrott. Marguerite Churchill, Ethel Wales. A card game is interrupted by an unmanageable furnace. Two reels.

6. *Stewed, Fried, and Boiled.* Fox (3/27/29), James Parrott. Sylvia Fields, Virginia Sale, Ed Brady. On gardening. Two reels.

Professor Benchley ingeniously describes *How to Figure Income Tax.*

7. *Your Technocracy and Mine.* Universal (4/15/33), no director credited. Two reels.

8. *How to Break 90 at Croquet.* RKO (1/4/35), Lee Marcus. Two reels.

9. *How to Sleep.* MGM (9/14/35), Nick Grinde. Academy Award winner.

10. *How to Behave.* MGM (4/25/36), Arthur Ripley.

11. *How to Train a Dog.* MGM (7/1/36), Arthur Ripley.

12. *How to Vote.* MGM (9/5/36), Felix E. Feist.

13. *How to Be a Detective.* MGM (10/17/36), Felix E. Feist.

14. *The Romance of Digestion.* MGM (3/13/37), Felix E. Feist.

15. *How to Start the Day.* MGM (9/11/37), Roy Rowland.

16. *A Night at the Movies.* MGM (11/6/37), Roy Rowland. Gwen Lee, Hal K. Dawson, Frank Sheridan, Jack Baxley, Ricardo Cezon. Nominated for an Academy Award.

17. *How to Figure Income Tax.* MGM (3/19/38), Roy Rowland.

18. *Music Made Simple.* MGM (4/16/38), Roy Rowland.

19. *An Evening Alone.* MGM (5/14/38), Roy Rowland.

20. *How to Raise a Baby.* MGM (7/2/38), Roy Rowland. Ricardo Cezon, Paul Clark, Robbie and Rolly Jones.

21. *The Courtship of the Newt.* MGM (7/23/38), Roy Rowland. Jacques Lory.

22. *How to Read.* MGM (8/27/38), Roy Rowland.

23. *How to Watch Football.* MGM (10/8/38), Roy Rowland. Joyce Compton, John Butler, Eddie Acuff, Diane Cook.

24. *Opening Day.* MGM (11/12/38), Roy Rowland. Harlan Briggs, John Butler. Benchley is to throw out the first ball of the baseball season in place of the mayor.

25. *Mental Poise.* MGM (12/10/38), Roy Rowland. John Butler. Psychiatrist Benchley has a lookalike patient.

26. *How to Sub-Let.* MGM (1/28/39), Roy Rowland.

27. *An Hour for Lunch.* MGM (3/18/39), Roy Rowland. Benchley tries to show how much one can get done during the lunch hour.

28. *Dark Magic.* MGM (5/13/39), Roy Rowland. Benchley tries his hand at amateur magic.

29. *Home Early.* MGM (5/27/39), Roy Rowland. Coming home early disrupts his entire household.

Benchley's perpetual screen wife, Ruth Lee, has a word for *The Forgotten Man*.

You're looking at Benchley's *Home Movies*.

30. *How to Eat.* MGM (6/10/39), Roy Rowland. Ruth Lee.

31. *The Day of Rest.* MGM (9/6/39), Basil Wrangell. Hobart Cavanaugh, Helen MacKeller, Sonny Bupp, John Butler, Shirley Coates.

32. *See Your Doctor.* MGM (12/16/39), Basil Wrangell. Hobart Cavanaugh, Monty Woolley, Helen MacKeller, Claire DuBrey.

33. *That Inferior Feeling.* MGM (1/20/40), Basil Wrangell. Mary Lee, John Butler, Jack Mulhall.

34. *Home Movies.* MGM (2/17/40), Basil Wrangell. Hobart Cavanaugh, Marie Blake.

35. *The Trouble with Husbands.* Paramount (11/8/40), Leslie Roush. Ruth Lee.

36. *Waiting for Baby.* Paramount (1/24/41), Leslie Roush.

37. *Crime Control.* Paramount (4/11/41), Leslie Roush. Ruth Lee. The war against stubborn inanimate objects.

38. *The Forgotten Man.* Paramount (5/23/41), Leslie Roush. Nobody ever talks about the expectant father.

39. *How to Take a Vacation.* Paramount (10/10/41), Leslie Roush.

40. *Nothing But Nerves.* Paramount (1/2/42), Leslie Roush.

41. *The Witness.* Paramount (3/20/42), Leslie Roush. Ruth Lee.

42. *Keeping in Shape.* Paramount (6/12/42), Leslie Roush.

43. *The Man's Angle.* Paramount (8/14/42), Leslie Roush. Ruth Lee. Sequel to *The Trouble with Husbands,* from the other viewpoint.

44. *My Tomato.* MGM (12/4/43), Will Jason. Ruth Lee, Monty Collins. Benchley tries to plant a victory garden.

45. *No News Is Good News.* MGM (12/18/43), Will Jason. Lon Poff. Benchley answers questions on various subjects from the audience.

46. *Important Business.* MGM (4/29/44), Will Jason. Ruth Lee, Connie Gilchrist. Benchley takes a train ride to Washington on "important business."

47. *Why, Daddy?* MGM (5/20/44), Will Jason. Ruth Lee, Fred Brady. Benchley goes on a quiz show with a know-it-all youngster.

48. *Boogie Woogie.* Paramount (6/15/45), Noel Madison. Barbara Matthews, Carmelle Bergstrom, Roland Dupree, Darryl Hickman, Frank Cook, Ann Shoemaker, Jerry James, John Kelly, Frank Faylen, Valmere Barman, Virginia Morris, The Hollywood Jitterbugs. Benchley lets his kids go out jitterbugging while the wife is away. Color; two reels.

49. *I'm a Civilian Here Myself.* Navy 1945. A wartime short.

"Screen Snapshots"

Since movies were invented the public has been curious about the people who make them. The screen, by its very nature, transforms its actors into larger-than-life figures who command a special kind of awe from the moviegoing public.

The fan magazines were the first to realize this and give the public what it was looking for: glimpses behind the scenes of movieland. At the same time, the magazines and the studios joined in a genial conspiracy to make these actors fit the larger-than-life images they projected on the screen. The result was what can only be called "The Golden Age of Fan Magazines," a time of the most wondrous nonsense ever seen in print.

There was also a film equivalent to the fan magazine: the behind-the-scenes short subject. Easily the major contender in this field was "Screen Snapshots," which lasted almost forty years. It was the brainchild of Jack Cohn, who was working for Carl Laemmle's Universal Pictures around 1917. Cohn was unhappy at Universal, however, and the "screen snapshots" idea gave him the impetus to leave the studio and become his own producer. It can truly be said that this series was largely responsible for the formation of Columbia Pictures, for with this property—and little else—Cohn, his brother Harry, and Edward Small formed C.B.C. Pictures Corporation, which evolved into Columbia several years later. (Cohn's partner in production of the shorts was Louis Lewyn, who spent the next twenty-five years making behind-the-scenes shorts for virtually every studio.)

This fact is an important clue to understanding "Screen Snapshots" longevity, an aspect of the series that we will examine later.

The short subjects were an immediate success and turned a handsome profit because they could be made for peanuts. For the sake of publicity, stars graciously posed for pictures outside their homes, at public events, on the golf course, and so forth. Nothing much happened in the shorts, but apparently even sequences of the stars enjoying a quiet home life were enough to keep the customers happy. Occasionally, the series would show films in production inside the studios—a feature of great historical importance for studying the shorts today.

Of course, Columbia was not alone in marketing this idea. Most studios, large and small, produced behind-the-scenes films at one time or another. One person who devoted himself to the idea more than most others was Ralph Staub. Born in Chicago, Staub became interested in motion pictures as a youngster and set out to learn the craft of photography. By the 1920s, he was accomplished enough to find work in Hollywood, filming comedies for Mack Sennett. Then he set out on his own to produce a series of life-in-Hollywood short subjects. Released by Artclass Pictures in the late 1920s, they had titles such as *Screen Star Sports* (showing Myrna Loy and Bessie Love playing bocci on the studio lawn, etcetera). At the time, Staub advertised himself in the trade papers as "The One Man Company: Director, Writer, Cameraman."

During the 1930s, Staub began working for Columbia's "Screen Snapshots," which were then being produced by Harriet Parsons. Miss Parsons tried to give the shorts some "production," instead of just patching odds-and-ends scenes together. (After leaving Columbia in the late 1930s, she hosted and produced a similar series for Republic in the early 1940s called "Meet the Stars".) Between "Snapshots" assignments, Staub established himself as a skilled director of two-reel comedies for Vitaphone (including the classic *Keystone Hotel*), and creditable B-pictures with Johnny Mack Brown, Olsen and Johnson, and others. He also produced "Jimmy Fidler's Personality Parade" for MGM in 1937. But his first love remained the Hollywood shorts, and when the opportunity arose to assume control of the "Screen Snapshots" series in 1940, Staub jumped at the chance; he devoted himself to that series exclusively from that time on, and, as producer, director, writer, and cameraman, turned out as many as twenty one-reel releases every year.

The 1940s entries in the series were lively and colorful and followed several patterns. Much of their best footage was taken at radio broadcasts and rehearsals, showing many of the stars at their peak: Bob Hope, Groucho Marx, Kay Kyser, Fred Allen, Rudy Vallee, Jimmy Durante, Marlene Dietrich, Jack Benny, to name a few. Staub also got a great deal of mileage out of USO tours and army performances starring stars like James Stewart, Edgar Bergen and Charlie McCarthy, Cesar Romero, the Ritz Brothers, George Jessel, Janet Blair, and so forth.

Then there were the usual publicity-oriented shots of stars at work and play, engaging in various sports, puttering around at home, cutting up on the studio lot during lunch hour. Finally, Staub devoted several shorts every year to looking at Hollywood's past, mining the vaults of Columbia, the "Snapshots" series itself, and public-domain footage for as much early material as possible. These shorts usually used a modern framework: in one, Alan Mowbray ran a movie house and showed the old footage; in another, Ken Murray was going through old film in the studio vault.

The series was surprisingly nonpartisan in showing various Hollywood stars, but every once in a while Staub would take advantage of his Columbia affiliation to secure the services of someone under contract for a one-reeler. While Billy Gilbert was making two-reelers at Columbia, for instance, the series devoted a reel to "a day in the life of Billy Gilbert"; when Jinx Falkenburg was being built up by the studio as a starlet, Staub featured her in the series several times.

Staub's connection with Columbia became a blessing in the early 1950s when his budget was apparently tightened. After 1950, virtually every "Screen Snapshot" was comprised of footage from earlier entries in the series, framed by a new introduction featuring Staub himself ("your 'Screen Snapshot' director") and a current star. Because the series still provided publicity of a sort, stars with no connection with Columbia (Gene Nelson, Jerry Lewis, etcetera) also appeared. But Staub was obviously happy to corral Glenn Ford, Jack Carson, Donna Reed, Jack Lemmon, Judy Holliday, Broderick Crawford, and even Fritz Lang (!) when they were working under contract to the studio.

Not that there was much time or effort involved for stars to make these "appearances." Each "appearance" consisted of the star standing or sitting somewhere on the Columbia lot, smiling, as Ralph Staub entered. Then the two exchanged amenities. The star would say something like "Gee, Ralph, I'd love to see some of that old footage of yours," and Staub would genially reply, "Well, I've got some right here!" and the film would jump into stock

Jean Harlow and Paul Bern sign their marriage license in 1932, as Jean's stepfather, Marino Bello, beams. A typical "Screen Snapshots" event.

footage, returning to Staub and his guest every few minutes for some unnecessary comments.

Many of these 1950s entries are hilarious in their ineptitude. In *Fabulous Hollywood* (1956), Staub is sitting with Jack Carson poolside at the Frontier Hotel in Las Vegas, where Carson is appearing. As they introduce some fifteen-year-old footage of Jack Benny and Fred Allen, the sound of the swimmers and, particularly, the noise of the diving board nearly drown out their conversation!

The original footage used in these flashback shorts is quite good for the most part, so these reels, modern intrusions aside, *do* have considerable historic and entertainment value. *Memories of Famous Hollywood Comedians* (1951), for instance, is a breakneck-paced compilation narrated by Joe E. Brown, with some fantastically rare behind-the-scenes footage of "Fatty" Arbuckle, ZaSu Pitts, Laurel and Hardy, W. C. Fields, Charley Chase, Andy Clyde, Louise Fazenda, Ben Turpin, the Marx Brothers, Olsen and Johnson, and many others, including Brown himself.

"Screen Snapshots" stumbled along through the 1950s, hitting occasional bright spots (like capturing Martin and Lewis's antics at the *Photoplay* Awards dinner), using and reusing footage old and new. With so many traditions going the way of all flesh in Hollywood during the 1950s, it seems amazing that this on-again, off-again series lasted so long. But one must remember the origin of the shorts: they put Columbia Pictures in business. And for all his gruffness; Harry Cohn was a loyal man—loyal, in this case, both to the series and to the man who had been heading it for so long a time. It is safe to conjecture that had Harry Cohn left Columbia, the series would have left with him. (Indeed, Cohn's death in 1958 may have been the precise reason for the series' demise.)

In 1957, in a surprising attempt to breathe new life into the series, Columbia gave Staub permission to shoot "Screen Snapshots" in Eastmancolor—surely an added boost for their marketability. There was, however, a problem. Shooting in color meant the end of endless black and white stock footage. It meant shooting everything new. And in 1957, the glamorous, lively Hollywood of the 1930s and 1940s was dead. What was left to shoot, in color or otherwise?

Staub did one reel, *Rock 'Em, Cowboy,* at a local rodeo, but it had little to do with Hollywood or movie-

Dean and Jerry performing at the *Photoplay* Award Dinner in 1952—a priceless piece of film.

Ken Murray goes through the film vaults for several "Screen Snapshots" reels.

When Ralph Staub gets Martin and Lewis on film at the height of their popularity, Columbia decides to cash in by making the reel a "Special."

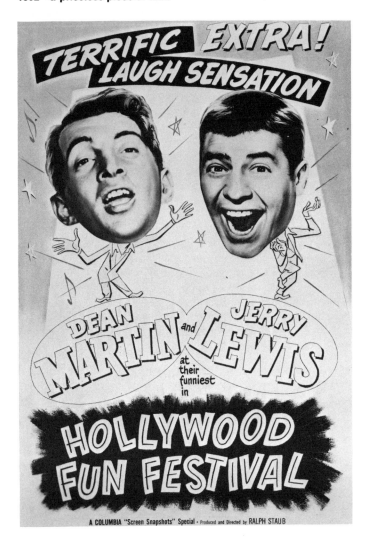

making, except for the presence of Audie Murphy, Frankie Laine, and his wife, Nan Wynn. Then Staub went to the benefit presentation of the *Ice Capades* for WAIF, the Hollywood orphans' welfare association. He set up his camera to film the celebrities arriving in true Hollywood-premiere style, with himself as interviewer-host. The short was called *Hollywood Glamour on Ice.*

Staub returned the next year, when WAIF sponsored another benefit, and repeated the same formula in *Glamorous Hollywood* (1958), one of the last films in the series. This time, Columbia had apparently given him exactly one reel's worth of color film to expose, and no more. That can be the only explanation for some of the footage that found its way to the screen in this entry. To begin with, no one seems to understand that they are in a film, and not on television. David Niven says cheerfully, "and I'll say hello to my wife who's in bed with flu." While Staub is talking to Lauritz Melchior, some anxious fan waves his hand in front of the lens, obscuring the picture. During an interview with Mr. and Mrs. Gary Cooper, Staub keeps shifting the microphone from the tall actor to his more diminutive wife—just in time to miss what each of them is saying. After Mickey Rooney goes into a harangue about what a wonderful night it is here in Hollywood, Staub says, "Mickey, we've just used up seventy-five feet of color film, but it was worth it!" The "The End" title seems to appear while Staub is in the middle of a sentence.

And on that discordant note the series came to an end, after thirty-eight years of showing movie fans what they wanted to see about life in Hollywood. Although a lot of trivia was set down for posterity and the series was often just plain clumsy, it did record a good deal of what was going on in Movieland. If much of it seems foolish today, the shorts are hardly to blame. They were only photographing the blissful foolishness that was Hollywood during the 1920s, 1930s, and 1940s.

There is no filmography for "Screen Snapshots"; accurate records of the films' contents, from 1920 to 1958, were not kept until the series' waning years, at which time a majority of the footage was lifted from earlier shorts in the series.

"John Nesbitt's Passing Parade" Shorts

The storyteller seems to be a dying breed. One of the best storytellers of recent times was John Nesbitt, a man who was endlessly fascinated with life, and who collected hundreds upon hundreds of true stories that he loved to tell. Born in Canada, Nesbitt supposedly got his start in

storytelling when his father, at various times a pastor and a British Intelligence officer (if one is to believe the official biographies), left him a trunkful of newspaper clippings accumulated during a lifetime of travel. When the young Nesbitt went into radio in the 1930s (getting his start doing one-hour adaptations of Shakespeare for station KXL in San Francisco), he developed a show of his own called *"Headlines of the Past,"* which gradually evolved into *"Passing Parade."* It was the success of this program that brought Nesbitt to MGM, initially to narrate the studio's newest series of shorts, "Historical Mysteries," the first being *The Ship That Died.*

Before long, Nesbitt's popularity dictated that he be given a series of his own, and after a year of narrating and writing various semidocumentary shorts, "John Nesbitt's Passing Parade" was born, at first including several topics on one reel, and then settling on one subject per film for the duration of the series.

In later years, Nesbitt said that his stories fell into four categories: men who never made headlines, men who changed the world, little-known facts about great men, and epic events. There was also a more general theme to the series, one which runs through all the shorts, namely, a great love for America and a desire to show its greatest attributes.

At first, Nesbitt was not especially subtle in his patriotic outlook. Films like *Yankee Doodle Goes to Town* (1939) are unabashed flag wavers, although done with great skill and intelligence. But they cannot compare with something like *Grandpa Called It Art* (1944), one of the best shorts of this type in the series. As it opens, Nesbitt talks about how, for years, Europeans have considered Americans skilled in inventing gadgets and using machinery, but fools when it came to the finer things in life. "And to a certain extent," Nesbitt admits, "they were right." He goes on to show some of the things that probably filled a typical American home fifty years ago: incredible pieces of bric-a-brac such as Venus de Milo with a clock in her stomach, which were supposed to be objets d'art. Then he contrasts that situation with modern America, which has produced some outstanding and distinctively American artists, each shown at work: Thomas Benton, Reginald Marsh, the Albright Brothers, John Sloan, etcetera.

Here is a perfect example of the Nesbitt style. He frankly kids the so-called artistic taste of Americans of the past, and then goes on to show, with great pride, the works of Americans today. The narration is intelligent and informative without falling into the traps of talking down to the audience or going above their heads.

Nesbitt also enjoyed Americana, and did a number of

shorts which were pleasantly nostalgic. *Our Old Car* (1945), told in an autobiographical style, was about the first car his father ever bought (which was also the first car on their block) in the late 1890s. The short shows each successive purchase and follows with the story of his family as he drove a jalopy in the 1920s when he was in his teens, and so on. The film ends as his parents are celebrating their forty-fifth wedding anniversary on the now-busy block with a car in front of every house. *Our Old Town* followed the same format with similar results.

Nesbitt was not a filmmaker; his only interest was in the stories themselves. He narrated each short, usually wrote the narration, and frequently created the screenplay for his films. But often the scenarios would be done by others, and he would simply adapt the narration to his own style. This done, a director would be assigned to make the short independently, to match the narration. The directors on the series ranged from MGM's young hopefuls (Jacques Tourneur, Fred Zinnemann, etcetera) to unknowns (Walter Hart, Herbert Morgan).

Nesbitt was a prodigious reader, and he claimed to have total recall. This provided him with many ideas for stories based on actual incidents in his youth or on people he had met. But many of his best shorts concerned great men of the past.

The Fabulous Fraud (1948), directed by Edward Cahn and photographed by Paul Vogel, was one of the best shorts Nesbitt ever made; it was also one of the most elaborate. The film opens in an atmospheric graveyard, where we discover the tombstone of one Franz Anton Mesmer, a colorful charlatan who, in the eighteenth century, stumbled onto the secret of hypnotism. A flashback takes us to his famous salon where he treated the rich and famous for their maladies, real and imagined, simply by talking to them softly, persuasively. (His name, of course, was adapted into the word "mesmerized".) The key sequence shows a poor man taking his little blind girl to Mesmer for curing. While Mesmer speaks to her, he inadvertently puts her into a hypnotic trance, but doesn't realize what he's done. For a moment he thinks she may be dead! He continues to treat her and eventually she *does* see, but her blindness returns when his treatment stops. Eventually he is run out of town as a phony, and dies alone in a far-off village, never having comprehended his own discovery.

The short is one of Nesbitt's all-time best, not only because of the fascinating story line (which, it must be admitted, is drastically compressed during the second half of the reel), but also because of its production. The costumes, sets, and lighting, especially in Mesmer's salon, are outstanding; the musical score is striking; the

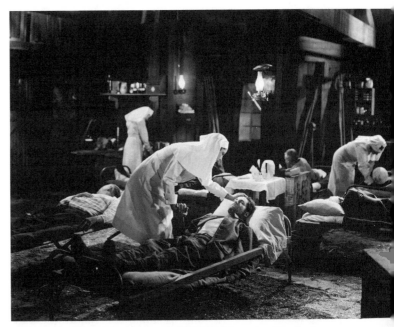

Barbara Bedford takes care of Cliff Danielson in *Angel of Mercy*.

performances by John Baragrey (as Mesmer), Morris Ankrum (as the father), and Marcia Mae Jones (as the blind girl) are excellent; and the directorial ideas are quite ingenious. As the narration tells us of Mesmer's failing in later years, a picture of the shingle outside his salon "melts" into nothingness.

Nesbitt often used the stories of men whose ideas were rejected in their own time. *The Magic Alphabet* (1942) dealt with Dr. Christiaan Eijkman, who discovered the importance of vitamins; *Stairway to Light* (1945) told the story of Dr. Philippe Pinel, the first man to treat the insane with compassion instead of brutality; *It Can't Be Done* (1947) collected the stories of Leonardo da Vinci, who was thought crazy when he invented an airplane; Tom Davenport, who invented an electric motor; Edward Jenner, who first used vaccination to cure disease, etcetera.

One of the better films in this series was a later entry, *Mr. Whitney Had a Notion* (1949), with Lloyd Bridges as Eli Whitney. Everyone knows that Whitney invented the cotton gin, but Nesbitt wanted to remind people that he made an even more important contribution to America with the development of mass production. The short shows Whitney, with the help of Thomas Jefferson, securing a contract with the army to produce ten thousand guns within a two-year time limit. The army believes it can't be done, and they grow doubly suspicious when nearly two years pass and not one gun has been seen. Whitney and his staff are working in complete secrecy. When some army representatives visit his workshop and demand to know what's going on, he takes them inside and reveals his secret: for nearly two years, he and his staff have been making the components for the guns. Before the visitors' astonished eyes, Whitney and his five workers each assembles a gun in seventeen minutes flat. It is the birth of the assembly line.

One of Nesbitt's most important, and most prophetic, shorts was a 1943 reel called *Forgotten Treasure*. The title refers to motion pictures that are disintegrating before our eyes. Nesbitt tells of the Museum of Modern Art's program to preserve historic film, and then shows a series of rare newsreel clips, many of which he says were saved barely in time: President McKinley in 1901, a day before his assassination; his successor, Teddy Roosevelt; the aftermath of the San Francisco earthquake; the Panama Canal under construction, and a visit there by President Taft; the funeral of Edward VII in England in 1910; the last gathering of the crowned heads of Europe before the turmoil of 1914; the Wright brothers' first flight; and many others. Nesbitt explains how vital it is for us to save the film we have, and speculates about future generations learning from this film. We see a group of students sitting in a theatre watching World War Two footage, labeled on the titles as a textbook might be. One kid turns to his friend, marveling at how students used to use books to learn history. "How primitive!" his friend replies.

Forgotten Treasure is an ironic reel to view today, since hundreds of films are crumbling every year because money and interest are not available to save them all.

Other entries in the series dealt with dreams (*Return from Nowhere*), weather (*It Looks Like Rain*), comic strips (*People on Paper*), and hobbies (*Hobbies*).

As the 1940s progressed, most studios spent less and less on short subjects. This was usually evident in the finished product, but the technicians at MGM, though subject to the same budgetary limitations, were much more clever at hiding the fact. Nesbitt's shorts made abundant use of stock footage from not only the MGM library, but also from earlier "Passing Parade" shorts. These could be brief clips used as a bridge between scenes (a shot of Peter Cushing from the 1940 short *Dreams* in the 1944 reel *Return from Nowhere*, or an entire sequence (showing the work of Dr. Joseph Goldberger from the 1940 film *A Way in the Wilderness* in the 1947 omnibus *It Couldn't Be Done*). In every instance, the editing and matching of shots were such that this trickery could easily go unnoticed.

The "Passing Parade" series, introduced with the impressive title artwork and a theme song from Tchaikowsky's Fifth Symphony, continued through 1949, when for reasons unknown, it was discontinued. In 1956 the series was revived, this time for television—at first presented as specials, and then in a filmed half-hour series made at the Hal Roach studio. Nesbitt's role as a collector of true stories was well known by then, and he told *TV Guide*, "If I had a quarter for every time someone has tried to convince me that the army is still searching all over the world for a cadet who disappeared mysteriously from West Point 30 years ago, I could retire to my cattle ranch at Carmel."

He did retire, after a year of the filmed half hour, but he never stopped reading, always searching for fascinating tales to be used sometime, somewhere. Nesbitt died in 1960 of a heart attack, at the age of forty-nine. With him went a tradition that is apparently out of style these days. Looking back at some of Nesbitt's "Passing Parade" shorts, however, we find that they still retain their original interest. Perhaps the art of storytelling isn't dead but is only dormant, waiting for another man with the expertise of John Nesbitt to bring it to life again.

"John Nesbitt's Passing Parade" Shorts

When he first came to MGM, Nesbitt narrated a number of shorts in the "Historical Mysteries" series, such as *The Ship That Died, The Face Behind the Mask, Forgotten Step, That Mothers Might Live,* and *Joaquin Murietta,* and a "special" called *They Live Again*. In 1942 he narrated another wartime "special," *A Yardstick for Rumors*. Following are all the films that were officially part of the "Passing Parade" series. *The Story of Alfred Nobel* was not originally scheduled as part of the series, but later was released with the others for exhibitor convenience. Likewise, the 1949 film, *Stuff for Stuff,* was not really part of the series. All the following were released by MGM, and were one reel in length.

1. *Passing Parade #1* (10/15/38). Basil Wrangell. Comprised of three episodes: *The Marriage Industry,* story of mail-order marriage; *Unclaimed Millions,* showing money that is left in banks indefinitely; and *Autobiography of a Car,* from factory to scrap-pile.

2. *New Roadways* (1/28/39). Basil Wrangell. New developments in industry; a look at plastic surgery; the wonder of scientific research.

3. *The Story of Alfred Nobel* (2/18/39). Joe Newman. Paul Guilfoyle, Eleanor Wesselhoeft, Gene Coogan, Lalo Encinas. After inventing dynamite, and realizing its power, Nobel is

determined to do something for peace. Originally titled *Am I to Blame?*

4. *The Story of Dr. Jenner* (3/18/39). Henry K. Dunn. Matthew Boulton, Fay Helm, Helen Browne, William Tannen, Raymond Severin. The story of the man who discovered vaccination. Later used in *It Can't Be Done.*

5. *Angel of Mercy* (5/20/39). Edward Cahn. Sara Haden, Ann Rutherford, Emmet Vogan. The story of Clara Barton. Later used virtually intact as *Flag of Mercy.* Originally to have been a Carey Wilson short.

6. *Yankee Doodle Goes to Town* (6/17/39). Jacques Tourneur. Albert Russell, Josiah Tucker. Throughout American history there have been sourpusses like Nathaniel Curdleface, who see only the worst. Uses stock footage from several MGM historical films like *Of Human Hearts.*

7. *The Giant of Norway* (6/24/39). Edward Cahn. Lumsden Hare, Hugh Sothern. The story of Fridtjof Nansen, who devoted his life to helping post–World War One refugees. Originally titled *The Man Who Couldn't Say No.*

8. *The Story That Couldn't Be Printed* (7/22/39). Joe Newman. Victor Kilian, Anthony Allan, Frederick Worlock, Vera Tattersall, Carl Stockdale, Emmet Vogan. The story of printer John Peter Zenger, who in 1784 tested the coveted freedom of the press in this country.

9. *One Against the World* (8/19/39). Fred Zinnemann. Jonathan Hale, Claire McDowell, Charles Middleton. The story of Ephraim MacDowell, the first man to attempt a surgical operation.

10. *Unseen Guardians* (8/26/39). Basil Wrangell. Focusing on the Postal Inspection Bureau, Children's Home Societies, and Underwriters' Laboratories.

11. *Forgotten Victory* (12/9/39). Fred Zinnemann. Donald Douglas. A tribute to the man responsible for the very bread we eat. Originally titled *Mark Carleton.* Released in sepia.

12. *XXX Medico* (3/23/40). Basil Wrangell. A miraculous new system which enables doctors to operate via long distance. Originally titled *S.O.S. Medico.* Released in sepia.

13. *The Hidden Master* (4/20/40). Sammy Lee. Peter Cushing, Louis Jean Heydt, Emmet Vogan. Historical examples of how important luck can be in a person's life. Released in sepia.

14. *A Way in the Wilderness* (6/22/40). Fred Zinnemann. Shepperd Strudwick. The story of an immigrant named Joseph Goldberger who came to this country and discovered the cure for the dreaded disease pellagra. Later used in *It Can't Be Done.* Released in sepia.

15. *Trifles of Importance* (7/13/40). Basil Wrangell. The slightest incidents can change entire lives, as is proven by three examples in history.

16. *The Baron and the Rose* (9/7/40). Basil Wrangell. The story of Henry Steigel, a Pennsylvania blacksmith who made and lost a fortune as a glassmaker. Originally titled *Black and White,* then *The Red Rose.*

17. *Utopia of Death* (10/12/40). No director credited. Mexico's Seri Indians live in preparation for the greatest of all existences, death.

18. *Dreams* (11/16/40). Felix E. Feist. Peter Cushing. What goes on in our minds as we dream, and how it can affect our lives.

19. *American Spoken Here* (11/30/40). Basil Wrangell. The history of slang is really the history of our country.

20. *Whispers* (2/8/41). Basil Wrangell. John Burton, Ken Christy. How some cunning men have turned small-town gossip into a profitable enterprise. Originally titled *Dark River.*

21. *More Trifles of Importance* (3/22/41). Basil Wrangell. Lumsden Hare, Eleanor Wesselhoeft, Vondell Darr, William Tannen. A teacup and a small flower prove again how minor items can play major roles in life.

22. *Out of Darkness* (3/29/41). Sammy Lee. Rudolph von Heinrich, Egon Brecher, Wolfgang Zilzer, Lotti Palfi, Charles Wagenheim. The story of a courageous underground newspaper in Belgium during World War One. Originally titled *Voice of Liberty.*

23. *Willie and the Mouse* (5/17/41). George Sidney. Yes, mice have brains, and this study shows that as with humans, there are smart and dumb members of the species.

24. *This Is the Bowery* (5/31/41). Gunther V. Fritsch. A realistic look at one of America's most unusual streets, and some of the tragic figures who live there. Originally titled *On the Bowery.*

25. *Your Last Act* (7/12/41). Fred Zinnemann. A look at some of the strangest wills of all time, including that of Charles Lounsberry.

26. *Of Pups and Puzzles* (9/6/41). George Sidney. Experiments with various animals make it possible to match men to the right jobs. An Academy Award winner.

27. *Hobbies* (9/20/41). George Labrousse. A look at some of the world's most interesting hobbies, including model railroad building and putting ships in bottles.

28. *Strange Testament* (11/15/41). Sammy Lee. The story of Julian Poydras, whose encounter with a girl at the Mardi Gras had a profound effect on his later life. Originally titled *The Strange Will of Julian Poydras.*

29. *We Do It Because* (1/24/42). Basil Wrangell. The origin of such customs as shaking hands, kissing, tipping one's hat to ladies, etcetera.

30. *Flag of Mercy* (1/31/42). Edward Cahn. Sara Haden, Ann Rutherford, Emmet Vogan. A reissue of *Angel of Mercy* with new framework footage relating it to America's involvement in World War Two.

31. *The Woman in the House* (5/9/42). Sammy Lee. Ann Richards. The story of a woman who is a recluse for forty years, fearing people will blame her for her lover's death long ago. Originally titled *Fear.* Released in sepia.

32. *The Incredible Stranger* (6/20/42). Jacques Tourneur.

Ann Richards in two stages of her life as the *Woman in the House.*

Paul Guilfoyle. A man refuses to accept the fact that his wife and child are dead, and continues to act as if they were still alive.

33. *Vendetta* (7/18/42). Joe Newman. Joe Kirk. The story of Carlo Pozzo di Borgo, a boyhood friend of Napoleon who later swears revenge.

34. *The Magic Alphabet* (10/10/42). Jacques Tourneur. Horace McNally. The story of Dr. Christiaan Eijkman, who discovered the secret of vitamins and their importance. Footage used in *It Can't Be Done.*

35. *Famous Boners* (10/24/42). Douglas Foster. Ian Wolfe, Ed McWade. Famous goofs in history: how Thomas Carlyle's manuscript on the French Revolution was burned, how a spy foiled a sabotage plot, etcetera.

36. *The Film That Was Lost* (10/31/42). Sammy Lee. The story of the film department of The Museum of Modern Art, and examples of the rare film they have saved.

37. *Madero of Mexico* (11/28/42). Edward Cahn. Paul

Guilfoyle. The story of the man who sparked the Mexican Revolution and sacrificed his life for his country's freedom.

38. *Who's Superstitious?* (5/1/43). Sammy Lee. Dave O'Brien. Looking at famous superstitions, and tracing their origins, including the seamen's "Flying Dutchman."

39. *That's Why I Left You* (6/12/43). Edward Cahn. A young man writes his wife that he is leaving, unable to stand the rat race they live in.

40. *Trifles That Win Wars* (7/17/43). Harold Daniels. Such items as an empty bottle, a spider, and chemical research on billiard balls have dictated the fate of several wars.

41. *Don't You Believe It* (7/3/43). Edward Cahn. Falsehoods are exposed in such legends as that of Mrs. O'Leary's cow and Nero's fiddling.

42. *Nursery Rhyme Mysteries* (7/3/43). Edward Cahn. Origins of some of the most popular nursery rhymes—and of Mother Goose herself.

43. *Forgotten Treasure* (7/24/43). Sammy Lee. More rare film clips from the Museum of Modern Art film library, including newsreel shots of the aftermath of the San Francisco earthquake, compared with footage from MGM's *San Francisco.*

44. *Storm* (10/23/43). Paul Burnford. How man has faced the forces of nature over the years.

45. *To My Unborn Son* (10/30/43). Leslie Kardos. Steven Geray. A Czech father writes to the son he will never see, to explain his resistance to the Nazi invasion.

46. *This Is Tomorrow* (11/27/43). No director credit. A look into the future of America, with planned cities and communities, etcetera. Adapted from Ralph Steiner and Willard Van Dyke's 1939 documentary *The City*.

47. *The Immortal Blacksmith* (5/20/44). Sammy Lee. Chill Wills, Pamela Blake, Hobart Cavanaugh. The story of Tom Davenport, a farmer who invented the electric motor. Used in *It Can't Be Done*.

48. *Grandpa Called It Art* (7/15/44). Walter Hart. Thomas Benton, Reginald Marsh, John Sloan, the Albright Brothers, Charles Birchfield, others. A survey of American art from its primitive days to the present, with scenes of many modern American masters.

49. *Return from Nowhere* (10/28/44). Paul Burnford. Don DeFore, Don Curtis, Morris Ankrum, Kay Medford, Naomi Scher; Peter Cushing shown in footage from *Dreams*. Story of a man whose subconscious takes over his mind one afternoon, so he cannot remember what he did.

50. *A Lady Fights Back* (11/11/44). No director credit. The story of the French luxury liner Normandie that refuses to stay down.

51. *It Looks Like Rain* (3/3/45). Paul Burnford. The importance of weather forecasting, especially to farmers, and what they can do to prepare themselves. Originally titled *It Always Stops Raining*.

52. *The Seesaw and the Shoes* (5/5/45). Douglas Foster. Arthur Space, Feodor Chaliapin, Gregory Golubeff. Those two objects inspired the invention of the stethoscope and the discovery of rubber's properties. Originally titled *Moments That Made History*.

53. *The Great American Mug* (10/6/45). Cyril Endfield. A nostalgic look at the barbershop of the 1890s.

54. *Stairway to Light* (11/10/45). Sammy Lee. Gene Stutenroth, Dewey Robinson. The story of Dr. Philippe Pinel, the first man to treat the insane with compassion instead of cruelty. Academy Award winner.

55. *People on Paper* (11/17/45). Herbert Morgan. A capsule history of comic strips, with film clips of these cartoonists and their creations: H. H. Knerr ("Katzenjammer Kids"), Bud Fisher ("Mutt and Jeff"), Fred Lasswell Jr. ("Barney Google"), Frank King ("Gasoline Alley"), Chester Gould ("Dick Tracy"), Dick Calkins ("Buck Rogers"), Milton Caniff ("Terry and the Pirates"), Chic Young ("Blondie"), Raeburn Van Beuren ("Abbie and Slats"), Ham Fisher ("Joe Palooka"), Hal Foster ("Prince Valiant"), Harold Gray ("Little Orphan Annie"), Al Capp ("Li'l Abner"). The closing sequence features Li'l Abner animation.

56. *Golden Hunch* (12/15/45). No director credited. The

stories of men who had hunches that led to great discoveries.

57. *Magic on a Stick* (1/19/46). Cyril Endfield. The story of an English chemist who discovered the principle of the sulphur match.

58. *Our Old Car* (6/11/46). Cyril Endfield. Nesbitt traces his life and the "history" of his neighborhood through the succession of cars his father owned.

59. *A Really Important Person* (1/11/47). Basil Wrangell. Dean Stockwell, Connie Gilchrist, Clancy Cooper, Chick York. A boy is assigned to write an essay for school on a really important person, and comes to realize how important his own father is.

60. *Tennis in Rhythm* (8/23/47). No director credited. Tennis champ Alice Marble shows how a sense of rhythm can aid a tennis game.

61. *The Amazing Mr. Nordill* (8/30/47). Joe Newman. Leon Ames, Clinton Sundberg. The story of one of the cleverest counterfeiters of all time.

62. *Miracle in a Cornfield* (12/20/47). No director credited. The story of a volcano that erupted in a cornfield at Paricutín, Mexico.

63. *It Can't Be Done* (1/10/48). No director credited. A trip through a Washington Hall of Fame recalls men whose great ideas were scorned in their day. Includes stock footage from *That Mothers Might Live* (with Shepperd Strudwick), *The Magic*

Dean Stockwell has to write about *A Really Important Person* for school.

A scene from **Goodbye, Miss Turlock.**

Alphabet, The Immortal Blacksmith (with Chill Wills), *The Story of Dr. Jenner, A Way in the Wilderness, The Magic Alphabet.*

64. *Goodbye, Miss Turlock* (1/24/48). Edward Cahn. A nostalgic visit to the one-room schoolhouse and its dedicated teacher. Academy Award winner.

65. *My Old Town* (2/7/48). No director credited. The idyllic life of small-town America in the early part of the twentieth century.

66. *Souvenirs of Death* (6/19/48). Edward Cahn. The history of a gun, from the German battlefield to the American underworld.

67. *The Fabulous Fraud* (8/28/48). Edward Cahn. John Baragrey, Phyllis Morris, Marcia Mae Jones, Morris Ankrum. The story of Franz Anton Mesmer, a charlatan who inadvertently discovered the secret of hypnotism.

68. *The City of Little Men* (11/20/48). Harry Loud. The story of Father Flanagan's Boys Town, focusing on one youth who goes there.

69. *Annie Was a Wonder* (1/29/49). Edward Cahn. Kathleen Freeman, Howard J. Negley, Ruth Lee, Hugo Sven Borg. A Swedish girl comes to work for an American farm family at the turn of the century. Nominated for an Academy Award.

70. *Clues to Adventure* (4/11/49). No director credited. How three unrelated incidents affected the Bill of Rights. Stock footage from *Nursery Rhyme Mysteries, The Story That Couldn't Be Printed,* and *The Face Behind the Mask.*

71. *Mr. Whitney Had a Notion* (5/7/49). Gerald Mayer. Lloyd Bridges, Erville Alderson, Howard J. Negley, Harry Hayden, Mitchell Lewis. Eli Whitney's bold gamble that introduced mass production to America.

72. *City of Children* (8/27/49). No director credited. The story of Mooseheart, Illinois, a home for parentless children.

"Joe McDoakes"

"Joe McDoakes" was the last long-running comedy series to be made in Hollywod. A consistently clever and well-made series of shorts, it stood virtually alone in the 1950s, when only Columbia was continuing to make comedies, and then, very cheaply. But while the McDoakes shorts flourished in the 1950s, the idea had originated some years before.

"The series was my idea," says director-writer Richard L. Bare. "I was running a theatre in Carmel, California, during the 1930s but wanted to crash Hollywood. I wrote a one-reel script entitled *So You Want to Give Up Smoking* and took it to Pete Smith at MGM. He read it while I waited and laughed but declined to buy it. So it went back in the trunk.

"Later, when I was teaching a course in cinema at USC, we needed a script to shoot in order to give the students some practical experience. Out came the script. I found George O'Hanlon, an extra, through my then wife (it seems he had once been in love with her and considered me some sort of ogre). But he agreed to play the lead in the short for nothing, thinking it might lead to something. I wrote the script, photographed it with my own 35mm Bell and Howell camera, directed, edited, and in all departments made the film, of course explaining each step to the students. When it was completed, I took it (unbeknownst to the university) to Warner Brothers. They bought it for $2500. I went back to the campus feeling somewhat guilty and wondering how I could explain and get my hands on the negative.

"When Warren Scott heard what I had done, he was most sympathetic. He asked me, 'What was the purpose of the film?' I told him, 'To train the students.' He asked me a second question: 'Did they get their training?' Again I replied in the affirmative. Then he went on to speculate that the negative was of no value to the University since they owned one copy of the print, and that if I would donate the sum of $1000 to USC he was sure the incident would be closed. I put the $1500 in my pocket, then wrote out a check for $250 to O'Hanlon; at the same time I signed him to a seven-year contract, anticipating that there might be more of these subjects.

"I sat down and wrote another, *So You Want to Wear*

The marvelous opening to the "Joe McDoakes" comedies, as Joe comes out from behind the eight ball.

Glasses. I took it to Warners, and they agreed to buy it (if it came out okay) for the same amount. Again George and I hustled about doing all the chores ourselves, borrowing talent from the university wherever possible. My conscience was clear, as Scott had clearly outlined the justification for the students' working for nothing: they were getting practical experience."

The war interrupted the upward climb of the aspiring production team, but when both Bare and O'Hanlon had simultaneous leaves and ran into each other in Hollywood, they quickly turned out a third comedy, *So You Want to Keep Your Hair,* which Warners bought for $4000. These early one-reelers were very much influenced by the Pete Smith shorts: They were shot silent, used overlapping narration (by Art Gilmore), and combined comic incidents with instructional hints. *So You Want to Wear Glasses* is as much an educational film about myopia as it is a comedy. Looking at these early shorts today, it is easy to distinguish them from the later Warners films, not only in approach to subject matter, but in the obvious economies of what was essentially an amateur production (sets, lighting, actors, etcetera).

After the war, however, Warner Brothers, pleased with these early efforts, asked Bare to do six Joe McDoakes comedies a year. "Naturally," Bare explains, "I jumped at the chance, and since the seven-year contract was still in effect with O'Hanlon, I controlled the package. For

ten years we operated on the Warner lot under Richard Bare Productions. George and I wrote; I produced and directed. My profit was always determined by how inexpensively I could make them, since I had a firm pick-up price from the studio. They started at $12,000, and ten years later had escalated to about $20,000 each. Warners liked the shorts because they were the only live-dialogue comedies on the market in the single-reel length."

They were also among the best short subjects ever made. Bare and O'Hanlon took the not particularly unique idea of exploring the trials and tribulations of Mr. Average, and infused it with their own wacky sense of humor. The results were always easy to mark for audience identification—everyday problems like finding an apartment, fighting with neighbors, going out to a nightclub—but while the fundamental reality was always there, the shorts had a ball with wildly funny exaggerations in every instance. The combination worked beautifully. No matter how outlandish the gags became, they always came across.

Other factors contributed to the success of the comedies: first, a great opening, showing Joe peering out from behind a giant eight ball; William Lava's theme and background music, which added immeasurably to the productions; O'Hanlon himself, a superb comic actor; the elaborate mounting of the shorts, which never belied their budgetary limitations; and finally, the ingenious casting, by Bare, filling every short with the best character actors in Hollywood.

The first short made as part of the official series, *So You Want to Play the Horses,* is Bare's personal favorite; it also won an Academy Award nomination as Best Short Subject of 1946. Narrated (as most of the early entries were) by Art Gilmore, it shows Joe as an incurable racing nut. He examines stables and takes things out of the blue as hot tips, with consistently disastrous results. His wife insists that he stop placing bets for good, and he agrees. When she leaves the house, however, the short goes into a spoof of *The Lost Weekend* (complete with discordant music) as Joe retrieves his hidden "fix"—a horse model in the chandelier, a racing form hanging outside the window on a string, and so on. Using a ridiculously complicated method, Joe picks his horse for the Porterhouse Stakes and bets one hundred dollars on him at a local bookmaker's. Incredibly enough, the horse wins, but the bookies pretend they've never seen Joe before and he's stuck for the money. Even after this, narrator Gilmore tells us, Joe is still "following the horses" —as a sanitation man.

The following year brought with it my candidate for the most ingenious short in the series, and certainly one of the most imaginative short subjects ever made, *So You Want to Be a Detective.* It begins with Art Gilmore giving his usual introduction about Joe McDoakes trying his luck as a detective. Suddenly Joe looks up, sneering, and interrupts the speech: "All right, Gilmore, I've had enough of those corny introductions." He explains that he's not Joe McDoakes, but Philip Snarlowe, private eye. He invites Gilmore to follow him as he goes out on an important case, and we (the audience) become Art Gilmore as the camera takes on the first-person, in a wonderful spoof of Robert Montgomery's *The Lady in the Lake.*

When we arrive at the house where the murder has been committed, Joe tells us to be inconspicuous, and pull down the brim of our hat. A hand pulls down a hat brim in front of the camera, as a butler opens the door and gives Joe a hard time about getting in. When Joe is persistent, the butler punches him, but misses, and sends his fist right into the camera. We (as the camera) reel back, and the image goes blurry. When it comes back into focus, Joe is looking down and asking if we're all right; Gilmore complains about his nose hurting.

Once inside the mansion, the spoof turns to *The Big Sleep,* with a voluptuous blonde innocently telling Joe that she discovered her uncle dead on the floor last June, but was too scared to tell anyone until now. Looking for secret panels, Joe opens a closet door and a body

Joe tries to act tough with Joi Lansing in *So You Want to Be a Policeman.*

falls out. Then another body . . . and another . . . and *another*—seven in all. The closet has a secret passage-way to a gambling casino downstairs, where Joe encounters Num-Num, the local boss, and tries to make him squeal. He does so only after being emotionally un-nerved by a visit from some local "boys" (who turn out to be little boys indeed) warning him to lay off the bubble-gum racket. "This looks like the right psychological moment," says Joe, and he tells Num-Num to sing. "I'll sing," he cries, "I'll sing!" Joe takes out a pitchpipe and

Rodney Bell, as Joe's pal Marvin, stops to think in *So You're Going to the Dentist.*

gives him a key, as he sings that the killer—none other than the infamous Tall Man—is in the bar. Joe goes in-side, confronts the Tall Man (so tall we see only up to his waist), and shoots him down.

Later, back in the lab, Joe tries to put all the clues together, when suddenly Gilmore picks up a gun lying on the table, and tells Joe he was just a little too smart. Gilmore is the killer! After a snarling speech, he shoots Joe who, moments later, wakes up to find it all a dream. Or that's what he thinks, until a man who can be seen only up to the waist walks by and asks directions.

It's hard to believe that *So You Want to Be a Detective* is only ten minutes long—harder still to believe that it was done in three days, on a small budget. The camerawork (by Wesley Anderson), sets, lighting, music, and acting all combine to create what is surely a minor classic of movie making.

If the world is full of thieves, as some think, they are all in the Joe McDoakes comedies. No one ever encountered more shysters than Joe. In *So You Want an Apartment,* he is locked into battle with Mr. McNasty, landlord of The McNasty Arms, who wants to renovate the building and is trying to get Joe and his wife to move out. Seeking help in finding a new apartment, Joe goes to someone called "The Laughing Irishman," who arranges a loan (laughing uncontrollably all the while) and sends him to his colleague, Shamus McShamus, who gets Joe to sign a contract guaranteeing an impossible sum of money every month as his finder's fee. After all this effort, the apartment that's been located for Joe is his old one in the McNasty Arms! For a punchline, Joe and wife are shown settled back in the old apartment with one exception: an elevator has been built in the middle of their living room!

Similarly, in *So You Want to Get It Wholesale* (1952), Joe uses his "contacts" to buy an oven as cheaply as possible. Going to a warehouse, he taps a salesman on the shoulder, asking, "Hey, would you like to wait on us?" Frank Nelson, Jack Benny's old nemesis, turns around and answers, "Ooooooh, *would* I!" in his distinctive voice. He buys the stove at a 15 percent discount, but then gets a tip where he can buy one for 25 percent off, and sends back the original stove to take advantage of the new offer. The fellow he goes to see is a sidewalk hustler who sells stoves like used cars. "Here's an oven that's practically new," he spiels, "Only two eggs been fried on it—it was owned by a little old lady who used it only on Sunday to boil water." He takes Joe over the coals, and while he's selling him one of his "hot" stoves, the cops raid the place and Joe is hauled into court.

So You Want to Play the Piano (1956) is a perfect example of the hilarious Joe McDoakes exaggeration within the framework of a concrete situation. Joe is no longer master of his household, since pianist Gregor Flatorsharpsky moved next door. Joe's wife, Alice, spends all her time listening to him. (We never see the pianist—only the candelabrum shining in his window across the yard.) Joe vows to learn to play the piano, and signs up for a super-duper three-week course from a con man at a department store (who is using a player piano, it turns out, for his demonstration). Joe buys a piano and struggles along, note by note, while the moving men, housemaid, milkman, and anyone else who passes by stops in and plays a few bars of music with ease, driving Joe crazy.

He gives up, but then hears a radio ad for a new magnetic teaching technique that will enable one to play many old favorites, including "Japanese Sandman." Joe looks up brightly and repeats, intrigued, "Japanese Sandman?" He buys the device, which hooks on under the keyboard. When the current is turned on, and you are wearing metal ringlets on your fingers, the gimmick guides your hand, to the right keys. One evening, as Alice, dressed in a flowing evening gown, is about to visit their neighbor Joe stops her and has her listen as he struggles along playing "Japanese Sandman." From next door we hear Flatorsharpsky pick up the melody with a concertized rendition, and Alice is drawn away to his house. Dejected, Joe decides to end it all, and gets his gun from the closet. While there, however, he spies his musty violin case, muttering that he'd forgotten all about it. Opening it up, he starts to play the violin—beautifully —and does so in counterpoint to Gregor's piano from next door. Outside, her skirt billowing in the wind, Alice is torn between the two musical forces, but finally comes back to Joe. "You never told me you played the violin," she says, hugging him. "You never asked," he replies. As he hugs her, he triumphantly begins to play the first notes of the McDoakes theme song, as the picture fades.

When one thinks of the level of quality reached by the standard two-reel comedy at this time, and the mundane nature of many television situation comedies, the Joe McDoakes shorts take on added stature. To be sure, there were mediocre entries in the series, but none were bad, and the large majority were bright and inventive. Joe's wife was originally played by Jane Harker, a pretty Warners contractee; then, in 1948, she was replaced by Phyllis Coates, an extremely winning B-picture heroine. While making the comedies, director Bare married her; the *real* marriage lasted seven months, but the *reel* marriage continued for several years. Joe's last screen wife was former singing star Jane Frazee, who displayed a wonderfully wry comic sense in the role. The virtual "stock company" that made up the supporting casts included Rodney Bell as Joe's pea-brained friend Marvin, Clifton Young (and, later, Del Moore) as his loudmouthed pal, and Joi Lansing, Fred Kelsey, Leo White, and Phil Van Zandt in a variety of supporting roles. Others who popped up from time to time included Lyle Talbot, Iris Adrian, Ben Welden, and Fritz Feld; but none of the supporting actors ever received billing in the films (except, curiously, in *So You Want to Be on a Jury*).

By the mid-1950s, Bare was shooting three one-reel comedies together in four days. "I brought a new, fast-pace production technique to what was then a cumbersome and expensive studio," Bare says. "So much so that when WB went into television, they asked me to produce and direct their first TV series, 'Cheyenne.' I declined the producer job, but accepted the director's job, a position I had for the first year. During these years I directed six WB features, and many TV shows, always managing to sandwich in the Joe McDoakes shorts, my first love.''

The new pace of making the shorts did not seem to affect their quality. O'Hanlon and Bare worked very carefully on the scripts before shooting began, so the films could be planned for filming with a minimum of wasted time and effort. Among the later efforts that maintained a high standard were *So You Want to Go to a Nightclub,* in which Joe and Alice go to a nightclub so crowded that when the band plays, they are pushed onto the dance floor with their tiny table suspended between them; *So You Want to Be Your Own Boss,* where Joe buys a restaurant without paying much attention to the quality of his food (A woman asks if they have trouble with cockroaches; as Alice assures her that they don't, a piece of French bread is carried away on one of the tables by a series of tiny feet); and one of the best of the series, *So You Want to Be Pretty.*

Evidently inspired by one of Charley Chase's famous silent films, *Mighty Like a Moose, So You Want to Be Pretty* has Joe and Alice happily married, although both are hideously ugly. Their buck teeth are so prominent that they've never been able to kiss (at the wedding they just shook hands, it's explained). On the pretense of visiting her mother, Alice goes away—to a nearby hospital where Dr. Von Slaughter (Fritz Feld), the famous plastic surgeon, restructures her face and makes her beautiful. Unbeknownst to her, Joe is in the room next door, undergoing the same process. Both are released from the hospital, and, at a nearby bar, Joe approaches Alice, unaware that it's his wife. She doesn't recognize him either, and begins to fall for his amorous pursuit. Then, going into a wonderful spoof of *Brief Encounter* dramatics, she tells him she isn't free. "Life is a masquerade," she explains, "and it's almost midnight." "Even a pumpkin has a right to a few moments' happiness," he replies earnestly. So they have an affair, over the next week, at which point they decide to tell their respective spouses and run off together to get married. When they discover that they're already man and wife, neither one is happy—in fact, they are furious at each other for having cheated. So they decide that the only way they can be happy, and continue to trust each other, is to get their old faces back from Dr. Von Slaughter!

The "Joe McDoakes" series won three Academy Award nominations, and appeared on the *Motion Picture Herald* poll of Top-Grossing Short Subjects for seven years. But by 1956, the short-subject market was considered dead, and the cost of making high-quality live-action shorts

Joe's restaurant advertises "Our Food Untouched by Human Hands" in *So You Want to Be Your Own Boss.*

prohibitive, so the Joe McDoakes series came to an end.

It is difficult to understand why the series has been forgotten so quickly. In Hollywood, director Bare found that once he got involved with dramatic TV shows such as "The Virginian" and "The Twilight Zone," no one would hire him to do comedy—ignoring the fact that he had done the "Joe McDoakes" shorts for thirteen years! (He now suspects that, having spent six years directing the comedy series "Green Acres," he'll never get a dramatic assignment again.) But film buffs, who usually have better memories, have also seemingly forgotten the comedies, which receive sparse distribution on television and the rental market. This is criminal. The shorts exist, waiting to be seen again, perhaps rediscovered, and fully appreciated for the comic gems they are.

The "Joe McDoakes" Comedies

All the following were released by Warner Brothers, one reel in length, directed by Richard L. Bare and starring George O'Hanlon. The erratic nature of supporting cast lists is due to the fact that no one (except O'Hanlon) was ever billed for appearances in the series. Plotlines are generally not provided for because, as with the Benchley shorts, the titles of these films pretty much reveal the content.

1. *So You Want to Give Up Smoking* (11/14/42). Narrated by Art Gilmore.

2. *So You Think You Need Glasses* (12/26/42). Narrated by Art Gilmore.

3. *So You Think You're Allergic* (12/1/45). Narrated by Art Gilmore.

4. *So You Want to Play the Horses* (10/5/46). Narrated by Art Gilmore. Jane Harker, Richard Erdman, Leo White, Clifton Young, Fred Kelsey.

5. *So You Want to Keep Your Hair* (12/7/46). Narrated by Art Gilmore.

6. *So You Think You're a Nervous Wreck* (12/28/46). Narrated by Art Gilmore.

7. *So You're Going to Be a Father* (5/10/47). Narrated by Art Gilmore. Jane Harker.

8. *So You Want to Be in Pictures* (6/7/47). Narrated by Art Gilmore. Nominated for an Academy Award.

9. *So You're Going on a Vacation* (7/5/47). Narrated by Art Gilmore. Jane Harker, Ted Stanhope, Clifton Young.

10. *So You Want to Be a Salesman* (9/13/47). Narrated by Art Gilmore. Jane Harker.

11. *So You Want to Hold Your Wife* (11/22/47). Narrated by Art Gilmore. Jane Harker.

12. *So You Want an Apartment* (1/3/48). Narrated by Art Gilmore. Jane Harker, Ted Stanhope, Clifton Young, Fred Kelsey.

13. *So You Want to Be a Gambler* (2/14/48). Narrated by Art Gilmore.

14. *So You Want to Build a House* (5/15/48). Narrated by Art Gilmore. Jane Harker, Clifton Young, Ralph Peters, Donald Kerr, Ralph Littlefield.

15. *So You Want to Be a Detective* (6/26/48). Narrated by Art Gilmore. Clifton Young, Donald Kerr, George Magrill, Kit Guard.

16. *So You Want to Be in Politics* (10/2/48). Phyllis Coates, Clifton Young, Fred Kelsey.

17. *So You Want to Be on the Radio* (11/6/48). Nominated for an Academy Award.

18. *So You Want to Be a Baby-Sitter* (1/8/49).

19. *So You Want to Be Popular* (3/12/49). Clifton Young.

20. *So You Want to Be a Muscleman* (7/2/49). Phyllis Coates.

21. *So You're Having In-Law Trouble* (8/27/49). Phyllis Coates, Clifton Young, Willard Waterman.

22. *So You Want to Get Rich Quick* (10/28/49).

23. *So You Want to Be an Actor* (12/3/49).

24. *So You Want to Throw a Party* (2/4/50).

25. *So You Think You're Not Guilty* (4/15/50). Ralph Sanford. Nominated for an Academy Award.

26. *So You Want to Hold Your Husband* (7/1/50). Phyllis Coates.

27. *So You Want to Move* (8/19/50).

28. *So You Want a Raise* (9/23/50).

29. *So You're Going to Have an Operation* (12/2/50).

30. *So You Want to Be a Handyman* (1/3/51). Rodney Bell.

31. *So You Want to Be a Cowboy* (4/14/51). Phyllis Coates.

32. *So You Want to Be a Paperhanger* (6/2/51). Rodney Bell.

George O'Hanlon and Phyllis Coates as Mr. and Mrs. Joe McDoakes, in *So You Want to Be a Cowboy.*

33. *So You Want to Buy a Used Car* (7/28/51). Phyllis Coates, Fred Kelsey.

34. *So You Want to Be a Bachelor* (9/22/51). Phyllis Coates, Ted Stanhope, Chester Clute, Jack Rice, Fred Kelsey.

35. *So You Want to Be a Plumber* (11/10/51). Phyllis Coates, Rodney Bell.

36. *So You Want to Get It Wholesale* (1/12/52). Phyllis Coates, Rodney Bell, Frank Nelson, Ted Stanhope, Charles Sullivan, Richard Reeves, Jack Mower, George Penbroke.

37. *So You Want to Enjoy Life* (3/29/52). Del Moore, Fritz Feld.

38. *So You're Going to a Convention* (6/7/52). Phyllis Coates, Connie Cezan.

39. *So You Never Tell a Lie* (8/2/52).

40. *So You're Going to the Dentist* (9/20/52). Rodney Bell, Frank Nelson.

41. *So You Want to Wear the Pants* (11/8/52). Phyllis Coates.

42. *So You Want to Be a Musician* (1/10/53). Maurice Cass,

Phil Van Zandt, Fred Kelsey, Chester Conklin, Paul Maxey, Fritz Feld.

43. *So You Want to Learn to Dance* (3/28/53).

44. *So You Want a Television Set* (5/23/53). Phyllis Coates, Rodney Bell, Phil Van Zandt, Fred Kelsey; gag appearance by Doris Day and Gordon MacRae, plus a color clip from their film *By the Light of the Silvery Moon*.

45. *So You Love Your Dog* (8/1/53). Phyllis Coates.

46. *So You Think You Can't Sleep* (10/31/53). Phyllis Coates, Ted Stanhope, Fred Kelsey.

47. *So You Want to Be an Heir* (12/19/53). Phyllis Coates, Phil Van Zandt; O'Hanlon as Joe, his Uncle Silas, half-brother Ellery, cousin Agatha, and grandmother.

48. *So You're Having Neighbor Trouble* (2/30/54). Phyllis Coates, Rodney Bell.

49. *So You Want to Be Your Own Boss* (3/13/54). Jane Frazee, Rodney Bell, Phil Arnold, Fred Kelsey, Lyle Talbot.

50. *So You Want to Go to a Nightclub* (5/1/54). Jane Frazee, Phil Van Zandt, Del Moore, Joi Lansing, Jack Chefe, Ralph Brooks.

51. *So You Want to Be a Banker* (7/3/54). Fred Kelsey, Snub Pollard.

52. *So You're Taking in a Roomer* (10/30/54). Jane Frazee, Rodney Bell, Joi Lansing, Fred Kelsey, Herb Vigran.

53. *So You Want to know Your Relatives* (12/18/55).

54. *So You Don't Trust Your Wife* (1/29/55). Jane Frazee, Fred Kelsey.

55. *So You Want to Be a Gladiator* (3/12/55). Jane Frazee, Del Moore, Phil Van Zandt, John Doucette.

56. *So You Want to Be on a Jury* (5/7/55). *Joi Lansing.*

57. *So You Want To Build a Model Railroad* (8/27/55). Jane Frazee, Arthur Q. Bryan, Minerva Urecal, Ted Stanhope.

58. *So You Want to Be a V.P.* (10/29/55). Emory Parnell, Del Moore, Joi Lansing, Minerva Urecal, Phil Van Zandt.

59. *So You Want to Be a Policeman* (12/17/55). Joi Lansing, Sandy Sanders, narrated by Arthur Q. Bryan.

60. *So You Think the Grass Is Greener* (1/28/56). Jane Frazee, Emory Parnell, Joi Lansing, Del Moore.

61. *So You Want to Be Pretty* (3/10/56). Fritz Feld, Iris Adrian.

62. *So You Want to Play the Piano* (5/5/56). Charlie Hall.

63. *So Your Wife Wants to Work* (7/14/56). Phyllis Coates, Emory Parnell.

Director-writer Richard L. Bare and George O'Hanlon are literally rolling in the aisles as they watch the latest rushes.

extra added attractions

"The Voice of Hollywood"

One of the most preposterous short-subject series of all time was "The Voice of Hollywood," produced in the early 1930s by low-budgeted Tiffany Pictures. The format was that of a radio show, "Station STAR," broadcasting from Hollywood. Each reel had a different host who introduced various movie stars. Those who could perform, by singing, dancing, or telling a joke, would do so. Those who could not perform would do so anyway.

Hosts included Bert Wheeler, Robert Woolsey, John Wayne, Franklin Pangborn, and Lloyd Hamilton. The hosts, and guests, were culled for the most part from the ranks of Hollywood's also-rans—often very creditable people, but seldom the really big stars Tiffany would have you think they were. A typical reel included fat-comic Walter Hiers telling jokes about his cars, Carlotta King singing "The Song of Siberia," and appearances by Dorothy Burgess, Leatrice Joy, and Ruth Hiatt. This reel, as well as several others, has the saving grace of a master of ceremonies who seems to be *aware* that the whole business is a farce, and treats it as such—in this case, Lloyd Hamilton.

The biggest joke of all was that at the end of every reel, your friendly announcer would implore viewers to write to Station STAR with suggestions of stars they would like to see in these films—as if any of the people the fans requested would ever show up.

"The Voice of Hollywood's" best footage usually came from public events, where they would set up their cameras. A priceless reel from 1929 features a ceremony welcoming former President and Mrs. Calvin Coolidge to Hollywood. They are introduced by a very tired-looking Mary Pickford, and greeted by Antonio Moreno, who says it's the most exciting thing that's happened since his mother came; Mack Sennett, who mumbles something unintelligible into the microphone; by Will Hays; and by the Duncan Sisters, who sing a special welcoming ditty written for the occasion. As soon as Silent Cal starts to speak, the sequence ends abruptly and we return to host Jack Duffy.

William K. Everson has written, " 'The Voice of Hollywood' must surely have been one of the most inept imitation 'Screen Snapshots' series ever perpetrated. Allegedly providing the fans with their favorite stars, on request, it was clearly largely limited to the has-beens

187

Mickey (Himself) McGuire is obviously in charge here. That's little Billy Barty, front and center.

(in Hollywood's eyes, if not in ours) and the nonentities. Awkwardly staged, underrehearsed (if at all), it provided most of the stars with an incredible paucity of material—as though their mere presence, democratically joking or hoofing it up like regular fellers, was enough in itself—while many of the emcees seemed downright disinterested in what was going on."

Still, "The Voice of Hollywood" shorts serve an academic purpose—to illustrate just how bad a short subject can be.

Mickey McGuire

In the wake of Our Gang, every fast-buck producer in Hollywood tried to score a hit wth kiddie comedies. The one who came closest was Larry Darmour, who bought the rights to the character of Mickey (Himself) McGuire, a tough street kid featured in the popular "Toonerville Trolley" comic strip. When auditions were announced, a Los Angeles stage mother decided that her son was the perfect choice to play Mickey. Since he was blonde-haired and everyone who read the comics knew McGuire had black hair, she rubbed shoe polish all over her son's head and brought him to see Larry Darmour. A combination of the young boy's natural talent and his

mother's perseverance won him the part. He would later be known as Mickey Rooney, though his real name at that time was Joe Yule, Jr.

Rooney later wrote, "The movie Mickey McGuire was much like the comic strip McGuire: brash, wise beyond his years, and stubborn. So he also was much like Joe Yule, Jr. The early McGuire movies were silent and I don't remember the plots. I do remember the plot of *A Midsummer Night's Dream,* in which I played almost as long ago. If they'd written the McGuire movies the way Shakespeare wrote *Midsummer Night,* I'd remember them, too."

The best way to describe these two-reelers is "cheap." They were very primitive and almost always shot outdoors to save the cost of building sets. Darmour was so cheap (according to Rooney's autobiography) that he tried to cheat the "Toonerville Trolley" cartoonist, Fontaine Fox, out of his royalty on the films by legally changing Joe Yule's name to Mickey McGuire.

The gimmick in these comedies was to have young McGuire act like an adult, taking charge of everything from making a movie to running a race. Following the tradition established by Our Gang, he had one black cohort, named Hambone, along with sundry other kids in his "gang." The silent comedies were often quite funny and, despite the economies, boasted of some impressive sight gags, as in *Mickey's Big Idea, Mickey's Movies,* etcetera. When talkies came in, however, costs went up, and the cheapness of the series was more evident. The sound McGuire comedies' quality plummeted.

Despite its shortcomings, the series did last for approximately six years, probably because the shorts were so inexpensive to make that profits came easily.

But others had their eye on this bright youngster playing Mickey McGuire (indeed, who now *was* Mickey McGuire), and Darmour lost his major asset when Universal signed the child actor to a contract. Thus ended the "Mickey McGuire" comedies—and few tears were shed.

Almost predictably, in the 1940s an enterprising producer decided to reissue the shorts to cash in on Mickey Rooney's subsequent stardom. Then he apparently watched some of the films and recoiled in horror. So the two-reelers were edited down to one reel, and a musical track was added. The results were quite pleasing, making the early-thirties shorts seem much better than they had originally looked.

"Hollywood on Parade"

Every studio, at one time or another, produced behind-the-scenes shorts. The most successful were Columbia's

"Screen Snapshots," but the best were Paramount's "Hollywood on Parade." Paramount's shorts stand out from the others because they are the only ones that actually seemed to shoot good, fresh material especially for the shorts, with their *top* stars.

The shorts never carried any credits, but it is assumed that Louis Lewyn was in charge of their production. Lewyn moved from studio to studio, and over the years supervised innumerable inside-Hollywood shorts, from the terrible "Voice of Hollywood" early talkies, to a famous Educational one-reeler from 1935 called *Hollywood Gadabout* (which, incidentally, took "Hollywood on Parade's" theme music), and later a number of Pete Smith Specialties at MGM.

Lewyn obviously had access to everyone working for Paramount at the time (1932–1934), as well as other stars who were willing to appear in the shorts, gratis, in exchange for the subsequent publicity. One of the very best films in the series is one of the first, #A-2, hosted by Stuart Erwin. It opens with Bing Crosby singing "Auf Wiedersehn." Then Bing introduces his friend, George Burns, and asks if he might meet his partner. George brings out Gracie Allen and says, "Gracie, this is—" She interrupts, "Oh, Morton Downey!" "No," says Bing with a touch of amusement, "I'm Rudy Vallee." "Well," says Gracie, "if you're going to keep changing your name, *nobody* will know you!" Next we are shown Olsen and Johnson cavorting at the beach, and then an incredible scene featuring Gary Cooper having breakfast and talking to his (off-camera) sweetheart. ("Well, dear, I see Louella has another item about us.") It turns out that his breakfast mate is a chimpanzee, whom Cooper dresses and takes to his car for a day at the studio.

(One can just imagine the publicity man who had to convince Cooper to shoot that sequence at his home one morning.)

Other entries in the series feature such tidbits as Cary Grant playing straight to a young girl who does a marvelous impression of Mae West; Viola Dana and her golfer husband Jimmy Thompson in an amusing encounter with Harry Langdon on the golf links; Cecil B. De Mille introducing Henry Wilcoxon and two slave girls to a convention of exhibitors at Paramount; a sketch featuring W. C. Fields, Tammany Young, and a Paramount executive; songwriters Mack Gordon and Harry Revel hosting an informal party after the repeal of Prohibition, with visits from Rudy Vallee, Ben Turpin, Ted Healy and the Three Stooges, Jimmy Durante, and delightful mimic Florence Desmond, who does Greta Garbo and ZaSu Pitts to perfection; the Earl Carroll girls returning to New York after a stay in Hollywood, recalling their various esca-

pades and playing "strip bridge" on the way home; and a would-be country-Western quartet consisting of Barton MacLane, on guitar, Buster Crabbe, Fuzzy Knight, and Randolph Scott.

An annual event in "Hollywood on Parade" was the introduction of the Wampas Baby Stars, a mixed blessing to be sure, even when one group (from 1932) included Ginger Rogers, Gloria Stuart, Mary Carlisle, Patricia Ellis, Evalyn Knapp, Lillian Bond, and Lona Andre. Here, where the series could have done something interesting, it missed the boat by presenting the young lovelies in a corny, ineffective manner.

But all in all, "Hollywood on Parade" remained a fascinating, offbeat collection of sequences, staged and impromptu, featuring some of the top stars of the day. At least it showed some effort, which is more than could be said for some of the rival behind-the-scenes short subjects.

"The Taxi Boys"

Hal Roach, in his constant search for a series to equal the success of his Laurel and Hardy films, decided to team Billy Gilbert and Ben Blue in a series called "The Taxi Boys," intended to be "another Laurel and Hardy." When Blue and Gilbert were introduced, Ben said, "You know, most comedy teams have a funny man and a straight man, and I'm pretty funny." Gilbert looked at him for a moment and declared, "Every man for himself!"

Indeed, "The Taxi Boys" is an example of everyone trying too hard. The series remains one of the greatest catastrophes in Roach's history, this in spite of the fact that the films included comics such as Gilbert, Blue, Franklin Pangborn, Clyde Cook, and Bud Jamison, and many were directed by comedy veteran Del Lord.

The Taxi comedies were designed as silent films, and that is how some of the problems arose. Although there was virtually no dialogue, it was sometimes necessary to set up a situation. So, after ten minutes of pantomime and sight gags, there would be a sudden burst of talk, and then silence again. In addition, many of the gags that might have been funny in Sennett silents simply didn't play in these shorts. One comedy, for instance, contained a scene in which Gilbert, pounding on a door, is suddenly flattened by a swarm of cabbies who knock down the door and run over it as they scramble for the hills. This kind of gag went over in silent films because it was so patently unreal; but here it seemed (and apparently was) genuine, and the laugh was gone.

Ben Blue and Billy Gilbert are "The Taxi Boys."

Another problem was that Blue and Gilbert both played complete nincompoops, to such a degree that there was no sympathy from the audience; there was nothing but disdain.

All in all, "The Taxi Boys" was a disaster, even though the parts were usually greater than the whole. The films, do, however, have some very ingenious sight gags. In *What Price Taxi*, Franklin Pangborn is trying to rescue Clyde Cook from angry Billy Gilbert's apartment by setting a large folding ladder on the roofs of the two cabs parked next to the building. As Clyde climbs down, and Billy follows, the cabs take off. Clyde and Billy desperately clutch the ladder, straddling the taxicabs, as they zoom along city streets and up and down hills. At one point Clyde hangs down from the top of the ladder by his suspenders, running along on the street between the two cabs, jumping up in the air over every car that passes under him!

Actually, the funniest short in the Taxi series wasn't really part of the series at all, although it was released under the same banner and starred Ben Blue and Billy Gilbert. An amusing two-reeler set in Gilbert's grocery store, it was titled *Call Her Sausage;* in keeping with the best part of the whole series—the titles of the comedies. Other examples: *Strange Innertube, Wreckety Wreck, What Price Taxi.*

The Masquers Club

In the 1930s, most of the professional acting fraternities made short subjects. The Lambs Club had a short-lived series for Columbia which featured, among others, Lynn Overman and Leon Errol; The Thalians did two-reelers for Universal for several years, combining the talents of comedy stalwarts like Franklin Pangborn and Grady Sutton wtih those of occasional guest stars. Easily the best of these shorts were those produced by the Masquers Club and RKO Radio Pictures.

If these two-reelers had one consistent quality, it was that they tried awfully hard. There was a conscious striving for offbeat humor, which at times was overbearing, but which often paid off. In *Rule 'em and Weep* (1932), the sound effects are always wrong. In a duel that runs through the film, every time the guns are fired, different noises are heard. And when a horse-drawn carriage pulls up to the country of Bulvania, where the story is set, the sound effect of a train slowing to a halt is heard.

Thru Thin and Ticket, or *Who's Zoo in Africa* (1933), directed by Mark Sandrich, is one of the wildest in the series. It follows Mrs. Chuzzlebottom's African Expedition into darkest Africa, where it encounters natives such as Trader Cohen, and the fierce jungle woman Tarkana (Dorothy Granger), whose yell sounds like a combination of Andy Devine and Johnny Weissmuller. Local reporter Scoop Skinner (Eddie Borden) tries to woo Tarkana; in one clinch between the two, a huge CENSORED sign is flashed in front of the screen. Messages are sent through the forest by a so-called homing pigeon, which looks more like a swallow, and makes more noise than ten airplanes combined.

The first Masquers short, in 1931, was *Stout Hearts and Willing Hands,* directed by Bryan Foy, and starring Frank Fay, Lew Cody, Laura LaPlante, Alec B. Francis, Mary Carr, Owen, Tom, and Matt Moore, Eddie Quillan, and Keystone Kop veterans Ford Sterling, Mack Swain, Chester Conklin, Clyde Cook, James Finlayson, Hank Mann, and Bobby Vernon. The second short, *Oh! Oh! Cleopatra,* starred Wheeler and Woolsey, with Dorothy Burgess as a lively Cleo. Stalwart Masquers such as James Finlayson, Max Davidson (particularly funny in *Cleopatra* as one of the royal musicians), Crauford Kent, E. H. Calvert, Maurice Black, Stuart Holmes, Richard Carle, and Matthew Betz turned up in most of the shorts, along with countless unnamed extras (all listed as Masquers Club members) and, of course, the special guest stars.

Wide Open Spaces (1932) starred Ned Sparks, Antonio

Director Mark Sandrich poses with two of his stars, Dorothy Granger and Eddie Borden, on the set of one of the Masquers shorts, *Thru Thin and Thicket; or Who's Zoo in Africa*.

go off the beaten track. Often they succeeded and sometimes they did not. But the ingenuity that went into them always shines through.

Moreno, Dorothy Sebastian, William Farnum, George Cooper, Claude Gillingwater, Frank McHugh, Tom Dugan, and George Chandler. *Rule 'em and Weep* (1932) featured Sam Hardy, Glenn Tryon, James Gleason, Eddie Kane, and Sid Saylor. *Two Lips and Juleps; or, Southern Love and Northern Exposure* (1932) starred Conway Tearle, Helen Millard, Edmund Breese, Robert Frazer, Alan Mowbray, and Lillian Rich. *The Bride's Bereavement; or, Snake in the Grass* (1932) starred Charles Ray, Montagu Love, Jed Prouty, DeWitt Jennings, Alan Mowbray, and Aileen Pringle. *Lost in Limehouse; or Lady Esmerelda's Predicament* (1933) had Laura La-Plante, Walter Byron, John Sheehan, and Olaf Hytten. *The Moonshiner's Daughter; or, Abroad in Old Kentucky* (1933) featured Mary Carr, Russell Simpson, Lucile Browne, Russell Hopton, and Frank McGlynn, Jr.

Familiar faces and far-out humor were the order of the day in the Masquers Comedies. They tried very hard to

"The Blondes and the Redheads"

After George Stevens left the Hal Roach studio he did some shorts for Universal, then moved to RKO. He had behind him approximately six years of training at the greatest comedy studio in Hollywood, and the experience paid off. He inaugurated a series at RKO called "The Blondes and the Redheads," in some ways reminiscent of his "Boy Friends" shorts for Roach, except that the emphasis here was on the girls—blonde, baby-voiced Carol Tevis, and redheaded, wise-girl June Brewster. Stevens also brought a more tangible asset with him from the Roach studio—delightful comedian Grady Sutton, who became a regular in "The Blondes and the Redheads" series.

In fact, the first entry in the series, *Flirting in the Park* (1933), is really a showcase for Grady. In it, he makes a date with the girls via telephone. When they ask him to describe himself, he sees a fan-magazine photo of Clark Gable in front of him and proceeds to describe Gable's various features. The film's climax is the rendezvous in the park between the boys (Grady and Eddie Nugent) and the girls, which slowly but surely turns into a slapstick disaster involving picnickers, boaters, and innocent bystanders as well. It's an excellent comedy sequence from every standpoint, reminiscent of the Roach comedies in more ways than one, and with good reason: it was directed by Stevens, written by Stevens and Fred Guiol, cophotographed by Len Powers, and it featured, in small roles, Charlie Hall and David Sharpe —all Hal Roach alumni.

The other Stevens shorts in the series do not quite come up to the first one, but they are all extremely enjoyable comedies, and full of wonderful touches.

Still another Hal Roach graduate—Dorothy Granger—joined the troupe when June Brewster bowed out of the series. By this time, George Stevens had gone on to features at RKO, and the shorts were in other hands, but the series continued to turn out very entertaining comedies, with more and more stress on slapstick. One of the best films from the entire series, *Hunger Pains* (1935), came from this period. The girls are flat broke, and absolutely starving. One day at the beach is spent in a fervent search for food—for which they are ready to beg, borrow, or steal. Their dreams come true when they run into wealthy Grady, a member of an exclusive surf club, who invites them to dine with him. Later that day, Grady's father (called Sylvester J. Sutton, Sr.) sends his lazy son out into the world with only ten dollars, to start at the bottom selling magazine subscriptions. Naturally, he ends up knocking on the girls' door. When they tell him they've got to have ten dollars to pay their back rent, he says, "I thought you girls were members of the Four Hundred." "Yeah," says Dorothy, "we're the two zeros!" After "borrowing" his money, they set up a scheme to sell magazine subscriptions but get into trouble and inadvertently save Grady's father from bankruptcy by foiling the plans of a shifty rival (Eddie Kane). The film is almost stolen by young Walter Brennan, as Grady's father's secretary, who, every time the boss faints, *sprints* across the room (a total of eight feet) to the water cooler, and sprints back again with a glass of water.

"The Blondes and the Redheads" series came to an end in 1935; the final short, *Pickled Peppers*, was hardly outstanding, but Grady, Carol, and Dorothy were still giving their all, and it's hard to see why RKO didn't try to keep the series going. It was a bright and amusing alternative to the tired marital comedies that seemed to comprise the bulk of the two-reelers made at that time.

Clark and McCullough

Most two-reel comedies were either slapstick or situation comedy. There were few true variations from this pattern, and among the few who trod their own path were Clark and McCullough.

Boyhood friends, Bobby Clark and Paul McCullough got their early training with minstrel troupes, in the circus (as clowns), in burlesque, and in vaudeville. By the time they hit Broadway in the early 1920s they were already experienced comedians: Clark shooting out hilarious rapid-fire dialogue, sporting "glasses" which were painted on his face, and wearing a hat that looked as if it should say "Press" on it, McCullough wearing a raccoon coat, a ten-gallon hat, and a "toothbrush mus-

Clark and McCullough are sanitation workers, but they're happy in their job, in *Jitters the Butler.*

tache." Many compared their style of mayhem to that of the Marx Brothers.

They were among the first Broadway headliners to make talking pictures, in 1928, for the Fox company. These early one-reelers were so successful that Fox brought the comedy duo to the West Coast to star in a series of all-talking featurettes, running anywhere from twenty to forty-five minutes, and directed by comedy experts Harry Sweet and Norman Taurog. Unfortunately, these shorts are not available today for reevaluation.

But a series of two-reelers Clark and McCullough inaugurated at RKO in the early 1930s do survive, and show what an inspired team they were. Gloria Morgan, then a script supervisor on the RKO shorts, recalls that "Bobby Clark was a very sweet, serious, hardworking man. Paul McCullough never said anything, and only came around for the shooting. Bobby laid out all the routines in a big rehearsal hall and they were shot the next three days in sets with two or three cameras, to save time."

The multiple cameras were not only a time-saving device, they were necessary at times to keep up with Bobby Clark, who would literally run all over the set during a given sequence. The Clark and McCullough comedies are full of way-out gags. In *The Druggist's Dilemma,* Clark prepares a sundae on top of the drugstore counter, and slides it down to a customer at the other end, explaining, "We're a little shy of saucers today!" In *In the Devil's Doghouse* our heroes (detectives Titwillow and Blodgett) are constantly plagued by practical jokes perpetrated by Alan Fun (Bud Jamison), president of the Fun Novelty Company. Every time Fun pulls some wheezy trick, he giggles uncontrollably and reminds them, "It's all in fun!" At the end of the film, when Fun is locked in a trunk, the sleuths convince burly Tom Kennedy to toss the trunk out of his apartment window. As it crashes on the sidewalk below, they call out to Jamison, "Remember, it's all in fun!"

But as zany as many of the plots and gags were, it was Bobby Clark's dialogue that distinguished the comedies more than anything else. Clark wrote much of the patter himself, along with such a fine comedy writer as Johnnie Grey. The patter seldom reads funny, since it required Clark's timing and delivery to put it across. In *In a Pig's Eye,* a central character is a pig named Ajax whom Clark and McCullough bring with them to a swanky party. Clark makes a beeline for the attractive hostess, who admires Ajax and says, "He's cute." Clark replies, "But not like you!" "Hardly," she snaps.

The shorts also benefited from the ingenuity of director Mark Sandrich, who loved working out crazy gag ideas. His successors, Sam White and Ben Holmes, also succeeded in capturing the comedy team's sense of lunacy quite well. Their films are full of little throwaway gags and bits of business that often go unnoticed in an initial viewing. In *Everything's Ducky,* they cook a dinner in order to sell their line of pots and pans. McCullough distractedly works at a meat grinder during his conversations with Clark while stuffing lettuce, Clark's hat—in fact, anything and everything he comes across—into the grinder. While Clark as a trial lawyer talks to a client in *Odor in the Court,* McCullough pours himself a drink into

Bobby Clark and Paul McCullough as "alibi photographers" in *Alibi Bye Bye.*

Clark's school bell, which he keeps nearby to call his secretary.

Odor in the Court is undoubtedly the team's best short, full of great dialogue, like the following exchange between Clark and the judge. It begins with the would-be lawyer shouting, "I object!" "On what grounds?" asks the judge. "None," Clark replies. "Overruled," declares the judge. "Content," says Clark, sitting down triumphantly. Later he delights in confounding the judge by shouting, "I don't object!" and then "It's a lie, but I don't object!"

Like the Marx Brothers, Clark and McCullough are almost surreal, definitely not quite in this world, as they run around passing themselves off as musicians, lawyers, detectives, exterminators, and spies, having no skill in any of those professions and caring not a bit. Their madcap humor was all too rare in the 1930s, and is more scarce today; we are lucky that they preserved their lunacy intact on film, so we can continue to enjoy their inspired antics for years to come.

Easy Aces

In the 1930s a delightful husband-and-wife team appeared on the radio scene with some of the wittiest comedy material ever performed. Known as "Easy Aces," they were comedy writer Goodman Ace and his dizzy wife (at least in character), Jane. Their popularity put them in demand for short subjects, which they did first for Vitaphone and then, on a more regular basis, for Van Beuren.

The Van Beuren shorts, Alice recalls, were made in one day. The Aces appeared on screen only fleetingly at the beginning and end of each short, as part of a movie audience. The titles would come on, superimposed over a large audience, and Jane Ace would read in her inimitable singsong fashion, "Van Beuren Productions presents Easy Aces in *Topnotchers* . . . oh, is this another short subject?" She would complain about having to sit through another dumb short, while her husband would try to shut her up. The balance of each short would be straight documentary footage—a travelogue, or newsreel—with the Aces providing a running commentary. Goodman would say something like "London has a population of three million people," and Jane, observing a bobby in the foreground, would reply, "There's one of them now."

The "Easy Aces" shorts are not belly-laugh provokers; the humor is very dry, and best appreciated by buffs of their old radio show. But one short, *An Old-Fashioned Movie,* is truly funny, taking a vintage silent melodrama and sending it up the river, not in the self-conscious way "Flicker Flashbacks" did years later, or with the optical effects Pete Smith used, but simply applying logic, with a humorous twist, to the silly going-on. "It was love at first sight," Mr. Ace comments about the two leads. "She must have been nearsighted," says Jane.

Goodman Ace says today of the one-reelers, "They were made for money, which was in short supply at the time." But whatever the motive, they were made by one of the finest comedy duos America had ever known, and they remain today very amusing shorts.

"The Glove Slingers"

Prizefight comedies have always been popular. In the early 1930s, Paul Hurst starred as a dumb fighter in a series of independently made two-reelers. The mid-1930s saw a short-lived "Joe Palooka" series at Vitaphone. In 1939, Jules White inaugurated a series at Columbia called "The Glove Slingers," also the title of the first film in the series.

The short has Noah Beery, Jr., as a timid young man who is goaded into the boxing ring by fight-manager Shemp Howard, who used to handle Beery's late father, and his dumbbell trainer, Paul Hurst. Noah's mother, Dorothy Vaughn, has made him promise never to become

Lloyd Bridges, Adele Mara, and Bill Henry in the "Glove Slingers" short, *The Great Glover*.

a fighter, so the whole enterprise must be carried out in secret.

The film was a passable two-reeler, and one could see where a series might be fashioned out of it. The trouble was that the series kept starting and never progressed anywhere! For four years, Columbia turned out "Glove Slingers" shorts, and nearly every one was written as if it were the first in the series. Another problem was that, since the series was done so erratically, the cast was always changing. Noah Beery was replaced by David Durand, at which time Sidney Miller and Joe Brown, Jr., were hired as his freshman buddies. When Durand left, Miller and Brown remained as Bill Henry, Dick Hogan, and others paraded through as the series "hero."

The comedy leads also changed from film to film; after Paul Hurst and Shemp Howard, the roles were played at various times by Guinn "Big Boy" Williams, Roscoe Ates, and Wally Vernon. Leading ladies included Adele Pearce (later known as Pamela Blake), Marjorie Deanne, Jean Porter, Gwen Kenyon, Adelle Mara, and Yvonne De Carlo. In one short (*The Great Glover*), Bill Henry's rival for Adele Mara's affections was played by none other than Lloyd Bridges.

The films ranged from fair to stupid, repeating the same

plot over and over again, featuring heavy-handed comedy relief, occasional songs, and an abundance of gee-gosh dialogue.

With such witty titles as *Mitt Me Tonight, Glove Affair, Socks Appeal,* and *Fresh as a Freshman,* the "Glove Slingers" series somehow stretched out over four years, and died a quiet death in 1943. Its chief interest today is in the cast listings; the films themselves have little value.

Hugh Herbert

It was only in the mid-1930s that Hugh Herbert, former dialogue supervisor, sometimes director, and straight actor, hit upon the characterization that was to make him famous. In such Warner Brothers musicals as *Dames* and, especially, *Colleen,* he became the screen's most delightful bumbler. His fluttery gestures, absentminded mumbling, and self-bemusement, typified by his cries of "woo-woo" (actually "hoo hoo hoo," or something like that, but so imitated and copied as "woo woo" that the copy eventually overtook the original), made him a much-sought-after supporting comic.

He had made some shorts in the 1930s—notably a bizarre RKO two-reeler called *Shampoo the Magician*

Hugh Herbert and Christine McIntyre in *Wife Decoy*.

Sidney Miller (in background), David Durand, Yvonne De-Carlo, Joe Brown, Jr., and Babe Kane in *Kink of the Campus*.

(1932), costarring Roscoe Ates and Dorothy Granger—but wasn't given his own series until the early 1940s at Columbia. The kind of musicals that Warners had been making in the thirties were now out of fashion, and Herbert found himself with fewer opportunities in good feature films—one of the most notable exceptions being Olsen and Johnson's *Hellzapoppin,* which may be his all-time funniest film.

By the time Herbert got to Columbia, he was, like so many others who ended up making two-reelers there, past his prime in many ways. In addition, his funny gestures and "woo-wooing" could only carry him so far; he needed good material. Nevertheless, he was still a familiar name and was capable of good things when given a chance. He stayed at Columbia making shorts until his death in 1952.

It is nearly impossible to tell the Hugh Herbert comedies apart; every one seems to have him married to a jealous wife who suspects the worst when he gets innocently involved with a local blonde (usually Christine McIntyre). Some of these, such as *A Pinch in Time* (1948), directed by Del Lord, were quite good. In a hilarious opening, Hugh runs the A-1 Memory Course—and can't remember the name of his only customer that day. But many others, like *A Night and a Blonde, Wife Decoy,* and *Who's Hugh,* for example, just limp along, with the same cast going through the same motions.

Another problem is the fact that Herbert *was* getting on

You just can't make conversation with some barbers. A scene from *Tall, Dark, and Gruesome.*

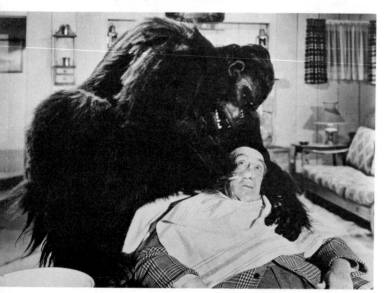

in years (he was born in 1887), and nearly every gag involving a fall or any kind of physical comedy had to be done by a stunt man—a fact that was all too obvious to the audience. In addition, his verbal humor was entirely dependent on pacing. Hugh's mumbled remarks are only funny when they seem spontaneous and off the cuff; when clumsy editing holds each shot too long, or there are "stage waits" between lines, the effect is ruined.

One of the few departures these comedies made from the woman-in-the-closet formula occurred when Herbert and black comedian Dudley Dickerson were featured in a series of haunted-house-type films. Since this was Columbia in the late 1940s, they had the advantage of using stock footage and building three or four shorts around the same material with only a minimal amount of new shooting. One of the best of these shorts was *Tall Dark and Gruesome* (1947), again directed by Del Lord. Hugh and his valet Dudley go to the country so that Hugh can concentrate on a book he's writing. While staying at a friend's cabin, he is the unknowing recipient of a crate that contains a live gorilla. Needless to say, the gorilla gets loose and starts playing havoc with Hugh's nerves. In a beautifully paced sequence, Dudley is shaving Hugh, who falls asleep. The gorilla comes in and takes over. Dudley, seeing him, faints. Then Hugh wakes up, sees the gorilla, and makes a beeline for the door. The gorilla gets into the chair, Dudley wakes up, and begins to shave the gorilla before he realizes what he's doing and nearly jumps out of his skin.

Like other comics, Hugh Herbert was a talented man who, with the right material, could be hilariously funny. On occasion, his Columbia shorts gave him that opportunity.

El Brendel

El Brendel was one of those vaudeville-oriented comedians who had a specialty (a Swedish dialect), did it well, and faced the problem of dwindling material when he got into movies. A typical vaudevillian could remain a headliner for years, and even appear in top Broadway revues, with just a few tried-and-true routines. When such entertainers began working in movies, they found that their backlog of material was used up very quickly, and that they were in the hands of their writers and directors.

Brendel worked in such notable silent films as *Wings,* but scored his biggest success when sound was introduced. He was under contract to Fox, and seemingly appeared in every major Fox picture for the first few years

El Brendel, unknown hillbilly, and Marion Martin in *Love at First Fright.*

Anne Jeffreys is El's leading lady in *Olaf Laughs Last.*

of talkies: *Sunny Side Up, The Big Trail, The Cockeyed World, Delicious,* and *Just Imagine,* to name a few. Generally he was quite good, and his material, like the delightful "Bla-bla-bla" song in *Delicious,* was excellent.

In the mid-1930s he started making two-reelers for Vitaphone; these were elaborate affairs, several filmed in Technicolor with musical numbers. (*What! No Men?* costars Wini Shaw and Phil Regan.) Even the straight comedies, directed by Ralph Staub, were quite well filmed, with titles like *The Lonesome Trailer* standing out. The Vitaphone shorts carried on Brendel's characterization of a simple-minded Swede with finesse.

But when Brendel started making two-reelers for Columbia in the late 1930s, there was virtually no thought given to characterization. The gags and plots were interchangeable with any other Columbia comic, and, without tailor-made material, Brendel's humor became tiresome. He was teamed with Tom Kennedy in a number of two-reelers built around a cemetery-haunted-house theme. These shorts, like *Ready Willing but Unable* and *Sweet Spirits of the Nighter* are only sporadically funny, laden as they are with predictable and overly mechanical gags. Brendel's portrayal of a simpleton had lost all its charm, and instead he emerges as an idiot. In one of the comedy department's less inspired moves, Brendel was then paired with Harry Langdon, whose innocent characteriza-

tion had also been lost in the shuffle. The results were dismal. In still other shorts he was costarred with Monty Collins. The studio's constant attempt to make El part of a team seems to indicate an awareness that he was not carrying his starring two-reelers. He was dropped from the comedy roster after 1945. One of his shorts, oddly enough (*The Blitz Kiss*), was nominated for an Academy Award.

Brendel's career limped along after that, sparked by occasional roles in such A-pictures as *The Beautiful Blonde from Bashful Bend* in 1949.

There is nothing sadder than talent being wasted. El Brendel had talent, but it was shown to its worst advantage in the starring shorts he made in the 1940s.

Vera Vague

In the late 1930s, a radio actress named Barbara Jo Allen created a hilarious spinster characterization for a radio staff party. She was asked to repeat the role on the air, and, before she quite knew what was happening, Miss Allen had achieved nationwide fame as "Vera Vague." She starred in her own radio show, and later became a regular on Bob Hope's program.

Miss Allen, a very attractive woman and not at all the dowdy type one would expect from her characterization, started a screen career in 1939, playing straight-woman to Leon Errol in some of his shorts, and taking supporting roles in such feature films as *Kiss the Boys Goodbye* and *Design for Scandal.* But by the mid-1940s, Vera Vague pretty much got the best of her; in 1943 she started her own two-reel comedy series at Columbia, which lasted

Vera Vague and Vernon Dent in *Clink in the Klink*.

Vera isn't too pleased that Christine McIntyre is getting all the attention from George Lewis.

into the early 1950s. She also made a brief series of travelogues called "Vera Vague Laff Tours."

Vera Vague *was* a very funny character, and Miss Allen adapted herself to the two-reeler with finesse. Unfortunately, her most frequent director was Jules White, whose fondness for violence and disregard for femininity sabotaged much of the series' potential. Aside from the usual whipped cream in the face and dousing-with-water, routines, he had Vera literally wrestling with a gangster, taking care of a rival (Claire Carleton) by breaking a light bulb in her mouth, and flying through a ceiling after being thrown by a hyperactive hobbyhorse. This not only went against the grain of her character, but was completely at odds with that quality known as good taste.

One of her best comedies soft-pedaled this violence, and the results were happy. The script was a scene-for-scene remake of Charley Chase's *Calling All Doctors,* with a simple change of gender; it was called *Doctor, Feel My Pulse* (1944). It cast Vera as a hopeless hypochondriac who is cured when her husband (George Lewis) and best friend (Christine McIntyre) pretend that she's going to die, and they're going to get married and live on her insurance money. This, plus the actions of nutty "Doctor" Jack Norton, get Vera out of bed and in the pink once more, with some very amusing side trips along the way. Another short, *The Jury Goes Round and Round,* was nominated for an Academy Award.

Miss Allen—or Miss Vague—tried her best at all times, and showed herself to be a skilled and versatile comedienne who was willing to "take it" in the name of comedy. One only wishes she could have been in better hands when it came to making her films.

"The Newlyweds"

When Edgar Kennedy died in 1948, one of the major assets of RKO's short-subject production vanished. In order to make up for the loss, the studio tried to get a few new series started; one of them was "The Newlyweds," best described as a situation comedy in a two-reel format. Suzi Crandall, a pretty blonde who had played Leon Errol's daughter in several two-reelers, and Robert Neil, who had also appeared in some RKO shorts, were costarred as the young marrieds.

Hal Yates, who had been writing and directing most of the Leon Errol and Edgar Kennedy shorts for the studio, worked on the "Newlyweds" films, but even when he came up with a fresh story line (which wasn't often in this series), it was usually overruled by the overbearing personality of Robert Neil, who sabotaged any hopes of audience empathy the series may have had. Yates directed the series with his customary rapid pacing, but speed does little good if nothing funny is happening.

Veteran players such as Polly Moran (*Prize Maid*) and Donald MacBride (*Newlyweds' House Guest*) were brought in to spice up the series, but nothing seemed to dispel the stale situation-comedy atmosphere of the two-reelers, not even a change of cast for the final two-reelers in 1952, which starred Robert Hutton and Elizabeth Frazer.

There were nine "Newlyweds" shorts in all. All things taken into consideration, it was nine too many.

Robert Neil and Suzi Crandall in one of "The Newlyweds" shorts.

Gil Lamb

In the 1940s, vaudevillian and eccentric dancer Gil Lamb was featured in a number of Paramount musical comedies and became fairly popular as a result of this exposure. In 1949, RKO signed him to star in a series of two-reelers. By this time, the RKO crew had the two-reel comedy down to a science. The Gil Lamb shorts, therefore, hold few surprises, and rely heavily on the two-reeler bag of tricks, but they move briskly, know where they're going, and come off much better than many more ambitious series of the 1930s and 1940s.

Lamb was given able support by leading lady Carol Hughes (best remembered as Buster Crabbe's vis-a-vis in *Flash Gordon's Trip to Mars*), and blonde foil Claire Carleton, who apeared in virtually all his shorts. In 1953, Andy Clyde costarred in two efforts, *Pardon My Wrench* and *Fresh Painter*. Gil, usually referred to as Slim, played a simple character who just seemed to run into trouble at every turn. The shorts tried to make the most of Lamb's physical dexterity (even in the live-action main titles) as well as his marvelous rubber face.

Probably the best short in the series was a 1952 entry called *Baby Makes Two*. Gil's brassy neighbor, Claire, has entered a baby-food company contest and won—except that she listed Gil as the father of her fictitious baby. She wants him to pretend to be her husband when the company president arrives to give her a $2000 check, and tells Gil to climb along the apartment ledge and "borrow" their neighbor's baby (since the neighbor refuses to loan the child out). All goes well until Gil's girl friend (Carol Hughes) arrives. Gil's attempt to make everything seem normal for her, and then to go along with Claire's scheme for the benefit of the company president (played by Frank Nelson), makes for a very enjoyable, frantic comedy.

The Gil Lamb comedies show that the two-reel comedy did not *have* to die in the 1950s—that while there was more reliance on formula in the fifties, when good production values and enthusiastic casts got together, the results could still do the two-reeler proud.

Carol Hughes has a powerful effect on Gil Lamb.

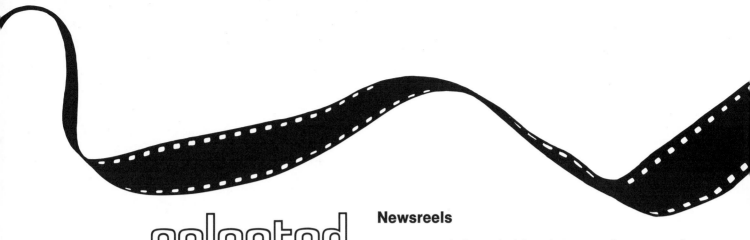

selected short subjects

Newsreels

In an age before television, the newsreel was one of the most important parts of a movie program. People seldom heard a news story for the first time in a newsreel, having read about it in a newspaper or heard it on the radio beforehand, but the newsreel brought every story onto the screen; people could see for themselves a presidential speech, a calamitous disaster, or a milestone event, whether it took place in Washington or Hong Kong.

Historically speaking, newsreels provide us with an invaluable living record of the twentieth century. Newsreel cameramen literally covered the world, and the footage they shot is among the most precious we have today.

If there is any disappointment in looking back at newsreels of the past, it is that they aren't *Citizen Kane.* In *Kane,* Orson Welles fashioned a mock newsreel called *News on the March* (more a spoof of the ''The March of Time'' than actual day-to-day newsreels). Nevertheless, it is so beautifully put together that it leaves an impression in the mind about newsreels that tends to cloud reality.

Newsreels were not, for the most part, brilliant—any more than any six-o'clock television newscast could be called brilliant. They were generally efficient, and at times they did something of an exceptional nature. Often the camerawork *was* brilliant, as when ''News of the Day's'' famous ''Newsreel Wong'' took his shot of a baby crying in the midst of a burned-out train station during the bombing of Shanghai. (The shot, incidentally, was blown up as a still for *Life* magazine.)

But normally, newsreels were produced under great pressure; often, if the reel simply got out it was considered something of a triumph. Most newsreels came out twice a week. Says Robert Youngson, who worked on the Pathé reel through the 1940s, ''The make-up days were Monday and Thursday. We would make up on Monday, and if the film got to the laboratory on time, in the wee hours of Tuesday morning, prints would start getting into first-run theaters on Tuesday.'' Particularly during the war the newsreel staffs had additional problems.

''What would happen was that you would make up a whole newsreel, and then suddenly a big story would break, and the film would come in from the Signal Corps, let's say, of a great battle. You would junk all the work

201

you had done and start from scratch, work all through the night and get out the newsreel. This was common practice."

Director Richard Fleischer also worked on the Pathé newsreel and recalls, "We would screen the dailies that would come in that morning in negative form. We only ran negatives, and we cut from negatives. Also I did all of the recording with the narrator, and it was all mixed together simultaneously with the voice, the music, sound effects. . . . I had to memorize all my own writing and all the cues, because I couldn't read the script and catch the cues on the screen."

The narrator had to be perfect, for in this age before tape, his narration had to be made on one continuous recording. The story is told of one evening where the narrator in question had an especially long script to read. Time after time, he started it and made a mistake midway through the reading. Finally, he did a smooth reading, but toward the end, unbeknownst to those in the studio, the engineer made a recording error. Embarrassed, he thought quickly and ran over and kicked the studio door with a loud bang. Running back to his console, he barked angrily, "Who did that? You spoiled the take!" Unfortunately, some of his colleagues caught him in the act.

Most newsreels had staff cameramen on the payroll in key cities around the country, plus innumerable "stringers" in every conceivable town and hamlet. These stringers may have been professional cameramen, or talented amateurs who accepted the slight responsibility

An official gathering outside one of Pathé News's new sound trucks.

in the hope that some day something worthwhile might happen and their footage would appear in one of the newsreels. The usual agreement was that a stringer could submit a story idea and, if it was accepted, he would send in his footage for approval; if it was not used, his footage would be replaced. When covering stories that did go into the reel, each man was permitted an expense account.

Robert Youngson recalls that Pathé had a stringer in Bar Harbor, Maine, a man who had been the official stringer there for many years, but who had been able to shoot little of value to the newsreel. Suddenly, in the late 1940s, there was a fire of gigantic proportions in Bar Harbor. It practically razed the town and destroyed many of the major buildings. Being the only newsreel cameraman on the scene, this man not only had an exclusive, but he shot exceptionally good footage that knocked out the Pathé staff in New York. Much of it was used in the reel, and Youngson used it again when he made his documentary short *Blaze Busters* in the early 1950s. When the cameraman's expense account came in, the only item noted was the cost of a new pair of galoshes.

Being in the right place at the right time was the story of many great newsreel shots. Had the flight of the dirigible, *Hindenburg,* been an everyday occurrence, the newsreels might have ignored its docking at Lakehurst, New Jersey, in 1937 and missed one of the most spectacular catastrophes ever captured on film. Had officials not been aware of impending disaster, a cameraman might not have caught the unique destruction of the Tacoma Narrows "Galloping Gertie" bridge in Washington in 1940—a bridge that swayed as if it were made of rubber before collapsing entirely. "News of the Day" caught a grim picture of one John Warde—who stood on the ledge of New York's Gotham Hotel for eleven hours in July, 1938, before jumping to his death—as he landed on the hotel marquee below.

Paramount's ace cameraman Damien Parrer (who shot "pool" footage for all participating newsreels during the war) virtually filmed his own death when an enemy sniper gunned him down in the South Pacific. Norman Alley had an exclusive when he filmed the bombing of the Navy gunboat *Panay* by the Japanese in China during 1937. It was such an explosive story that Universal fashioned a special two-reeler from it.

One of the newsreels' biggest assets was use of their studio's music library. Each reel had a music editor whose job it was to comb the files for music that might match certain kinds of stories, and have it ready on a moment's notice. Paramount and Warner-Pathé benefited most from this, Paramount using everything from "One Hour with You" under a fashion story to the score from

A frame blowup from a newsreel of Charles Lindbergh, about to take off for Paris.

Five Graves to Cairo during the North African campaign of World War Two. Later, Warner-Pathé made use of the great Warner Brothers music by Max Steiner, Franz Waxman, and others.

When sound came in, in 1927, Fox Movietone News led the field by immediately dispatching cameramen to capture as wide a range of subjects as possible with direct sound recording. For this purpose, sound trucks were designed and built—a considerable innovation when one considers how long it took some companies to get their sound equipment manageable within studio walls. In addition to normal news events, Movietone filmed interviews with such luminaries as Benito Mussolini, British Prime Minister Ramsay MacDonald, King Alfonso of Spain, and George Bernard Shaw. Shaw remained a newsreel favorite for many years, and he apparently reveled in the glory of being a pet subject. On a trip to America during the 1930s, he was asked what his recommendations were concerning the Depression. "There's no use asking me questions about this country," he replied. "I was here before, I told you exactly what to do, you didn't do it, and you're up to your neck in trouble in consequence."

The newsreel really put itself on the map by shooting a talking reel of Charles Lindbergh's takeoff for France in May, 1927. When Lindy landed in Paris, the Roxy Theater in New York stopped the show midway during the feature, made the historic announcement, and flashed Lindy's takeoff on the screen. The audience stood and cheered.

Universal's newsreel, not surprisingly the cheapest in the business, started one important trend quite unintentionally. Because Universal could not afford a fleet of sound trucks to record sound on the spot, they hired Graham MacNamee, one of the country's leading radio newscasters, to narrate their reel and save the cost of live recording except in special instances. The idea of a narrator caught on immediately, and Hearst–Metrotone News hired Edwin C. Hill, famous "globe-trotter," shortly thereafter. By the end of the decade, moviegoers came to identify newsreels not by style or content, but by the personalities whose voices were used.

But here again, Fox got an edge on the competition. The company hired playwright Laurence Stallings to act as editor of their reel, and he decided to fashion the newsreel like a screen magazine, with regular departments, and with different individuals to head each category. Each story would begin with an inset of the narrator in the upper corner of the screen, by way of introduction. One of the men who rose to fame through this format was Lew Lehr, a member of the Movietone staff who started narrating the lighter human-interest stories in a burlesque-German accent. His catchline, "Monkeys is de cwaziest peoples," caught on like wildfire and made Lehr a radio personality. Lehr was one of the most popular aspects of the Movietone reel, along with sportscaster Ed Thorgeson. Still another distinction of the Fox newsreel was that it was the first to give screen credit to its cameramen.

Paramount News was widely considered to be the best in the business. Certainly it had the most impressive titles, with the familiar "Paramount on Parade" theme, and, at

Pathé tries to cash in on the excitement over Lindbergh's landing.

the end of each reel, the anonymous cameraman turning his lens toward the audience as the slogan "The Eyes and Ears of the World" jumped out from the screen. Beyond this, Paramount had more verve than some of the other reels; it tried for the offbeat, and worked very hard to get different angles on familiar stories. Paramount would frequently devote an entire reel to one subject, or in many cases save the biggest story for last, steadfastly refusing

Pathé covers the opening of the RKO Mayfair Theatre in New York, which just happens to be showing one of the studio's films, *Check and Double Check.*

to become a staid and predictable newsreel. In so doing, it won the respect of everyone in the business as well as in the audience.

Hearst-Metrotone News was also efficient, but too often, some felt, it was merely voicing the view of its owner, William Randolph Hearst; there were incidents of booing in many theatres when the newsreel's main title flashed on the screen. In 1936, the name was changed to "News of the Day," which turned out to be a smart tactical move.

Universal had the least intelligent reel on the market. Often there were more human-interest stories than news features in a typical reel, but the most incredible story

Lew Lehr, who rose to fame on the soundtrack of the Fox Movietone News.

about the Universal newsreel ("Covers World Wide Events" was its unimaginative subtitle) is told by Robert Youngson; it concerns the reel's treatment of the atomic bomb. Here was, after all, not only one of the biggest newsreel stories of all time, but certainly one of the most important events in the history of mankind. At the time of the announcement, actual footage of the explosion was unavailable, so Universal used footage of a bombing mission on Tokyo, after which it cut to a typical human-interest-type shot of a sailor sitting on a destroyer with his dog. As the camera cut to a close-up of the canine, narrator Ed Herlihy concluded, ". . . the atomic bomb: it shouldn't happen to a dog!"

Oddly enough, the war, which affected so many industries in America, gave a shot of adrenalin to the newsreel. Unlike the war in Vietnam, which can only be shown in TV footage as a small group of men crawling through the underbrush, World War Two was war on a grand scale; it was not coincidental that the term "Theatre of War" was used to describe various centers of activity. The war lent itself to being filmed, and since each newsreel was given access to tons of government-approved material, as well as having individual and "pool" footage by their own cameramen, the newsreel staffs in New York

had a field day. In many cases they could cover one battle from many different angles, a luxury of editing that had been denied them before. They had electrifying footage of numerous battles and attacks, with eye-riveting highlights like the U.S.S. *Franklin* being blown up bit by bit, with men staying aboard to fight the flames, and of course the landing at Normandy, at which a newsreel cameraman must have been one of the first to hit the beach, in order to get the shots he did!

The newsreel was also a boon to moviegoers, who got a firsthand glimpse of war involving American troops. It was not uncommon for many families to eagerly await the latest newsreels in the hope of seeing a son, husband, or sweetheart among the many faces that passed by the camera.

When the war was over, newsreels were never quite the same again. Their prime source of material—and great material—was gone. Similarly, audiences found it hard to get excited over postwar domestic news after four years of exposure to war footage. Television dealt a further blow, and before long was reporting the news to people at home. Television became the new eyes and ears of the world, and the function of a theatrical newsreel became more and more obsolete.

Most of the newsreels petered out in the 1950s; Fox Movietone and Universal lasted the longest, but their newsreels of the 1960s were sorry affairs indeed, stressing human-interest and sports stories, and ending up as "filler" on the program instead of the center of attraction.

The last one to go was the Universal newsreel, whose final episode appeared the last week of 1967. *The New York Times*'s Richard F. Shepard attended the last recording session for the final two six-minute reels and concluded, "The last newsreel was laid out Wednesday night and the old movie-house staple has now gone the way of the fountain pen, the dirigible, and the dodo bird." In the final year of production, Universal abandoned its staff cameramen and bought footage from UPI's television department. Ed Herlihy, the voice of Universal for twenty-five years, recalled, "The most trying moment for me was the assassination of President Kennedy. When I saw his picture on the film, I burst into tears. They all walked out and left me alone."

So ended tradition, and with it an era. It is difficult to imagine a newsreel today, with the issues as heated and many-sided as they are, and with many Americans showing an increasing awareness of current events and seeking information that goes beneath the surface level.

The newsreel belonged to what we like to regard as a simpler time. Perhaps it wasn't, really; perhaps it was just

Some great newsreel shots:

Babe Ruth and Al Smith as a golfing twosome . . .

. . . Lou Gehrig making his farewell speech at Yankee Stadium . . .

. . . and the American flag being raised on Iwo Jima.

that *people* were simpler, and found it easier to look at things in terms of black and white, without exploring the many shades of gray in between. The newsreel reflected this attitude, and suffered a rude awakening after the war, when many Americans began searching for deeper answers to life's many problems.

Travelogues

With the invention of the movie camera, it became possible to bring the world onto a movie screen in any town, anywhere. People who were destined to spend their whole lives in a small farming community, or those too caught up in big-city life to leave, could now see what it was like in parts of the world they could never hope to visit.

Thus, the travelogue had a surefire appeal from the start. It continues to flourish today, for two main reasons. First, it can be made with an absolute minimum of expense (no actors, no sets, no costumes, canned music, postrecording, and the like), and second, it remains one of the most effective forms of advertising for tourists. A majority of the travelogues that show up in theatres today are sponsored by chambers of commerce or

ministries of tourism around the world. Given to theatres without charge, they manage to find their way onto scores of movie screens, while professionally made short subjects (which have a rental fee) sit gathering dust.

There seems to have been a theory, from the beginning of movies, that one needn't worry about trying to make a travelogue interesting as long as there were pretty pictures on the screen. Thus, over the years, travelogues have been accountable for some of the dullest moments spent in movie theatres.

Even the two most famous entrepreneurs in the business, Burton Holmes and James Fitzpatrick, were responsible for many yawn-provoking reels. Holmes's reputation was based on his live appearances with films, presentations which, it is said, were quite good. But most reviewers agreed that he fell flat on film. Fitzpatrick's "Traveltalks" were a part of MGM's short-subject product for some thirty years, but "The Voice of the Globe," as they were known, were often stuffy, dehumanized films that failed to maintain interest even though they depicted some of the world's most beautiful sights. Fitzpatrick hired some of the best cameramen in the business, and was shooting his pictures in full Technicolor before most of his competitors, but, despite this potent selling point, they tended to be static, seldom if ever showing any signs of life, and concentrating instead on inanimate structures.

In 1932, Fitzpatrick got some publicity hoopla out of two shorts filmed in Russia. "Congratulations, Mr. Fitzpatrick," read an MGM trade ad. "You are the first to film *RUSSIA TODAY* as it really is!" The ad then addressed the exhibitor, saying, "He has done an amazing, courageous thing for the screens of America."

Oddly enough, the best travelogues over the years were usually one-shot items, or short-lived series, which often took the audience by surprise when they showed intelligence, wit, or imagination and broke away from the standard formula. In 1932, for instance, an independent firm produced a two-reeler about Charleston, South Carolina, called *An Old City Speaks,* and hired famed humorist and Southern storyteller Irvin S. Cobb to do the narration. It was extremely well received.

In 1939, United Artists released a series of foreign travelogues under the title "World Windows." These shorts were photographed in Technicolor by Jack Cardiff, perhaps the greatest color cameraman of all time (later famous for such British films as *The Red Shoes* and *Black Narcissus*). They played the art houses of New York but were considered too highbrow for mass audiences because they carried no narration and featured decidedly artistic photography instead of the usual straightforward camera work. UA eventually dropped the series, and Paramount released several more of the imports under the title "Fascinating Journeys."

That same decade saw some real imagination for the first time on the part of several studios in adding life to their travelogues. Columbia initiated a short-lived series of gag shorts called "Vera Vague Laff Tours," with such titles as *A Lass in Alaska* and *Sitka Sue,* beginning in the late 1940s. Universal-International also tried the humor route, starring Phil Foster in a series called "Brooklyn Goes To . . .," with the New York comic touring the United States and adding his comic observations to the sights displayed. And who should come forward with an innovation in 1955 but James Fitzpatrick, who, concurrently with his MGM series, inaugurated another line of shorts for Paramount called "Vistavision Visits . . .," using that studio's prized photographic process.

In the 1950s Warner Brothers seemed to corner the market on great travelogues. They released some interesting one-shots, such as *Charlie McCarthy and Mortimer Snerd in Sweden* (1950), a comedy with Edgar Bergen and his dummies on a trip through Bergen's homeland, filmed in Technicolor. In 1952, Errol Flynn directed and narrated *Cruise of The Zaca,* another Technicolor two-reeler filmed on an oceanographic expedition undertaken by Flynn, his father, artist John Decker, Howard Hill, and scientists from the California Institute of Oceanography, on Flynn's schooner, *The Zaca.* It was a refreshing and extremely well-made short with lovely South Sea scenery complementing the action.

Owen Crump, who wrote Flynn's narration for *Zaca,* also supervised a series of beautiful travelogues in Technicolor and CinemaScope that Warners made in the 1950s. These are among the most breathtaking travelogues of all time, with the superb photography aided by Crump's enjoyable narration (spoken by Marvin Miller) and fine musical scores. The travelogues, as well as all Warner shorts were aided immeasurably by fine music tracks written by Howard Jackson and William Lava.

The 1950s and 1960s saw an increase in the number of sponsored travelogues shown in theatres; besides the fact that these are often amateurishly made, they have an annoying tendency to focus on happy vacationers enjoying their holiday. Since the vacationers are seldom professional actors, the results are often unintentionally funny. Furthermore, hair styles and fashion trends change so quickly that many of these shorts look old before their time. Judging from reactions heard when these two- to ten-year-old films turn up on local screens, there is apparently no worse insult to an audience than to show it an old travelogue.

There are few things worse than a bad travelogue. The annoying part of sitting through one is knowing that *good* travelogues can be most enjoyable. But sponsoring companies, and film companies as well, have seldom cared enough to hire filmmakers with the taste and skill to furnish a really enjoyable product.

Documentaries

"Documentary" is a very distinguished word to use in reference to the kind of live-action shorts that the majority of studios released in the 1930s and 1940s. For the most part, "in depth" was an unheard-of phrase, and indeed, rather than "documentaries," the factual live-action shorts most companies produced were known as "novelties." The use of that word is far from incidental —it tells exactly what kinds of films the studios had in mind when they released their "Pictorials" series. The "Pictorials," released by Pathé, Paramount, and Vitaphone, were composed of odds and ends—human-interest material, for the most part, ranging from a woman who painted holding the brush between her teeth to an inside look at how Oriental rugs are made.

One expert in the field of novelty, and one who made it pay off, was Robert L. Ripley, who brought his popular "Believe It or Not" phenomenon to movies in 1930, for Warner Brothers. Among other choice tidbits, his first short featured a lady from the Sudan whose eyes were padlocked for a month. Reviewers noted that Ripley was a very pedantic host and that the short was extremely static. Taking heed, Vitaphone immediately tried to change the format, and by the fourth entry in the series, there was some experimentation involved. Number Four featured child-actor Billy Hayes, who fell asleep and dreamed he was on a tour with Ripley through "Believe It or Not Land." The next short, directed by Alf Goulding, took the form of an interview between Ripley and a woman reporter. Then it was decided to have someone else narrate the shorts, and Leo Donnelly, who had been writing them, was recruited. Nothing seemed to help, and the series expired after twenty-four episodes. In the late 1930s, it was briefly revived by 20th Century-Fox in an entirely new format: Ripley introduced a story and presented the balance of the film as a dramatization of a true incident. These shorts weren't bad at all, but for reasons unknown the series didn't last very long.

Ripley's closest rival, John Hix, sold Universal on a short-subject series based on *his* newspaper column, and in 1931 "Strange As It Seems" made its way to the screen; even though it was filmed in color, the critical reception was no better than Ripley's. Even so, "Strange As It Seems" enjoyed a long stay at Universal (moving to Columbia in 1937), followed by the similar "Stranger Than Fiction" in the 1940s.

This whole genre of films was royally spoofed by radio comedian Colonel Stoopnagle with his one-reel shorts, "Cavalcade of Stuff." The Colonel's bemused narration, and the sequences themselves (one lady who is to give a recipe absolutely cannot remember the instructions), made for several truly funny outings.

There were, of course, great documentary shorts being made all during this time by people like Pare Lorentz and Willard Van Dyke, but they were not being financed by studios, nor were they, in most cases, receiving much theatrical distribution. Some famous films, such as *The River, The Plow That Broke the Plains,* and *The City,* did get wide release. Even so, pioneer documentary filmmaker John Grierson advised his colleagues to shun theatre distribution, because he felt it carried with it commercial desires and the temptation to dilute a message or idea to make it more palatable to a large audience, instead of keeping the film pure for the audience for which it was originally intended.

The breakthrough in theatrical documentaries in this country came in 1935 with the inception of "The March of Time [MOT]," sponsored by the Time-Life company and produced by Louis de Rochemont. At the end of its first year, the series' ad in *Film Daily Yearbook* summed up its birth and initial success:

Last year, U.S. citizens relaxing in their favorite cinema theaters discovered a new experience in motion pictures, the March of Time on the screen. It dealt with news, but neither in the manner nor with the kind of news to which the screen was accustomed. Subjects, familiar as backgrounds for cornerstone layings and official ribbon-cutting, were disclosed as thrilling ventures in national planning. People long in the headlines but barred from the screen by traditional taboos on politics and debate, appeared in informative, arresting dramas of modern life. Schemes, isms, and international entanglements, their obscure beginnings, little-known developments and headline-making climaxes portrayed in sequences so swiftly and sharply revealing that the cinema public reacted instantly to the combined impact of news and drama. Wary at first, cinema critics and theater men watched audience reception, gave hearty support when issue after issue proved that here was a new cinema "natural." The March of Time goes into 1936 an established success . . .

But "The March of Time" didn't have to blow its own horn; there were many others who were lavishing words of praise on the series, among them John Grierson:

"March of Time" does what the other news records have failed to do. It gets behind the news, observes the factors of influence, and gives a perspective to events. Not the parade of armies so much as the race in armaments; not the ceremonial opening of a dam but the full story of Roosevelt's experiment in Tennessee Valley; not the launching of the Queen Mary but the post-1918 record of British shipping. All penetrating and, because penetrating, dramatic.

To an isolationist country, a country so wrapped up in its own Depression troubles that it didn't want to know about what was happening overseas, "The March of Time" brought background stories on crucial developments around the world. To a naïve country ready to believe the words of persuasive charlatans, "The March of Time" exposed inhabitants of the "lunatic fringe." To a country too reliant on headlines, "The March of Time" provided the essential story-behind-the-story.

The very first issue, released on February 1, 1935, featured three stories: how New York's "21" nightclub kept two large storerooms of liquor intact through the Prohibition era; the influence of former premier of Japan Prince Kimmochi Saionji on the fate of his country during perilous times; and Giulio Gatti-Casazza announcing his resignation as director of the Metropolitan Opera after twenty-five years and watching his last opening night, a performance of *Aïda* with Lawrence Tibbett, Giovanni Martinelli, and Elisabeth Rethberg.

The series followed up with stories on Hitler's strategy, convict-composer Huddie "Leadbelly" Leadbetter, the new transpacific flights which hoped to open the door to extensive trade with China, an interview with Chief of Staff General Douglas MacArthur on what would happen if the army were called into action, and the popularity of Father Charles Edward Coughlin, who preached to an enormous audience over the radio.

"The March of Time" is an invaluable record of America during the 1930s and 1940s, precisely because it does not only concentrate on Hitler's plans, but also takes time to look into a phenomenon like Father Coughlin. So great was the desire to do in-depth studies of each subject that by 1938 the filmmakers decided it was foolhardy to divide their monthly reel among several stories. From that time on, each "March of Time" issue turned its attention to one topic, ranging from an inside look at Hitler's peace proposal (*Peace—by Adolf Hitler,*

August 1941) to a capsule history of the movies (*The Movies March on,* July 1939).

If there was one aspect of "The March of Time" which could be criticized, it was the dramatization technique. Despite the fact that the filmmakers would capture as much live material on the spot as possible, and add Westbrook Van Voorhis's stentorian narration, there was always the need for newly staged sequences, because for the most part, "The March of Time" was discussing events after the fact, and going behind the scenes.

Sometimes these sequences worked perfectly, as in films where the MOT merely wanted to show people going about their work in an everyday fashion. Outdoor scenes were always more natural than indoor scenes, which used obvious artificial lighting, detracting from the realistic look of the films. Staged scenes, even when clearly phony, had one unexpected advantage: like the less obvious "cinéma vérité" films of recent years, they enabled us to see a person conscious of the fact that he was being filmed—and showing us exactly how he wanted to be viewed. MOT's scene of Gerald L. K. Smith talking to himself in a mirror says more about the man than any hidden-camera technique could. In the same way the wonderful MOT reel on Fiorello La Guardia, where, at the end of a long day, the mayor returns home to his loving mother, has helped to perpetuate an image of the New York mayor that has remained indelible over the years.

Where the dramatization technique often failed was in giving this treatment to everyday people—to poor farmers affected by the dam-building of the Tennessee Valley Authority, for instance, who were required to read their eviction notices and comment on them to each other. Here, the MOT technique seemed hopelessly stilted and ineffective. But the series' mentors found that focusing on the human angle of various stories brought them the greatest success, and they continued in that tradition.

The end of the war did not mean the end of good material for the series; postwar topics included an explanation of the atomic bomb, a look at the nightclub boom, the story of public relations, a study of divorce in America, etcetera. But by the 1950s the short-subjects market was dwindling, and the opportunities for a theatrical series of "The March of Time's" caliber were few. In August, 1951, the series' last reel, *Formosa—Land of Promise,* labeled Volume 17, Number 6, was released to theatres. The makers of MOT then turned to educational film and television production, and one of movies' great chapters was closed.

"The March of Time" had a profound effect on the movie industry; it paved the way for other "popular documentary" shorts. When MOT moved from RKO to 20th Century-Fox distribution in mid-1942, RKO and producer Frederic Ullman, Jr., decided to produce their own documentary series. By early 1943, "This Is America" was in release, producing, like MOT, one short every month, and focusing, like MOT, on sundry aspects of life in our country.

Like MOT, "This Is America" also tried to emphasize the human angle on every story; one of the first releases, *Boomtown, D.C.,* a story of wartime Washington, centered on a soldier standing guard duty at the Capitol building. Several other releases during the first year, such as *Medicine on Guard, Lieutenant Smith,* and *Sailors All,* were directed by the famed montage expert Slavko Vorkapich, whose talents were too often ignored in Hollywood.

Another young director who got his first break on the "This Is America" series was Richard Fleischer; his shorts won him the opportunity to do a feature-length documentary, *Design for Death,* which won the Best Documentary Academy Award in 1947. The series' most durable director, however, was Larry O'Reilly, who was with it from its inception through the final releases in 1951.

For the most part, "This Is America" was a successful and well-made series of shorts, but it suffered in comparison to "The March of Time." "America" simply lacked the depth and intelligence of MOT, and while MOT's dramatizations were sometimes annoying, "America's" use of silent footage with a narrator was even more restrictive. It particularly became a bother toward the end of the series, when director Edward Montagne tried to do some Pete-Smith-like shorts—one with Arnold Stang called *Expectant Father,* for example—and to disguise the fact that there was no live sound recording.

Some of the series' best entries were Larry O'Reilly's unremarkable but sure-handed, straightforward documentaries like *The MacArthur Story* and *Lone Star Roundup,* both from the series' final year, 1951.

Meanwhile, another filmmaker had his sights on a different kind of documentary short. Robert Youngson, on the staff of the RKO-Pathé newsreel, got his chance when Warner Brothers bought the newsreel and its assets and became Warner-Pathé. Youngson convinced the head of Warner-Pathé, Norman Moray, to let him make a series of shorts using Pathé's enormous newsreel backlog, which dated back in strength to 1905, with scattered material going as far back as the 1890s. Moray gave him the go-ahead, and Youngson subsequently made forty-seven shorts, of which two won Academy Awards and six others were nominated.

The Youngson shorts are outstanding productions in

every respect, from the imaginative title sequences to the always-great Warners music scores. One of the reels, *Blaze Busters,* the story of fire fighters, with clips of some of the most spectacular fires of all time, was even released in sepiatone. Many of the clips included in the films are priceless, from the building of a zeppelin inside a huge airplane hangar (in *Lighter Than Air*) to Al Smith leading a community sing of "The Bowery" (in *I Never Forget a Face*).

During this period Youngson also made use of vintage movies in the Warners library. *Magic Movie Moments* features footage from the late silent spectacle *Noah's Ark; Thrills from the Past* highlights the earthquake scene from *In Old San Francisco; A Bit of the Best* has the original Rin-Tin-Tin in *Trapped by the Police; An Adventure to Remember* spotlights an obscure early-talkie action film called *Isle of Lost Ships;* and *When the Talkies Were Young* shows some of the top stars in early performances—James Cagney and Joan Blondell in their first film, *Sinner's Holiday,* John Barrymore in *Svengali,* Clark Gable in *Night Nurse,* etcetera.

In 1950 Youngson directed a feature-length documentary called *Fifty Years before Your Eyes.* But because he did not have total control over the feature (as he did on the shorts—"a rare opportunity," he admits) when it was completed, he decided to do a series of shorts tracing the first half of the twentieth century the way *he* wanted to. The shorts that were made as a result were *I Remember When, This Was Yesterday* (including the legendary newsreel footage of Pancho Villa taken on his Mexican expedition of 1915), and *It Happened to You.*

With the death of Warner-Pathé, Youngson's idyllic filmmaking opportunity came to an end. He remembers the shorts as "just a delight to work on. I would decide a subject, and then go through great masses of film, screen hundreds of thousands of feet of film, and eventually emerge with that subject. It was a delightful personal enterprise . . . there was nobody looking over my shoulder, nobody telling me what to do."

Youngson *knew* what to do, judging from these fine shorts and from the feature-length comedy compilations that have followed.

But just as TV situation comedies brought an end to the theatrical two-reeler, television news spelled death for the newsreel and the documentary. Serious documentary films never had it easy during the 1930s and 1940s, but "The March of Time" producers and other filmmakers with integrity proved that it *was* possible to explore subjects intelligently and present them to a mass audience. Their work remains one of the true high points of film history.

Musicals

One of the major breakthroughs of the talking picture was the ability to put great musical performers on film; among the first talkies ever made were shorts featuring the New York Philharmonic and great opera stars of the day in renditions of classical works.

Thus, from the very beginning of sound, the musical short established itself as a staple of film production, and, during the next twenty years or so, literally hundreds of shorts were made. For most of that time a conflict existed in the method of making musical shorts; one school of thought believed that the camera should be set up and the performers should perform, period. The other school favored having a story line and working in the musical numbers as part of an overall plot.

There were good arguments on both sides. Having the performers simply do a musical number for the camera presented the material in its purest form, without the aid of gimmickry. Looking back on such shorts today, they provide a wonderful filmed record of some of the all-time great entertainers and musicians. But, admittedly, they *can* get dull, and that is the cardinal sin of the movies.

On the other hand, most story lines in musical shorts were so hopelessly inane as to make one wish they would throw out the plot and just let the performers perform. Apparently, there was no happy medium.

A typical victim was Ruth Etting. Her first short was a half-reel item for Paramount made in early 1929. Called *Favorite Melodies,* it consisted of Miss Etting standing in a homey setting and singing two songs—no frills, no introductions, no story. The short is good because *she* is so good, but somehow it leaves one with an empty feeling. In 1930 Miss Etting began making two-reelers for Vitaphone; she did thirteen in all over the next few years, and then an additional dozen for RKO from 1934 to 1936. Each short had a simple story that enabled Miss Etting to sing three or four numbers. Some of them were harmless enough, like *Artistic Temper* (1932), in which she shows a friend how she makes her husband a perfect three-minute egg by singing a certain song that times out exactly.

But others weren't quite so charming, and the plot portions of the films became dreary fillers between songs. In addition, although Miss Etting was famed for bringing sincerity and emotion to the songs she sang, she was not much of an actress.

The story of Ruth Etting's short subjects is true of many of her contemporaries', and examples could be cited endlessly. Instead, we would like to pinpoint some of the

Ruth Etting and Tom Kennedy in *Derby Decade,* **one of her two-reelers.**

shorts that overcame these difficulties—those that stand out among the many, many musicals being made at the time.

One of the most original musical series was made independently in 1930 by art-director–designer William Cameron Menzies. Noted for his dazzling visual effects in such films as *Things to Come* (which he also directed) and *Foreign Correspondent,* as well as the production design for countless films (including *Gone with the Wind*), Menzies developed the idea of shooting one-reel live-action shorts to match some of the great classical themes, much in the way Disney did *Fantasia* ten years later.

The results were eye-popping shorts, using existing sets and costumes, transformed by Menzies's fantastic imagination into impossibly extravagant backgrounds and decorations for his visualizations of *Zampa, The Sorcerer's Apprentice, The 1812 Overture, The Hungarian Rhapsody,* and other great works of music. These shorts are as impressive today as they were when they first came out.

Most musical shorts, however, were made on much smaller budgets than Menzies's, by men of less daring

and ingenuity. One problem they faced was the lack of fresh song material. Unable to pay the necessary fees for popular hits of the day, they often hired young songwriters to compose tunes especially for the shorts. Understandably, these varied sharply in quality, and it was a shame to force some of the top musical talents to sing such second-rate songs.

Warner Brothers found one way to get around this problem, and for several years they produced two-reel versions of musicals and operettas which had already been made as feature films by the company. Thus, there were no additional fees involved, and they had use of some of the greatest songs of the day. Indeed, when Vitaphone starred Alexander Gray and Bernice Claire in a two-reel version of *The Desert Song* called *The Red Shadow,* the duo easily eclipsed the stars of Warners prestigious 1929 feature, John Boles and Carlotta King.

Mack Sennett, of all people, was the first one to spot movie potential in Bing Crosby, and he starred the crooner in a series of two-reel comedies which were liberally spiced with songs, and titled with the names of Crosby's biggest hits: *I Surrender Dear, Blue of the Night, Just One More Chance,* etcetera. These were primarily slapstick outings, carried by the now-famous Crosby charm, good costars (Babe Kane, Franklin Pangborn), and good songs—ingredients that others making musical shorts often sought to provide, in vain. Crosby also did two-reelers for Pathé and Paramount at this time.

Warners then signed Crosby's closest rival, Russ Columbo, to star in a two-reeler called *That Goes Double.* While Columbo lacked Crosby's easygoing style, he wasn't a bad actor, and did quite nicely in a dual role as himself and a meek office worker lookalike whom Columbo hires to pose as the real item for personal appearances. Warners also wisely included two of the singer's biggest hits, "Prisoner of Love" and "You Call It Madness."

Sometimes musical shorts flopped for the simple reason that the talent involved was inept. *Variety* reviewed one 1930 opus, *Tapping Toes,* thus: "A bunch of young people who look like the students of a dance school. . . . Whole thing seems a waste of celluloid because of no talent. It's stuff like this that inflames the giddy youth of the country and starts many a boy or girl into a 'stage career' that ends, starving, back home, if no worse. There ought to be a law." The review was written, incidentally, by *Variety*'s colorful founder, Sime Silverman.

Other times, shorts had audience interest because they were so offbeat. A 1931 "Vitaphone Variety" called *George Jessel and His Russian Art Choir* was disliked when it came out, but it is a slyly funny reel today. Jessel comes out on stage and does a humorous introduction of an art choir he encountered on a recent trip to Russia. Just when you think the whole film is going to be a gag, the choir appears and starts singing, quite seriously. After their first number, Jessel reappears to introduce the next selection, a cossack song. "The cossacks, what wonderful men," says Jessel. "I'll never forget how they shot my uncle." Quick exit, and on to authentic cossack song. The finale, which is almost surreal, has the choir singing the Negro spiritual "All God's Chillun Got Shoes" in phonetic English, joined for a closing chorus by Jessel himself, whose Southern twang bears the marks of the Lower East Side.

The first short to be given an Academy Award, in 1933, was a three-reel musical comedy, *So This Is Harris,* directed by Mark Sandrich. Sandrich had been doing offbeat things at RKO for the past few years, working mainly with Clark and McCullough, but this short gave him an opportunity to go wild with the camera, spend a little more money than usual, and bring his imagination to the staging of several musical numbers with the film's star, Phil Harris, and a bevy of chorus girls. Colleagues who worked on the short remember that it was earmarked as "something special," and that it became, with Sandrich's multiple-exposure camera gyrations (photographed by Bert Glennon) and rhythmical dialogue, an offbeat gem. Indeed, the short was so successful that RKO gave Sandrich the go-ahead to do a feature immediately thereafter, also starring Phil Harris, called *Melody Cruise,* which expanded many ideas that were used in the short.

Big bands were a fixture in musical shorts, and these films provided even more problems for the filmmakers than most. After all, you couldn't very well write parts for an entire band and put them into a book musical. So, generally, band shorts were pretty staid affairs, with obligatory attempts to liven things up by putting the band in a strange setting, with offbeat costumes, or cutting away from the musicians to show a dramatization of the song.

This is not to say that every band short was bad, but good ones were the exception, not the rule. A Warners reel from 1939, *Symphony of Swing,* for instance, is an example of an outstanding musical reel, starring Artie Shaw and his band, with Helen Forrest, Tony Pastor, and clearly visible on drums, Buddy Rich. The short is unusual, first, because its four songs, "Alone Together," "Jeepers, Creepers," "Deep Purple," and "Lady Be Good," are all first-rate. Additionally, it is ingeniously photographed, showing various pictorial arrangements of the musicians, using superimposition, and varying the

lighting from song to song. The only weak spot in the reel is a rather limp dramatization during Helen Forrest's vocal. But *Symphony in Swing* stands out as a first-rate band short in every department, and seems better and better as one sees the more mediocre band shorts.

The photographic trend of *Symphony in Swing* continued when Warners moved operations to the West Coast, and the "Melody Masters" series was taken over by fledgling director Jean Negulesco, who, with noted cameramen like George Barnes and Charles Rosher, did incredible things with such placid bandleaders as Leo Reisman and Henry Busse, by shooting in mirrors and at bizarre angles, and so forth.

Universal shot most of its big-band shorts of the 1940s in a nightclub set, hired extras to sit at the tables, and then paced each short so fast that there was never any time for applause. Instead, at the end of each piece, there would be an optical effect of some sort and the band would already be playing its next number!

Hal LeRoy goes into a tap routine in *Rhythmitis,* as Toby Wing looks on from the table at right.

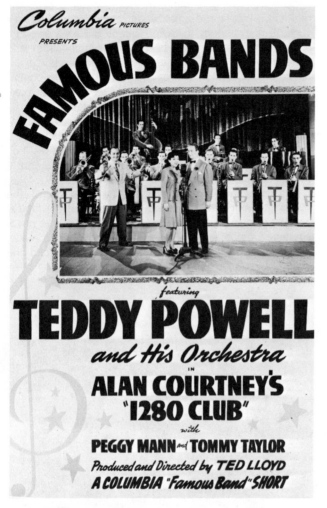

An advertisement for one of Columbia's band shorts.

There were many variations on the standard musical short—indeed, the studios must have been grateful for some new ideas and willing to try anything. Paramount established a series of songwriter shorts featuring both veterans and modern-day composers singing their own works, and Columbia had a series called "Community Sing" that was either the highlight or the nadir of the program, depending on personal taste. When shot in California, the singalongs at least made use of Columbia contract actors and standing sets; but when production was moved east and assigned to an independent producer, cardboard became the order of the day.

MGM worked very hard to make its musical product

distinctive. For its handsomely mounted two-reel musical comedies featuring such contractees as Virginia Grey, Johnny Downs, and Dixie Dunbar, the studio hired songwriters Robert Wright and George Forrest (best known for their later show *Kismet*) to do the tunes. In 1937, they sent director George Sidney and a forty-man crew to the Fort Worth, Texas, Centennial to film "Billy Rose's Casa Mañana Revue," the famed showman's extravaganza featuring Harriet Hoctor, a large supporting cast, and Rose's famous six-foot show girls, the Glamazons. The following year, Metro had a unique one-reeler in production, *An Optical Poem,* filmed by Oskar Fischinger; shot in color, it used geometrical abstract figures to evoke a mood created by Liszt's *Second Hungarian Rhapsody.*

One of the finest musical shorts of all time was made under the auspices of Warner Brothers in 1944 and directed by famous photographer Gjon Mili and shot by Robert Burks. It was called *Jammin' the Blues,* and an introductory explanation told the audience, "This is a jam session. Quite often these great artists gather and play hot ad-lib music. It could be called a midnight symphony." The soloists were Lester Young, saxophone, Red Callender, bass, Harry Edison, trumpet, Marlowe Morris, piano, Sidney Catlett and Joe Jones, drums, Barney Kessel, guitar, John Simmons, bass, and Illinois Jacquet, tenor saxophone.

The film is a highly stylized one, beautifully conceived and shot, with high-contrast lighting of the musicians against a stark black background, the smoke from their cigarettes rising slowly as they improvise a blues. We first see vocalist Marie Bryant in a reflection on the piano; then, as she sings "On the Sunny Side of the Street," the background becomes bright white, and as she and Archie Savage go into a jitterbug dance, the effect is almost that of a silhouette. Despite all that's going on, the short has a very relaxed, casual quality about it, befitting the blues songs on the sound track. *Jammin' the Blues* is a small masterpiece.

Remembering the success others had had by rushing a new musical star into short subjects, an independent producer named Berle Adams sensed the potential of singer-musician Louis Jordan when his record "Caledonia" became a hit in 1945. He hired Jordan to do an inexpensive two-reeler in New York, called it *Caledonia,* and succeeded in getting bookings immediately. It was billed on many marquees, and proved anew that short subjects could have strong drawing power and didn't necessarily have to be good to make money.

In the mid-1940s, Paramount produced a series of Technicolor musical two-reelers which were often unin-

A scene from one of MGM's unpredictable, elaborate musical shorts, *Over the Counter*, filmed in Technicolor.

tentionally funny and sometimes inept but which gave opportunities to such people as Olga San Juan, Billy Daniels, Marie McDonald, Pat Phelan, Noel Neill, Peggy Lee, and (of all people) Mikhail Rasumny, who received star billing for perhaps the only time in his career in a short called *Gypsy Holiday.*

Ironically enough, it was the worst kind of musical short that lasted the longest: the big-band reels. These were the easiest and cheapest to make, so they endured while the companies were cutting down on short-subject production. Universal continued to release ten musical two-reelers a year well into the 1950s. In 1946, RKO, which hadn't done much in the way of musicals, suddenly decided to make some two-reelers featuring big bands, weaving them into some sort of plot. Typical was *Let's Make Rhythm,* which features the short-lived device of jukeboxes that required you to call in your request to a central switchboard. The switchboard girl falls in love with a young sailor whom she's never met, but only spoken to through the jukebox. When the turntables break

down from a short circuit, she runs into the recording studio next door and prevails upon Stan Kenton, who's cutting some records, to broadcast live to the jukeboxes so she can keep the lines open and hear from her sweetheart that evening.

RKO also had one of the few successful musical series, "Ray Whitley and His Six-Bar Cowboys," which lasted through eighteen two-reel Western musicals. They were without a doubt the dullest Westerns ever made, using their Western themes as an excuse for country-style music and comedy of the grizzly-sidekick variety. Although there were nominal leading ladies, there was little romance, and although the settings and costumes were there, there was seldom any action. The series probably lasted because it was unique and served the demands of country-Western music fans. In 1949, Universal followed up with a series of shorts starring Tex Williams.

Mixing comedy and music was a natural idea that was employed too infrequently. The problem was coming up with good comedy *and* good music. Hal Roach experimented with a series of musical comedies in the mid-1930s, and while they starred such reliables as Eddie Foy Jr., Billy Gilbert, Patsy Kelly, and singer Jeanette

Ray Whitley and his Six Bar Cowboys are obviously wrapped up in their work in this exciting scene from _Ranch House Romeo._

A scene from the Pinsky production of _The Barber of Seville_ in _Apples to You._

Loff, they were curios at best, with one notable exception, a wild two-reeler called _Apples to You._

Billy Gilbert stars in this short as Pinsky, the famed burlesque impresario, who is hired to add life to the failing Cosmopolitan Opera Company. He reopens the theatre with _The Barber of Seville,_ advertising "20 Beautiful Barberettes." The performance turns out to be a wild combination of legitimate opera and burlesque, complete with a runway, undulating chorus girls, and a production number, "Would You for a Nice Red Apple?" Between acts, Pinsky comes on stage to give a curtain speech to the highbrow audience which concludes, "Remember, when you see a Pinsky show, you know you're getting the best."

Gilbert also starred in another first-rate musical comedy for RKO several years later. Called _Swing Fever,_ it co-starred Jack Norton and Christine McIntyre. Gilbert plays the head of Dr. Van Loon's Sanitarium ("We Use No Pills to Cure Your Ills"). The entire place is run on music; there are notes all over the walls, and snatches of dialogue like "Nurse, take his tempo." The cure for everything is music, and when Doctor Gilbert asks for his instruments, a violin is brought forth from the sterilizing cabinet. Critically ill patient Norton is finally cured when Christine sings him a "swing" aria.

One of the last inventive short-subject musical series was made in 1953–1954 by 20th Century-Fox to show off its new CinemaScope process, and, in at least one case, stereophonic sound as well. The color shorts would consist of Alfred Newman conducting the 20th Century-Fox "symphonic orchestra" in some outstanding work of music—the sight and sound of color, CinemaScope, and stereo taking care of everything else.

Although the quality of musical shorts ran the complete gamut, their chief aim was to put the top musicians and entertainers on film. For this, audiences were grateful then. Today, music buffs are doubly appreciative, for we have living records of Bessie Smith, Rudy Vallee, Duke Ellington, Ruth Etting, Louis Armstrong, Bing Crosby, Russ Columbo, Cab Calloway, Gene Austin, Ethel Merman, Artie Shaw, Woody Herman, Fats Waller—virtually every music "name" of the late 1920s, 1930s, and 1940s.

Sports

The early 1930s saw a mad rush in Hollywood to sign the biggest sports figures in the country to do short subjects. The studios realized that many athletes who were "marquee names" in their various fields could also be marquee names at the box office. Thus began one of the great rivalries of all time.

Universal was the first one to start the ball rolling by hiring Knute Rockne to host a seires of football shorts. Because it was a fresh idea, Universal managed to get maximum publicity out of the contract signing, and photos of Rockne with appropriate captions appeared on sports pages around the country. The other studios fell into line with MGM signing tennis star Bill Tilden, Warner Brothers hiring golfer Bobby Jones, Pathé signing another golfer, Johnny Farrell, and Universal then topping itself by contracting with Babe Ruth for a series of baseball films.

With so many entries in the running, studios found it harder to get free newspaper space; MGM tried to overcome this cold shoulder by posing Bill Tilden in gag photos. But the Warners publicity department worked the hardest, giving the Bobby Jones series an exploitation campaign that many feature films never received. A combination ticket entitling the buyer to attend showings of all twelve Jones shorts for $3.00 was sold to golfing clubs, for example. Many other tie-ins and gimmicks were sent out around the country in anticipation of the heralded series.

Pathé went to work and produced their Johnny Farrell short quickly, to get it into theatres before Jones's initial reel appeared. They succeeded, but the Farrell film was a loser due to the golfer's uninspiring personality, but also because of the hokey nature of the short. Shortly thereafter, Warners released the first of the Bobby Jones shorts; the series was called "How I Play Golf," and the first short, *The Putter,* was acclaimed by critics and audiences alike.

Warners hired George Marshall, veteran comedy director, and a golfer, himself, to handle the series. He brought Jones to Hollywood, along with an Atlanta newspaperman and golf expert named O. B. Keeler, who was set to write and narrate the series. The crew set up production at Flintridge Country Club in Los Angeles. Warners agreed to have some of its top stars appear in the shorts, for marquee value, but soon stars from every studio were beginning to work in the films without pay, just for the fun of it, and for the thrill of playing golf with the legendary Jones.

Robert Cantwell explained, in his excellent article on the series in *Sports Illustrated:* "Flintridge was used for most of the shooting because it was more remote and not so well known as Lakeside, and it was felt that less of a crowd would be likely to gather to bother Jones or make

Guy Kibbee and Glenda Farrell watch Bobby Jones on their TV console in the short called *Position and Backswing.*

A casual-looking walk along the green requires careful preparation on the part of a crew. William B. Davidson, Bobby Jones, and Warner Oland stroll along for a scene in *Hip Action,* accompanied by camera, microphone, and reflectors. Director George Marshall can be seen at left of picture, with back to camera.

him self-conscious. But, as it turned out, Jones was probably the most assured man involved in the venture. Any difficulty that arose came not from movie fans gawking at stars, but from movie stars gawking at Jones."

The format of the series was established at the outset. Instead of having Jones go through pedantic recitations of how to do this or that, each reel was given a plot that involved some celebrities playing golf. They would do something wrong, which would give Jones an opportunity to set them right, and demonstrate, himself. The effectiveness of this formula depended on Jones himself, and he came through beautifully, his bearing, modesty, and winning personality making the shorts a thorough delight.

Author Cantwell explains that serious golfers in the audience may not have always agreed.

The nonsense and slapstick and fast ad-libbing of the stars sometimes jarred against Jones's serious feeling about golf. Even more, the byplay clashed with his desire to make golf interesting and intelligible to the average moviegoer. But his natural dignity and his mastery of the game made most of the story episodes seem so outlandish and irrelevant that they did not interfere with his essential message. The message was summed up in his words to the disconsolate Frank Craven: "The whole idea, it seems to me, is to do the thing in the simplest and most natural way."

The initial series was made in 1931; two years later, Warners signed Jones to do a second series called "How to Break 90." In these, director Marshall tried some interesting gimmicks, such as dressing Jones in a half-white, half-black outfit against a black background to make the demonstration of various shots all the more striking. This series was more solidly instructional than the earlier one, but equally successful.

The talent roster involved in the Jones shorts reads like a *Who's Who:* W. C. Fields, Warner Oland, James Cagney, Edward G. Robinson, Loretta Young, Walter Huston, Leon Errol, Richard Barthelmess, Frank Craven, Louise Fazenda, Joan Blondell, Douglas Fairbanks, Jr., Richard Arlen, Claude Gillingwater, Joe E. Brown, Warren William, Guy Kibbee, Glenda Farrell, Charles Winninger, Evalyn Knapp, Zelma O'Neal, Huntley Gordon, William Davidson, Harold Goodwin, and John Halliday, among others. It was by far the most notable sports series Hollywood ever produced.

In 1932, Universal came up with another winner, however, in their Babe Ruth series. Timed to be released during the baseball season, there were six one-reelers in all. Each one had a slight story line as an excuse for Ruth to go into some baseball sequences and provide incidental instruction. The films wisely capitalized on the Babe's great following among young boys. In *Perfect Control,* Franklin Pangborn appears as a stuffy schoolteacher making his class recite the multiplication table; one youngster dozes off and dreams that Babe Ruth comes by and disrupts the class, calling the boys out onto the field for a baseball game. In this sequence, Babe shows the kids how to pitch, demonstrating the proper technique for throwing a curve ball, fast ball, and so forth. Pangborn joins in the game as catcher.

The shorts were a big success, mostly because of Ruth's engaging personality. Four years later, Warner Brothers starred him in an odd baseball musical, *Home Run on the Keys.*

Bobby Jones compares clubs with Walter Huston between takes on *The Spoon.*

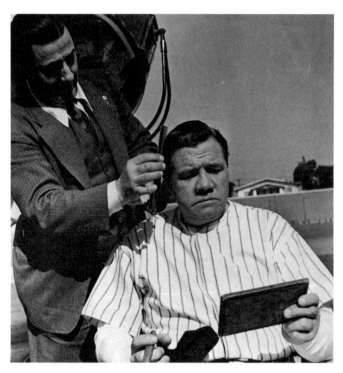

Babe Ruth, star of a series of short subjects in the 1930s, gets made up for a scene in *Pride of the Yankees.*

Perhaps on account of this early oversaturation, sports films with leading athletes soon became passé, and after the early 1930s few were made. Instead, each studio released regular sports reels, such as the long-running "Grantland Rice Sportlight" series, and Pete Smith's annual "Football Thrills" reels.

Most of the sports reels, like the Rice series and RKO's "Sportscopes," tried to stay away from familiar games like baseball and football, figuring that audiences would prefer something more offbeat. As a result, most sports reels focused on deep-sea fishing, quail-hunting, skiing, and the like. Specific events were avoided, since these were usually covered in the newsreels (which employed leading sportscasters like Clem McCarthy and Ted Husing to narrate the sports sequences), so most sports shorts had a hard time coming up on a regular basis with fresh and interesting material. None of them ever attained the quality of the early special series with Bobby Jones, Babe Ruth, and other "stars," for these were the only sports shorts that were given the kind of first-class treatment accorded a comedy or dramatic reel. Most sports reels were done as quickly and cheaply as possible, with footage often purchased from free-lance

Grantland Rice, sportswriter and host of the "Grantland Rice Sportlights."

shorts and B pictures and save their arguments for the important films.

Edward Bernds has vivid and painful memories of what happened to him while directing two-reelers for Columbia in the late 1940s and early 1950s. The short-subjects unit was under direct orders from Harry Cohn to comply with the Code office's every request for cutting and changing.

Bernds recalls:

On the first Hugh Herbert picture I directed, I cast a pretty young girl named Rebel Randall. She wanted to be well gowned, and since (strangely) she wasn't going to be doused with water or plastered with pies, I gave her permission to wear her own evening gown instead of using something from our wardrobe department. In the film, a faint shadow of "cleavage" showed. I wasn't even aware of it as we were shooting—it was, believe me, utterly modest, a mere shadow. Those sick, thwarted Jesuits cut the hell out of my poor, innocent, antiseptic little two-reeler. We had to cut out most closeups of the

Buddy Hackett is having problems in a comedy bowling short made for Columbia.

photographers. Thus, the variation in quality was understandable, and bull's-eye shorts were the exception rather than the rule.

The men responsible for the Jones and Ruth series were also very canny when it came to gauging audience reaction. They knew that not everyone who went to the movies—certainly not many women—would sit still for a sports reel on its own, and they set about to maintain the basic sports element while providing either a story line or a guest cast to give the nonsports fans something to enjoy. The result, of course, was a compromise for both parties, but it was a formula that paid off the way few "straight" sports films ever did.

A Note on Censorship

It may come as a surprise to many people, but during the days of the Production Code in Hollywood, even short subjects came under the scrutiny of those guardians of American morals, the censors. And, unfortunately for the people who were making the shorts, they had little bargaining power. Apparently, the studios felt that they should give the Code people what they wanted in

A scene from one of Hugh Herbert's "naughty" comedies, *Should Husbands Marry*, with Matt McHugh, Vernon Dent, Dorothy Granger, Marion Martin, and Christine McIntyre.

girl. When we had no other film to cut to, we either had to "blow up" the film, making ugly, grainy big-head closeups out of nicely composed waist figures, or, if the offending scenes were two-shots, we had to double-expose shadows over those horrid, lewd, lust-provoking little bits of cleavage.

Most amazing of all are the notations made by the Production Code people on the script of Bernds's Hugh Herbert comedy *Honeymoon Blues*. The film is a typical Herbert two-reeler, written by Clyde Bruckman, in which his boss corners Hugh immediately after his wedding ceremony to do an important job for a big client—he's got to get to one Fifi LaRue and obtain some love letters written to her by the client. The inevitable mix-ups ensue, especially since Hugh doesn't want to let his bride know what's going on. In the final scene, all is straightened out, and Hugh's wife says dreamily, "This is heaven

—just you and I." As she turns to her husband, she finds that Hugh, exhausted, is fast asleep. With a sigh, she starts to play solitaire as the film fades out.

Here are the censorship notes from the MPAA (Motion Picture Association of America) office. In Scene 5, Hugh and Betty Lou are married by a justice of the peace. The office comments, "We assume this speech by the justice of the peace will be read straight." In Scene 6, Hugh, embarrassed at kissing his bride, absentmindedly kisses the best man on the cheek as the best man is kissing the bride. Says the MPAA, "We regard it as very questionable that Hugh actually kisses the best man on the cheek. We think it would be well if he stopped just short of kissing this man."

In Scene 8 Hugh's boss corners him for the special assignment. "You know who J. P. Mott is?" asks the boss. "The banker?" replies Hugh. "Right," his boss replies. "He's in a jam with his girl friend . . ." The MPAA suggests, "It might be well to change 'banker' to something else, possibly 'big businessman.' "

In Scene 12, the Boss gives Hugh his instructions; he must get those letters immediately. "Me?" says Hugh.

"Boss! Not tonight! What about my wife?" "Don't bother me with trifles," snaps the boss. "Trifles!" says Hugh. "Mr. Wright, I—I hate to say this, but I'm *not* leaving this building tonight!" The MPAA says, "In Hugh's speech 'Not tonight,' we request that this either be deleted or possibly changed to 'not now.' In his next speech, 'I'm not leaving this building *tonight,*' we request that the underscored word be dropped."

Other notations include, "Here and elsewhere please minimize the drinking and showing of drinks," and "Care should be exercised as to these kisses of Fifi and Hugh that they be not lustful, passionate, or open-mouthed. This same caution applies on page 25 where Bruno kisses Betty Lou, and scenes 73 and 75."

But the topper comes in the last scene, where Hugh's wife finds her bridegroom asleep and starts playing solitaire. Says the Production Office, "The greatest care must be exercised as to this concluding scene where Betty Lou decides to play solitaire. There must be no suggestion of sex frustration about her action at this point."

To use the current expression, the mind boggles.

index

Other Da Capo titles of interest

Available at your bookstore